THE PROPHET'S WILL

I had been in the Fundamentalist Church of Latter Day Saints (FLDS) from the moment I was born. It was all I knew and the only way I could imagine living. From his teachings, I knew that the prophet's job was to dictate what was best for us, and that the words he spoke came straight from God. I believed that my impending marriage was God's will, and therefore nothing could be done to stop it. But still, I had to try.

I also knew that I was different from other FLDS girls. I wanted to get an education, and maybe even become a nurse or teacher someday. I'd come to realize things were possible that I'd never dreamed before. Sure, I knew that I wanted to be a mother, but not at fourteen. I wanted children *and* a future, and I dared to think that both were possible.

"[Wall's] book helps to bring to life those opaque, tight-lipped FLDS believers who appear on television like time travelers from the nineteenth century. . . . You finish *Stolen Innocence* wrestling with the question of what limits a decent society should place on religious freedom."
Houston Chronicle

STOLEN INNOCENCE

My Story of Growing Up
in a Polygamous Sect,
Becoming a Teenage Bride,
and Breaking Free of
Warren Jeffs

ELISSA WALL

with Lisa Pulitzer

WILLIAM MORROW
An Imprint of HarperCollins*Publishers*

HarperCollins books may be purchased for educational, business, or sales promotional use. For information please write: Special Markets Department, HarperCollins Publishers, 10 East 53rd Street, New York, NY 10022.

First William Morrow paperback edition published 2012.

ISBN 978-0-06-162803-0 (pbk.)

12   13   14   15   16   [RRD]   10   9   8   7   6   5   4   3   2   1

This is my story. The events described are based upon my recollections and are true. I have changed the names of some individuals to protect their privacy.

To Sherrie and Ally; you remind me every day of what I'm fighting for.

And to the memory of Daleen Bateman Barlow, my mother-in-law, who was one of the first to find the courage to stand up for herself and her children.

CONTENTS

PART TWO

PART THREE

A TEENAGE BRIDE

I clutched the delicate silk nightgown and embroidered robe of my bridal gown as I hurried to the bathroom. Though it was just a few feet from my bedroom, the bathroom seemed like a sanctuary, the one place I could be alone. With a turn of the lock, I slid to my knees and leaned my back against the door—for the moment I was safe. Over the past several days, I'd cried myself out of tears, and now I felt strangely numb, unable to cope with what was going on.

When I'd awoken that morning, I was a fourteen-year-old girl hoping for the miracle of divine intervention; my prayers, however, had gone unanswered. With no other choice, I'd submitted to the will of our prophet and had married my nineteen-year-old first cousin. As a member of the Fundamentalist Church of Latter Day Saints (FLDS), I'd been raised to believe that marriages were arranged through a revelation from God, and that these revelations were delivered through our prophet, who was the Lord's mouthpiece on earth. As a faithful follower, I'd embraced this principle and believed in it wholeheartedly, never imagining that at fourteen, a revelation would be made about me.

Ever since that revelation, I'd spent every last ounce of energy begging the prophet and his counsels to grant me more time or select a different man for me to marry. Not only was my new husband my first cousin, we had never gotten along, and I was having trouble believing that God would want me to marry someone I loathed. But my repeated pleas and desperate attempts to stop the marriage had failed, and that morning, I'd been driven across the Utah border to a motel in Nevada, where I was sealed for marriage in a secret wedding ceremony performed by our prophet's son, Warren Jeffs.

Now, with the lock on the bathroom door securely fastened, I felt the full weight of the day for the first time. As I lay sprawled out on the cold tiles of the floor, I was uncertain I would be able to muster the courage to join my new husband in the bedroom. I ran my fingers along the expertly sewn long nightgown and pink satin robe that my mother had given me in honor of my wedding. So much tedious work had gone into the delicately embroidered flowers scattered across the robe's lapel. I knew I was supposed to feel exalted. Marriage was meant to be the highest honor an FLDS girl could receive, and I was devastated to admit to myself that I didn't feel that way.

I pictured my husband waiting for his bride, and the thought of sharing a bed with him terrified me. I had no idea what happened between a man and his wife in bed, and I didn't want to find out. I'd never been allowed to touch a boy, even to hold hands. Girls of the FLDS were taught to view boys as poisonous snakes until their wedding, at which point girls were expected to morph instantly into women and obey the direction of their new husbands. It didn't matter if you were fourteen or twenty-two.

Nausea overtook me, and I raced to the sink, digging my palms into its porcelain edge and trying not to vomit. Looking up, I caught sight of my red-rimmed eyes in the mirror. I had no idea how long I'd been in there, but I knew I had to leave the comfort of the bathroom. I knew these stolen minutes behind the locked door were my last solitude. From that time on, I would be the property of my husband, and would have to obey him completely. All I wanted to do was run to Mom's room right next door and curl up beside her, but it couldn't be done. I would always be her daughter, but I was no longer her little girl.

This is what the prophet has told me to do. I have no choice but to do it.

I peeled off my dress slowly, still wearing my long church undergarments, panties, bra, and tights. After some debate, I resolved to leave everything on underneath my nightgown. Tying the belt of my robe over my many layers made me feel protected, like I was wearing a suit of armor.

My heart was heavy as I reached reluctantly toward the knob and turned it. I ached for Mom but knew that even if she were standing here right now, her hug would not be enough to calm my nerves. Breathing deeply, I fought back the tears building up behind my blue eyes.

Now is not the time to cry; I must keep sweet.

PART ONE

CHAPTER ONE

A NEW MOTHER

For us, it is the priesthood of God or nothing.
—FLDS PARABLE

I can still smell the Dutch-oven roast on the table the night Dad announced we were getting a new mother. Even though there were already two mothers in our house, receiving a third was cause for celebration. I was nine years old and a little bit confused, but mostly I was excited because everyone else at the dinner table was acting so happy for our father.

It didn't seem at all unusual that we would have a third mother—or that our family would continue to grow. That was just a part of the only life I had ever known as a member of the Fundamentalist Church of Jesus Christ of Latter Day Saints (FLDS), a group that broke away from the Church of Jesus Christ of Latter-day Saints—more popularly known as the LDS Mormon Church—so that they could continue to practice plural marriage. Sure, our home already had two mothers and almost a dozen kids, but many of the children I knew had far more than that in their families. It seemed to make sense that we would get another mother. It was just that time.

Back then, I didn't really understand much about the

FLDS, but I knew that we were different from the people living around us in our Salt Lake City suburb. For one thing, we weren't supposed to play with other kids in the neighborhood, and we usually kept the curtains in the house drawn to protect our privacy and the secret life we led. Unlike most of the neighborhood kids, we didn't get on the yellow school buses and go to public schools. Instead, we went to a special place, Alta Academy—a huge, unassuming white brick house that had been converted into a school for members of the FLDS. We also dressed differently from everyone else, wearing long church undergarments that covered our entire body and stretched from the neck to the ankles and the wrists. On top of these, the girls and women wore frilly long pioneer-style dresses year-round, which made it hard to play in the backyard and even harder to stay comfortable in the summer heat. Whereas most kids would go out in shorts and a T-shirt, we didn't own either, and even if we did, we would not have been allowed to wear them.

At the time, I didn't really know why everything had to be so different; all I knew was that I had to "keep sweet" and not complain. We were God's chosen people—and when Judgment Day came, we would be the only ones allowed into heaven. Judgment Day was known to the FLDS people as the day the destruction of the Lord would sweep across the earth, bringing fire, storms, and death in its wake. The wicked would all be destroyed and when it seemed like none would survive, the Lord would lift the worthiest people— us—off the earth while the devastation passed beneath us. Then we would be set back down and would build Zion, a place without sadness or pain. We would reside there with God and enjoy a thousand years of peace.

My father, Douglas Wall, was an elder in the FLDS Church. For him, and indeed for our whole family, receiving a third wife was a major blessing and an important milestone on the long road to eternal salvation. The idea of having more than one wife had become an integral part of the Mormon religion after Joseph Smith founded it in 1830, but the Mormon Church officially abandoned the practice of polygamy in 1890, in part, so that Utah could gain state-hood. Still, some of its members continued to practice in secret at the risk of being excommunicated. By 1935, some of the men who'd been expelled from the Mormon Church formed their own breakaway sect, first known as "The Work" and decades later as the Fundamentalist Church of Jesus Christ of Latter Day Saints. They viewed plural marriage as a central tenet—and the only way to attain eternal salvation.

Members of the FLDS believe they are following the true Mormon religion as it was first envisioned by Joseph Smith. One of its central teachings is the idea of celestial marriage, in which a man must have a minimum of three wives to gain admittance to the highest of the three levels of heaven. That Dad was getting a third wife meant that he had begun to secure a place in the Celestial Kingdom for himself and his family.

Eleven of Dad's twenty-two children were still living at our home in Salt Lake City, Utah, when he broke the news that Saturday evening in October 1995. Many of my older siblings were married and had moved out to start lives of their own. My family lived on a quiet street in a suburb called Sugar House, about thirty blocks southeast of Temple Square, the headquarters of the Mormon Church, located in downtown Salt Lake City. Established in 1853, six years after Brigham Young guided the Mormon pioneers into the Salt Lake Valley, Sugar House was named for the sugar mill whose contruction had never been completed there. Still, the name stuck.

Our house was set back about twenty feet from the road, with views of the Wasatch Mountains in the distance. Large pine trees and shrubs in the front yard obstructed much of the view and made the house appear smaller than it really was, but Dad had always loved this location because it had a big backyard where the kids could play. More importantly, it afforded a degree of privacy, which was crucial, since we didn't want people to know too much about us. Because plural marriages were forbidden in Utah, our family, like all families in the FLDS, was concerned about the attention we could receive if the outside world knew what was going on inside our house.

What helped families like ours stay under the radar in Salt Lake was the fact that our numbers were few and we were all scattered throughout the Salt Lake Valley. At the time, there were about ninety FLDS families residing in the area, and if we had all lived together in the same location, our way of life may have drawn more attention and brought repercussions from the state government.

My father was beaming that Saturday night as he sat at the head of the dinner table. On either side of him sat his two wives, the mothers of the family, who would have to make room for one more at their table. Sharon, my biological mother, was my father's second wife. Audrey, my father's first wife, was known to me as Mother Audrey. The atmosphere was filled with excitement as we looked at one another with the expectation of a good future. My father's face seemed to swell with pride as we talked about how we would prepare for the ceremony and make room for our new mother. My older sister Rachel and some of my other family members began preparing a song that we children would sing in honor of our new mother's arrival.

But when the revelry of the night gave way to the realities of daylight, the anxiety of the situation became palpable. Receiving another mother into the family is supposed to be a wonderful, joyous occasion; we had always been taught that this was a gift from God to be celebrated and revered. But beneath our outward joy, a larger, ominous tension lurked, as no one—not my father, my mother, Mother Audrey, or my siblings—was sure how this would impact the volatile chemistry that was already at work in our house.

For as long as I could remember, there had been an undercurrent of contention and unrest in our family. The relationship between Mother Audrey and my mother was complex and often fraught with misunderstanding as their natural feelings of insecurity and jealousy created problems for us all. Trying to coexist in a single-family home with multiple children and two women sharing the same husband had presented challenges that began soon after my mother arrived more than twenty-five years earlier.

Dad met Audrey when he was fifteen. They attended the same high school and traveled there on the same bus. Dad was class president and a football star in his junior year at Carbon High School when a friend set him up with Audrey, a beautiful and vibrant senior. Audrey was smart, educated, and outgoing. The chemistry was right, and they became sweethearts, marrying in August of 1954.

Since neither was raised in the FLDS Church, they came to the faith by chance. After Dad and Audrey had been married for several years, Audrey's parents converted to the fundamentalist religion. Eager to bring them back to mainstream Mormonism, Dad and Audrey began to study the FLDS religion to learn all that they could about the faith. At the time the church was still known as the Work, and Dad and Audrey's plan was to scrutinize The Work's teachings and find its flaws, but instead they found themselves swayed to its views.

A few years after joining the FLDS, my father saw my mother, the woman who would become his second wife, through a chance encounter during a trip down to southern Utah. Dad's training as a geologist made him a valuable resource to the FLDS community, and at that time he'd been working a lot with the main community in the twin border cities of Hildale, Utah, and Colorado City, Arizona, helping them to find sources of potable water.

My mom grew up in an FLDS family in southern Utah and was a member of the church choir. My father first noticed her during a service he attended one Sunday, as she sat with the choir waiting to perform. She bent down and whispered something to her father, Newel Steed, the conductor of the choir, and the slight movement caught my Dad's attention.

Dad later told me that at that moment, he heard a voice

telling him, "Sharon Steed belongs to you as your next wife and you will speak next." Dad was extremely surprised when he was called up to the podium just minutes later to address the people. Men of the FLDS are taught they hold power to receive some direct revelation from God and Dad believed this was God's message to him. Following church teachings at the time, my father returned to Salt Lake City and began to pray about his revelation. To his amazement, a few months after he arrived back in Salt Lake, Audrey told him about her own revelation. She had dreamt that a woman named Sharon Steed belonged to their family, and she asked Dad if he knew who she was. Up until this point, my father hadn't told anyone about his revelation, so hearing this from Audrey was a surprise. That day, he told her about Sharon and they began to pray together.

More than a year passed and nothing happened. Soon afterward, Dad heard that Sharon was going to be placed with another man. Disappointed and worried that he had misunderstood the revelation, he confided in Audrey's brother, who suggested that Dad speak to the man who was then the head of the church—the prophet Leroy S. Johnson, commonly referred to as "Uncle Roy." (In the FLDS religion, the term "uncle" is commonly used to refer to the patriarchs and presiding leaders and conveys endearment and respect.) During his conversation with Uncle Roy, Dad learned that there was no marriage planned for Sharon, and the prophet directed him to go home and pray so that Uncle Roy could "take it up with the Lord."

When it comes to marriage, members practice something called the Law of Placement, in which all marriages are decided by the prophet and based on a revelation that he receives from God. Everything the prophet proclaims is said to be the word of God, and thus if he directs a union, it is akin to God commanding the union.

Several weeks after his conversation with Uncle Roy, during one of Dad and Audrey's visits to southern Utah, the revelatory word came from the prophet. At the direction of Uncle Roy, Dad and Audrey drove to the home where my mom lived with her family to make an introduction. Mom was in the living room when they arrived, and not knowing what was about to take place, she rose to leave when her father instructed her to stay and meet her husband-to-be. My mother had already been told of the prophet's placement for her, but when nothing immediately happened she worried she would not be married because traditionally, marriages are "sealed" by the prophet within days, and sometimes hours, of a revelation.

My parents were married that very same day. With no time to sew a wedding dress, Mom made do by wearing her favorite pale pink dress for the ceremony. That night, she was on her way to Salt Lake City to start a new life with my father and Mother Audrey in their six-bedroom house on the "benches" of the Wasatch Mountains.

This would be one of the first nights my mother had ever spent away from her large family. Though it was a difficult and sudden change, her steadfast faith allowed her to see it as positive. The union represented an important milestone: the prophet had found a place where she could start to build a new family. More than anything, Mom was thankful to have been placed.

My mother came of age during a time when the local authorities in southern Utah and northern Arizona were very committed to ending plural marriages. For a time, her father, my Grandpa Newel, had become a target of routine raids, with police turning up unannounced at his ranch in hopes of finding plural wives. As a result, much of her childhood was spent hiding her family's polygamous living arrangement from authorities and moving between Utah and Arizona to evade detection and capture. In an effort to avoid arrest and possible imprisonment, Grandpa Newel had begun stashing the women and children in various locations around the region. My mother was sent to live in a home near the Arizona border, where some of her siblings could attend school. However, authorities somehow learned of their location, and an anonymous call was placed to my biological grandmother, Alice, alerting her to their knowledge and offering friendship and a way out. Much to the astonishment of law enforcement, none of Grandpa's wives were unhappy or seeking help. In fact, all five of his wives wanted little more than to be left in peace to live out their lives according to their religious teachings and beliefs. It has often been said that Grandpa Newel and his family were a model to be followed by all.

As traumatic as the moving around and evading authorities might seem, it only made my mother's faith more entrenched. She firmly believed in the traditions of plural marriage and the teachings of the church, and her positive experience growing up shaped every part of her outlook. Whenever she spoke of her childhood, her voice resonated with affection—even when she spoke of the family's persecution. Nostalgic stories of living on her father's ranch would mix with dramatic scenes of evading capture, leaving me scared and imparting the clear lesson that all strangers—especially the police—were not to be trusted. One story in particular about my mother and her young siblings crawling through a hole in the backyard fence of their "safe house" near the Arizona border to escape the authorities always sent my stomach lurching. I would sit there listening and imagining how terrified she must have been, a little girl out there in the dead of night squeezing through a fence to escape the officers who'd come to round up her family. Mom used stories like this one to deepen the faith of her own children, and to help us to understand why it was so important to keep our lifestyle hidden from outsiders—particularly outside law-enforcement officials.

At the time of her wedding, Mom was only eighteen years old, while Audrey was thirty-three. Despite their age difference, Audrey eagerly anticipated the addition of another wife to the family, thinking that she would have a confidante and a friend. However, it was soon apparent that the different ways in which the two women had been raised made it difficult for them to understand and appreciate each other. Although Audrey's parents were converts to the FLDS religion, Audrey herself had grown up in a monogamous household. When my mother became the second wife, it was the first time that Audrey had ever experienced a plural marriage firsthand.

Understandably, having a much younger woman come into her home and share her husband's love brought up strong feelings of resentment and deep jealousy for Audrey. She was Dad's first wife and first love. She had established a home and family with my father and had been his mate for nearly fifteen years before my mother arrived. My mother was talented and beautiful and had youth on her side. She could cook and sew and was very artistic, with a gift for painting that she had inherited from my grandmother. Sharon was known for her lovely singing voice and vibrant personality. With soft brown eyes that revealed the kindness in her soul, she appeared to captivate my father. That my mother was brought into the family by a revelation from God only seemed to make her union with Dad more significant and intimidating to Audrey.

There were also practical issues. Audrey had always played an integral role in the family's financial planning and had a clear idea of how money should be spent. It seemed that in Audrey's opinion, Mom had left her home a child and had no experience with budgeting for a family.

My mother, in turn, had her own feelings of inadequacy. Audrey had a long-established, strong relationship with my dad; she'd borne his children and knew his wants and desires. As first wife, Audrey had primacy, which elevated her in the eyes of my father and gave her authority. Later I realized Mom saw Audrey's concerns over the household budget as demeaning and felt she was trying to monitor her spending. Mom had never known money to be such a contentious element in her life. Growing up on a self-sustaining farm, money didn't have the same kind of relevance. Her family had little but made do, living frugally. Still, everyone was content and provided for. In Salt Lake, Mom tended a garden in our backyard, and harvested fruit and vegetables for the family. She was unaccustomed to having to provide reasons for items she felt she needed to care for herself and her children. It was even harder when the questions were coming from a sister wife.

As the years went on and their families grew, these problems and insecurities did not fade away, but only amplified. Even after my mother began to have kids of her own, the two women were often at odds over everything from raising children to the affections of their husband. Each woman suffered doubts about the household as she tried to practice her individual parenting style and run a house full to the brim with children. To make matters worse, each mother felt that the other's children were being treated better than her own. Frequently, communication between Mom and Mother Audrey was strained with my mother taking the onslaught to prevent further conflict. Neither had total authority over the household, and both seemed to feel somehow robbed of the chance to be in charge of their own home.

Growing up, I always heard differing sides to the story, and blame for the problems in the family was always being passed around. By the time I came along, my brothers and sisters were older and the dynamic in the household had changed significantly. For my elder siblings, memories, as well as their understanding of the source of the troubles, varied tremendously depending on their age and involvement in the family strife. From my perspective, there seemed to be frequent fights among various family members that often resulted in raised voices and angry tones. It seemed like both mothers constantly pointed out each other's faults, with one accusing the other of a lack of cooperation and disrespect toward the children. Each complained of being overworked, and each felt that she was carrying the heavier load. As Sharon's daughter, I naturally tended to support my mother's point of view. I looked up to and adored my mother and strove to be just like her.

Mother Audrey liked a tidy house, and she tried to create an organized system for family members to accomplish their individual responsibilities. In theory, it was a good idea, but with so many people in the home it was hard to keep track of everyone's role. Although the chores did somehow get done, the strained communications in the family prevented repeated attempts to implement a workable system. Despite the flaws, there were moments the family took pleasure in working together. We all knew the faster we finished, the sooner we could play and escape the inevitable complaints that our jobs had not been completed to satisfaction.

All this tension between the mothers frequently spilled over to the kids, who also harbored feelings of resentment, believing that the sons and daughters of the other mother were receiving special treatment. Church rules forbade us from outwardly showing displeasure, so the bitterness remained just below the surface. We were taught to always put on a good face, even when things are going poorly. We were told to "keep sweet," an admonition to be compliant and pleasant no matter the circumstance. Since we couldn't reveal our angry words and feelings, they got bottled up inside, and often there was no communication at all. Despite our teachings, many times our true feelings came out, erupting in arguments, with each group of children naturally siding with their biological mothers.

Over time the bickering between Mother Audrey and my mother took its toll on my father and endangered his standing with the church. Dad's role as patriarch of the family was to control his wives and children in strict accordance with the teachings of the church and the directives from the priesthood. *Priesthood* in the FLDS, is a hard concept for outsiders to understand. First, to "hold the priesthood" is to hold the power and authority of God, delegated to men. To hold priesthood, a man must prove his worthiness by showing his absolute devotion to the work of God through strict obedience to the key holder of the priesthood, the prophet. The prophet is the president of the priesthood. In the FLDS, it is believed that God (or the priesthood) is funneled through the prophet to the elders of the church.

Lines of priesthood authority are patriarchal and strictly observed. In this system all women and children basically belong to the priesthood—not just to their husband or father. In reality, they are possessions of the priesthood and the prophet, and revelations from God determine their ultimate fate. When the prophet decides to award a wife to a priesthood man, it is viewed as a transfer of a possession to the man. The prophet decides when two people should marry, when families can form, and when families that are not working are to be reorganized. From my earliest memories, I was taught that I should never do anything to go against the prophet and priesthood. Doing so would ultimately be going against God himself.

It was common practice to expel men, and in extreme cases women, whom the priesthood considered a threat and could weaken the faith of other members. It doesn't take a religious ordinance or excommunication for a man to lose his priesthood. All that's required is for the prophet or someone acting at his direction to say: "You have lost your priesthood." The significance of this is enormous for believers, as it creates a culture of fear. If a husband loses his priesthood, his family is literally no longer his. In addition, he has to leave his land and home because his home is owned by the FLDS Church and controlled by the priesthood. Faithful wives and children will accept these decisions and wait to be reassigned to another man. In the meantime, the father is told that his only chance to win back his family is to leave and repent at a distance.

If men want to remain faithful members of the church and not lose their home and family, they must obey the priesthood's rules and teachings in every facet of life. An important part of this responsibility is running a happy and obedient household. Because of the friction between Mother Audrey and my mom, it was no surprise that my father was apprehensive about the prophet getting involved in our family's domestic issues. Men had been kicked out for far less serious problems, and it seemed only a matter of time before the difficulties at home would become apparent to the priesthood.

But even this risk was not too great to stop my mother from enlightening the prophet to our problems once she'd reached her limit. Mom had long ago learned that trying to fix problems herself wouldn't change anything and she could no longer allow her children to be blamed for troubles in the home. Not long before the night we learned that my father would have a third wife, my mother had contacted the prophet, alerting him to the trouble in our household. This bold move was a huge violation for a woman, as it disrespected her husband and went against the church code of female behavior. Women are not supposed to complain; they are taught and expected to willingly and "sweetly" obey their husbands, who are their "priesthood heads."

The fear of displeasing God and failing our religious responsibilities is so great that it pushes most members to do anything for the priesthood. For many women, this means they must sacrifice their own desires, needs, and feelings to conform to those of their husband and their religious beliefs. The FLDS believes that women cannot gain entrance to the highest of the three levels of heaven on their own; they must be married to a man who holds the priesthood and has at least three wives, or they will go to a lower level of heaven or to hell.

From birth, girls are prepared for this role. Their way of life is chosen for them by the priesthood. They are told whom to marry, what to believe, and how to live their lives. Women are taught that they have already chosen their destiny before their birth, at which point they chose to willingly place their lives in the hands of the prophet and priesthood, having everything dictated for them.

For my mother to alert the prophet without my father's knowledge meant risking our chance of going to heaven together as a family, but things had gotten so bad in our home that my mother felt something needed to change.

When my father learned of my mother's actions, he feared that he would never receive a third wife—or attain celestial marriage. But he held faith that the prophet would see him as the good man he was. He was well aware that men who prove unable to control their wives are looked upon as "weak sisters" and that he faced the possibility of losing his wives and his children to another man the prophet deemed more worthy.

So Dad was quite relieved several weeks later when he received a call from Rulon Jeffs, the prophet at the time. It seemed that Uncle Rulon had "another lady" for my father, and that my mother's concerns had not jeopardized his standing after all. All my father's worries were put to rest. Clearly, the prophet must have been confident that my father could handle his family issues.

My mother's complaints may have been brushed aside, but there were reasons to be optimistic that another mother would bring stability into our home. The whole house seemed to light up at the mere prospect, and the two days after the announcement were consumed by a flurry of activity. All of the kids had fun rehearsing the musical presentation to welcome our new addition. Even my mother and Audrey seemed to put their differences aside as they began preparing for the wedding.

Dad had been assigned to marry Mom's twenty-four-year-old niece, Laura Jessop. Laura's father was married to two of my mother's sisters and one of them was Laura's mother. In the FLDS, it's not uncommon for members of the same family—even sisters—to share a husband. Our family and the Jessops had been close for many years, but the choice of Laura was still a big surprise because we had been so closely tied to her growing up. It would be an adjustment to now call her "mother" instead of cousin.

The wedding was to take place at the prophet's home in Salt Lake. Laura was driving up with her family from Hildale, Utah, home of an FLDS-only community. For years, Hildale and its sister town of Colorado City, Arizona, were called Short Creek, named after a stream that came out of the mountains and disappeared into the sand. Many of the locals just refer to the twin towns as "the crik," and to the residents as "crikers." Although these are not the proper spellings, residents of Short Creek long ago adopted these unusual pronunciations and spellings: "crik" and "criker."

Nestled close to the awe-inspiring red rock mountains of El Capitan and surrounded by hundreds of miles of parched, rough country, Short Creek was a refuge for members who wanted to practice their religion and plural marriage without the risk of persecution. Though barren and desertlike, the area's rugged landscape and great expanses of open space offered scenic beauty and served as a buffer between the FLDS community and the outside world. The remote sites appealed to followers because they'd long been taught to be suspicious of all outsiders and to regard them as evil.

My family always stayed with the Jessops on the Utah side of Short Creek when we made the long drive south for church meetings and events. Likewise, the Jessops stayed with us in Salt Lake during visits to the prophet's compound or as a pit stop on their way to visit their relatives in the FLDS-only community of Bountiful, British Columbia, just across the Canadian border. The community in Canada was much like the one in southern Utah in that its thousand or so members lived isolated from outsiders. Members of all three FLDS communities operated under the same umbrella of priesthood leadership and convened in Short Creek several times a year for important religious events and community activities.

Our new mother, Laura Jessop, was fourteen years older than I was, and she and I had rarely spoken during our family visits. I was much friendlier with her three younger sisters, who were closer to my age. Still, I shared everyone's optimism about Laura and hoped that her addition would mark a positive turning point for our family. Mom hoped for a friend in Laura. So did Mother Audrey. I just wanted the fighting in our house to stop and for us to all be a happy family.

Unfortunately, things would only get worse.

CHAPTER TWO

GROWING UP AND KEEPING SWEET

We follow the prophet.
—FLDS PARABLE

It hadn't always been so tense in the Wall household. Growing up, I remember many good times with my family. There were camping trips, picnics in the mountains, and countless visits to the FLDS communities in Canada and southern Utah for festivals, celebrations, and group events. There were struggles, but I remember so much happiness, and how much I loved my dad.

Sixteen of Dad's children were still living at home when I was born on July 7, 1986. I was the eleventh of my mother's fourteen children, and number nineteen of Dad's eventual twenty-four. My father was in the delivery room for my birth, and he always said that I came out smiling and continued to smile throughout my childhood. He nicknamed me Goldilocks because of my long silky blond hair and the way I skipped around the house reciting the Grimms' fairy tale and performing it in skits for my family.

I was still quite young—only a few months old—when a dramatic fire changed the course of life for our family. At the time, we were living in our new nine-bedroom house on Claybourne Avenue. One crisp morning in November my mother was in the kitchen preparing breakfast for three of her young boys and cleaning up from a hectic morning of getting eleven children off to school. After putting some raw honey on the stove to melt, she went down the hall to the nursery to check on me. I had awakened and had decided I was hungry, so my mother lovingly took a few minutes to address my needs. While she was feeding me, my older sister Rachel called from Alta Academy, and my mother talked to her as she nursed me.

The blaze started when she was out of the room. The boys were happily eating oatmeal when a heating element on the old stove exploded and turned the pan of honey into a fireball. The flames quickly spread to the cabinets, which were made of a highly flammable material; upon seeing the flames, my brother Jacob ran into the nursery to alert my mother. My mother was still on the phone with Rachel, and it took her a few minutes to ask Rachel to call back and to calm Jacob enough to comprehend what he was saying. Her heart was pounding as she raced after Jacob to the kitchen only to be greeted by the grim sight of flames licking at the kitchen walls. Justin, Jacob's twin brother, stood at the sink throwing small cups of water onto the flames to try to put them out.

Just then the phone rang, jolting my mother into action. She rushed to answer it, hoping that whoever it was could send help. It was Rachel calling back, and Mom screamed into the phone that the house was on fire, instructing her to get word to my father. Mom immediately herded the twins and my two-year-old brother, Brad, to safety, but the fire spread rapidly. Windows of the house exploded from the heat as she came back in to pull me from the nursery. In the end, I escaped uninjured, but my mother needed medical treatment for burns she received during the rescue.

After a frantic search for my father, who was volunteering as a teacher at Alta Academy, Rachel found him and shared the catastrophic news. As Dad raced home, he could see the thick black smoke rising from halfway across the valley. His heart dropped and a sick feeling entered his stomach as he realized the seriousness of the blaze and the danger we were all in. He arrived home to find the street packed with fire trucks, but to his relief we were all collected safely outside.

Once the flames subsided and the trucks had dispersed, the damage was assessed, and it was crushing: the top floor of our house had been completely destroyed, and the basement had suffered damage as well. Our neighbors on the block immediately came to our aid. Even the local Mormon bishop arrived with donations of clothing and offered a place where we could stay temporarily. Our family was shocked by the outpouring of kindness from people outside our church. Their actions contradicted what we had long been taught about the "evil" character of outsiders. Here were so many non-FLDS people offering help in our time of need, despite knowing about the secret and misunderstood life our family led.

While the loss of our home was traumatic, it was nothing compared with the loss we suffered later on that day. That night, November 25, 1986, as we were recovering from seeing our home and possessions go up in flames, we received word that our prophet, Leroy S. Johnson, had passed away at age ninety-eight. The entire FLDS community was devastated, and suddenly the fire in our home took a back burner.

To say that the prophet is the most important figure in the FLDS is an understatement. He is viewed as an extension of God. His words and proclamations are equal to the word of God on earth. A prophet's death was a profoundly tragic occasion, one that forced us to set aside our own situation and focus on the church.

In particular, Uncle Roy's death took a huge toll on the FLDS community. Part of what had endeared him to us was the important role he played in reuniting the people after the notorious raid of 1953 when members of Arizona law enforcement stormed Short Creek, arrested 36 men, and sent 86 women and 236 children on buses to Phoenix in an attempt to put a stop to their polygamous lifestyle. The governor of Arizona at the time, J. Howard Pyle, said the raid was in response to reports of child abuse and men taking young girls as brides, but the governor's goal of abolishing polygamy failed after graphic photographs of children being ripped from their mothers' arms surfaced in the media. In the days after the raid, Uncle Roy vowed to reunite every single family in the community, and in the years to come he followed through on his promise, showing his love and loyalty to his people.

For a few years before his death, we'd been told that Uncle Roy suffered from shingles and deteriorating health. According to what people were saying, Rulon Jeffs and several other church elders had been overseeing the meetings and taking care of church business. There were a number of church elders with more seniority than Rulon Jeffs, but a disagreement between members of the priesthood council over the interpretation of key church ordinances ended with Rulon, the religion's oldest living apostle, as our prophet's likely successor.

With nowhere to live, we moved in with another church member, Woodruff Steed, and his family. Woodruff owned an enormous home in Sandy, in the southern end of the Salt Lake Valley. His house accommodated not only his seven living wives and dozens of children but now our large family as well. His ten-acre property was big enough for both a small dairy operation and several of his sons' homes.

Woodruff was my mother's uncle, but that was not why he offered to let us stay with his family. My father had helped design Woodruff's house, and the two had cultivated a lasting friendship. In return for lodging our family, Dad agreed to share the two thousand dollars he was receiving each month from the insurance company to cover our family's living expenses while our home was being rebuilt. In addition to the dairy, Woodruff owned an excavation company, and business had been slow. The insurance money would help to feed his large family.

Woodruff was not the only one experiencing financial difficulty at the time. For almost a year, my father had been in the process of selling the company he'd founded with a partner in the late 1970s. The company, Hydropac, sold components, parts, and seals used in hydraulic and pneumatic equipment and pumps. In its prime, it had about twenty employees and contracts with numerous branches of the U.S. military as well as NASA.

The sale of the company was taking place at the behest of Uncle Roy, who wanted my father to discontinue his frequent business trips and be at home with his family. This was not the first time that my father had sacrificed a high-paying position at the prophet's direction. Back in the spring of 1967, Uncle Roy had instructed Dad to leave his job at Thiokol Corporation, where he worked on secret, high-tech rocket-development programs. The prophet told Dad that his business travel was interfering with his time with his family and exposing him to outside influences he deemed "worldly." Uncle Roy wanted his followers close to him, and with little explanation, he told my father to resign from his post and move his family from their Brigham City residence to the Salt Lake Valley. A strong believer in FLDS teachings, Dad trusted in the prophet and, without questioning, did as he was told; he quit Thiokol and moved his family to Salt Lake. The move exacted a huge financial toll on the family, from which they would not recover for years.

A similar scenario played out when my father later went to work at Kenway Engineering, where he had secured a high-paying position as a program manager. There he oversaw projects valued at forty to sixty million dollars and supervised a large staff, but sure enough, after a little while, Uncle Roy told him he had to leave that job for the good of his family.

Because of these two incidents and the financial burden they had placed on our family, my father was understandably reluctant to sell Hydropac, fearing he would lose a small fortune in the process. With two wives and nineteen children, many of whom were still living at home, he had to be careful with his finances. He postponed selling the company for about a year, hoping that Uncle Roy would relent and allow him to keep it.

That hope died with Leroy Johnson. In the wake of Uncle Roy's passing, Rulon Jeffs became prophet, exerting renewed and vigorous pressure on my father to sell the company. The sale would be for a fraction of Hydropac's true value, to three FLDS members, among them Brian and Wallace Jeffs, Rulon's sons, who had been working at the company for about two years. It didn't matter that none of the men buying Hydropac had experience running a high-tech company, it was what the prophet wanted, and so it had to be done. In the end, my father proved no match for the newly consolidated power of Jeffs, finally acquiescing to priesthood demands and putting his family in financial straits in the process.

After the sale was finalized, Dad had more free time to spend with us at Woodruff's house, and during this period our family grew further enmeshed with the Salt Lake Valley FLDS community. Woodruff was an influential person in the church, with strong ties to its followers. Since my dad was a convert and didn't have a real family connection to the religion, we'd always been a little bit segregated from the church. Our time with the Steeds brought us closer not only to their family but to the FLDS way of life.

The eight months at the Steed compound offered Dad, Mom, and Mother Audrey a reprieve from their typical routine and helped them to get along better. These were happy months, and in the years that followed, my older siblings would often share with me their fond memories of that time. It provided a chance for the kids in our family to play with the other children, roaming free on the Steeds' expansive property and forming close links with the Steed family.

We returned to the house on Claybourne Avenue in time to celebrate my first birthday on July 7, 1987. While most of the money from the sale of Hydropac went to the church, my father had held some back to make improvements to expand and redesign the house, which had been built with a much smaller family in mind. This time my father designed much of the interior to accommodate our large family, and everybody was pleased with the way it turned out. We all hoped the new home would give us a fresh start. After eight months living in four bedrooms at the Steeds' property, we were finally able to stretch out and make the most of our new surroundings.

I shared the nursery on the main floor with my twin brothers and Brad. Our room was just across the hall from my mother's, which was kitty-corner to Dad's suite. Mother Audrey's room was at the far end of the same hall. All three of the adults' rooms had queen-sized beds. The living room now had carefully crafted floor-to-ceiling windows, and in the mornings the sun would fill the entire first floor, which Dad had finished in a lovely pale blond wood. Most of the bedrooms for the older kids were in the basement, and unlike the rest of the house, those rooms always felt dark and grim to me, even though there were some windows at grade level. The basement was also where Dad kept his hunting rifles and bows safely secured behind a panel inside an enormous walk-in pantry. The floor-to-ceiling shelves of this pantry were filled with home-canned food, enough to last us for six months. Many members of the FLDS had similar storage spaces, since we were taught that the end of the world was coming and storing food was one way to prepare. It could take several months once we'd settled back on earth after the destructions before we'd again be able to start planting and harvesting our own crops.

At first, living in the nursery room with my brothers was fun. I was born smack dab in the middle of the younger boys in my family and found myself stuck playing with them much of the time. There were two bunk beds, and we liked to jump back and forth from one to the other. We spent hours doing this or tying sheets across the two beds to make a hammock. As my brothers and I jumped around the room, my ankles would sometimes get caught in the hem of my long dress. Like me, my brothers had restrictions on what they could wear. In order to cover their church undergarments, they wore long-sleeved shirts and long pants, even in summertime. Our wild games made the boys hot and sweaty; they were constantly tugging at their collars in discomfort.

We were typical, rambunctious kids with lots of energy and not much to do at home all day long. Mom let me read the American Girl doll catalog from time to time, and I dreamed of the day that I might be able to get a Molly doll for myself. Dad provided us with toys to fit his budget, but with so many birthdays in a year, he could not afford a doll so extravagant. Still, our family made a big deal of birthdays. Dad always marked them with a special dinner out or a gift he'd carefully selected, and Mom prepared beautiful hand-decorated cakes. On the months when there was more than one birthday, we'd have one big party with a cake and presents for each child celebrating.

Dad didn't allow us to leave the property without an adult, and our school friends lived too far away for frequent visits. With nowhere to go and little to play with, we found sanctuary in the backyard. My brothers and I were always out there, making up games and bickering. Being trapped at home all day forced us to be creative. We'd spend hours playing cowboys and Indians or hide-and-go-seek. On sunny summer days, we would climb high into the branches of the trees around our house and leap out with bedsheets tied to our wrists and ankles, aiming our landings for the big trampoline we positioned to hopefully break our fall. Given the dangerous nature of our play, there were occasional mishaps that would send Mom into a panic, but luckily for us, we got by with a few broken bones and minor scrapes and bruises.

My sisters were much older than I was, and they rarely included me in their activities. Teressa, who was closest to me in age, was still seven years my senior. I adored her and all my other sisters, and I couldn't wait until I was old enough to move downstairs with the big kids. Sometimes I'd sneak down to my sister Michelle's room and slip into bed next to her after everyone went to sleep.

When I got sick Michelle was always there to take care of me. I'd climb into her bed because Mom's was often full with some of her other children. Like a lot of FLDS families, we didn't have private health insurance. My dad didn't believe in living off the government, so instead of getting Medicaid or food stamps like many members did, we went without coverage. My mother was an herbalist who believed you should use God's natural remedies before turning to the medical community. Her skeptical view of conventional medicine was shared by most FLDS members, who were quite suspicious of the professional medical community because they were afraid the government was using medicine to spy on people. For this reason, we were also not fully immunized because a suspicion circulated around the community that the government was putting tracking devices in the vaccines, or that they were making the vaccines bad to hurt the people. I rarely went to a doctor or an emergency room as a child, and when I had an ear infection I usually did not have access to antibiotics or other pharmaceuticals. I remember nights when I would cry myself to sleep because my ears hurt so badly.

By the time I turned five, the financial crunch from the sale of Hydropac was beginning to ease. Dad had found good work as a mining consultant, but the job unfortunately took him away from home to remote mining sites throughout the West.

My father was somewhat strict and expected a lot from us, but he loved us and we knew it. He would tell us that we could do anything with hard work. Seeing him in the evening was the highlight of our day. We didn't get to leave the house much, except to attend church on Sundays, so when we heard Dad's car pull into the driveway, we all raced to greet him in the carport, hoping he would have a stick of gum for us. Dad kept his stash of Big Red cinnamon gum in his Buick Le Sabre and we were crazy about that gum. If we were lucky, sometimes he'd invite us along to the supermarket, where he did all the grocery shopping from a list that his wives would compile.

Since Dad was often away on business during the week,

it was important to him that we spend time as a family on weekends. We would sometimes share quiet evenings in front of the TV, watching *Little House on the Prairie* or a National Geographic special that Dad deemed appropriate. All the kids would crowd around the TV in the living room to enjoy Saturday-morning cartoons. In college Dad had played football, and he passed his love for the game on to us. On some Saturday mornings, he would take the older children to see his alma mater, Brigham Young University, play football, and when they returned he would recount the game's best plays to me. I couldn't wait until I was old enough to go with them. Sadly, religious pressures and new priesthood teachings began to restrict these trips to outside sporting events, labeling them as "worldly" entertainment. By the time I was old enough to attend, our family no longer went. The priesthood expected the members to dedicate their Saturdays to donating labor for the church work projects instead of partaking in family fun. I never got to have my own experience with my dad watching his favorite team play.

Every summer we enjoyed a one-week vacation camping in the Uinta Mountains. The endless expanses and quiet solitude gave us a reprieve from our hectic and often chaotic existence. Somehow when we were in the mountains, our problems seemed to dissolve. With room to breathe, we all put our anger aside and remembered what it means to be with family. We had a special campsite there, a big meadow with lots of privacy. Being in the wilderness was the best part of our summers. Since he was a geologist, Dad would teach us about rocks, fossils, plants, and how to be smart in the wild.

Dad was amazing with a Dutch oven and liked to prepare large breakfasts of pancakes, bacon and eggs, and hot chocolate with mini-marshmallows. After a day enjoying the great outdoors we would have the treat of Dad's special roast and potatoes for dinner. At night, under a blanket of stars, we'd have big campfires and sing hymns or family songs. My mother has a beautiful voice and my sisters all played violin. Together, they would end the day with the sweet harmony of "Danny Boy," my Dad's favorite song. Oftentimes, my dad's father and stepmother, who were not members of the FLDS, would come on our camping trips. Even though they did not share our lifestyle, Grandma and Grandpa Wall loved us just the same. Mom slept with us in a little pop-up camper, and Dad shared a tent with Mother Audrey. I never thought to question why Dad had two wives and Grandpa Wall didn't. It was all I knew. Mother Audrey was the "other" mother and that was that. It was never explained. That was just how it was.

When I was six years old in the fall of 1992, I started the first grade at Alta Academy. My turn had finally come to leave the house for a few hours each day, and I was looking forward to being among my older siblings.

Alta Academy was a combination school, place of worship, and birthing center for the FLDS people who lived in the Salt Lake Valley. In 1972, with many of his children grown and no longer living at home, Rulon Jeffs had converted his twenty-plus-bedroom white brick residence into a school for FLDS children, moving himself and his wives into a smaller, more elegant Colonial-style house that the people built for him just next door. The school would be called Alta Academy, and it became the center of church life in the Salt Lake Valley. Rulon's son Warren had just graduated with honors from the local public high school, and Uncle Rulon directed him to serve as Alta Academy's first principal. To many church members, Warren seemed intelligent and knowledgeable about the church's religious teachings—the ideal candidate to help mold the young minds of Salt Lake's FLDS community.

Uncle Rulon used church donations to fund the conversion of the drafty old house into a school, but much of the building remained as it was when he lived there. It was littered with secret cubbyholes built into the walls and hidden doors that blended in with the décor—hiding places that may have been used for plural wives and children in case of an unexpected raid by the police or other authorities. They could be locked from the inside to protect those in hiding from being discovered. There were also locks on the outside, and rumors circulated, but were never substantiated, that the hidden crawlspaces were used to correct a disobedient child or wife.

In two of the converted bedrooms on the second floor, Uncle Rulon opened a birthing center that was staffed by his wife Sharon, who became the midwife for the Salt Lake Valley's FLDS community. The delivery room was makeshift and had barely changed since it had been a bedroom in the original house. With blue shag carpeting on the floor and the lower half of the walls, it was wholly unlike anything you'd expect to see in a regular hospital. There was no sink or other running water in the room, and the midwife had to use an elongated sink in a nearby bathroom to wash the newborns. An adjacent bedroom was used as a recovery room for the mothers and their babies.

Though the birthing center provided only basic medical equipment and services, it offered members one distinct advantage over hospitals: husbands could be present when their plural wives gave birth. Before the birthing center, men rarely accompanied their plural wives to give birth because it risked attracting attention from outsiders. Such was the case when my mother gave birth to her first daughter, Rachel. Mother Audrey had accompanied Mom to the hospital, with Dad relegated to the waiting room.

Before Alta Academy opened its doors, children in the Salt Lake area had attended the public schools. My older brothers and sisters who grew up then had gone to the elementary school just up the road. Mothers enrolled their children under fictitious names to hide their status as plural wives.

On that first day of school I was incredibly excited, but it didn't take me long to figure out that the drive to school was fraught with the same tension that permeated my home life. Since Mother Audrey worked as a teacher at Alta Academy, it was her responsibility to get us into Dad's big blue Chevy

Suburban, which we all called "Big Blue," and shepherd us
to class on time. Of course, rounding up nearly a dozen kids
was no easy task. My sister Teressa was always ready first.
Eager to get a move on, she'd go outside to the car and wait
for the rest of us to file out. After about ten minutes she was
back in the house, screaming at everyone to hurry up. Then
she was back at the car, where she'd honk the horn wildly to
let us know that she meant business.

Inside the house chaos reigned as we shoveled oatmeal
into our mouths and scrambled to get dressed. The drive to
Alta Academy took about twenty minutes in good weather,
but there was often fog and snow. On some days, the ride felt
like an eternity to me, sitting squished between my brothers
in the third row of Big Blue. There was usually a lot of commotion in the truck, with everybody trying to talk over everybody else. At times, fights would break out and Mother
Audrey would step in to take charge. She didn't like us hors-
ing around when she was trying to concentrate on the road,
and she wasn't afraid to tell us.

Mother Audrey differed from Mom in the way she handled discipline. She had a clear idea of how things should be
run, and her preoccupation with order pervaded every aspect of her life, including her appearance. While Audrey's
eyeglasses would shift within the bounds of popular fashion, everything else about her style remained constant. The
long skirts and blouses she wore during my childhood had
become a kind of uniform, and she never changed her hairstyle: one wave on each side of her head, with the rest swept
up in the back. During the rides to school, Mother Audrey
tried to impart her beliefs about how we should conduct
ourselves both at home and in school. Often her lectures
upset my sisters. Sometimes they'd argue back. Other times
they'd fester in silence, telling Mom about the confrontation
when they got home.

Part of what made the car rides so tumultuous was that this
was one of the only times during the day that we were alone
with Mother Audrey. Because our mother was concerned
about the way that Mother Audrey reprimanded us, she tried

to keep us separated from her. If we wandered into Audrey's room, we would be shooed out. By that time, to ease the pressure, Audrey rarely interacted with our side of the family, spending much of her time in her bedroom with her own children. After school, Mom and Dad would hear about the day's drive and inevitably the friction would grow, frequently culminating in an angry blowup in which Mom defended her children against being deemed as the only source of the trouble.

Every school day began with a class called Devotional, taught by Warren Jeffs. The meeting room on the ground floor, which was used as a religious hall for Sunday and priesthood meetings, was enormous, half a football field long, but it still could not accommodate all of the Alta Academy students for Devotional, so the fourth- through twelfth-graders met in there, while students in the lower grades listened over the PA system from their classrooms. Every student, no matter his or her age, was expected to take notes, which were always reviewed and graded. The content of the Devotional was mostly religious teachings, with readings and homework assignments from the Book of Mormon.

Most of the students had to enter through the door at the very back of the room, and the age and grade level determined the section you sat in. This explained Teressa's morning panic; at thirteen she'd have to walk all the way to the front with the older kids, directly in Warren Jeffs's line of view. If she walked in late, she would meet one of his signature stern glares—no one wanted to receive one of those. We were all expected to treat Uncle Warren with the highest respect; he was not only our school principal but also the son of the prophet.

Uncle Warren would start every morning by saying, "I am only here to do the prophet's will," a statement that always made it seem as though the lesson that followed had been dictated by his father and thus was the word of God. As students, we all strove to gain Warren's approval. Having his good opinion and acknowledgment meant much more than the small prizes he would sometimes hand out for good deeds and high marks. Life at school could be miserable if you were not in Uncle Warren's good graces.

One night in the spring of first grade, our family was eating a thick, mushy spaghetti dinner—Mother Audrey was frugal with the sauce—when my father revealed some exciting news: our family was blessed to have a daughter marry the prophet. My sister Rachel was twenty-two years old, and Dad had received word that she was to be married to Uncle Rulon, who was eighty-one at the time. It seemed that all the prettiest girls were chosen to hold the honor of marriage to the prophet, but no one would dare say that out loud. My oldest sister was no exception. Rachel was lucky to inherit our mother's rich dark hair, slender figure, and wide, bright smile.

In addition to Rachel's marriage being a tremendous honor for our family, it was also incredibly exciting to me that we would be invited to attend the wedding ceremony at Rulon Jeffs's sprawling thirteen-plus-bedroom residence in Salt Lake. For us, Uncle Rulon's tan brick house was considered a mansion. It was constructed of top-of-the-line materials and equipped with expensive appliances, and it had an enormous garage to accommodate his fancy Cadillac. We would be able to witness the ceremony in the prophet's living quarters on the main floor, which was treated as his private sanctuary.

The wedding took place on April 30, 1993. Because it was the prophet getting married, the marriage was "sealed" by my father, who had been temporarily ordained to fill the role usually played by the prophet. Not only was Rachel's marriage important for religious reasons, it also afforded my sister many opportunities that other women in the community didn't have. As a wife of the prophet, she was elevated in status, viewed as a worthy angel on earth. She was well provided for and had access to credit cards and cash. Even though it appeared to us that Uncle Rulon's wives were lucky and blessed to be members of his family, like all

FLDS women, they were still considered property of their husband and the priesthood. They were expected to keep sweet and be submissively obedient.

After the marriage, Dad sometimes allowed me to stay over with Rachel at Uncle Rulon's Salt Lake compound, where she had a room on the second floor. In my young mind, I always felt that I was staying at Buckingham Palace. It was a great honor to any member to be graced with the opportunity to be on the prophet's property. During my sleep-overs, I sometimes got to watch a kid-friendly video on the small TV that Rachel kept hidden in her closet.

While we had been able to watch TV when I was much younger, life had grown more constricted under Rulon Jeffs's direction. In an attempt to cleanse the people of all outside influences, he'd banned television, films, and video games. Through Uncle Warren, we'd been told that the prophet had ordered all the books in the school library that were not priesthood-approved be burned, claiming that those who read the unworthy books would take on the "evil" spirit of their authors. The library was then restocked with books that conformed to priesthood teachings.

Warren also had a house on his father's compound, where I was sometimes invited to play with his daughter Shirley, a classmate at Alta Academy. While his house was nowhere near as big as his dad's, it had plenty of space for his five wives and their many children to spread out.

Though he was harsh and intimidating at school, I liked Uncle Warren and he seemed like a caring father to my friend. But my feelings about him began to change when I entered the second grade. I was in the middle of schoolwork in Mrs. Nicolson's class when I heard my teacher's name called over the loudspeaker. I watched her pick up the telephone and look in my direction. I was to report to the principal's office at once. I had no idea why I'd been summoned, but I'd been at Alta Academy long enough to know that it wasn't a good thing to be singled out to see Uncle Warren.

My legs felt heavy as I climbed the carpeted stairs to the third floor, where he had his office. The walls of his office were covered in cheap wood paneling, and he was seated behind a large desk that faced the door. Our eyes met as soon as I stepped into the doorway. He was smiling when he told me to sit down in one of the chairs facing his desk. I was about to receive my first lesson on boy/girl relations.

Warren had been told that I was holding the hand of my seven-year-old male cousin while playing outside earlier in the day. This was true, but I had no idea why he was bringing it up. As he explained, what I had done was absolutely not to be tolerated. I was never to touch boys; I was to treat them as poisonous reptiles, as "snakes." Even thinking about a boy was "unclean."

It was a strange lecture, but I took it to heart, vowing to obey him and not touch a boy again. Unfortunately for me, that was not the only thing that landed me in Warren's office that year. A few months later, I was back there for unknowingly breaking the dress code. As a souvenir from one of his trips, my father had given me a gold heart-shaped ring and necklace set that was accented with pink sparkles. It wasn't super-expensive, but it meant a lot to me because it was from my dad. I didn't want to take it off and had worn it to school so that all my friends could see. Again, I climbed the stairs in dread. When I arrived in Warren's office, he greeted me kindly.

"That's a beautiful necklace and ring," he said. "Can you please put the pieces on my desk?"

I wasn't sure what was going to happen, but given his gentle tone it didn't seem like I was in any trouble. Uncle Warren spoke in a mild tone and was formal. He always addressed me as "Miss Wall."

"Miss Wall," he began, as he turned the sparkly pink and gold necklace over in his fingers and admired it. "Are you aware of the restrictions on what the priesthood people can wear?"

I had no idea, and didn't immediately answer. Now I was intimidated and worried, not knowing how to respond.

"This jewelry is quite nice," he continued.

I began to exhale a sigh of relief.

He told me that it was wrong to adorn our bodies with worldly possessions. "Now, I want you to walk over to the garbage can and throw them away."

I was devastated and embarrassed, but there was nothing I could do. Lowering my eyes, I obediently dropped the jewelry into the can, losing them forever.

I cried as I related my terrible experience with Uncle Warren to my mother that afternoon. She was sympathetic but firm. She told me that from that day forth I should not wear unacceptable items to school. I had to obey what Warren said. I was too afraid to tell my father, feeling ashamed to have lost something that he had given me, so I kept the incident to myself, oftentimes sulking in private when I thought about how my precious gift had become Uncle Warren's trash.

The summer following second grade, I was officially baptized into the priesthood in the sacred "baptismal vault" in the basement of Alta Academy. I knew about the room, but I'd never actually been inside it until I had come of age. Descending the stairs to the basement in my pretty white full-length dress, I felt a rush of apprehension. I was excited to be participating in the sacred rite of passage, but also a bit scared. It was the way I felt about all of our rituals: it was good to know that my time had come, but there was always mystery surrounding the observance. Still, the thought that my father would be waiting for me in the waist-deep water calmed me down.

My mom and some of my siblings were standing just outside the door as I took off my white lace socks and white shoes and prepared to enter the room. I walked through the door of the sacred space slowly and descended the white tile steps that led into the enormous tub that took up much of the room, my clothing growing heavier with each step.

Three church elders had to be present for the ceremony; one was my dad, who was already in the water waiting for me to join him. The water was deep, just about up to my shoulders when I reached the section where Dad stood. For the ritual to be performed properly, every part of the body had to be completely submersed. My father had to submerge me three times because my foot kept popping out of the water.

Climbing back out of the tub, I was met by the other two elders standing just inside the doorway. They were there to perform a laying on of hands and anoint me with the special olive oil that had been blessed by three church elders for the occasion. I should have been freezing because the water in the font was so cold, but I was too overwhelmed to care.

I was officially a member of the church now and responsible for all my actions. It was an important moment in my life as an FLDS believer. The baptism signified that I was now accountable for my choices. All my childhood sins were instantly wiped away and I was given a "clean slate" to begin my life as an official member of the priesthood. From here on out, making the wrong choices could result in a permanent "black mark" on my slate that would remain until I was judged in heaven.

The moment I exited the cold tub of water I began to think carefully about how I behaved. I was in the church now, and I had to obey all the rules. If I didn't, there would be consequences.

CHAPTER THREE

GOOD PRIESTHOOD

CHILDREN

Your family must be united.
—RULON JEFFS

In the weeks immediately following Mother Laura's arrival in October 1995, the tension in the house had, for the most part, subsided. We'd cleared one of my sisters' bedrooms on the lower level to make room for our new mother, and at the start we were all on our best behavior.

Mother Laura's entry into our lives came at a time when many things in the Wall house were changing. In the span of a few months, my sisters Kassandra, Sabrina, and Michelle were all married according to the prophet's revelation. Kassandra, at nineteen years old, joined Rachel as one of the many wives of Rulon Jeffs, who by that point was eighty-three, while Sabrina was married to a member of the FLDS community in Canada. Michelle stayed closer to home, marrying Uncle Rulon's son Seth. All of my sisters had been over the age of eighteen at the time of their marriages, and Dad had been chastised for keeping them in the home so long. But my father just wanted to give his girls the opportunity to grow up.

Of these departures, Michelle's hit me the hardest. She had the gentlest soul of anyone in my family and had always looked out for me—comforting me when I was sick, making sure that my hair was combed, and that I was dressed neatly and appropriately. There were so many children in the Wall household, and as the nineteenth, I sometimes fell through the cracks. But Michelle made every effort to ensure that didn't happen; she was like a second mother to me. For the eldest sisters in the home to help with the care of the little ones was a common practice for families of the FLDS. Mom had thirteen children of her own still living in the home, and with Audrey up and out early to teach at Alta Academy, that left most of the domestic duties on Mom's shoulders, so she needed Michelle, Kassandra, and Sabrina around to provide us extra attention. Of course, nothing compared to Mom's healing touch, but in many ways Michelle had become another anchor for me. Losing her was unthinkable. I cried right up until the day of the wedding, begging her not to go away.

With all these changes in the family, it was beginning to feel like our house had a revolving door with people constantly coming in and going out. However, though we lost many of my older sisters that year, we had gained a mother and there was hope in that new relationship. I looked to Mom for advice on how to welcome Mother Laura. She had grown up knowing and wanting this lifestyle, but I now understand that our years of turmoil had made many of us skeptical about what her arrival would do to the already touchy atmosphere in our household.

Mom had endured years of compromising as she'd tried to pattern this home after the one she'd grown up in. I know that she had obeyed her priesthood head as she was directed, but over the years she'd grown increasingly disheartened at the way her relationship with her sister wife and husband had affected her children.

Mom's firm religious convictions reminded her to hold her tongue and keep sweet. I admired how she welcomed Mother Laura with open arms. Seeing her embrace our new mother made me hopeful that this new element in the equation would balance our home out. Because Laura's age was close to that of my older sisters, I felt optimistic about the prospect of forming a bond with her like the one that I shared with them. At first this seemed possible. Mother Laura and I had lots of fun, playing games with some of my other siblings. Her presence helped to alleviate some of the emptiness I'd felt since my sisters' departures. But I watched helplessly as it soon became worse than before. Mom's gentle personality and unwavering commitment to her faith were no match for the others in the home. It distressed me to see the lonely look in her eyes as she tried to keep the pieces together and shield her younger children from a repeat of the past.

But by the end of that first month, the newness of having Mother Laura in the house had begun to wear off. It was quickly becoming clear that Dad's third wife had her own unique set of expectations and would present certain challenges. She was yet another person who wanted things done her way. We'd seen glimmers of that stubborn side during family get-togethers, but her desire to take charge held a different significance now that she was part of our household.

While Laura's presence was problematic in itself, it served to aggravate another long-simmering tension in the family, involving my twenty-one-year-old brother, Craig. As he came of age, my oldest brother from my mother had finally been able to quiet some of the tension between the mothers and the children in our home. But adding Laura to the family had again made the equation unbalanced. It was not long after she arrived that old feuds were rekindled. She and Mother Audrey quickly became friends and their newly formed bond seemed to have the two women pitted against Mom and her children. Seeing his mother and younger siblings being improperly treated forced Craig to step in and do what he could. We were still recovering from losing three of our sisters and it had been hard for my mother's children, especially Craig.

In conversations with Craig since, I have come to see that my brother, like most young men his age, had long been contemplating what he had been taught growing up. He found that many aspects of our religion had glaring discrepancies and didn't make sense or feel right.

Craig possessed a fiery intelligence and a quick mind. When he was still a high school student at Alta Academy, he had begun to examine aspects of our religion in his quest to gain a deeper understanding of our faith. Uncle Warren didn't seem to like Craig because he wasn't just another sheep willing to follow the flock. He was an enthusiastic student, and in priesthood history, he often asked pointed questions that would back Warren into a corner in front of the whole class. While he was eagerly trying to understand how the teachings and our culture all fit together, Warren was threatened by my brother's inquisitiveness and labeled him as trouble. The two often clashed.

Warren seemed to single out Craig and watch for any misstep he made. He was always ready to chastise him and often made an example of him in front of his classmates. One particularly shame-inducing consequence for acting out in school was to have your father called in, and Warren was not afraid to subject the students to that humiliation.

Warren's attitude toward Craig and many of my siblings seemed to come not just from displeasure with their behavior but from a larger, more fundamental problem with the Wall family. It was almost as though he felt threatened by us. The fact that many in my family were smart, strong-willed, and unafraid to ask questions when things did not feel right made it hard to keep a tight hold on us. Warren didn't like having to deal with disobedience and questions concerning the priesthood. Our religion left no room for logical reasoning and honest questioning. Warren made no attempt to understand or tolerate any of this, deeming it as absolute rebellion.

By the time Craig was twenty-one, doors had been opened and he began to objectively examine our culture. He was still a believer, but was growing skeptical. He had lost trust and faith in the church and its leaders because he was having trouble reconciling the way they were teaching to the way in which they were conducting their actual lives. Seeing our sisters get placed for marriage to men who were so much older than they were only confirmed for Craig that there were many unjust and illogical elements to the FLDS belief system. In particular, the marriage of our half-sister Andrea disturbed him.

Andrea had wed Larry Steed, who was also married to Mother Audrey's daughter, Jean. Because Jean was one of the oldest girls in our family, the younger children were not close to her, and Andrea feared that life in the new home would be difficult. Before her marriage, we all worried about the prophet's revelation that she should marry Larry. We were skeptical that the union would make her happy, and doubt began to swirl that the placement had truly been God's will.

Though Craig had been raised to see Andrea's placement as a revelation from God, he questioned more than ever the arrangement. At the time, he worried that Larry and others had contrived the marriage and suspected it had little to do with any divine inspiration. He was coming to question the most fundamental aspect of our way of life: divine revelation from God regarding placement marriage. A thought like this went against everything we knew, but with no outlet for his questions, Craig continued to struggle inwardly.

When Mother Laura moved in, his internal debate began to bubble over in noticeable ways, and he was sometimes confrontational. It wasn't just about how Mother Laura behaved; her presence was a constant reminder that the church's values were flawed and that plural marriage was not working in our home. Laura had a forceful personality, a trait that combined with Audrey's similar personality seemed to drown out our mother. I was too young to really know what was going on or see the dynamic, but I could tell that Craig's concern only grew as he came to feel that Mom was not being treated properly.

Looking back, I wonder if a lot of the fights may have arisen because neither Dad nor Audrey knew how to live in plural marriage. Even if you're raised in plural marriage and have a model for it, it's difficult to make it work—to know when to compromise, when to complain, and when to involve the father. If you're not careful, minor scuffles can snowball into ugly conflicts. Since Audrey grew up in a monogamous family, it seemed hard for her to take a conciliatory tone, and with the addition of Laura's assertiveness, my mother's needs frequently got lost in the fray.

My mother's background only made things more complicated, because she knew all too well that plural marriage, with all its intricacies, could work under the right circumstances. Mom had been raised in a household that was held up as the ideal plural family, where the mothers got along and *all* the kids truly saw one another as siblings. Mom embraced her faith and the FLDS teaching in regard to women, and desired a peaceful household. As it wasn't Mom's way to engage in fights with the other women in the house, she would often retreat instead of getting in the middle and making things worse. Everyone on Mom's side felt that Dad should stand up for her more, and we were upset when he allowed the more forceful wives to take charge.

The situation failed to improve with time. Craig, being my mother's oldest son, took on the responsibility of advocating for her and her children when no one else would. When his conflicts with Mothers Audrey and Laura escalated, my father was often pulled in, leading to contention between him and Craig. Some fights got so heated that they turned physical. I had always seen my dad as an even-tempered and reasonable man, but now it was slowly beginning to show that he was consumed by the situation and having trouble controlling his feelings. It appeared that in Dad's mind, Craig was affecting the other boys in the home and tainting their beliefs, and in trying to solve this problem, he was losing his grip on our family and on himself.

Dad tried to address the family's dissension during our regular Sunday-school lessons in the living room. As our priesthood head, he was in charge of educating his children on our religion and its principles. Everyone, even the mothers, was expected to attend Sunday lessons. Typically, the kids fought for a seat on one of the two couches. Whoever didn't get a seat on the couch got relegated to the floor.

Dad was a stickler for punctuality, and the lesson began promptly at 10 A.M., usually with a reading from the Book of Mormon or the Bible. The lesson usually lasted about an hour, during which Dad would select one or two of us to stand and bear witness, while he sat on the couch in front of the big windows. I could always tell when he was about to raise the family issues because he'd begin talking about the "United Order," a teaching that stressed the importance of oneness and reinforced the other teachings we'd been hearing our entire lives. He said we couldn't attain it in our home without complete harmony in the family. Ideal FLDS children were expected to be "humble, faithful servants" of their priesthood head and the prophet. That meant the daughters needed to "quit arguing," the mothers needed to "stop fighting," and we all needed to "keep sweet and keep the spirit of God." Unfortunately for him, his words seemed to be falling on deaf ears, and they did little to quell the growing unrest. While I believe my father tried not to point fingers, by my perception it appeared that Dad was singling Craig out as the cause of our family's problems.

I was just a couple of months into school's fall session when Dad made a fateful pronouncement: Craig was to be out of the house by November 1, 1996. Since he was over eighteen, it was considered too late to send him away to reform, as was customarily done in cases such as this. Instead, Dad just wanted him to leave.

I will never forget the day that Craig asked Mom if she could drive him to the highway, where he would hitchhike out of the area. Some of us younger kids piled into Mom's little brown Buick sedan to join her for the ride and say good-bye to our older brother. The hour-long drive was mostly quiet, and our silence said everything about the sadness and fear we all felt. My sister Teressa was taking it the hardest. She had become very close to Craig, and now he was one more person leaving our lives. With little money in his pocket and raw emotional wounds, Craig set off to find his own answers to his many questions.

I could barely watch him get out of our car and walk away. The final image I had of my brother Craig is with a backpack strapped to him and a sign reading DENVER in his hand. Years later, my mother would tell me that leaving Craig by the side of the road that day was one of the most painful things she ever had to do. At the time, though, she was as silent as any perfect FLDS wife should be. Casting out her son was her duty. She could not object, and even if she did, her opinion would not matter. She had to follow the orders of her husband; that was the command of the church, and she obeyed it no matter how much pain it caused her.

Even so, it took her several minutes to find the strength to shift the car into drive. As we wound down the gray asphalt of the highway heading home, I watched tears trace the soft skin of my mother's face. She was still beautiful, but in that moment she became a shadow of her former self. She had lost her eldest son, her protector. It was a wound that would never completely heal. I saw Teressa beside her, hands folded stiffly in her lap and her pained eyes staring into space. She had just watched her dear friend and brother walk away and did not know if she would ever see him again. I wanted so badly to reach up from the backseat and hug both of them, to offer the only form of consolation that I as a ten-year-old child could provide, but I knew better. The best and only option was to keep my mouth closed.

It was not until many years later that any of us heard from Craig. He purposely avoided reaching out to our family for fear of further affecting his younger brothers and sisters. Over time I came to understand his choice to put distance between himself and our family, but back then I thought of him frequently, which would always make me feel a bit sad and discouraged. I didn't really understand the concept of questioning, but I felt sympathy for the way things had turned out between Craig and my dad. I was not alone in my concern for him, but I kept my pain to myself; it was not something to be spoken of. At home, I noticed a marked change in my mother. She seldom sang or hummed around the house anymore, and she began to look drained, somehow older. A general sadness permeated the household and made me miss Michelle all the more. I wished so dearly that I could hold on to my mother as I had once done with Michelle. Without my nurturing older sister around, I had no one to make me feel safe in the unrest that had taken over our home and irrevocably changed our lives.

In the weeks after Craig's departure, a pall set over the house, and even Mother Laura's pregnancy and impending delivery didn't lift the mood. Having Craig leave was even hard for Dad, but he hoped it would bring our family's turbulence to an end. Dad had been optimistic that without their older brother's brooding influence, the younger children would fall back into line. Instead, some of them began to exhibit their anger at having lost so many older siblings.

The summer before Craig left, my brother Travis, four years Craig's junior, had begun to question his faith in much the same way that Craig had. The church leaders decided to send Travis to Short Creek to reform so that he would become more faithful. Sending children to reform was the church's way of dealing with those who got out of line. Because Travis was younger than Craig there was still "hope" for him in the eyes of the priesthood, and this retreat was supposed to bring him back into compliance. On a reform retreat, the boys do manual labor for the priesthood, while immersed in the teachings of the church and isolated from their families. At the end of their time, they are supposed to return to their homes behaving and thinking properly.

Travis was placed with a family in southern Utah known for its good priesthood children. The hope was that being in their household would remind him of his role as an obedient and active member of the church, but the reality was that reform was a harsh environment. Shut off from communication with his family, Travis was mistreated by those in charge of his attitude adjustment.

Even without Travis in the house, his doubts began to trickle down to the twins, Justin and Jacob, and Brad, all of whom adored their older brothers and used them as examples. The younger boys now displayed their own doubts about the church's role in our family, and Mom was powerless as she watched the same fights that Craig and Travis had with our father and mothers happen all over again. The departure of Travis and Craig had done little to change Dad's manner or the feeling in the house. Desperate not to lose yet another son, I later learned that Mom had begun confiding her fears to my sister Rachel. She was worried that my father had lost his ability to control and unite our family, and she believed we needed outside help.

Though we knew things were bad, none of us were aware that Mom was losing faith in our father. All we knew was that every day the problems seemed to get worse and the options seemed to grow fewer.

CHAPTER FOUR

IN LIGHT
AND TRUTH

The prophet can do no wrong.
—WARREN JEFFS

After all the struggles in our home, I longed for my mother's pain to subside and for peace to be restored. That previous August I'd returned to Alta Academy a fifth-grader. While I wasn't in an upper classroom yet, I was now in my second year with the big kids in the meeting hall for Devotional.

In addition to being our principal, Warren also taught a number of our classes. One of them was a class in priesthood history, which occurred every day and was considered the most important lesson in school. Uncle Warren would teach us everything about our religion's history, starting from biblical lessons to the Book of Mormon and going through the life of Joseph Smith as well as the more recent developments in the FLDS. Uncle Warren would always use priesthood-approved scriptures to teach the lesson, and then he would explain them using his own words.

Part of the curriculum for older girls was to study *In Light and Truth,* an FLDS publication. The book was a collection of condensed sermons and teachings by Joseph Smith, Brigham Young, Uncle Rulon, and many others. Warren would read the various lessons to the girls, applying his own spin. He would even read the words of his own sermons in such a way as to make us believe that the words were coming directly from God.

We were encouraged to listen to tapes of Uncle Warren's important sermons as frequently as we could. Often in school we would hear these tapes wafting out of the loud-speakers as we went about our day. We also listened to them at home the way other families would listen to music, and as I grew older, I took to listening to them on my own. I was dedicated to being a good student, even if I didn't entirely understand every aspect of my religion. I searched for answers in the tapes and in my school lessons, rarely asking for help when I felt confused. If I didn't understand something, it was better not to say it aloud than appear to be questioning priesthood principles.

Ever since the age of eight or nine, I had been taking a home-economics course along with the rest of the girls in which we learned the basics of running a household. Taking these courses brought us closer to our ultimate goal— becoming perfect priesthood wives. Kitchen abilities were an extremely important element of our lessons. Our individual teachers would separate us from the boys and lead us to the huge industrial kitchen just off the meeting hall. There, we learned basic cooking and cleaning skills that would ready us for the large families that would someday be ours. There were also classes in sewing. We all needed to be able to stitch our special church undergarments and the ankle-length prairie dresses that were a staple in our wardrobes, and some day our own wedding dresses. Most of my dresses were hand-me-downs from my older sisters. On special occasions, like my birthday, Mom would sew one just for me, and I looked forward to doing such things for my own daughters someday.

One afternoon in early December, it became clear that God was continuing to test my family. I was at school and had just finished enjoying my lunch of a tuna sandwich and an apple when Uncle Warren's assistant, Elizabeth, poked her head into my classroom and summoned me to the principal's office.

My legs shook as I followed Elizabeth down the hallway. I'd made this journey several times, and it had usually been for a "correction." Turning the corner, I found myself holding my breath as I approached Uncle Warren's office. I pushed open the door and nervously exhaled when I saw five of my siblings along with my mother sitting in Warren's office. Uncle Warren was seated at his desk, as always. Mom's brown eyes looked as if she'd been crying, and I knew something serious was going on. I quickly sat down in a chair facing Warren's desk. No one was speaking, which made me even more scared. I could see the confusion and fear on everyone's faces, and my heart began to race. Uncle Warren's low voice cut the silence.

"I'm delivering a message from the prophet," Warren began in an icy tone. "The prophet has lost confidence in your father. He is no longer worthy to hold the priesthood or have a family."

Shocked and confused, one of my brothers asked for an explanation. "How can that be?"

After a momentary pause, Uncle Warren glared down at him, his irritation visible from behind his thick eyeglasses. "Are you questioning the prophet and his will?"

No one—especially not a child—could argue with that. Still, we Wall kids had trouble accepting things when they didn't seem fair. Just like my brother Craig, we all looked for the truth in any given situation.

My brother Brad spoke next. "Where will we go?" he asked timidly.

"It's up to the prophet to decide," Warren told him. "You will no longer be attending school."

The silence was deafening as he told us to return to our classrooms and gather our things. Looking at my mother, I saw pain and sadness on her face. We would not be returning to our home or to school. Confusion took over my mind.

In a daze my brothers and I filed quietly out of the room, leaving my mother and my older sister Teressa behind with Warren.

I felt so ashamed knowing that my classmates were watching me as I collected my belongings. We hadn't been given a clear explanation as to why Dad had lost the priest-hood or what had led to this life-altering declaration. We were just to follow the prophet's direction. I was still gain-ing an understanding of the world I was raised in and the workings of the priesthood. Even though we had always lived to please the prophet and do his will, everything still felt so wrong. How could our father just be taken away from us? Why were they breaking up our family? What about Mother Audrey, Mother Laura, and their kids? Would Dad lose them as well? The questions burning in my mind would go unanswered, and I kept my mouth shut out of fear.

Once we gathered our things from our classrooms, we went to the meeting room on the main floor and were uncer-emoniously escorted across the blacktop driveway and through the gate that led to the prophet's home. We were told that we would spend the night there and that in the morn-ing we would leave for southern Utah, where my mother had grown up. Staying overnight at the home of the prophet made me feel safe and comforted, if only for the moment. I had always dearly loved my visits there. Many of Uncle Ru-lon's wives had been kind to me, and I loved and looked up to my elder sisters.

The drive down to southern Utah the next morning was a blur, and I remember it now more as a collection of images and feelings than actual events. The crunch of the tires on freshly fallen snow as we left. The thought that my brothers and I should have been making snowmen in our backyard instead of being packed into the back of a van. Wiping the fog off the inside of the van's window and watching our school disappear around the corner. Even if we had been scrambling to get to school on time in our traditional morn-ing rush, I would have felt infinitely happier. None of us knew if we were ever coming back or going to see my dad again. I was a child faced with unspeakable loss, completely confused, with no one giving any answers.

Rachel and Kassandra had joined us in two of Uncle Rulon's family vans for the four-hour drive to the prophet's other home in Hildale. They were there to help pass the time and keep the younger kids entertained. I didn't know then, but Rachel had played a role in Mom's decision to involve the prophet in our domestic problems. Over time, I learned that both Rachel and Mom believed that our home had become a battleground, with innocent children caught in the crossfire. For some time, Mom had been confiding in Rachel her fears about losing more of her sons and had sought her help drafting a letter to the prophet. Meanwhile, Rachel had independently gone to Uncle Rulon for advice. She and Kassandra knew that the previous morning Mom had gone to see Warren, who'd been acting for his father. To ease the severity of our situation, it had been arranged that my two sisters would accompany us on the long drive south. They tried to play games with us to lighten the mood, but I was too old and too aware to be distracted.

During the ride I searched my mother's face for answers, but unsurprisingly, it offered none. I knew I wasn't to question the prophet—or God—but I was desperate. "Will we ever see Dad again?" I asked Mom.

"I don't know, Lesie," she replied, using the nickname, pronounced "Lee-see," that I'd had since I was very young. "Put it on a shelf and pray about it."

This was Mom's and the FLDS's standard response to questions that had no easy answers. Between Craig's departure and the troubles at home, my shelf was already full. Now I worried it would tip over.

At the time I was so focused on my own experience that I didn't stop to think about how that day affected my father, and it was not until years later that we had a chance to talk about it. In the hours before we were gathered in Uncle Warren's office, Dad had been summoned to see the prophet at his home in Salt Lake. He was immediately shown to the prophet's private office, where he found Uncle Rulon and his son Warren. As had become the case in recent years, Warren was there to speak on behalf of his father. Although Uncle Rulon was still officially the prophet, he was in his mid-eighties and not as active as he once had been. Warren had taken on many of the traditional responsibilities of the prophet. A year earlier, it had been Warren who performed Dad's marriage ceremony to Mother Laura, and here he was, once again, delivering his father's directives. Taking a seat across from the men on one of the chairs, my father didn't know what to expect as he adjusted himself and waited to be addressed. Warren did not waste any time getting to the point.

"The prophet has lost confidence in you as a priesthood man and is taking Sharon and her children away," he blurted out.

The words were an assault and Dad was too overcome by emotion to respond. It seemed like only yesterday that he had been honored with the addition of a third wife. Now, as Warren had bluntly put it, Dad was losing Sharon and all of their children. He sat there listening to Warren speak, and the reality of the situation began to sink in: Dad had been stripped of his priesthood duties as they pertained to Mother Sharon and her children, but Mothers Audrey and Laura would remain under his control. As he sat listening, he wondered how everything could have slipped through his fingers so quickly. Rising to leave, he was too besieged by emotion to speak and left in bewilderment. My father later explained that he'd felt as if he'd become detached from his body as he heard the prophet's revelation that day. The words had been spoken, but Dad just couldn't make them feel real inside.

When he returned home, he found the belongings of Mother Sharon and her children had already been taken away. Mothers Audrey and Laura were shocked by the news. They too had been unhappy, but they'd never thought it would come to this. In the weeks ahead, Mother Audrey felt a devastating loss. While things had not been working in the house for quite some time, losing Mother Sharon and her children was much more upsetting than she ever imagined.

When our two vans arrived at the prophet's Hildale home, my mother's brother Kevin was waiting for us. He'd been instructed to take us to the Steed family ranch, some 150 miles outside of Short Creek near Widtsoe, Utah. My heart was momentarily warmed as I watched his hug seem to give my mother strength. It had been a long time since she'd lived there, but I sensed that she felt a certain relief to be going home.

Since Grandpa Newel's death at the age of eighty-six, many of his sons had cared for the ranch where he had raised his large family. Uncle Kevin and his family lived in the main house and had started a home school for their children on the sprawling grounds. The ranch had been in the Steed family for about eighty years, ever since Grandpa Newel settled it in 1916 at the tender age of fourteen. Despite his youth, Grandpa Newel had traveled alone with sixty head of cattle to the remote and barren land in southern Utah that his father had homesteaded, and it was there that he made good on his promise to his father that he would establish a fully functioning ranch. He spent hours alone caring for the stock, milking the cows, and churning fresh butter, barely making it through that first long, hard winter. But even as the isolating snow and ice cut through the valley, Newel Steed endured it all in the name of his dream: living a life where he could practice Mormonism as it was originally envisioned by Joseph Smith, a life where he was free to practice plural marriage.

Grandpa Newel's belief in the principle of plural marriage first took root when, at the age of ten, he accompanied his father to a clandestine meeting of men still in the Mormon Church who continued to embrace the practice in secret. This was in the early days of "The Work," decades before it was known as the FLDS Church. In time, Grandpa Newel was not only free to practice his religion, he also became one of the most respected members of the FLDS in southern Utah. When the Steed family arrived at a community event, all eyes were on their perfectly styled hair and their attractive homemade clothes. The Steeds were known for their taste in fabrics and their unique, trendsetting interpretation of the church-mandated dress code.

Although there was this rich tapestry of family history at the ranch, I had not spent much time with Uncle Kevin and his family. Still, he seemed genuinely happy to see us. I will never forget riding in the back of his white truck with the camper shell on it. The drive to Widtsoe seemed to take forever, and a little bud of excitement formed inside of me. I had rarely had the opportunity to visit the Steed ranch since my grandfather Newel's passing in 1988, and despite the acute sadness and confusion I had experienced over the past couple of days, I couldn't deny my eagerness to get there.

When we arrived, the house looked cozy, the snow-covered ground and the white picket fence that surrounded the historic wood residence giving it a homey feel. After such a long, emotional journey, it felt good to be received with love by Uncle Kevin's many wives and children. Mom's brother was a faithful follower and he and his family did all that they could to move aside and open a place for us to stay in their home.

We were moved by their generosity, but the accommodations were difficult for a family that had been used to more modern living. This was the original home that my mother had grown up in and it had not been updated. There was no power or central heat. The home was run on a generator and heated by an old wood-burning stove. Uncle Kevin had cleared a bedroom for my mother, sisters, and me, but my brothers had to bunk with some of Uncle Kevin's sons. Uncle Rulon had allowed my sister Kassandra to stay with us full-time, and Rachel traveled to see us when she could. At various points, there were as many as seven children in some of the rooms.

My mother's spirits seemed to lift immediately upon our arrival at the ranch. I sensed her relief and joy at being back in her childhood home. Having her and my older sisters close helped us get through this scary and trying period. But there were moments when I longed for my home in Salt Lake and to hear my father's soothing voice leading the family in evening prayer.

Even though everyone was willing to adopt us into the family, life was still not easy—especially for Teressa and my brothers. I was young enough not to understand everything that was going on, but they were fully aware of our situation's harsh realities. As we tried to process complex emotions, we couldn't help but feel that Dad had been unjustly dealt with. While those outside our family may have thought that the prophet and Warren were saving us from a father who could not control his family, I never saw it that way. Things were not perfect at home and something did need to change, but breaking the family apart would not solve the problem. It was just another wound from which our family would never recover.

We'd been at the ranch for a few weeks when Mom suddenly went away, leaving us in the care of Kassandra and Teressa. While I trusted my older sisters, I was worried about my mother's unexpected and secretive departure. We were told only that she'd gone to Hildale to see the prophet. During her absence, I became so ill I nearly collapsed. Perhaps it was the change of climate or the stress of losing my dad that had me fighting off constant colds and spells of the flu. I'd never really gotten over the Lyme disease I'd contracted the previous summer during our camping trip to the mountains, and I often felt weak and tired. Fevers plagued me during repeated bouts of illness, and as the snow and cold of winter set in, I found it impossible to get warm. I walked around much of the time with inflamed tonsils and a general feeling of ill health.

Kassandra and Teressa took care of me as best they could, but the homeopathic remedies of cayenne pepper, garlic, and echinacea could not prevent my deterioration. There were moments when my throat seemed to almost completely close up, and my tonsils became severely infected. Even if my mother had been there to take care of me, with no health insurance and no doctors nearby, there was not much more she could have done to help. Nevertheless, I longed for her comfort and presence at my side.

At the ranch, we were expected to share in the workload. Our names were placed on the job chart and we worked alongside everyone else, but because I was so sick, it was difficult for me to do my share. We were also required to attend morning lessons with our family members, where we would listen to the taped sermons and teachings of Warren Jeffs. There were days when I felt well enough to ice-skate and sled, and I was able to enjoy the big New Year's Eve party when we made homemade candy and played games with our many young cousins.

In addition to Uncle Kevin's family, my uncle Lee and his wife, Debbie, were living at the ranch in a smaller home. Some of my older male cousins shared a "bunkhouse" just behind the main house, where they had been sent from Hildale by their fathers to help care for the ranch. One of these was my fifteen-year-old first cousin Allen Glade Steed.

From our first contact that winter, I didn't like Allen one bit. He was gangly and awkward, but that didn't stop him from teasing my younger siblings and me because we didn't have a father. Though he probably knew that his words stung, he would remind us with a gleeful smile that we didn't have a "priesthood father." We were quick to defend Dad's honor, and it led to many arguments. As a ten-year-old girl, I was very self-conscious and insecure. For most of my childhood, I had kept some baby fat, and even though Allen seemed to know it scorched my feelings, he took to calling me "Tubba-Tubba."

He seemed to enjoy embarrassing me. One day, I had been ecstatic about going ice-skating because illnesses had kept me from many other skating trips. The reservoir on the Steed ranch was too far from the house to walk, so we would usually drive over. I waited patiently for my brothers and sisters to get ready, and we all rushed outside to pile into the trailer attached to Allen's four-wheeler. They got in one by one as I waited for my turn to hop on. Just as I stepped toward the trailer, Allen let out a loud, cruel laugh and sped away, throwing me off balance and causing me to hit my head. Tears stung my eyes, but rather than act like a baby, I stood back up and shouted "Stop!" and asked him to please return for me. He simply went on laughing, not even hearing my words as he left me behind in the snow.

Although he was particularly mean to me, I wasn't Allen's only target. My younger brother Caleb and I were in the milk shed one day watching a few of the Steed siblings milk the cows. I was feeling shaky after another bout of illness, and the bitter-cold winter air was hard to ignore. Allen, with a menacing smile, started to spray us with the hose he was using and continued until our clothes were soaked. I begged him to stop, but he wouldn't. Caleb was bolder than I, and picking up a nearby shovel, he threw some manure at Allen. Allen left in a rage, telling Kevin that Caleb had tossed manure at him while he was working and claiming that the attack had been unprovoked.

I couldn't even stand seeing Allen at the dinner table in the evenings. The Steeds ran their home much like a business, with meals served at set times and in shifts; those who found a seat at one of the two dining tables in the kitchen ate first. When the rations ran out, there was often nothing more to eat. Unlike Salt Lake and even Short Creek, Widstoe was a kind of ghost town, with no grocery stores in close proximity. The town and the surrounding area had long been abandoned due to a lack of water. Our nearest neighbor was about fifteen miles away. Much of the food was harvested from the big vegetable garden on the property and pickled and stored for use throughout the winter. Sometimes we would go to bed hungry.

The run-ins with Allen were not the only problems between the Steed kids and the Wall children. After Mom had been gone for a while, a dispute broke out between my brothers and some of Uncle Kevin's sons. Despite the fact that both families belonged to the same religion, our father had raised us differently than Uncle Kevin raised his family, and these disparities became a point of contention. With Mom temporarily out of the picture, some of Uncle Kevin's older sons took it upon themselves to impose their more rigid form of FLDS observance on my brothers. They were constantly proclaiming their faith in the prophet and quickly became impatient with my brothers' apparent lack of conviction. The Wall boys resented the perpetual, uninvited tutorials, and Kassandra and Teressa were forced to step in to mediate.

By January of 1997, the benefits of the arrangement had begun to erode. Personalities were conflicting and the harsh winter in such a remote place was becoming problematic. While there had been some fun and lasting memories during my short stay at the Steed ranch, I was ready to go home.

Just as we started to wither in these frustrations, news came that changed everything: Uncle Rulon had decided that Dad had acknowledged his shortcomings and repented so that his priesthood could be fully restored. The thought of a warm hug from the man whom I had missed so dearly filled me with hope. At last, it felt as though my family was being glued back together. Home had never been perfect, but it was the only place I wanted to be.

CHAPTER FIVE

THE RISE
OF WARREN

The time is short.
—FLDS PARABLE

It wasn't until we returned to the house on Claybourne Avenue that we learned Mom had been in Salt Lake City for several weeks, redecorating our house with help from my sister Rachel. It turned out that both my parents had gone to the prophet separately about reconciliation, but in order for my mother and her children to be welcomed back into my father's home, certain things had to happen. The prophet had directed my parents to be rebaptized and remarried. They'd even gone off to California for a second honeymoon.

Another stipulation was that Mother Audrey and Lydia, Audrey's youngest daughter and her only child still at home, had to move out. At the time, there was no explanation given for their departure, only that Audrey was to repent from afar. In truth, our problems were never the product of any one individual; they were the result of living in a complicated family with complicated issues under tremendous religious pressures. But in the prophet's search for a solution to make us all whole again, he decided the only answer was to divide our family once more, this time in a different way.

Many years later, Mother Audrey would confide to me how difficult our departure to the Steed ranch had been for her. It had left her feeling empty and drained, and she worried that something was terribly wrong with the prophet's decisions for our family. She'd been so elated when she heard that we were finally coming home, but her joy quickly turned to pain again when she was informed that she would now be the one who had to move out.

Audrey faced the challenge of finding a place to stay, and it was only after several phone calls to her children that her son Richard and his wife took her in. She'd have to come to terms with the fact that she and her husband would remain married but live apart. As a believer, she would continue to keep the faith, praying to the Heavenly Father that they would soon be reunited.

For my mother and father this really did seem like a chance for a fresh start. I can still see the look on my mom's face when Dad returned home one night holding a dozen red roses and a brand-new wedding ring that she'd helped to design. It had rubies and diamonds, and Dad had it wrapped in a small box tied with a bow. I lingered in the living room, watching my parents share a few romantic moments, heartened to again see them expressing their love for each other. Mom hadn't looked that happy in ages, and seeing her like that renewed my hope that everything would work out.

With Craig gone, Travis packed off to reform, and Audrey no longer living with us, the house felt eerily quiet. Emotions were high, and everywhere there was a lingering emptiness. As a result, we eagerly anticipated the upcoming April conference for all FLDS members in Hildale, Utah, and Colorado City, Arizona. This would give us not only a chance to see Travis but the opportunity to get our family back on track.

The April conference was just one of many annual events that required the entire community—including those of us who lived in Salt Lake City and Canada—to travel down to Short Creek. The FLDS does not celebrate traditional Christian holidays such as Christmas and Easter. We had our own events to observe throughout the year, three of which took place in the summer months. The first was on June 12, commemorating the birthday of our former prophet Leroy Johnson. Throughout his life he would gather the people together on his birthday and serve them all watermelon. People so dearly loved and respected him that after his passing they continued to gather on this day to remember him. This was followed by Independence Day on July 4 and Pioneer Day on July 24, with the traditional Pioneer Day parade. Of these events, Pioneer Day was by far the biggest community celebration, as it marked the day in 1847 that Mormon pioneers first settled in the Salt Lake Valley. The summer gatherings were followed in the fall by Octoberfest or Harvest Fest, in which members would all gather in the "crik" to help harvest the potatoes and other crops on which many of us would rely throughout the winter months.

Of all these yearly occasions, the April conference was the most sacred, and the people would come to the twin towns for religious teachings. For the men, this was also the time for the priesthood ordination meeting. During this important meeting, male members of the community learned their worthiness and whether or not they would be honored with an elevation to a higher level of priesthood. Young men are ordained into the priesthood at the age of twelve, when they become priesthood deacons and gain admittance to the sacred male-only priesthood meetings. As they get older, they can rise to higher levels within the church, so long as they have their father's recommendation. Once a man reaches the age of eighteen, he can attain the level of church elder, at which point he can have a wife and family through a revelation from the prophet.

Because of the celebratory nature of all these gatherings, I had always associated southern Utah with joy and togetherness. Our time there was always marked by jubilation and relaxed fun. When I was a child, those events gave me the precious freedom to run around and play with the other children at the park. I also loved going to the zoo at the center of town that had been created by Fred Jessop, the bishop of

Hildale/Colorado City and a beloved figure in our community. The zoo was home to many exotic animals, including
zebras and llamas, and he built it so that children wouldn't
have to leave the community to enjoy such amusements.

Uncle Fred, as he was known, owned an enormous white
house perched atop a small hill overlooking the community
and visible from most parts of town. Like the Jeffs compound in Salt Lake City, Fred's house was vast enough to
accommodate a birthing center for the local FLDS community, but Fred Jessop didn't have any biological children of
his own, as a childhood disease had rendered him sterile.
Instead his children came from the wives of husbands who
had lost the priesthood, and had been reassigned to him.

Since he was so involved with the community, I had always had a good feeling about Uncle Fred. Though I didn't
know him personally when I was younger, I would hear stories of his life. From the little that I did see of him, he seemed
to be a kind and loving man who had the people's best interests in mind, a man who represented all the good things
about the community.

Short Creek was a place where we didn't feel strange or
outcast. It was the only place I knew where I was free to
socialize and roam about the town. There was a deep sense
of unity in knowing that we all believed the same things and
didn't need to feel ashamed in one another's company. Back
in Salt Lake, outsiders would scoff at our long dresses and
unfashionable hairstyles, but down in Hildale and Colorado
City, everyone looked and acted just like our family did. The
twin towns felt like home to everyone; there everyone knew
one another by name and many were related by blood or
marriage. If anything could ease our troubled family, it was
a trip to Short Creek. As the car jam-packed with Walls made
its way toward southern Utah for the April conference that
year, I was optimistic about our chance to heal our family's
wounds and assuage my own overwhelming loneliness.

Unfortunately, that year's conference weekend was not
what I had hoped for. When I first arrived, my anxiety
seemed to disappear as friends and relatives greeted me.

Together we had fun and began to relax, and for the first time in months, I felt at ease. But one day, with spring-flushed cheeks glowing from hours of play, I walked into a room to discover Mom sitting in a corner, crying. I asked her what was wrong, and through tears she said that she had seen Travis and heard the truth of what was happening to him. The family that had taken him in felt that he was corrupting their children and disapproved of a group of boys he'd befriended. Like Travis, many of his new friends were struggling with the teachings of our faith and finding ways to rebel. At this point, Travis had somehow gotten his hands on a car, and to escape the oppressive atmosphere in the household, he began sleeping in it.

Mom didn't feel it would be appropriate to share many of the details with me, but her devastation was clear. This was the second time I had seen her crying like this, and memories of the day we left Craig on the side of the highway flooded my mind. Later, I would look back on this occasion and wonder whether Mom was crying solely out of love and regret for her sons' pain or for the dual failure that the situation represented. A priesthood mother is expected to raise her children to be virtuous and good, and if a child strays, it is viewed as the mother's fault. Mom was heartbroken enough to share her true feelings with me, and somehow I understood what that meant. I hadn't yet finished the fifth grade, but it was in this bitter moment that I witnessed the continuation of my family's unraveling.

In the end, it appeared Travis's resentment of his circumstances at the reform retreat proved too great to endure. Shortly after we'd returned home from the April conference, we heard that he finally left Short Creek and moved into a house in southern Utah with some friends who had also left the church. Most were lost and searching for a way to make life work outside their religious upbringings. When I heard he was with them, I was pleased because it sounded like they'd formed a kind of family bond that would help them get through whatever rough times they would face. My parents, on the other hand, sensed that he was living with a bad crowd, but they could not access him and control his actions; Mom was consumed by worry—and Dad by frustration.

In early summer of 1997, our family was invited to join many of the Salt Lake members on an organized camping trip to Bear Lake, Wyoming, which would be one of just a handful of times in my lifetime that the people in Salt Lake organized their own community event. For much of my life, playing in the water had been off-limits because Dad felt it was too dangerous. On several occasions, I was told that the Devil controlled the water and swimming for pleasure would prevent the Lord from protecting us from him.

Because of this teaching, I was excited but also a little scared at the prospect of spending a few days at the lake. When I asked if the Devil would be in the water, I was told that because the prophet had approved of the trip the water would be blessed. This completely set my mind at ease, and upon our arrival, I splashed and played in the water in my long dresses to my heart's content. At night we stayed in tents on the beach and the sound of water lulled us to sleep.

At one point during the festivities, my attention was drawn to another group of children in swimsuits frolicking in the water. They were not from the FLDS, but they too were with their families on vacation. Like a scientist, I paused to study them. I was curious because I had been taught that outsiders were evil, but at first glance they didn't look that way to me. The longer that I looked at them, the more I came to realize that they looked nothing like I had imagined. Of course, I had seen non-FLDS strangers before—after all, we were a small minority in Salt Lake City. But I had never really studied them, to see how they acted and how they treated one another. These kids looked so nice. Sure, they were dressed in modern styles, but I found their clothes attractive as opposed to immodest. Secretly, I envied their bare legs, their sense of freedom, and the fun in their style. My ankle-length blue dress may have matched my blue eyes, but suddenly it no longer reflected how I felt inside.

As I watched them eat, laugh, and play with their families, I realized that those kids actually seemed similar to us, and that the only difference was their clothing. Even from far away, I could tell that there was love in this family's eyes, that they cared for one another and would care about us too. I was young enough to still believe what I had been taught, simply because it was all I knew, but seeing that family gave me a shocking new point of view about the church's teachings. I didn't say anything to anyone. I kept it to myself.

Later on in life, I would realize that standing there and watching those kids was the first time I ever questioned FLDS teachings, even if it was only subconsciously.

Unfortunately for me, the excitement of our trip to Bear Lake was tainted by my chronic illness. My tonsils were so infected that they'd ruptured and infectious fluid was circulating through my system. My father finally realized that the severity of my situation required a visit to the doctor and was advised that surgery was in order. Doctors told my parents that I would need my tonsils and adenoids removed, as well as surgery to reconstruct my collapsed nasal passage.

Unaware of what was to come, I enjoyed all the attention I was receiving in the hospital. I had only been to the doctor a handful of times, once for a tetanus shot, another time for ear tubes, and another to treat my Lyme disease. I was given a gown to wear, and seeing my parents worrying over me made me feel cherished, like for that moment I was the only one of their children who mattered. Before my surgery, an anesthesiologist administered a shot to put me to sleep. It hurt so much, and I remember the burning sensation traveling up my arm. Suddenly, my arm went numb, and I drifted off to sleep.

When I awoke, it was a day and a half later. My parents had been keeping vigil at my bedside. Through an error, I'd been given an adult dose of anesthesia, and it had nearly cost me my life. I was told that at one point I had "coded" on the operating table. While I remembered waking up once and feeling as though I couldn't breathe, I had no idea that my heart had actually stopped and I'd been rushed to a nearby children's hospital for intervention. After all of that, my tonsils were never removed. My condition had been too grave to perform the surgery, and it would be weeks before another doctor would operate. In the days after I recovered consciousness, I suffered repeated mini-seizures that terrified my mother. True to form, my parents used this near-fatal accident as evidence for why we should avoid doctors and conventional medical care.

As my health slowly returned, our family settled into a routine, and at first it appeared that with Mother Audrey out of the picture, life would be more manageable. But in time it become obvious that as long as there was more than one woman in the Wall home, the situation was unsustainable. Mother Laura was allowed to stay and continued to live in the house with her newborn son. Because it was her first child, Mother Laura seemed like a mother bear with a newborn cub. She wanted her space and decided that things in the house needed to be done her way. To make matters worse, she exerted a lot of influence over Dad, causing him to dole out punishments to my brothers Jacob, Justin, and Brad. All three boys were constantly in trouble with Mother Laura, who appeared to expect my father to prove his love by "correcting" their behavior.

Mother Audrey's absence had done little to change the explosive atmosphere. In fact, things got even worse. From what I could see, Mother Laura used Audrey's absence to extend her influence over the family, and suddenly what had once looked like a solution created a bigger fissure in our disjointed family. Even more bothersome was how paranoid and worried Dad had seemed to become. Losing his family had been devastating, and now with pressure from the priesthood to shape up our home, he was becoming stricter toward my siblings in an attempt to regain his tentative grasp on all of us. My mother was no exception, and she too was under constant surveillance. Worried that she would again go to the prophet, Dad grew anxious each time he saw her talking on the phone, and eventually it got to the point where she could only talk to Rachel and Kassandra when he was not around.

That September, I was back at Alta Academy, entering the sixth grade, but by then the school had become yet another source of unhappiness. For many years, Warren Jeffs had been teaching that boys and girls shouldn't associate; as I had learned back in the second grade, we were to treat each other as "snakes." But this year, his teachings became increasingly rigid, and he decided to physically separate the two sexes into different classrooms and different buildings on the compound. The curriculum for the sixth-grade girls' class was wholly unlike that of the sixth-grade boys. Our scheduled recess times and grade-level activities were different, and there was no longer a time during the school day when the boys and girls had any contact. Warren told us that the separation was "the will of the prophet and God," but it seemed to make little sense.

As we advanced into higher grades, the religious aspects of our education, which had always been present, became all-consuming. Little by little, Uncle Warren had been removing traditional age-appropriate curriculum and replacing it with teachings from the church, as well as many of his own. While for years the church had openly taught us to hold prejudices against anyone whose skin color didn't match ours, now Warren's language became even harsher. He taught us that nonwhite people were some of the lowest, worst sinners on earth and that association with them was one of the most disobedient things an FLDS member could do.

In addition, he had rewritten our coursework to fit his designs. Books by authors outside the church were destroyed and replaced with church-approved ones. Subjects such as science and current events became less important, and instead the focus was on our religious teachings. Unapproved pictures were removed from textbooks, and anything that had to do with evolution or human anatomy was excised. In fact, anything that did not conform to our strict religious teachings and beliefs was removed from the lesson plans, and pages of books that dealt with conflicting subject matter were simply ripped out.

One example of this slow conditioning process was the evolution of the school paper, the *Student Star,* which was later renamed *Zion's Light Shining.* What had begun a number of years before as a fun school newspaper filled with lighthearted stories, school announcements, and other items of interest had transformed into yet another vehicle for strict religious indoctrination. Warren had taken hold of the newspaper and revamped it to include sermons and teachings from past prophets and church leaders. Nothing could be printed without his seal of approval. Interestingly, it was not actual scripture but his interpretation of various scriptures that made the paper. Soon it became an integral part of the learning process at Alta Academy and a major part of the curriculum. We were required to read it from front to back and were tested on its content.

Through these and other methods of indoctrination, Uncle Warren was slowly cultivating a generation of loyal followers. Most of us had attended Alta Academy since our youngest years. Almost everything that we knew about the priesthood had come from him. Warren had shaped our vision of the religion and the world; and we had learned only what Warren wanted us to. The students who passed through Alta Academy were taught to fear and obey Uncle Warren as more than just our principal. He was the person with the closest connection to the prophet, and as such, we soaked up his every word.

Over the years, the prophet had gradually put Warren in a position of authority over the people. "Warren speaks for me" is a phrase that I heard many times from Uncle Rulon's lips. The wheels had been set in motion, and the FLDS people had begun to look to Warren as one with the prophet in authority over them. As Uncle Rulon aged and grew more feeble, it was natural that the people accepted Warren's words as his father's and became accustomed to the slow transfer of power. We all wanted to be saved and we knew that following the prophet and Warren was the only way to make sure we would be.

The scope of Warren's extended power became quite apparent in 1998 when he took us one step closer to Judgment Day with a startling announcement: he was closing Alta Academy, and his father was selling the property. Together they would relocate to the prophet's other home in southern Utah. The year 2000 was rapidly approaching, and soon Zion would be redeemed in the new millennium. They began requiring select families in Salt Lake to move with them to southern Utah, so that our people would be united and "lifted up" to heaven when the end of the world came.

This directive tapped into one of the most fundamental aspects of our religion. "Time is short" had long been a kind of mantra for the leaders of the church. For years, the people had been instructed to stay worthy and prepare because the end of the world was near. We believed that any day destruction would cover the land and only the pure and righteous would be saved. Everyone who was not a "worthy" member was wicked and would not be saved. If we were not faithful in the prophet's eyes, we would be left behind to be destroyed.

That May, the final graduating class at Alta Academy walked out the doors of the building and the school was closed for the last time. Through the summer, Michelle's husband, Seth Jeffs, and several other church followers worked diligently to copy and distribute the school's curriculum, so that families who stayed in the Salt Lake Valley could homeschool their children. Over the next few years, more and more families were commanded to make the three-hundred-mile move. The communities of Hildale and Colorado City became flush with an influx of people.

Despite Uncle Rulon's declining health, everyone in the FLDS believed he would live for hundreds of years, even after he suffered a stroke in the summer of 1998. As one of Uncle Rulon's wives, my sister Kassandra was living in his home when the stroke occurred and was one of a few people who knew the reality of his condition. Kassandra later told me Rulon was at his compound in Hildale attending a family gathering when he was found slumped forward in a chair. Thinking he had just dozed off, those around him left him alone until they realized something was terribly wrong. Uncle Rulon was carried to his room, and Warren was contacted immediately.

When Warren arrived in Short Creek, the paramedics were called and it was determined that Uncle Rulon had suffered a stroke. Later Kassandra was with Rulon at the hospital where tests were run to determine what part of the brain had been affected and how severely. Initially, Rulon did not remember any of his wives or the other familiar faces around him, reverting instead to the memories of his childhood.

As Uncle Warren came to see the extent of his father's impairment, he began directing his father's care and regulated the people who had access to him. Nothing would happen to Uncle Rulon without Warren's knowledge and approval. To justify his behavior, Warren led Rulon's wives to believe that as the prophet's son, he would have heavenly inspiration concerning those who were "faithful" enough to be in Uncle Rulon's presence. Someone who did not have enough of the "Spirit of God" would hinder his recovery process. Warren even controlled which wives were faithful enough to room with the prophet after his return home from the hospital.

As Uncle Rulon's conditioned stabilized and started to improve, Warren arranged to have him taken back to Salt Lake City so that he could oversee the recovery until the family's move to Short Creek. Concerned over how the people would receive the news of his father's deteriorating health, Warren continued to monitor access to the prophet, directing all the women in the house not to permit anyone to see Uncle Rulon, instructing "We cannot let these people see the extent of Father's stroke."

Shortly after Uncle Rulon returned to Salt Lake City, there was to be a monthly priesthood meeting at Alta Academy attended by some of the most senior church elders. Among them were the "Barlow Boys," Danny, George, Sam,

Louis, and Truman, all faithful and well-respected priesthood fathers. Before the meeting, it was customary for this group of patriarchs and elders to greet Uncle Rulon in his private quarters at the compound, but fearing that the men would discover the severity of his father's condition and his inability to carry out his duties as prophet, Uncle Warren told some of his brothers to stop the visit. Kassandra overheard Warren issuing a directive to his brother Isaac: "Do not let them see Father. Tell them he's resting. If we let them see how severe he is, we will have a problem on our hands. We must tell them that our father is doing fine. The Lord will take care of him, and they need to lend their faith and prayers."

When Warren eventually allowed people to see Uncle Rulon, only a select few family members were permitted to visit with him alone because Warren was always there. Uncle Warren told people that God had inflicted this stroke on his father as a means of giving the prophet some time to rest. He was ill but would be renewed, Warren said, and the unquestioning faith and prayers of the people were the only things that would heal him. We truly believed that if we were faithful enough, he would be made young and strong again.

Unbeknownst to us, in the immediate aftermath of his stroke, Uncle Rulon was barely able to move and had to be assisted in everything from dressing to eating. Although he improved enough to attend and preside at countless meetings and continued to make it known that Warren spoke for him, he never fully recovered and would struggle with his memory for the rest of his life. Warren took over his father's appointments. Anyone trying to get in touch with or see the prophet would have to go through him. Knowing his father was unable to handle any church responsibilities, Warren also took over conducting church meetings and priesthood dealings, giving him complete control of the operations of the church.

It appeared as though Uncle Warren had been preparing himself to fill this role for years. He was not Uncle Rulon's oldest or youngest son, but he had worked hard to position himself as his father's natural successor. Even as a teenager, long before Rulon was prophet, Warren had opted out of playing with the other kids, instead going out of his way to spend time with his father, which was considered a very honorable thing to do. When he became principal at Alta Academy, he would counsel with his father closely, and their relationship evolved from there with Warren becoming Rulon's eager right hand, the son who could always help the prophet get things done.

Being the head of Alta Academy, Warren led us to see him as a figurehead, and by the time of the stroke, people already knew that if they couldn't approach Rulon, Warren would be the next person to talk to. Out of respect for his role as the prophet's son, the people blindly listened to and obeyed Warren. All of the faithful trusted him and believed that he was merely speaking on behalf of his father, our prophet and God. No one would dare to suspect otherwise, and Warren used that confidence to his advantage as he began manipulating us and making it impossible for us to see the rise of a new and unforgiving power.

Before the mid-1980s, authority in the FLDS had been divided between the prophet and a priesthood council, but a disagreement over who had the authority to arrange marriages had put an end to this shared hierarchy, ceding all power in the church to the prophet. The dispute came about because a number of council members had been arranging marriages at the same time—sometimes unwittingly promising the same young woman to more than one man based on claims of revelation.

Leroy Johnson, the prophet at the time, balked and said that was not acceptable, insisting that all marriages should be arranged by him. The council members objected. Ultimately Uncle Roy won the argument and assumed sole authority over the priesthood and placement marriages. It was a historic event in our church and marked the beginning of the doctrine of one man rule.

Dismayed, some council members who favored a more traditional leadership structure left the FLDS to form their own church that came to be known as the Centennial Group. For church members, this was a pivotal period and resulted in what has come to be known as "the split." Those who left our church to form the new group were deemed apostates and were no longer considered "worthy" by the FLDS. Uncle Rulon and members of his inner circle strongly discouraged even casual contact with members of that sect, which established itself about a mile from the Crik.

The danger of course with the post-split power structure was that all control over the FLDS people resided with the prophet. This did not prove to be a major issue during the waning years of Uncle Roy's life, but with Rulon and Warren at the helm it held a great many risks.

CHAPTER SIX

OUT OF CONTROL

I want to be the humble servant of the prophet.
—FLDS PRAYER

In the fall of 1998 our family was still living on Claybourne Avenue and, much to my surprise and everyone else's, Mother Audrey returned home. Her youngest daughter, Lydia, had been married not long before, and with no more children at home, Mother Audrey strengthened her friendship with Mother Laura, who was now in her mid-twenties and raising her young son. The two women had bonded from the beginning and had grown closer in our absence. But the house that Mother Audrey returned to was not the one that she had left the previous year. All of a sudden, it seemed Laura had become Dad's favored companion. It was Laura accompanying Dad to the supermarket. It was Laura scrutinizing the other mother's shopping lists about whether certain items were truly necessary.

Just as Mother Audrey had struggled with the addition of Dad's second wife, now Mom had a hard time coping with Laura's presence. This is one of the natural drawbacks to a plural marriage. The husband experiences pride and excitement with a new wife in the household, but for the women already there, resentment and jealousy sets in. Making matters worse for my mother was that the old wounds between her and Audrey had yet to heal. Once again, Mom found herself on the outside, with the blame for the family's domestic troubles laid at her feet. No one was completely innocent, but no one was willing to accept responsibility for the problems that continued to plague our home.

While my mother got the brunt of it, everyone pointed fingers. To me the other two mothers were ganging up on my siblings and me. When a problem arose in the house, Dad was quick to side with one of the other mothers, dismissing the children's version and agreeing that punishment was in order. From my perspective, it seemed that to Dad, Audrey, and Laura, Mom's kids could do no right. My brothers had taken to escaping the tension with forbidden trips to the local arcade and Toys "R" Us, where they met friends and played video games. Meanwhile, my sister Teressa began standing up to Dad and his other wives and advocating for our mother just as Craig had, a rebellion that landed her on the dark side of Dad's anger.

Terrified of losing the family he loved for a second time, my father only grew more paranoid as Teressa and my brothers stretched their teenage wings and became more openly confrontational. Though they were merely acting like normal teenagers, they were seen as defiant and Dad suffered great anxiety over how their behavior would affect his priesthood standing. As sad as it was, it was clear to us all that Dad was coming apart as he fought to rein in his wives and children according to the priesthood's design.

Thinking back on his battle to control our family, I have wondered if Dad's own difficult childhood had left him emotionally unequipped to handle his twenty-four kids and three wives. When he was just a small boy, his mother had abandoned his family; the way Grandpa Wall told it, she just didn't want to be married anymore. Unable to care for his two young children and continue to earn a living, Grandpa Wall had no choice but to send Dad and his sister to live with relatives. In time, a different arrangement needed to be made and Dad ended up on a working farm for orphans in

Utah. Because Grandpa Wall was away working in the coal mines, it took a while for him to realize that the farmer was abusing the children, including my father. When Grandpa finally learned what was going on, he promptly moved Dad back with him. Over the years, they moved around a lot and ended up in Utah, where Grandpa eventually remarried. But problems in the home forced Dad to move out when he was sixteen. Still, he completed his high school education. After graduation, Dad joined the National Guard and received training in combat engineering. He served as a reservist for eight years. Later, his discipline and desire for education helped him earn advanced degrees.

Dad desired order and wanted his boys to be good priest-hood men; however, as my brothers grew into teenagers, it became impossible to form them into the proper FLDS mold. Faithful boys were expected to serve their fathers in a humble manner, greeting them by saying things like "I am here to do your will. What do you want me to do? I want to be the humble servant of the prophet" and to constantly ex-press their "undying love and loyalty" to the prophet and priesthood. But my brothers listened to a deep inner voice telling them that this type of behavior just wasn't right. As hard as Dad tried through example and scripture, his sons struggled to live the principles of our strict faith.

The fact that Teressa—not just my brothers—was now openly dissenting only added to the friction. While I'm sure it broke her heart to be at odds with Dad, the situation be-came so unbearable that she began to sneak out of the house to escape conflict, if only for a few hours. I'd always looked up to Teressa and admired her strong and stubborn person-ality. She wasn't afraid to display those attributes and do what she felt was right. To exhibit this type of attitude and behavior was bold, as it was not acceptable for FLDS women to have a voice or a say in their own destiny. Despite these social pressures, she never hesitated to speak her mind, much to my father's great dismay. It was with great sadness that my mother looked on, helpless to fix the situation.

Teressa's rebellion invited pressure to marry. Now I see

that it was a common practice that a girl who had "problems" with obedience should be married and made pregnant as soon as possible to help pull her from her wicked ways and push her to conform to the FLDS ideal of womanhood. Our mother and some of our older sisters began urging Teressa to "turn herself in to the prophet for marriage," but true to herself, Teressa refused. In response, my parents coaxed her into a meeting with Uncle Rulon and Warren. During the meeting, my sister sat stubbornly silent, refusing to answer Uncle Rulon's questions. She'd warned my parents that if they forced her to see the prophet, she wouldn't speak a word. Offended by her behavior, Warren later ordered her off church-owned land, allowing her only to go to the community in Bountiful, Canada, to work, repent, and learn about her proper role in our society.

Not long after Teressa was sent to Bountiful, my twin brothers Justin and Jacob joined her there. They had continued to question elements of our religion, and in order to prevent the situation with the twins from getting out of control, they too were sent to Canada for reform. As with Teressa, my parents hoped that time away would solidify their beliefs and bring them home more faithful.

The three of them went to work at a church-owned post and pole manufacturing mill in remote Alberta, almost seven hours north of Bountiful. Once there, they were all put to hard manual labor alongside other boys and occasionally a girl or two who had been sent there to reform. "Work them so they can't find time to get into trouble" was the saying. Their primary task was to turn trees into poles. This was rigorous for all three of them, but especially hard on Teressa in her long prairie-style dresses. Frequently they worked the night shift, even in subzero temperatures; and there was little safety equipment. They received no pay, only room and board.

There was little attempt to hide the purpose of subjecting Teressa to this regimen. The point was to break her spirit by working her into submission. Marriage was dangled in front of her as the only reprieve from the work. It was a battle of wills and they were determined to undermine hers. After many months, Teressa finally gave in and it was announced that she would marry Roy Blackmore, the eighteen-year-old son of my sister Sabrina's husband and one of his other wives. While it was an unwanted marriage for her, at least her husband would be her age, not to mention the fact that at the time, Teressa wholeheartedly believed Uncle Warren's prophecies that the end of the world was imminent. Convinced that she was not worthy of eternal salvation, she believed she would have only two years in the marriage before the destruction of the world landed her among the wicked in hell for all eternity.

It had taken the bitter cold of Canada, manual labor, and intense pressures, but finally Teressa had been broken. She was seventeen years old when she got married, and the most beautiful bride I'd ever seen. She had golden blond hair and fiery blue eyes. She was stunning on the surface, but beneath that veneer, I knew she hated that they'd defeated her.

I was only twelve when Teressa was "sealed" in marriage and became a permanent member of the Canadian FLDS community. Being the pesky little sister, I had never been able to have a close relationship with her. I secretly idolized Teressa and wanted to be just like her. Watching her spar with the members of my family, I learned that it was important to stand up for yourself if something was wrong. Though she had eventually given in to marriage, she advocated for her beliefs and her personal rights, even though her opinions went against the church. Her actions were bold and insubordinate, but I was old enough to recognize that there was something admirable in them. I didn't know it at the time, but seeing Teressa's defiance through the eyes of an impressionable young sister changed something in me. Only years later would I find out just what that something was.

On July 7, 1999, I celebrated my thirteenth birthday with my family in Salt Lake City, not knowing that it would be the last time that I would ever observe any event with my father.

I was now the oldest girl in the house, and I took on many of the domestic tasks previously performed by Teressa. With no school to attend, I began to do a lot of the cooking and cleaning, often busying myself with chores and the care of my mother's two youngest daughters, Sherrie and Ally. Many times I lovingly tended to Mother Laura's little boy, but I had to be careful about the way I treated him. Mother Laura was still playing the role of mother bear and remained highly protective of him. While her behavior could be frustrating, Mom encouraged me to see that Laura's actions were understandable. She had been the same way with my brother Travis, ultimately quitting her job at Dad's company so that she could care for him and her other kids during the day.

A sad look came over her eyes, as she no doubt thought of Travis, who wasn't faring well. His living situation with the other boys who had left the FLDS had eventually deteriorated and become unsustainable. Most of the boys forced out of the community were mere teenagers themselves and had been raised in such a closed community with little real education. While they banded together to help one another, there was little they could do beyond working menial jobs. Finally it got to a breaking point, and when Travis decided he could no longer live like he was, he returned to Salt Lake City for a fresh start. Years of hard work as a member of the FLDS community helped him land a construction job, and he again moved into a house with other former FLDS boys. The move did little to change his fortune, and the hard times that had begun in southern Utah continued back in Salt Lake, leaving him in need of help.

Because he'd left the church in the middle of his "reforming" in Short Creek, he was now labeled an apostate. To be an apostate was even worse than being a gentile. *Gentile* was the term given to all non- FLDS people, no matter their religion, but an apostate was someone who had lost faith or had left the church, turning their back on the priesthood.

Apostates were viewed as one of the worst kinds of evil. FLDS teachings demanded that all members abandon people who choose to apostatize—even members of your own family. The severity of this requirement was such that we had to be extremely careful about our association with our brother. We'd been warned that the punishment would be harsh, but none of us knew exactly what that meant. Still, we were not prepared to abandon a brother and son completely.

After months of being away, Travis became a presence in our lives again, and periodically he would stop by to check in on his younger brothers and sisters. Usually, he would come just to say hello, but he would end up staring at our dinner with hungry eyes. Mom and Dad couldn't stand to see their child in that condition, and on occasion they would allow him to have a plate of food, despite the risk. No matter how much he was suffering, Travis couldn't bring himself to ask my dad for help. Mom and I would sneak him care packages during his forbidden visits home. Though it went against the church's teachings, we couldn't stand to see him starve.

It was devastating to watch the members of my family being slowly destroyed in the name of our religion. Even as our home life spiraled out of control, Dad continued to hold our annual camping trip and picnics in the mountains in an attempt to recapture the good times we all remembered. But the realities of our situation were glaring, and the absence of so many of my siblings made it hard to enjoy the trips as I had in the past.

The sad truth, as I learned later, was that our family's struggles were making their way to Uncle Warren's ear. Mom had again been talking with Rachel in secret, confiding about how my father was not in full control of his family. Rachel naturally took my mother's side without seeking out my father's perspective, eventually concluding that Dad was not leading the family correctly and that he had no power over what was going on under his roof. In turn, Rachel often relayed stories to Warren, a practice that grew more frequent after Rulon's stroke had put our prophet in the backseat while he recovered.

When Rulon Jeffs became the prophet, he expanded the prophet's role regarding marriage beyond simply revealing who was allowed to marry. Before Uncle Rulon, if a couple was having marital problems, they would be encouraged to handle them on their own, save for serious matters such as adultery and apostasy. Rulon began performing a sort of marriage counseling supposedly aimed at resolving marital conflict, but it was less about solving problems and more about control over husbands and wives.

With his new practice, the prophet became privy to members' most intimate secrets, and Rulon was not afraid to put this information to use. Under the guise of counseling, the prophet—and later Warren—began making life-altering decisions such as controlling the sexual relations of spouses and at times going so far as to divide families by banishing men, and remarrying their wives.

As Uncle Rulon's stroke placed Warren more firmly in the seat of power, these irrational directives started becoming even harsher and more far-reaching in their implications. Now FLDS men had to worry about any misstep in their household—even those that did not impact the marriage. Warren effectively began to encourage some women to spy on their husbands in the name of the Lord, wanting them to come forward with any infraction, no matter how small. He probed everything from the possession of worldly music to more serious infractions such as religious doubt or disloyalty.

No violation was too small, as far as Uncle Warren was concerned, and this was bad news for our family. It was no secret in our house that Warren had long had it in for many of the Walls. Now, with our problems, it was only a matter of time before he used this information to serve his purpose.

When Justin and Jacob returned from Canada, they had a hard time adjusting to family life. It had been rough for them in the closed FLDS community, a far cry from our routine in Salt Lake. There were fewer outside forces to entice them, no big stores or shopping malls or video arcades packed with children. If they had made any progress in their faith while in Canada, it evaporated shortly after their return.

The fact that Travis was around again only made the twins more restless. Travis had developed an interest in techno music and went to parties known as raves. The music had a strong beat and vocals like nothing he had heard before, and he would tell the twins about it whenever he came by our house. Even to me, just a child, I could see his effect on them was apparent, as both the twins wanted to do what their older brother was doing. At the time, I didn't have a full grasp on the situation, but I did understand that Travis wanted to share his new world with my brothers.

Then in July of 1999 came the day that changed our family forever. Travis had excited Justin and Jacob about the raves to the point where they badly wanted to go to one. Since Travis wasn't living with us, he was planning to go separately, and the twins had no ride. Desperate to get to the party, they begged my mom to drop them off there. Dad warned her not to do it. He was fed up with what had been going on at home, and if the twins went to that party, he would be upset.

Membership in the FLDS didn't stop Dad from facing the kinds of concerns that plague all parents of teenagers at one time or another. His twin sons were not yet eighteen, and as far as he was concerned, it was still his duty to protect them when he felt that they were placing themselves in harm's way. We'd all heard about the worldly music and dancing that went on at these rave parties, and it didn't seem out of the ordinary for Dad to be worried. Besides, if Uncle Warren were to find out that Justin and Jacob had gone to a party even though they didn't have Dad's consent, he might use that as an excuse to further damage my father's standing in the priesthood, and Dad might risk losing his family again.

The Saturday of the party came around and, in keeping

with family tradition, that day my mother wanted us to wash the family's Suburban so it would be clean and shiny for church the following afternoon. Most times, we would scrub the truck right in our driveway with sponges and buckets we had around the house. Mom tried to make this chore fun for us, and on this occasion she decided to take us to the car wash up the hill from our house.

The beginnings of summer dusk were spreading across the sky as we pulled up to the car wash and began to feed quarters into the machine. We had finished spraying the soapy lather over the truck and were applying the final rinse when we noticed a figure running up the road toward us. I felt a chill rush through my body as, all at once, I saw his scuffed-up face and the way he was limping—and recognized that it was Brad, my fifteen-year-old brother.

Brad approached my mother and clung to her like a small child, his arms draped around her body and his shoulders heaving. It was startling to see my older brother, who I had always found so strong, dissolve into tears. Mom asked us to give her and Brad some privacy and instructed us to move to the other side of the vehicle. Worried, we peeked around the truck to see what was happening. As Brad shared the story, I watched a look somewhere between fury and pain sweep across Mom's face. Though it would not be until years later that I learned the details of what had happened, it was clear from her expression that something bad had taken place.

Dad had returned home to find the family gone. While we were at the car wash, the twins had secretly gone to meet up with some friends. With no one there to inform Dad where we were, he grew worried that perhaps Mom had given in and agreed to drive Justin and Jacob to the party. As the minutes crept by with no word from Mom, Dad's imagination began to take hold of him. It was at that point that Brad came home from whatever he'd been doing. Right away, Dad asked Brad where his brothers were.

Since Brad had no idea, he issued a typical teenage response: "Why do you care?" Angry at his son's lack of respect, Dad left the room for a moment to take a breath.

This was when Mother Laura got involved and everything spun out of control. Furious at how my brother had spoken to Dad, she took it upon herself to give Brad a scolding. While I wasn't there to witness what happened next, years later, I was told that the conversation grew heated, with Laura becoming so angry that she raised a hand to Brad, who reflexively grabbed her arm to protect himself. As Dad walked in the room, he saw this and thought that Brad was attacking Laura. What followed was probably one of the most dramatic moments in the Wall family history, as the confrontation between Brad and my father turned dangerously physical and ended with Brad escaping up the hill to the car wash.

After hearing Brad's awful story, Mom moved quickly. She instructed us all to get back into the Suburban and buckle up. I wondered where we were going and what Mom planned to do, but I knew I shouldn't ask any questions or offer an opinion. I didn't know what Brad had told her, but Mom seemed very upset.

Mom drove fast, fueled by sadness and despair. She made her way down the road, pulling abruptly into the first place that had a pay phone. She grabbed my hand and pulled me beside her into the phone booth. Crammed next to her in the glass encasement, I knew right away that she was on the phone with Uncle Warren; she had reached her breaking point and didn't wait to hear Dad's explanation before calling.

She gave Uncle Warren the details of the day's events and waited intently as he told her what to do. I didn't understand what Mom was trying to do, but I realize now that she was just trying to do the best for her kids. There were so many painful events that had happened even before I was born, and it placed Mom in the position where she felt she had nowhere else to go for help and turned to the only thing she had faith in. There was little we kids could do except watch helplessly as the events unfolded. I stood there with my head pressed against my mother, listening as Uncle Warren's voice floated out of the receiver and into the air that seemed to be closing in on us. Without hesitating, Warren rattled off a list of instructions, including that we were not to go home. I had already been removed from my home once, and I couldn't bear to go through it again.

When she got off the phone, my brothers and I sat in the truck begging her to let us go home, trying to convince her that everything would be okay. We were afraid of what would happen to us next, and how long we would have to be gone this time. The knot that had taken root in my stomach began to grow large and painful. I was filled with dread from the realization that nothing would ever be the same.

That summer we were removed from my father's home for the second and final time. Warren and the prophet never even spoke to Dad, giving him the chance to explain or try to find a less severe resolution. While we did return home one last night to sleep, the following morning we piled into the Suburban and Mom took us to the home of a church elder, who was directed to arrange our transportation out of town. This time, Dad would lose not only Mom but also, soon, Mother Laura. For my dad, this was the most painful blow imaginable. He was told that he had not only lost his priesthood and family but also his place in the Celestial Kingdom. To an FLDS member, this was losing everything. As with our first departure, his heart was broken, but now it was clear it would never mend.

CHAPTER SEVEN

REASSIGNMENT

For time and all eternity.
—FLDS WEDDING VOW

I have no recollection of how we got to Hildale or who drove us there. Instead, what I remember is the painful silence of the long car ride and Brad's overwhelming guilt. Even though the altercation with my father hadn't been his fault, he was horribly distraught over it and blamed himself for what was happening to our family. If he hadn't become so entangled with Dad the previous day, our lives might have remained as they were. While things were far from perfect, they were what we knew. Now, once again, we were uprooted and facing an uncertain future.

The next morning, Mom assembled her kids and prepared to bring us to the home of the church elder in the Salt Lake Valley. We didn't know anything except that we were leaving. As Mom was trying to herd us into the Suburban, Justin and Jacob refused, informing her they wouldn't go until they knew where we were being taken. They had urged Mom not to leave, assuring her things would change, but I knew in her heart she was committed to carrying out the will of the prophet. It seemed like all that mattered was what Warren had told her, and blinded by what she thought was the will of the prophet, I suppose she did the only thing she knew and chose to leave her sons in the name of her religion. In a flurry of emotion, we left the twins at the house, with my mother telling us that someone in the church would make sure they joined us later. That never happened.

Without the twins, only five of us, Brad, Caleb, Sherrie, Ally, and me, drove out of town with Mom that day. I was too young to draw any conclusions on my own, and I felt helpless as I watched the busy city streets of Salt Lake give way to the parched, red earth of southern Utah. Even for Brad our departure was bitter. Over the last months, Dad had been trying to work on his relationship with the boys. He'd bought four-wheelers and had been taking them into the mountains to ride on weekends. Growing up, Dad had forbidden such things, even bicycles, because they would take us off the property, but riding in the mountains with the boys had started to bring them closer together.

What none of us realized that day was that we had been taken from Dad not because of his abuse. In the FLDS, physical abuse is not nearly the taboo that it is in the outside world, and kids often suffer harsh punishments at the hands of their parents. What had happened to Brad was tragic but would not ordinarily be grounds for an FLDS man to lose the priesthood. Perhaps the reason that Warren and his father felt such a drastic step was necessary was that my father had lost control over his house, and it seemed clear that he would never get it back. With each group of younger kids falling under the influence of the older ones, my father's family was growing up doubting and sometimes defiant toward him and the church. If the priesthood allowed this trend to continue, it might spread to other kids and other families. That was too great a risk for a religion that relied on absolute control over its members. The only solution to this was to remove the rest of the family from that environment in the hope that a new home and a new priesthood father would mold us into ideal church members.

"Let us go back, Mom," I begged, overcome by a sudden urge to cuddle up to my mother and hold on to her skirt as if I was a toddler. "Please, let us go home."

Her face was drawn and her eyes had lost their glow, and behind them I sensed the same fear that we were all feeling. Turning toward me, she could muster no other response than "Just pray, Lesie."

Brilliant hues of orange and red illuminated the late-afternoon sky as we pulled up to the home of Uncle Fred Jessop, the local bishop. It would have been difficult for me to find any source of comfort at the time, but at least we were at the home of Uncle Fred. Because of his important role in the community, he commanded respect, and even though I had never known Uncle Fred myself, I looked up to him. Still, dread gripped my stomach as we approached his doorstep with the small bags that contained the few items we'd had time to gather: a few changes of clothing and a single pair of pajamas.

The stark contrast between Uncle Fred's house and the house I grew up in was undeniable. His expansive U-shaped residence was one of the largest in the community, with more than forty-five rooms spread over two floors and three large wings connected at the center to the original home. Fifteen of Uncle Fred's living wives and more than thirty of his children lived there when we arrived in late July. While I'd long seen his sprawling compound from the playground several blocks away, I'd never actually been inside.

The front door opened onto the huge dining room, where the Jessop family was seated at two long tables holding about eighteen on each side as well as four shorter tables. Although I had been raised in what many would consider a very large family, there had never been anywhere near this many people seated in our dining room. I immediately spotted Uncle Fred at the head of one of the two long tables. The air was full of chatter and the inevitable clanging of a dish or squeal of a baby.

When we stepped inside, it was like something out of a movie: a hush fell over the noisy room and everyone stopped eating to look at us. The arrival of a family in trouble was nothing new to them. Indeed, many such women and children like us had found themselves here. Still, I felt terribly awkward and ashamed as I followed my mother to an enormous living room packed with couches and chairs arranged in rows. Like all FLDS families, the Jessops held prayer services in their home, and the sheer number of people in the house required the space to be large and specialized. Upon entering the huge oblong room, I was overcome by the strangeness of the place.

Weary from the emotional turmoil of the last several days, I took a seat close to my mother. A commotion drew my attention to the doorway, where some of Fred's children were peeking in at us as if we were on display. Everyone was curious, and in the days ahead I would discover that many of Fred's children had stories much like mine, but people hardly ever talked about them. In many ways, it felt like we were all a bunch of outcasts forced to put our pasts behind us and find our niche in this large mixed family.

During the ten minutes that it took for Uncle Fred to finish up his dinner, I soaked up my surroundings. Like many members of the FLDS, Uncle Fred had added to his home a number of times over the years as his family grew. The room that we were in was part of his original home, but I could tell that it had been recently updated with new carpet and a fresh coat of paint. Vaulted ceilings and large windows lent the room an open feel, much like the Claybourne house that Dad had remodeled for us. In the center was a big, comfy-looking La-Z-Boy chair that I was certain belonged to Uncle Fred.

Sure enough, when he shuffled in, he made himself at home in that very seat. Out of respect, we all rose and one by one shook his hand. I was initially intimidated by the way he stared at us, and I didn't speak a word. Finally, a grin formed on his face and in a jovial tone, shaking his head, he mused to all of us, "What am I going to do with you?"

Even though his manner was kind, I was intimidated by him. This was the typical dynamic between women and children and church elders, especially men in a position of leadership. Fred Jessop had been assigned to be our caretaker until the prophet could decide where we belonged, and it was clear that he took the role seriously from his effort to set us at ease. Motioning one of his wives to join us, he instructed her to check on our accommodations and make sure things were ready. Then he invited a handful of his young daughters to gather around us and introduce themselves. We sat among them as Uncle Fred regaled us with a few stories of his youth before sending us to the second floor to settle in for the night. He'd graciously offered us a meal, but we were all too numb to eat and went to bed that night with empty stomachs and heavy hearts.

We were given two rooms in the south wing. Brad and Caleb shared one room, while Mom, my younger sisters Sherrie and Ally, and I moved into the larger room, which had a queen bed for them and a small pullout chair for me. Both rooms were at the end of a long hallway with a door leading to a small terrace where we could sit outside and enjoy dramatic views of the Vermilion Cliffs encircling the community like fortress walls. At first I found the scorched red landscape too grating to enjoy, but with time, I came to appreciate the raw beauty of the rugged crimson mountains that surrounded us.

I was miserable those first few nights and cried myself to sleep. I begged my mother to take us home, and I was so confused about what was happening to us. Nobody would explain to me why Uncle Warren and the prophet had ripped us away again, and I would not know what had actually happened until many years later.

Though I was incredibly homesick, I held out hope that Short Creek would prove a welcome home. I had so many positive associations with it from all of the years of summer festivals and FLDS gatherings. Hildale was the place where we didn't have to hide our lifestyle within the confines of our house and backyard. I found myself drifting into daydreams and remembering Pioneer Day celebrations from years past, envisioning how much fun it would be to encounter that kind of communal spirit on a daily basis. One of the centerpieces of Pioneer Day was a parade. It was an important and eagerly anticipated community event and every member worked hard to contribute. Beautiful floats, lines of marching boys, and groups of girls dancing to music would stretch for a good mile through the center of town, where everyone would line the streets to watch. The sheer number of people attending was astonishing.

There were a couple of years when I had the excitement of being one of the dancing girls. My sisters Kassandra and Rachel were in charge of the choreography for this and many other community performances. Their artistic and musical talents earned them a degree of respect in the community. For weeks before the parade, hundreds of girls would gather to rehearse the steps my sisters had helped to arrange until they had them down perfectly. It was impressive to see row after row of girls dressed alike performing their routines in precise harmony as they twirled their way along the town's roads.

Like the dancing girls, the marching boys, or Sons of Helaman, would meet weeks beforehand to prepare for their biggest performance of the year. Uncle Rulon's Sons of Helaman was a program to teach young boys unity and discipline. During the summer break, the boys of the community would meet to learn and practice military-inspired marching. Each platoon was directed by a church elder, who was to act as leader and mentor. Every Monday at dawn you could hear the steps of hundreds of boys marching to commands. It was an honor to every young man to earn a place in this assembly. The boys performed their carefully timed formations at many community functions.

After the morning parade, everyone would go to Cottonwood Park, where there was a large breakfast spread set up in a carefully manicured spot planted with greenery and lined with picnic tables. Donations to fund the breakfast were accepted but not required, and no one was meant to feel excluded. FLDS families cooked up every kind of breakfast fare imaginable. For me, this had always been a welcome change from the typical morning offerings of lumpy oatmeal that lined the counter of our long kitchen island.

Throughout the day the people would socialize and enjoy one another's company. The children were free to let their imaginations run, while adults could take a day off from the daily grind. Laughing children weaved their way through the crowd and played for hours on the playground. The park had an actual working mini-train, and standing in line for a ride, I could barely contain my excitement.

The day would come to a close with a community dance held in the Leroy S. Johnson Meeting House, an enormous Colonial-inspired structure—it spanned the entire block—that my father had helped to design. The dances were far from modern—we did the waltz, the two-step, and square dances. You could feel the energy in the air at the sight of twirling girls in flowing dresses and boys in their best Sunday suits. These special events were the only time that physical contact between members of the opposite sex could take place. We were allowed to chose our own partners and touch just enough to be able to perform the dance steps. When the night came to a close, we had to view each other as poisonous reptiles once again.

After summer's warmth had vanished and the children had all been in school for over two months, Octoberfest provided a reprieve from the daily routine. Much of the potatoes, dairy products, and meat consumed by community members were raised on the farm of Parley Harker, which was homesteaded in Bural, many miles outside of town. This was a time when many could come together to help harvest the crops we would consume throughout the year. The event, also dubbed Harvest Fest, was one of the most anticipated celebrations of the FLDS, with festivities lasting for three or four days, ending with Saturday work projects.

Much like the summer events, Harvest Fest days were spent at the park, where all could enjoy food and musical entertainment. Some of the stores in town closed early to celebrate, and many families participated in the organized program set for each day. The park was lined with booths offering every food item a child could dream up—candied apples, pie, cotton candy, popcorn, canned items and home-made knickknacks. Harvest Fest even allowed an annual football game for men and older boys, held in Maxwell Park, a huge sod field where there was also a baseball diamond. It was one of the few chances for men from all of the FLDS communities to come together to enjoy the raw aggression of a contact sport. Women were prohibited, of course, even from attending as spectators. Still, some of the older girls would drive by slowly enough to take an unnoticed peak from the road while "pretending" to be en route to another activity.

While I knew that these were special occasions, I still held out hope that the communal atmosphere that permeated those days would carry over to the rest of the year. There weren't many things about the move to Hildale that I had to look forward to, but the hope of finally fitting in was one of them.

It didn't take long for this optimism to fade. Trying to mesh with the home's many occupants at Uncle Fred's proved quite difficult for my family. Dad had raised us differently from the way many of the children in Fred's home were raised. We'd grown up exposed to non-FLDS people, and Dad shared my mother's desire to educate us in music. It had always been Mom's dream to play the violin, and even though it wasn't encouraged, Mom had the tenacity to seek out musical instruction for her children, developing in us all a deep love and appreciation of classical music. I remember from my youngest years her efforts to expose us to the world of music, taking us to concerts, the symphony, and instrumental performances in Salt Lake. As busy as my father was, he had always tried to find time for family, whether it was picnics, camping trips, or family music lessons. And since Dad traveled so much, we'd learned about other places in the world from his stories.

The breadth of our experiences was quite different from what most people in Hildale had grown up with. For my siblings and me, life in the closed community of Short Creek gave us something of a culture shock. Until we moved, I'd never realized just how isolated the people who lived there really were. Complicating matters was the fact that there was a trace of skepticism about us because we were from Salt Lake. Growing up, I'd always sensed an undercurrent of competition between the communities of Salt Lake City and Hildale/Colorado City, and as the days turned to weeks, that silent rivalry I'd felt as a visitor seemed to take root in Fred Jessop's home.

It seemed that almost from the very first day, the other mothers living in the house kept close tabs on all of us, including Mom. My brothers and I were often singled out and humiliated for the kind of small incidents that would be ignored when they involved other members of the household. Uncle Fred had no qualms about shining a spotlight on us during prayer services when he felt we'd done something wrong. It felt to us like the people in Fred's home were trying to break our spirits in order to make us conform more strictly to the FLDS religion as they knew it. Even so, I held on to my belief that the spunk which had gotten us into trouble so many times in the past was also what would help us to stay strong and true to ourselves.

Several days after we'd settled in, I began the eighth grade at the public junior high school in Colorado City. It was so exciting to join the public school, and from the moment I first arrived, I loved my time there because it kept my mind off my family situation. Every day, I rode to and from school in one of Fred Jessop's family vans with other kids from his family because Uncle Fred's house was so far up the hill that there was no bus stop nearby. At the end of the day, Mom would pick us up from school. Those trips home were just about the only moments when we were all together with no one from the Jessop family around, and we cherished that time. On the days when she couldn't come, sometimes I would walk the couple of miles back home after school, taking the opportunity to enjoy time by myself before returning to the bustle of Uncle Fred's house.

Almost all of our school's administration and teachers and most of my classmates were FLDS members, but unlike the curriculum at Alta Academy, which was rooted in our religious teachings, the coursework at Colorado City School District #14 conformed more to state mandates. Those who were not FLDS were from the surrounding area, including members of the Centennial Group. Being able to mix with kids outside of the FLDS religion was a wonderful change. I quickly found friendship with a girl from the Centennial Group named Lea, but the long-standing feud between the two sects prevented me from socializing with her outside of school. By church declaration the members of the Centennial Group were apostates, and I was not to associate with them.

As I became more accustomed to life in Short Creek, I was lucky to find a very dear friend who was also an FLDS member. Her name was Natalie, and she was one of the most enjoyable people I'd ever met. She was the first young person in Hildale who seemed to accept me as I was— something that I'd been unable to find in Uncle Fred's home. For the first time since I'd arrived, I felt I could trust someone, and I finally started to come out of my protective shell and blossom.

Friends weren't the only thing that I liked about school. Public school opened my eyes to a varied curriculum that gave me a thirst for learning. Given the focus on religious learning at Alta Academy, I had missed out on several important subjects, and had to struggle to catch up to my grade level. With so many distractions at home, at first I had a hard time with the rigors of public school, but with the help of my science teacher, David Bateman, I felt my eyes open up to a whole new academic world. I had never really studied science at school, and Mr. Bateman challenged me to come up to par, and even spent extra time helping me to discover science at work in the world around me. We had our fair share of difficulties and teacher-student arguments, but I loved his class and he became my favorite teacher. I also developed a love of writing and history and found that I was good at both. I finally started to adjust to my new school life, although I found it impossible to adapt to my new home. Since arriving at Fred's house, I'd endured weeks of backstabbing and name-calling from the other girls in the home. My near-fatal reaction to the anesthetic during my "attempted" tonsillectomy had resulted in a number of lingering effects. One was the retention of water, and that, coupled with the baby fat I'd always had, had contributed to the little bit of pudge I'd put on over the months. Being a bit heavier had placed me at the center of cruel taunts, as some of Uncle Fred's daughters looked to cut me down. With fifteen girls between the ages of twelve and seventeen living in the home, it had become like a dormitory with various cliques forming and relentless teasing everywhere. I was already very self-conscious about my appearance, and their comments only made it worse. I was so hurt and humiliated that I began starving myself to lose weight.

Had it not been for Mom's intervention, the situation could have turned far more serious. She'd noticed that I wasn't eating my meals and immediately took steps to correct the problem. Mom recognized how this was hurting my spirit and lovingly assured me that no matter what anyone else was saying, I was special and beautiful and didn't need to be ashamed of myself. I was just a normal young teenager struggling to find my place in a house full of teenage girls.

The problems didn't end with my weight. Every time I spoke about my father, the other girls in the house teased me, apparently deriving pleasure from informing me that he wasn't my father anymore. I'd been involved in several heated arguments over the weeks and had simply refused to abandon Dad or agree that he was a wicked man.

"You just watch," they'd say in rebuttal. "Your mother is going to marry Uncle Fred."

I should have realized that they were speaking from experience, as it had already happened to them and their mothers. Nevertheless, I refused to let go of my hope that somehow we'd all be reunited.

Finally, the day came when the idle gossip became real. After helping some of the other Jessop girls pick corn from the community garden, we all had just arrived back at the house when one of Fred's daughters approached me.

"Your mom's going to marry Father," she said, in a know-it-all tone.

"No she's not," I quickly retorted, trying my best to sound sure of myself. "We're going to go home someday."

I was not going to give up on my dad. If Mom really did become Uncle Fred's wife, it would mean that all of her children would then belong to Uncle Fred, and from the day of their wedding forward we would have to address him as Father. As far as the church was concerned, the man who had raised me, the man I had loved and called Dad for thirteen years, would no longer be my father. We could no longer even think of him in that way. In fact, we could no longer think of him at all. If Mom and Uncle Fred married, we'd literally belong to Fred Jessop and be expected to immediately transfer our love and loyalty to him.

It would also mean we would have to drop our proud family name of Wall and take on the last name Jessop. When a woman and her children were passed from one man to another—regardless of the reason—they were forced to forsake the legacy of the father, as though he had never existed. Warren preached that when a family remarried to another man, God changed their blood and DNA to match that of the priesthood man they now belonged to. If we did not have worthy blood running through our veins, we could not gain entrance into the kingdom of heaven.

But I didn't want a new name or new DNA, and I most certainly didn't want a new dad. I wanted my old dad, and the thought of these things taking place was incomprehensible. And I wasn't going to allow it.

Upset after yet another confrontation with the girls of the house, I ran upstairs to see Mom. Pushing open the bedroom door, I found her standing before a mirror trying on what appeared to be an unfinished wedding dress as my sister Kassandra altered it. I was stunned and completely speechless. In one moment the realization that she was indeed going to marry Fred hit me. For weeks, my relationship with my mother had been a bit strained, and the fact that I was entering my teens only fractured our already weakened mother-daughter bond. It was too much for me to come to grips with the fact that Mom would give up on Dad, but there she was, standing in front of me, preparing to marry someone else as though my father no longer existed. As I stared at her, all my hopes were shattered. There was a familiar sparkle in her soft brown eyes that had been missing for quite a while, a sparkle that contained hope and said that everything was going to be okay. Those were emotions that I hadn't felt in myself for a long time.

Too devastated to say a word, I raced onto the house's large balcony, where I found solace in a wicker porch swing. When I calmed down, Mom explained that Uncle Rulon had directed her to marry Uncle Fred, but I was livid. She hadn't even taken the time to tell me. Hearing it from the house rumor mill had made it that much more difficult to swallow. The news was even worse for my two brothers Brad and Caleb. Life in Short Creek was very hard for them, and without the twins, they had banded together to survive. Brad and Caleb shared my feelings about Mom being married, and the idea of becoming another man's children was something they could not accept.

Not long after my discovery, Rachel joined Kassandra at the Jessop house to help us make dresses for the ceremony. In the days that followed, everyone in the household was nice to us. While I hated to admit it, it felt good to be noticed and included in things for a change. Mom's marriage to Uncle Fred would elevate our status in the home to actual children of the church bishop as opposed to "refugees."

I was heartbroken as I stood in the living room of Uncle Rulon's house that September 2, 1999, and watched as my mother was passed on to another man. On the outside, I was the picture of a beautiful priesthood child. My sisters had sewn my special pink gown with a three-inch lace sash at the waist, and my hair had been styled for the occasion by Felita, the well-known "Hair Queen of Hildale." But inside I was falling apart. As hard as I tried, I couldn't stop the tears from stinging my eyes. When the ceremony began, I beat myself up for having harbored angry feelings toward my father over things that had happened. Standing there, staring at my mother, I suddenly forgot any problems our family had ever had. All I could think was that we would never be reunited, and I deeply regretted not having cherished every moment we'd spent together. Had I known this was going to happen, I would have savored my times with Dad, and the whole family.

Uncle Fred looked old standing next to my mother, who was elegant in the delicate white lace gown my sisters had sewn for the occasion. It didn't make any sense to me that Mom could become another man's wife. How could she go from loving my dad for so long to suddenly loving Uncle Fred—all because of the prophet's words? Even through the eyes of an FLDS child, those words were not enough to take away that love. The priesthood, God, the prophet—none of it could justify what was happening. Mom entered into this union out of hope for a better future for us all, because she truly believed that the prophet knew what was best for her and her children. It took a heavy toll on her as well, but it was hard for me to see that at the time.

I didn't dare let on, but for a while I'd been wondering about aspects of our faith. I couldn't understand how our family had ended up so fractured and why the Lord would take children away from their father. I struggled with the fact that Mom seemed happier and maybe even excited over her new placement as Fred Jessop's wife. While the union had elevated her status in the family, it did little to ingratiate her to my brothers and me, but ultimately, we knew she had little choice. Since arriving in the Crick six weeks earlier, we hadn't been allowed any contact with my dad. Every time I asked for an explanation, I was told that it was what Uncle Warren had directed. They said my father needed to repent and we did not need his influence in our lives. I know now that they were afraid if we talked with Dad he might ask us to go back home and the priesthood could lose control of us. I was also upset that my mom hadn't pushed harder to get Justin and Jacob to Hildale. It was like she'd abandoned both her husband and her children, all in the name of God.

I listened as Uncle Warren sat at the right hand of the prophet reading a sermon. I held my breath, praying that Uncle Warren would not seal this union "for time and all eternity." Sometimes, a couple is sealed merely for time, as is the case for a woman who has lost a husband to death and needs a caretaker on earth until she can join him in the Celestial Kingdom. I might have been able to accept the marriage had it been a union simply for "time." That would mean my brothers and I could still be with Dad in heaven. But that Uncle Warren had sealed her to Fred for "time and all eternity" took away any lingering hope of being reunited with my father in the next life.

CHAPTER EIGHT

PREPARING FOR ZION

Where we may have children who are leaning away,
we must keep working them until they declare themselves
against the Priesthood; and case by case, they are brought
before the Prophet and handled.
—WARREN JEFFS

We'd been living at the Jessop compound for a little more than three months when fear that the world was going to end became overwhelming. All our lives, it had been ingrained in us that we were to prepare for the "Great Destructions" and the redeeming of Zion. The new millennium was upon us, and we had been told that when it arrived, God was going to send destruction upon the world, and only the most worthy would be preserved.

Warren made it clear that the coming apocalypse, which had been the impetus to move the prophet to Short Creek, was going to occur soon. Speaking on behalf of his father, he commanded all FLDS members remaining in Salt Lake to move south so that all of God's worthy chosen people could be one as we were lifted up to meet the Lord.

While the coming of Zion was supposed to be a good thing, I worried about how it was going to happen. As with many of our religious prophecies, I felt confused by it. We had all been told that if we were not 100 percent pure inside, we risked being destroyed alongside the wicked. I reflected over my thirteen years and contemplated all of the times I had doubted my faith, all the times I had not been perfectly obedient or not kept perfectly sweet. Because of the times that I had questioned the word of the prophet since coming to Uncle Fred's house, I knew that I was not 100 percent pure, and I was terrified.

Even with the apocalypse looming, there was a New Year's Eve party at Uncle Fred's house and several FLDS members who had passed through his home over the years as his "children" returned for the festivities. Despite the energy that filled the space, I could tell I was not alone in my worries. We popped a ton of popcorn for munching as we all waited for the moment when the Lord would descend.

As 2000 came and went and the world didn't end, everyone was pretty confused. In the days ahead, Uncle Warren would tell us how lucky we were that God had blessed us with more time to prepare. Satisfied with the explanation, many of us went about our lives feeling gratitude for the reprieve, and the extra time to cleanse our souls.

Being a full member of Fred Jessop's family soon lost its luster. While Uncle Fred preached in church that a father should reprimand his sons and daughters in private, he'd often hold my brothers and me up as examples during his prayer services at home. "Sharon, I don't like the shirt your son is wearing," he'd say to Mom in front of the entire family. On more than one occasion, he singled me out, correcting me in front of everyone for a variety of reasons: I wasn't helping enough around the house, my clothes weren't up to the dress code, or he didn't like the music I was listening to in the privacy of my room. It seemed like nothing I did was acceptable to him. But sooner or later, he would make all of my family fall in line.

The music in particular became a point of contention. At Fred's home, as in other FLDS homes, it was preferred that we listen to Uncle Warren's tapes, including his home-economics classes or church-distributed music. While I listened to those tapes over and over, I also had classical music that I had been listening to all my life, which was comforting to me and helped me to relax. Even that small outside influence was too much for the Jessop household, and Fred made no attempt to hide his disdain for my choices. This would have been hard in any environment, but what made life in the Jessop home so unbearable was that it was impossible to trust any other family members. One time, another mother went so far as to hide in Mom's closet to spy on us and catch us listening to "worldly" music. When I noticed her behind some dresses, she became very upset with me for questioning her authority. She didn't feel that she'd done anything wrong and in fact got me in trouble for the incident. In response, Fred demanded to see our entire music collection and threw out any titles he deemed "worldly."

Incidents like this made it that much harder to accept Uncle Fred as my new father, and the sting of his corrections did not seem to go away. Ultimately he struck at the one thing I loved about my new life—school. It all started when one of my new stepsisters tattled on me to Uncle Fred for having a friendship with a boy at school. Austin Barlow had been nice to me in class when I was still "the new kid" struggling to fit in, and throughout the year, we shared many classes, developing a friendship in the process. He was the first boy I'd ever met who didn't make fun of me. It was a new experience for me not to have so many restrictions and to be able to forge an actual friendship with a boy. Being treated kindly by someone of the opposite sex felt good, and for a time I even had a secret crush on him, though it was never anything more than an innocent schoolgirl feeling.

Still, my associations with Austin became a source of great pain when my stepsisters saw us talking after school one day. One of them felt it was her duty to report it to Fred. That night Uncle Fred stood me up in front of the entire family during prayer time and reprimanded me for these boy-girl relations that would "taint" my future. I hung my head in shame as he made me feel so guilty for something I hadn't even done. I tried to get a word in, but he refused to stop the tirade, forcing me to defend myself against his accusations.

"Did you kiss him?" he demanded.

"No way," I insisted with a trembling voice, as every pair of eyes in the room bore a hole through me. "I would never even touch him."

But for all my denials, Uncle Fred wouldn't let it go. I wanted to run and hide as my cheeks grew fiery from the embarrassment. I already felt like an outcast, but now I was on a life raft all by myself.

Until then, school had been my lone refuge from the chaos of the Jessop house. It was the one place I felt safe. Back at Alta Academy, I had always been afraid of Uncle Warren. His critical eye was always upon us, and any minor infraction would be taken very seriously. In this new school, I felt free in a way I never had before. Because it was a public school, the principal was not required to adhere to the strict mandates of the FLDS Church. With some room to breathe, I grew comfortable in my own skin and enjoyed socializing with children from other polygamous sects outside of my faith.

All that changed with one word from Fred. While it was not against school policy to talk to members of the opposite sex, Uncle Fred insisted that the principal, an FLDS member, suspend me. Suddenly I was cut off from the few friends I had. With a fresh feeling of betrayal and anger, I later confronted my stepsister, and though she denied what she had done, I knew better. With that incident, it became clear that all the things I had appreciated about my new school were fleeting. The priesthood wielded just as much power in the public school as it had at Alta Academy. No matter where I was, Uncle Warren and the FLDS Church permeated every aspect of my life.

When I finally returned to school, I could never speak to Austin again. Everybody was watching us to make sure we had no further contact. In spite of this, I still tried to maintain friendships with the girls and boys in my grade. One of my science teacher's sons, Steven, and I had been friends that year, and after I returned from my suspension, he, along with my two friends Natalie and Lea, were the few kids who did not make comments about my absence.

Brad had also been struggling ever since we arrived in Hildale, and without the twins for support, every day seemed to grow harder for him. In an attempt to lift his spirits, Dad had sent him the four-wheeler he'd bought for him when he was in Salt Lake, along with our belongings, and Brad had happily parked it in the rear lot of Fred's house. But a few days after it arrived, Brad woke up to find that Uncle Fred had confiscated it. Although many people in the Creek, including some in Uncle Fred's own family, had ATVs, Fred took Brad's without even speaking to him about it. It seemed he wanted to punish Brad for any trouble that Fred felt he'd caused. Despite Brad's petition to have it returned, Fred was immovable on the subject.

This was the last straw for Brad, who had been a constant target of Uncle Fred's scrutiny since his arrival. It all started when Fred singled Brad out for not adhering to the dress code. The long-sleeved knit pullovers that Brad wore over his church undergarments were frowned upon by church elders, who wanted only button-down shirts for the men. Brad's looser-fitting pants were also outside the limits of acceptable garments and earned him repeated scoffs from Uncle Fred. His clothes weren't the only problem, though; his attitude also began to get him in trouble. He refused to call Uncle Fred "Father," or accept him as such, and he started to skip family gatherings. When he was at home, he stayed in his room and listened to unapproved music with Caleb. Whenever I could, I would sneak into their room and join them to hear some of the forbidden CDs.

With so few Wall children together, we had all grown close, however, after the confiscation of Brad's four-wheeler, we knew deep down that our time together was about to end. When Brad learned what Fred had done, he was furious. The ATV had been the only thing he had left from our true father.

Mom did what she could to hold on to the last two sons she had with her. She would beg and plead with them to read passages from the Book of Mormon and other church teachings, telling them it would help them to understand their mission. She promised to help them find the way by praying for them, but Brad was sixteen and his inner voice was taking him in another direction. He refused to conform to Uncle Fred's design, and from that point forward things only got worse for him.

One day when I was in his room, several police officers who were members of the FLDS broke the door down and began a "professional" search of his belongings. Supposedly, they were looking for firearms that he was "rumored" to have in his possession, but we all knew that they were searching for anything that could get him into trouble. Despite the authority they had over me, I was furious at the intrusion, and I nervously watched as they ransacked the room, eventually confiscating a small TV my brother had secretly purchased from a kid at school, his CD player, a handful of his "forbidden" CDs, and some sketches he had made of a motorbike.

Uncle Fred's fingerprints were all over the search, and we all knew it from the moment the police showed up at the door. With the evidence found in Brad's room, the church elders became convinced that he was in need of reform and decided to send him to Canada.

Having heard the twins talk about their experience in Canada, Brad knew that it was not a place he wanted to go. Not only was the work site in a remote location in Alberta, but he would be living in a portable trailer with other "fallen" kids and few of the comforts of home. With temperatures often dipping as low as twenty-five degrees below zero and much of the work being done outside, Brad would need a strong will and a passion for the priesthood that he simply didn't possess. He was fed up with the church and those who led it, and he knew that he had to find a way out. The only question was how.

Against his will, he began the long drive up to Canada with the priesthood men in charge of him. They stopped to spend the night at a hotel in Salt Lake City, and not missing a beat, Brad saw his opportunity. With his guardians sleeping nearby, he silently tossed his belongings out of the window, then jumped out after them, landing in a heap on the cold, hard ground. From a pay phone, he called our brother Travis for help.

Over the next few days, they tracked Brad to Dad's house and Warren himself tried to convince him to come back to Hildale. When he refused, Dad received a call from a church leader, stating that he should take care of Brad and the twins, and that my mother would take care of the girls and Caleb. It was one of the few times that the priesthood had split up children in this fashion.

Brad's absence hit me incredibly hard, leaving me with an emptiness that I struggled to conceal. As if losing another brother wasn't bad enough, the school that I had come to love so much underwent a change. Shortly before Brad's escape, I graduated from the eighth grade, but sadly that marked the end of my public school career and signified the last time I'd see many of the friends I'd made there. All year I'd looked forward to my first-ever graduation ceremony. This would be the first time I'd ever be recognized for having completed something. Standing among my friends in the school auditorium in the beautiful lavender dress my sister had helped me sew, I felt such a sense of accomplishment. Mom had even bought me a corsage at the local florist—another first—and I was so excited to pin it on.

The occasion proved bittersweet. I'd finally found an outlet for my inner struggles in learning, and my inclination toward science had gotten me thinking in new directions. Suddenly dreams I had never had began to fill my mind. For the first time, I felt that I had the power to shape my own destiny, that everything wasn't predetermined for me. All I had to do was continue to excel at school, and I might be able to reach my goals and chart my own course.

But Uncle Warren would crush this dream, too. That summer, he stood up in church and told the people that they needed to take their children out of the public schools. "The time is short," he said from the pulpit. "The prophet has directed the people to pull your children out of the schools of the world and start priesthood school."

He'd already commanded the FLDS people to separate themselves from apostates, warning that anyone caught associating with them would be dealt with severely. Now his directive to pull the children from the schools resulted in the closing of the Colorado City Unified School District and a huge loss of jobs and income for many in the community. There had been more than a thousand students enrolled at the time I arrived, but that number dropped to just a handful in the days following Uncle Warren's decree.

Of course, Warren started his own private school in Hildale, and enrollment was coveted. It seemed that only the very righteous were admitted. There was also a school run by Fred Jessop called Uzona Home School, as well as several other private schools organized by various local families. As one of Fred Jessop's children, I would be attending his school, which, oddly enough, he opened in the building that had housed my junior high the year before. Many former teachers from the public school would now work for Uncle Fred, mostly on a volunteer basis, as is expected of FLDS members. At the public schools, the teachers had been salaried and their families were dependent on that income. Though monetary donations to the private schools were encouraged and spread among the teachers, the money was rarely enough to make up for the loss of the salaries.

In order to make sure that no one broke his ban on the public school, Uncle Rulon, through a speech delivered by Warren, stopped virtually all contact between the FLDS people and outsiders. Uncle Warren said that our prophet's call was "Leave apostates alone, severely." We were told that the prophet would lose confidence in anyone who associated with apostates. Those who lost that confidence would lose their family and home—both of which were the property of the priesthood. Warren made it clear that the prophet "means business."

That summer we celebrated Mom's fiftieth birthday and I

turned fourteen, but I found it difficult to rejoice in either event. Our lives were growing more restricted by the week. Everything had become unpredictable, and all that appeared certain about our future was that it would hold more rules, warnings, and fears. Turbulence was spreading, and it was just a matter of time before it came to my bedroom door.

CHAPTER NINE

A REVELATION

IS MADE

For his [the prophet's] word, ye shall receive as if
from [God's] own mouth.
—D.C. SECT. 21

In August 2000, I started the ninth grade at the Uzona
Home School, and it was a massive disappointment. For
one thing, everyone there was FLDS, and that familiar con-
formity was frustrating. The curriculum at Uzona also had a
stunting effect. With the focus back on religion as it had
been at Alta Academy, I realized I would not be able to continue the many subjects I had come to love. Public school
had been filled with possibility, but here I felt claustropho-
bic, knowing that it would never help me to learn in the way
that I needed.

Almost from day one, I was on my own a lot at Fred
Jessop's school. None of the friends I'd made at the public
school had enrolled here, and starting over was not easy. At
home, I didn't fare much better, as many of the other girls
my age continued to treat me poorly. While there were some
kind ones who were also suffering from poor treatment by
the other girls, the emotional difficulties we were all experiencing made it a challenge for us to really connect and rely
on one another. As a result, we all had to fend for ourselves.

This lack of acceptance led me to spend most of my time in my room with my mother, Sherrie, and Ally. The isolation was hard to tolerate, but it gave me a chance to support my two younger sisters. In their short lives, they had been through an amazing amount of hardship and confusion watching our family struggle. Though I hoped that their age had insulated them from the difficulties of the past four years, I understood the hurdles that they would face as they tried to come to terms with our family's past and shaky future. In response, I had a sort of idealized vision that if I could be there for them, if we could lean on one another to make a close-knit little group within the larger Jessop family, maybe they wouldn't have to feel the pain and betrayal that had tainted our recent lives. We were a part of a large family and an even larger community, but all we really had was one another.

Eventually I learned that much of the resentment I was feeling from the other girls was due to my domestic abilities, which were sometimes recognized and praised by Uncle Fred. Because there were so many people living in the house, my skills were frequently called upon, as I had to pitch in to get all the chores done. Every mother was assigned to cook a meal during the week, and my mother had Friday lunch. I would help her, and we always tried to make it special, creating a three-course meal or adding a fun theme such as Mexican or Italian. We would serve a soup or salad, an interesting and different main course, and a homemade dessert, like my specialty cheesecake. For us, the fun wasn't just making the food but also decorating the dining room with our own personal flair, perhaps spicing up the plastic tablecloths with fresh flowers from the backyard and around town. Our goal wasn't just to make a good meal but to create a pleasant atmosphere, a place that felt more like home.

The vast Jessop family came to look forward to my mom's lunches. I enjoyed sharing this weekly task with my mom, which offered us mother-daughter time, while giving us a chance to showcase our culinary talents. I took great satisfaction in my work and tried to do everything perfectly. Having carefully watched my sisters and mother for years, I'd honed my own skills and felt fulfilled when others enjoyed our creations. The fact that our Friday lunches had become so popular filled me with a sense of accomplishment, and I liked to stand back and watch as the family fussed over the menu and complimented our aesthetic. But even this effort to please was met with some disdain from most of the other girls and a few of the mothers in the house. I couldn't understand why something that came from the heart and was meant to delight others could cause such contention.

Unable to find a place either at home or at my new school, I started to spend more time with my sister Kassandra, staying over with her at the prophet's home whenever I could. She had a cozy room on the ground level with an elaborate daybed and a trundle, where I'd sleep. Over the last couple of years, I had been able to bond with a few of my older sisters, and Kassandra had become a close friend. For many different reasons, she was also growing restless in her home life. Increasingly, Uncle Warren had been encouraging Rulon's wives to cut ties with their own family and turn their sole attention to Uncle Rulon. Whereas before, Uncle Rulon's wives experienced special freedoms, now they were pressured to stay at home and pray. This did not sit well with my sister, who was twenty-three, full of life, and reluctant to fully succumb to these new restrictions.

One advantage of Kassandra's position was that she had access to a car and finances, and we began escaping to St. George, a city forty miles away, on secret shopping trips. I felt grown-up as Kassandra and I wandered through stores and shared lunch at a restaurant. Many times we'd take Mother, Caleb, Sherrie, and Ally along. Of course, we knew we were defying the rules by not bringing along a priesthood man as our escort, but a tagalong would have spoiled the adventure. However, it was not all fun and games. We ran the risk of getting into serious trouble. All it would have taken was a suspicious member of the FLDS to tell on us for being out unescorted.

When trips to St. George were not possible, sometimes we would quietly borrow ATVs or horses from people we knew and spend time out in the vast expanses of open desert around Short Creek's twin towns. In those fleeting moments, it felt like we were free to do whatever we wanted, like we were living on the edge and challenging the expected codes of conduct.

Though these jaunts from the twin towns were exciting, we had to be on the lookout for the police wherever we went. It was widely known that the local police squad was composed almost entirely of FLDS members, who many believed that in addition to purportedly enforcing state and local laws also used their authority to enforce the directives of the priesthood. Even though we were doing nothing to break the laws of the land, our behavior went against the laws of the church and we feared religious retribution far more than anything else.

While the local police didn't often catch us on our excursions, my brother Caleb wasn't so lucky. With Brad in Salt Lake, Uncle Fred and his family's focus had turned to my twelve-year-old brother, who, like Brad, was having difficulties in the Jessop house. Already he'd been set up by some of Uncle Fred's sons when they convinced him to return a video of a community play that they'd taken out of Fred's office without permission. As a new kid in the home, Caleb accepted their instructions without a second thought, but when one of Uncle Fred's wives saw him in the office returning the tape, she immediately assumed that Caleb was stealing money from Uncle Fred and called the police.

I was in the room when they arrived, handcuffed my twelve-year-old brother, and put him in the patrol car. I screamed at them to leave him alone, but they drove off in the direction of the town meeting hall. Uncle Fred was there attending one of the Friday-night socials he oversaw. My brother was dragged before the entire gathering by the police and placed before Uncle Fred. Outwardly annoyed that the officers had humiliated him by alerting the community to a private family issue, Fred instructed the officers to take Caleb home, where he would be dealt with later.

Incidents like this gave me the sinking feeling that Caleb would not last at the Jessop house for much longer. He had also started attending Uncle Fred's private school that year and was not adjusting well. I could see that without his brothers, he felt completely alone, forced to cope with his questions about the church and its teachings on his own. Many of the older boys in Fred's house took it upon themselves to try to keep him in line. He refused to be broken, and sure enough, about six months after Brad's departure, Mom frantically woke me up in the middle of the night, saying, "I think I heard something downstairs. I think Caleb is leaving."

"What?" I asked groggily, wiping the sleep from my eyes. "Caleb's going where?"

"I think he's trying to leave the house. You have to go and stop him."

Instantly I leapt out of bed and ran downstairs. I had been left behind by all of my older brothers, but I couldn't stand to lose a younger one. He was the only brother remaining in my life whom I was allowed to speak to. My heart pounded in my chest as I got to his room to find it empty. I sprinted outside, arriving at the driveway only to see a car speeding away from the house. Something in me knew it was Brad. He had come to rescue Caleb, but they had forgotten me.

In the darkness of the chilly night, I took off behind them, chasing after the car on foot until I couldn't run anymore. Exhausted, I put my hands on my knees and stood there gasping for air. As I slowly returned to the house, my heart sank in my chest. I had drawn strength from my recent closeness with Brad and Caleb. Although Brad and Caleb were both young, I'd still felt a certain sense of protection with them in the house. They were my brothers and they cared about me. They helped me through things. I had become so isolated from the other family members that without their companionship, I couldn't imagine how I could continue. I was all alone to help Mom with Sherrie and Ally.

Losing her two remaining sons proved incredibly difficult for Mom. Devastated, she talked to them both on the phone and pleaded with them to return. She told them that she needed them and that they'd abandoned her. But they felt abandoned too, and they begged her to come back to Salt Lake and take care of them. When she said she couldn't, they accused her of choosing her religion over them. Her heart was torn in two, but the reality was apparent: her faith required that she choose the prophet and religion over everything else. It didn't matter how much she loved us, missed us, or wanted us by her side. She could not forsake her duty to the prophet and priesthood.

I couldn't understand how my mother could make such a choice. For me, it seemed clear that she should be with Dad and her children. In many ways the situation with Brad and Caleb mirrored what had happened with Justin and Jacob, and I was still upset with her for having left them in Salt Lake City with my father. But as time went on and I experienced the truth of life at Uncle Fred's, I was glad they'd never had to endure it. Still, I missed them terribly.

As it turned out, things weren't much easier for Justin and Jacob in Salt Lake. The crushing pain Dad suffered after having his family taken from him and given to another man had almost destroyed him. But instead of reaching out to the twins and trying to heal their pain together, it seemed like he became immersed in trying to understand why Warren and Uncle Rulon had removed us and in taking the steps they deemed necessary in order to repent.

Justin and Jacob still didn't have the father we had grown up with, and they were sent again into reform, this time beginning in Idaho which was harder than before. For months they bounced around from one reform home to another, and in each they were subjected to harsh work and terrible living conditions and forced to fend for themselves. They were subjected to this to deepen their faith, but it only made them more resentful toward the priesthood. When it was clear that they would not conform, they were sent back to Dad's house in Salt Lake.

Upon their return, the tension with Dad continued, and it didn't take long for similar divides to open up between Dad, Brad, and Caleb. While I imagined all of them happy with Dad at home, they too struggled to put pieces of the family together and survive in a shattered household. Since Dad and Brad had left issues unresolved between them before our parting, their relationship remained strained. Being back at home in Salt Lake reopened the wounds of the past and ultimately resulted in Brad entering foster care. Much of the problem stemmed from the emotional toll that the last few years had taken on Dad. He must have been overwhelmed. Just a few days after we had been commanded to leave him, Mother Laura was removed from his home as well. She was nine months pregnant at the time and immediately became the fourth wife of Fred Lindsay of Hildale, giving birth to Dad's son a few days following the wedding. Sadly, Dad's new son would never have the chance to know his biological father. According to priesthood law, Laura and her sons now belonged to Fred Lindsay.

With Laura's children as with us, Dad had no visitation rights. While rights could be awarded by the courts, the FLDS typically hold the courts and the laws of men in contempt. Going to court to address problems is seen as a clear betrayal of the priesthood, and court orders are routinely disobeyed. Like Sharon and Laura, Mother Audrey had also been directed to leave, but she bravely refused and remained in the home by my father's side.

Robbed of almost all my familial support, I receded even further into myself, taking refuge in my time with Kassandra, which thanks to Warren's mandates for Rulon's wives became less and less frequent. The weeks and months passed slowly until one day more than a year after my arrival at the Jessop house, when everything ground to a sudden halt. That was the day that changed everything for me—the day when Fred Jessop announced to the house that the prophet had a revelation that centered on me—a revelation about marriage.

In retrospect, I can see that Uncle Fred had been dropping hints for some time, but I was fourteen. I hadn't understood the true implication of his words and brushed them off as simple signs of encouragement. It had started in the early spring of 2001, while Mom was in Canada visiting two of my sisters. She'd hitched a ride with another church member heading to the community up there, leaving me on my own to cook Friday's lunch. Because of the amount of work it took to prepare a meal for fifty family members, I'd gotten up extra early to start cooking. People of the FLDS commonly believe that God is an early riser, so we had breakfast at 5:30 A.M, and all of our meals were scheduled for a specific time each day. It was best to get to each meal for the blessing and in line early for the food so that you could eat before the tables were cleared and the dishes had to be done.

When the hour for lunch rolled around, I enthusiastically announced over the intercom that "lunch is served" and waited anxiously in the dining room for the family to start arriving. As people came in, I walked over to the enormous windows, which offered an impressive view of the town with a small patch of our garden in the foreground, and stood for a moment basking in the generous light of the day, feeling a sense of pride and accomplishment for having prepared such a large meal all on my own. At the age of fourteen, I had pulled off the task without complaining or asking for help.

As the mothers filed in, I could tell they were impressed, but never did I expect any overt recognition. Surprisingly, Mother Katherine told me how pleased she was and that I had done an "amazing job." She was one of the few other mothers who was nice to me, and I'd grown fond of her during my time at Uncle Fred's house, enjoying her kindness and authenticity, qualities I'd always admired in my sister Michelle.

As we began eating, I overheard Mother Katherine telling Uncle Fred that I had prepared and served the beautiful meal on my own. While her intention was to call Uncle Fred's attention to my accomplishment, I quickly sensed the undercurrent of annoyance among the other girls at the table. Their displeasure grew when Mother Katherine expressed her wish that the other girls in the house would take some responsibility like I did.

"You are going to make a man very happy someday," Uncle Fred declared, his tone full of pride. "You will make a good wife for someone."

It felt nice to have Fred's approval instead of a reprimand. Even though I was only fourteen, I knew that this was the best compliment a girl could get. Becoming a wife was the ultimate goal and dream of all FLDS girls. Not certain how to respond, I giggled and continued eating my lunch. As usual, Uncle Fred's words would invite more scorn toward me from my stepsisters, but I didn't care. I was pleased with what I had done, and even when my annoying cousin Allen Steed showed up to grab a bite, it didn't break my mood.

Over the past six months I'd begun to see a lot of Allen. He was a frequent volunteer at Fred's house, taking care of the zoo, helping with odd jobs, and lending a hand where it was needed. His family lived just a few streets away, but he had begun sticking around to join the large Jessop crew for meals. It seemed that he was mainly interested in watching the many daughters. It gave me the creeps. Although I still loathed my cousin, the feeling was different now. When we had lived together at the Steed ranch, Allen had been lanky and awkward but a bully. Now he had grown stockier and his oddness made me uncomfortable.

At nineteen, he could no longer treat my siblings and me the way he had in the past. Nonetheless, there was something that just didn't seem right about him. The other girls and I talked behind his back about how strange he was. Whenever he would come around, we would giggle and talk about how he stared at the pretty girls who flitted about the house taking care of babies or helping their mothers prepare dinner. When he spoke to me, he tried to make it seem as though he had lost his meanness, but I knew the real Allen. The truth about him might have been masked behind a bigger frame, but he was very much the same person who left me fallen in the snow, laughing loudly as he drove off to go ice-skating. In the evenings, I was always happy when some of the mothers would tell him that it was time for him to be on his way. He never seemed to pick up on the subtle and not-so-subtle cues that he'd overstayed his welcome. But as irritating as he was, Uncle Fred seemed to like him and continued to find things for him to do.

After that Friday lunch, Uncle Fred began to pay more attention to me. During the time I'd been living in his home I'd had little interaction with him aside from regular corrections, but suddenly he seemed to want to talk to me. It was just a few days after my solo debut in the kitchen that I crossed paths with him in the hallway and he stopped for a moment to chat.

"How old are you?" he asked in his usual friendly tone.

"Well," I said, smiling, "I just had my fourteenth birthday."

"Ah, you're joking with me, right?"

"No, I'm fourteen," I replied, unsure why we were having the conversation. But my confusion quickly passed when Uncle Fred chuckled, and I joined in.

A few weeks later, Mom and I were preparing another Friday lunch. Together we were running around, washing and cutting everything in the kitchen. I was standing at the sink when Uncle Fred came up behind me and put his arm around my shoulder. "Very soon, you are going to make a good wife to a man," he said softly into my ear.

Mom was standing nearby, and I instantly saw a look of astonishment come over her face. Even though I was somewhat alarmed by the comment, Uncle Fred was my priesthood head, and knowing that he was pleased with me felt good. His compliments were rewarding, even if they came with these cryptic remarks about marriage. Besides, he couldn't honestly want me to get married "soon." I was only fourteen.

Mom, however, remained worried. Her trepidation only increased when Uncle Fred invited me to join him and three of my older stepsisters on a trip to Phoenix, where he purchased provisions to replenish our six-month food supply and for the community storehouse, which was a metal shed where some FLDS members got food at no charge. Fred's pantry was the biggest I'd ever seen, and the walk-in refrigerator was bigger than one you'd find in a sizable restaurant. Because he frequently made these trips to Phoenix, Fred had a home there. It was considered a great honor to be one of the family members invited to go with him. Since I had come to Fred's house, I had watched a number of girls and boys have the chance to go, but never before had he selected me. Though I tried to shrug it off at the time, the reality was that not being chosen had left me feeling disappointed and a bit jealous—just one more thing that demonstrated I was on the outside of the family.

I should have known that something was up when he extended the invitation to me, but I was blinded by my excitement at being included. All I could think about was that for the first time since I had left Salt Lake, my "father" was beginning to approve of me. I thought maybe I was starting to belong somewhere in the Jessop house, and perhaps it would only be a matter of time before the other girls started to accept me as well.

The trip was a fun break from our normal routine. We got to eat in restaurants, and I enjoyed meeting some of the girls who had accompanied the other church elders on the trip. In the euphoria of the moment, I didn't think much about the fact that the last two daughters who'd accompanied Fred to Phoenix had been married soon after their return. When it did occur to me, I dismissed it right away, knowing that at least eight of Uncle Fred's daughters were older than I was. Surely they would be placed in marriages long before me.

We'd been back home just a few weeks when Uncle Fred made an announcement during our weekly prayer service in his living room. Everyone was assembled when he informed us that the prophet had found a "place" for three of his "girls" at the side of priesthood elders. We all knew what that meant; the three unnamed girls were going to be married. When the prophet arranged a marriage for a girl, it was often referred to as a "place." For the prophet to tell your father he has a "place" for you is supposed to be one of the greatest moments in the life of an FLDS girl. We all looked around excitedly wondering who they would be. Some of the girls tried to pry it out of Uncle Fred, but he maintained his big secretive grin and said nothing.

Several days passed and everyone was still eagerly awaiting word of who the lucky three were and when the marriages would take place. One night, as we were all gathered for evening prayer, the chosen girls were subtly revealed. After prayer, it was customary for the boys to shake Fred's hand and the girls to receive a light hug from him. I joined the line behind my mother to hug Uncle Fred, and as I went to put my arms around him, he also gathered my mother in the embrace. Bending down, he smiled and said to me in a soft voice, "You are one of the three girls."

My eyes instantly widened and my jaw dropped. It took me a second to fully process what he had said. I wondered if I had heard him correctly.

"You probably have me mixed up with someone else," I stammered. "You know I'm only fourteen, right?"

He assured me that yes, indeed, it was me, and I needed to prepare myself. A sick, heavy feeling crawled into my stomach as he again pulled my mother and me in for a celebratory hug. A look of glee stretched across Fred's wrinkled face; he was clearly pleased to deliver the news. It was supposed to be joyous. It was supposed to be celebratory. But I felt like my heart had stopped, and my feelings of revulsion started to grow. I knew that many girls still in their teens were married. I'd even heard of girls who had been married as young as fifteen. There were stories from Uncle Roy's time as prophet when really young girls like myself and even younger had been married.

But I hadn't heard of anyone getting married at fourteen for some time. I knew that marriages of girls under the age of eighteen had been performed a lot more carefully as of late. Not that long ago, Uncle Rulon had actually said we would stop the practice after laws were passed forbidding the marriage of girls under eighteen. In church one day he said that we would "follow the law of the land" as it pertained to child brides. However, Uncle Warren later said that the Lord couldn't stop his work on earth just because the laws of the land had changed. Those laws had been put in place to hinder the priesthood's work, therefore they were not to be followed. It was one of the increasingly frequent moments when Warren assumed power and authority publicly. Warren was taking over, and his will seemed to prevail over his father's. The FLDS people simply accepted the result. And so the marriages of underaged girls continued but were performed cautiously and in secret, since the prophet who presided and those officiating ran the risk of prosecution by the government.

Shocked and in a total daze, I walked away with my mother and tried to convince myself it couldn't be true, but something inside me knew better.

CHAPTER TEN

THE CELESTIAL LAW

Take this revelation, or any other revelation that the
Lord has given, and deny it in your feelings and I promise
that you will be damned.
—BRIGHAM YOUNG

I had been in the FLDS Church from the moment I was born. It was all I knew and the only way I could imagine living. From my teachings, I knew that the prophet's job was to dictate what was best for us and that the words he spoke came straight from God. I believed that my impending marriage was the will of God and therefore nothing could be done to stop it. But still, I had to try.

I also knew that I was different from other girls in my community. I wanted an education, and maybe even to become a nurse or teacher someday. During my year in public school, I'd come to realize things were possible that I'd never dreamed before. Sure, I knew that I wanted to be a mother of good priesthood children, but not at fourteen. I wanted children *and* a future, and I dared to think that both were possible.

It took a little while for me to absorb what Uncle Fred had said. As I turned it over in my head, I couldn't digest the idea that the prophet wanted me to marry, and it didn't feel right. Still thinking that perhaps Uncle Fred had confused me with one of the older girls in the house, I decided to speak with him. I climbed the stairs to Uncle Fred's office on the second floor and waited in the hallway for him to notice me. When he saw me standing in the doorway, a kind smile widened across his face and he invited me in to talk. I swallowed my fear and took a seat, eager to tell him how I really felt about the pronouncement. The office appeared much like Uncle Warren's office at Alta Academy, with a big desk, a couch, and a few chairs for those who came to seek counsel. As a respected member of our community, Fred held a lot of clout. He had been appointed the bishop of Short Creek by Leroy Johnson long before Uncle Rulon took over as the prophet, giving him the position of second counselor to the prophet and placing him third in the leadership hierarchy, right behind Warren, who was first counselor.

Taking a seat in one of the brown leather chairs, I held my tongue until I was invited to speak, and when Uncle Fred signaled me to share what was on my mind, the words almost spilled out of my mouth.

"I want to make sure you understand that I'm fourteen," I said, mustering a soft, respectful voice despite my anxiety. "I'm worried that you have me mixed up with someone else." Uncle Fred was well into his seventies, and sometimes he'd forget things, even people's names.

"No, you are going to be married," he replied with certainty.

Panic swelled inside of me, and I searched my mind for what to say next. "I don't know if this is right for me," I told him after a long pause. "I don't feel ready. I don't feel like that is what I should be doing, because I'm really young. And I think there are so many other girls in the house who would be more ready for this calling."

Undeterred, Uncle Fred instructed me to "go and pray about it."

I was at a loss for words, and I realized that he intended for me to go forward and marry. I asked if he could at least share the identity of my future husband. Perhaps if I knew who God had chosen for me, it would set my mind at ease.

"That will be revealed to you at the right time," he replied.

I felt physically ill as I stood to leave. The conversation was over, and there appeared to be nothing more I could say.

In the days ahead, I was flooded with congratulatory words from my family and many stepsisters, who, much to my surprise, knew that I was among the three girls chosen for marriage. I struggled to hide my true feelings as they told me how lucky I was, and at moments it felt nice to have so much attention. Getting married is the highest honor for a girl in the FLDS Church. It was what women lived for—our dream and our mission. Even though I was only fourteen, it was hard not to get caught up in all the excitement. Soon, though, those feelings would pass, and the anxiety returned.

I discovered I wasn't the only young girl who had been assigned a husband. The prophet had also chosen my stepsister Lily, who was only a few months older than I was. She would be celebrating her fifteenth birthday before me. The third girl chosen was Nancy. She was a few years older than Lily and me and seemed excited at the prospect of achieving what she'd been preparing for her whole life.

As we looked at our similar situations, Lily and I formed a bond in our attempt to come to terms with our futures. Like me, Lily had been through a difficult time. A few months earlier, she'd begun a secret friendship with an older FLDS boy who had recently moved to Hildale from Salt Lake City. Since the prophet is the only person who can authorize romantic relationships, this friendship went against church teachings. Inevitably, Uncle Fred found out what was going on and forbade her from seeing the boy again. Lily was beside herself with sadness, and she tried to take her own life using Tylenol and ibuprofen.

Her attempt failed, but her marriage announcement seemed to be in reaction to her improper friendship, as though the powers above her thought that marriage would force her back into the correct FLDS mindset. At moments, it even appeared to be working, as Lily seemed to share

Nancy's excitement. But my resistance never wavered, and despite everyone's words, I remained unconvinced that this was my time.

In the days after Uncle Fred's announcement, I wrote down my thoughts about what was happening in a journal.

> *Sunday, April 15, 2001*
> *It sure has been an amazing weekend. Many things have happened to make things feel a little upside down. Yesterday was quite a nerve-shaking day. It was about . . .*

My mother came into the room, and I could feel her standing over me as I began to put my worries and questions on the paper.

"Lesie, you should be careful what you write," she cautioned, interrupting my stream of consciousness. "Your words are not private."

Looking up at her, I expressed surprise. "What do you mean? Who would be looking at my personal journal?"

"Well, what you write about this important time will be your legacy for your children, and it should be proud things. So you don't want to regret it later."

Mom's words overwhelmed me. I was being told that I shouldn't express how I was really feeling about what was happening. I was horrified that my private writings might not actually be private, and that these personal reflections would be seen as disobedient and unfaithful. This new pressure to write only what I should have been feeling engulfed me. I flipped the page of my butterfly-covered spiral notebook and started over.

> *Sunday, April 15, 2001*
> *Today was the most beautiful day. It was as though the Lord sent it just for me. The morning was so peaceful that it gathered peace to my soul. This weekend has been quite a time. Many things have happened to make my world go up-*

side down. There [are] many things that are very weighty on my mind. If it wasn't for the Lord, I would be feeling quite overwhelmed. Yesterday was quite an experience. It was about ten o'clock when Mother Amy called up to the room and told me that Father wanted to see me. As I was getting ready to go see him, I was trying my hardest to think what it might be about. A dozen things or happenings went through my head. I walked in his office when he was talking to someone else, which gave me a few minutes while I stood there by his side. Soon he saw me and turned and began talking. He stated to me that he had talked to Lily and me on the subject of getting married. When he had said anything before he had talked about things happening some time in May. Well he told me that the prophet was thinking to do it sometime next week. It caught me by such surprise that I just stood there. I will never forget the emotions that went through my head. For a long time now, I have been pleading with the Lord to please prepare a place for me by a man who will love and teach me. Most of all I pray that the Lord will give me a testimony that I will be able to know with all my heart that where I am placed is where I am supposed to be.

In the days that followed, I consulted with Uncle Fred several times. While I was following Mom's advice of keeping obedient even in my writings, in reality I was terrified about my future. After a couple of visits with Uncle Fred, I told him I wanted him to know that I wasn't trying to resist the will of the prophet; I just needed more time. I would be more ready if I could just have two more years.

"I can't do this," I told him during another conversation. "You know, I just don't think this is right for me. I have prayed about it. I don't feel good about it. My heart and my gut just tell me that I need to grow up a little. And I need to prepare myself for this kind of responsibility."

Uncle Fred's tone was gentle yet firm. We had been talking about this for a few days, but finally he gave me a new response: "This is the prophet's calling, and you will have to take it up with him if you feel like you're not prepared."

A wave of relief swept over me. I had his blessing to contact the prophet about my situation. I walked out of Uncle Fred's office pondering what I would say when I got Uncle Warren on the phone the following morning. That night I barely slept, worrying about how Uncle Warren would react to my request to see the prophet, and I was lying in bed awake when the black night sky gave way to the purple lines of daybreak. I hadn't had much contact with Uncle Warren since my days at Alta Academy, and I knew I had to first speak with him before I could see his father. The thought of our conversation filled me with the same dread that I'd always felt as I climbed the steps to his office at Alta Academy.

That morning, Mom sat next to me as I picked up the phone to dial his office. Eventually, I was patched through to Uncle Warren, and in a shaky voice, I told him why I was calling. Trying my best to calm my nerves, I explained that I didn't feel the marriage was right for me, making it clear to him how old I was. "I don't feel like it's right for me to marry at this point in time. It's just that I'm not ready for this kind of responsibility."

I was frightened by the eerie silence on the other end of the phone. The lull was broken by the sound of his hypnotic voice. "Are you questioning the prophet and his revelations?" he asked.

Stumbling over my words, I tried to clarify that I wasn't trying to defy the prophet. "I just want to make sure he knows that I'm only fourteen and how I feel."

"I will speak to the prophet," Uncle Warren assured me. "I will tell the prophet that you feel that you're too young and need some time. Say your prayers." He said he would contact Uncle Fred after he had spoken with Uncle Rulon.

Not only would I pray, I would fast in the hope that God

would understand my concerns. The phone call with Uncle Warren had drained the last of my energy, but a piece of me felt better knowing that I'd told him my thoughts. Honestly believing and trusting that the priesthood leaders would listen to me, I felt my anxiety begin to ease.

Back in my room, I knelt by my bed and spoke to God as if he were my friend. "I believe you are listening to me," I said, closing my eyes and envisioning him before me. "And that you have my interest in mind. I'm begging you." Fighting back sobs, I gathered strength. "I know you are up there and you can hear me. If I have proven myself worthy, then you can change this situation for me."

When I awoke it was the middle of the day, and I was on the floor next to my bed. I'd been so exhausted from not sleeping the night before my conversation with Uncle Warren that I'd fallen asleep in the middle of my private prayer session with God. But I was sure God would see that I was a good person and hear my pleas. With that realization, my mood began to lift, and the darkness that had lingered over me for days temporarily receded.

Over the next few days, both of my stepsisters were told whom they were going to marry. Lily was invited for a drive around the town with our twenty-three-year-old stepbrother Martin, whom the prophet had revealed as her husband even though they'd been raised as brother and sister for a few years. Nancy's intended husband, Tim Barlow, was already married to one of Nancy's blood sisters as well as one of her stepsisters.

For members of the FLDS, dating is not permitted in any traditional American way. However, once a girl has been promised to a priesthood man, sometimes the new couple is given a chance to spend some quiet time alone together. The man will typically come by the girl's house and pick her up for a ride in his car. Both Nancy and Lily had the chance to meet and talk to their future spouses like this, yet for some reason I was still in the dark about whom I was to marry. It was troubling, but I held out hope that it meant now was not my time after all.

My hope turned out to be short-lived. When a few days passed and Uncle Warren still hadn't responded, my anxiety returned and once again the future became uncertain. I kept replaying my conversations with Fred and Warren in my head, insisting to myself that they just didn't understand how old I was.

Finally, Uncle Fred summoned me to his office. "Uncle Warren has contacted me, and the prophet wants you to go through with the marriage."

His words hit me like a sharp slap. I could barely stay focused as he continued, "This is God's calling and your mission. You must open your mind and heart and do what has been revealed for you."

"I just don't know if I can do it because I don't feel like it's right," I pleaded, swallowing the knot in my throat. Carefully I explained that I didn't want to disobey the prophet; on the contrary, I believed that following his word was the key to my eventual salvation. I'd be much more willing to accept any decision from the prophet if he'd just let me wait a couple of years until I felt more ready.

Fred heard me out but continued to state that this was the will of the prophet and of God. Still, something inside of me kept pushing back. Uncle Fred insisted that this was the path that God had chosen for me. It felt like I was being punished, and I wasn't sure why. Though it was hard to see a way out, I remained resolved to fight for what I believed was right.

By the end of the week, I'd grown tired of everybody talking to me about my impending marriage and of the spiteful attitudes of some of my stepsisters. I could feel that many of the older girls were worried that they'd been passed over for someone so much younger. If it were up to me, I would have gladly traded places. I said as much to Uncle Fred during one of my conversations with him, but he'd frightened me when he told me that if I refused to follow the destiny that the prophet had revealed for me, I was not likely to get another opportunity. Eternal salvation depended on marriage to a priesthood man. I believed his words and was terrified of that fate—being alone for all eternity, stuck between worlds forever.

When I arrived at prayer service on Thursday night, I was emotionally exhausted. I'd been in my mother's room for hours sobbing over my situation. I knew that she too had doubts about my marriage, and even though I was being viewed as disobedient, she encouraged me to stand up for myself. Nevertheless, she had to tread carefully. All it would take was Uncle Fred getting wind of her support for me, and she herself would be subject to reprimand from the prophet. There would be extreme consequences for her if she overstepped her role as a submissive wife, and her eternal salvation, for which she had already sacrificed so much, could be taken away in an instant.

I was comforted by Mom's presence as we walked into the living room for prayer that night. I took a seat right next to her and waited for the rest of the family to assemble. As the room began to fill, I noticed that some of the mothers were sitting on the floor. "Please come and sit here," I told one of them out of respect, motioning to the empty chair just beside me. "Or at least take my chair."

When she declined, preferring to remain on the floor, I grew worried. Maybe everyone was angry with me. Many people viewed my actions of late as immature, and their attitudes made me feel like a child throwing a temper tantrum. To them, accepting the will of the prophet was simply what you were required to do. There were no questions involved, no other options. Even though the temperature in the living room was comfortable that night, I felt cold and wrapped myself deeper into my fuzzy jacket. It was then that I saw Allen standing in the doorway.

Great, I thought; the night couldn't get any worse. It was hard to imagine that I was related to him. I was hoping he wouldn't even look my way; in my current state I couldn't even pretend to be polite. I watched as his bulky frame clumsily stepped into the room, and I grew immediately unnerved when I realized he was walking in my direction. He would never come straight toward me in a setting like this—unless there was something else going on.

Watching Allen lumber over, I kept hoping he was going to turn and walk in another direction, but he didn't. He walked directly toward me, then without a word sat in the only empty chair in the room, right beside me. In an instant, the realization of my fate hit me, robbing my lungs of air. I could feel the eyes of everyone in the room taking in my every move. Overcome with disbelief, I could no longer handle the pressure, and without thinking, I jumped from my chair and sprinted upstairs. I was afraid, disgusted, and angry at everyone. They knew how I felt and how much I did not want this, but no one seemed to care.

Winding my way through the halls and rooms of the enormous house, I felt tears flow down my face. Part of me wanted to pass off Allen's actions as happenstance, but I knew that for him to make such a public display and sit in the one empty chair beside me meant something. The fact that the mothers had chosen to sit on the floor instead of the seat next to me meant that this had been arranged. The whole family was in on it. They all knew who I was going to marry before I did. Not only would they force me to get married at fourteen, they would force me to get married to the one person I had come to loathe in my short life.

In between my footsteps, I could hear my mother behind me urging me to slow down and tell her what was wrong. I was sobbing uncontrollably when I reached her bedroom door and blindly pushed it open. The four walls of my mother's room were my only sanctuary, and I flopped down on Mom's bed before my legs collapsed beneath me.

"I know who I'm going to marry!" I shouted.

"Really? Who?" Mom asked, sounding completely in the dark.

"Allen!" I yelled back without even raising my head from the pillow. I couldn't believe Mom hadn't been hit with the same realization the minute he sat down next to me.

"He's your first cousin," she assured me. "They wouldn't

do that to you." Then she began to cry herself. When I finally calmed down, I sat up to hear Mom out. "If you're really concerned, you need to go and talk to Father about it," she said, trying to console me.

"I will not get married!" I announced defiantly, emboldened by my mother's words. "I will not marry Allen!"

It wasn't ten minutes before I was paged over the house intercom. "Elissa, Father wants to see you."

"Oh, great. What now?" I thought. I didn't even try to make myself presentable. I was almost beyond feeling as I made my way across the house to Uncle Fred's office. I expected that he'd be angry with me for my outburst and was a little surprised to find him seemingly unfazed.

"Sit down, Elissa," he instructed, motioning to the leather chair facing his desk. "How are you doing?" he asked casually.

"Father, I know who I'm going to marry," I blurted out.

I watched the corners of his lips lift into the beginnings of a smile. "Oh, really? Who?" he asked.

"You are going to place me by Allen."

It took him a moment to validate my suspicions. But I was right. "Well, yes," he said. "That is what the prophet has revealed for you."

"No! I want you to know that I won't do it. I will not marry Allen. I just don't want to marry that man!"

I was momentarily surprised at my own courage. I hadn't even hesitated before saying those words. A week before, I would have stumbled and tripped over my own tongue, but now I was determined. Knowing that Allen was to be my husband had only strengthened my resolve. I paused to take a breath. To this point, I'd clung to the hope that Uncle Rulon would come to see that this was not right for me. But at that moment, I realized that I needed to speak to him myself.

The look of puzzlement on Uncle Fred's face quickly faded and was replaced with a stern stare. "You would defy what the prophet has revealed to you?" he retorted.

"You realize Allen is my first cousin?" I reminded him.

"This makes no difference in matters of the Lord," Uncle Fred told me. Members of the FLDS believe that intermarrying among family members is okay if it is what the prophet reveals. Even concerns over birth defects are diminished with the explanation that a child who comes to the earth "imperfect" was sent that way by God because the child was "too special" and would again be whole in the Celestial Kingdom. Birth defects are never blamed on cousins marrying or incest but rather occur because "God wanted it that way." While rumors continuously circulated outside of our community that babies born with birth defects were drowned at birth, it was simply not true. These children were held with reverence because of how special God thought they were. That my marriage had been a revelation from the prophet negated any worldly concerns about interfamily marriages and their consequences.

"Well, I want you to know that I'm not going to be able to do this," I huffed. "I just can't bring myself to do this. I will not marry that man."

"Well, then, you need to go and speak to Uncle Warren, because this is something that has been revealed for you. So, you need to talk to the prophet and tell him this."

I don't even remember who answered the phone when I called Uncle Warren the next morning. Usually it was one of Uncle Rulon's wives or sons.

"I need to come up and see the prophet," I told whoever was on the other end of the line. I was unyielding in my position that I would not get married unless I heard of the revelation from the prophet's own mouth. After several moments, I was given an appointment for the very next day.

I tried to calm myself as I thought about everything that had happened in the last few days. By this time tomorrow, I would know whether I was getting married to Allen, but before that decision was reached I would get the chance to approach Uncle Rulon myself, to speak to him and tell him in person that I didn't feel this wedding was right for me.

While I was anxious, I was also hopeful that seeing me in person would bring him a new revelation from God, a revelation that I was too young, that I was destined for something beyond being a fourteen-year-old bride. I was destined to do other things, to learn, to grow, to get an education—possibly even become a nurse. I could see this destiny for myself, but in the end, the only thing that would matter was whether the prophet could see it as well.

CHAPTER ELEVEN

THE WORD
OF THE PROPHET

Your heart is in the wrong place.
—WARREN JEFFS

Later that morning after I set up the appointment, Mom and Kassandra, under priesthood pressure to convince me that the marriage was the right thing, tried to excite my interests by taking me to prepare for the "fun part"—the wedding dress.

Together we traveled to St. George to the fabric store, where we browsed through various materials and patterns to assemble the look for my wedding day. What I didn't know at the time was that even my sisters had gone to Uncle Warren with their concerns about my marriage—and had been directed to encourage me to go along with it. When our visit to the fabric store failed to elicit any enthusiasm in me, we walked around the strip mall, where we spotted a pair of gorgeous white crushed satin shoes in one of the windows. They were so pretty, with a delicate buckle across the ankle and a little heel. Kassandra said they'd be perfect with any wedding dress, but even the glamorous shoes couldn't lure me into the store.

"I don't need those shoes," I angrily declared. It should

have been an exhilarating time for me—planning my wedding, picking out materials for a dress, and getting those special shoes—but it felt like I was being asked to design an outfit for my funeral. I was bordering on rude by the time my mother and sister dragged me from the shoe store, where Kassandra had purchased the shoes over my objections, to the Chili's restaurant. Eating out with Mom and Kassandra was bittersweet. With this terrible event looming over my head, it was hard to relax during what would turn out to be my last few moments as a carefree teenager. I was hurt that I was being pushed in this way, and that no one who could do something about it was listening to me. Most of my sisters had married young, but with the exception of Teressa, they had been allowed to reach the age of eighteen. I didn't know if any of them could understand what I was going through. They tried to console and encourage me, but it didn't make me feel any less afraid.

Aware that I would be meeting with Uncle Rulon the following morning, I went through my closet to pick out my best dress when we returned home. A meeting with the prophet, especially on a subject like this, was very important. I wanted to look both pretty and respectful—the image of a perfect priesthood daughter.

The next morning I settled into Mom's old mustard-colored Oldsmobile and restlessly smoothed my dress. Uncle Rulon's compound was too far to walk to, and I felt comforted by mother's company during the short ride. She'd seemed a little withdrawn over the past several days, and while I believed that my situation had a lot to do with it, she had spoken little about what she was experiencing. She tried to assure me that everything was going to be fine, but I knew that inside she was fearful. I appreciated that she was willing to stand by me.

As I sat in the waiting room, I rehearsed what I would say to Uncle Rulon. In the past, when I had been a guest of Kassandra's or Rachel's, I had been invited to dine with Uncle Rulon and his family. It was a great honor after the meal when I was welcomed to approach the prophet and shake his hand, but this meeting would be different. This time, it was about me.

The waiting area was busy, with people coming and going. After some time, Uncle Warren finally came out and greeted me. Wearing a wide grin and his predictable dark suit and tie, he addressed me with a warm, welcoming voice.

"Elissa, how are you?" He motioned for me to follow him into the office.

Exhausted, I quickly sat down in the dark upholstered chair closest to the door. I'd been up most of the night praying, and I felt light-headed from my ongoing fast. Warren sat down at his father's desk, which faced the wall, and swung his chair around to face me. Now there was no desk separating us as there had been at Alta Academy.

"Tell me what's going on," he began in a low, inquiring voice. "What is the issue?"

I hesitated, wondering when Uncle Rulon would be coming in to join us. When he didn't immediately arrive, I felt obligated to go over my concerns a second time with Uncle Warren.

"Well, I know you've told me to get married. And I know you feel like this is a revelation. I don't think that this is right for me because I feel like I need to have some time to grow up. I'm just not prepared for this kind of responsibility. And I'm not willing to marry my cousin."

Uncle Warren looked surprised. "Your cousin?"

"Yes," I said. "You asked that I be married to Allen Steed, who is my first cousin."

"Well," he began, wearing a look of confusion that worried me, "have you been praying about it?"

"Yes, I am. And everything is telling me not to do this. Every part of my soul and heart is telling me that this isn't right for me."

"Have you told your father?"

"Yes, I've met with Uncle Fred several times. And I've told him that this is something that I'm not willing to do at this point, that I would prefer to not get married. And he has instructed me to come to you. I need to let you know of my concerns."

Uncle Warren sat contemplatively for a brief moment. "Well," he announced, rising to his feet, "the prophet has directed you to do this."

"I know, but I need to hear it from him," I replied, my stoic façade suddenly crumbling as I broke into tears. "I need to know that he is aware of the situation and at least ask him if he can give me two years. I just want two years before I get married."

"Elissa," he replied, offering me a tissue from the box on his desk, "this is a revelation from God. This is an honor to have the prophet place you in a good priesthood marriage. Are you declining to do this?"

"No," I said, erasing tears from my cheeks. "I just want you to know where I stand, where I am, and why I feel the way I do."

As I sat nervously shredding my tissue, I noticed a rainbow of flowers standing at cheery attention in the garden just outside of the expansive bay window. My tissue was in tatters, with small pieces falling onto the floor, as I made my position clear. "If I am going to go through with this marriage, then I need to hear it from the prophet's mouth," I petitioned.

Perhaps realizing that I was not going to back down until I saw Uncle Rulon, Warren went to speak with his father on my behalf. I watched as he exited through a second door in the office that opened up to a private hallway in Uncle Rulon's personal living quarters.

A few minutes later, Warren reappeared in the doorway.

"The prophet has a few minutes to see you now," he told me. Rising to follow him down the long corridor, I grew terrified of what Uncle Rulon was going to tell me. I was going to meet the most important man in the church, the living embodiment of God on earth, and I was going to tell him that I thought he was wrong about his vision for my future.

Pushing through a pair of lovely French doors that led to

the dining room, I gathered my courage. I'd been speaking with the Lord for days, and surely he knew how I was feeling. Now it was up to Uncle Rulon to deliver his verdict on my situation. In the dining room there were two long shiny wood tables draped in colorful tablecloths, and Uncle Rulon was seated at the head of one of them, his plate still filled with food. He wore a gentle smile as he motioned for me to come closer. I could feel his whole body shaking from age as he took my hands in his.

"What can I do for you?" he asked.

I was overcome with emotion as I knelt by his side; I tried to remain calm, but my throat grew tight and tears began to fall. Uncle Rulon had experienced a second stroke and was now hard of hearing, but he seemed to listen intently as I started to tell him my feelings. In my mind, I thanked God for granting me this moment. All this time, I had been fasting and praying to the Heavenly Father for help, and I believed that he'd allowed me to be before the prophet that day.

In a hesitant voice, I explained to Uncle Rulon that I was not trying to defy him or God's directions for me but that I felt like I was too young to be married. "All I'm asking for is to have two more years to grow up a bit," I begged. "If nothing else, could you please find someone other than my cousin Allen for me to marry? Allen is the last person I can ever imagine being a wife to. So, please, just if there is any possible way, can things just not happen now?"

A confused look crossed his face as I stared into the prophet's eyes. "Now, what did you say, sweetie? Will you repeat that, please?" he asked solicitously. I took a deep breath and desperately tried to slow my heart down so I could compose myself as I repeated my worries and concerns.

Just then Uncle Warren leaned down from his towering six-foot-plus height and jumped in on the conversation: "This young lady feels like the place you have found for her to be married is not right and she knows better," he began.

I didn't like the way Warren was distorting my words, making it sound as though I was ungrateful and thought I knew better than the prophet. It was disquieting and made me seem more defiant than I was, but I was too frightened to speak up.

"She feels like you haven't decided right and she wants your permission not to be in the marriage," Warren continued as I looked up at him in frustration. He was trying to make me feel terrible for even making such a request, for questioning the word of the prophet and God.

Puzzlement swept over Uncle Rulon's face as he looked up to Warren and back down at me. For a moment he said nothing, and then he smiled kindly. "You follow your heart, sweetie, just follow your heart," he told me, gently patting my hand.

While he'd not given me a direct answer, his words were clear and relieving. My heart leapt into my throat. Finally, someone was listening to me and going to give me the chance to decide. Rising to my feet, I felt as if a thousand pounds had been lifted off my chest. The prophet had told me to follow my heart; the will of God was for me to listen to my own judgment.

"God bless you, and keep sweet," Rulon said, smiling, and he turned back to his lunch.

Uncle Warren ushered me out of the dining room and back down the hall. I expressed my relief aloud: "The prophet told me to follow my heart, and my heart is telling me not to do this."

Suddenly Warren's pace slowed. "Elissa," he said, turning his gaze in my direction. "Your heart is in the wrong place. This is what the prophet has revealed and directed you to do, and this is your mission and duty."

Confusion rocked me. I had just walked out of a meeting with the prophet where he himself had told me to follow my heart, and my heart was telling me that this was not right. Now Warren, who in my mind was only second in command, was telling me that my heart was in the wrong place.

"Well, he told me to follow my heart," I reminded him. "And my heart is screaming no!"

Uncle Warren looked astonished.

It was like he hadn't heard a word I'd said. Despite Uncle

Rulon's declaration, Warren remained unmoved. The prophet's statement was irrelevant; all that mattered was what Warren wanted.

It was dinnertime when I arrived back at Uncle Fred's house that Saturday evening. Everyone was assembled around the tables. I'd been crying for four days straight, I hadn't eaten, and I'd barely slept. My life had become so full of drama, and it felt like people were constantly stopping in the middle of meals to focus on me whenever I entered the house. Racing upstairs to my room, I assumed what had become my new position—facedown on the bed in a puddle of tears.

Mom followed me upstairs and sidled up next to me on the bed. "Are you gonna be okay?" she asked, gently stroking my hand.

"No, Mom. I would rather die right now than ever have to go through with this."

"Lesie, maybe being that it is the Lord's will, this will work out. Allen can't be that bad."

"There is no way I could ever marry Allen and have it work out," I told her forcefully.

"So, what are you going to do?"

"I would rather die than go through with this wedding." I could see that my words upset my mother, but at that moment I didn't care. All I cared about was saving myself from this horrible fate.

I'd been home for less than thirty minutes when there was a knock on the bedroom door. One of Uncle Fred's wives was there to deliver the message that Uncle Fred wanted to see me. I knew what he was going to say, and I dragged my feet all the way to his office. Another mother was on the couch in his office when I arrived.

"Can't I just do this alone?" I thought to myself as I assumed my seat.

"Well, how did it go?" Uncle Fred asked, looking out at me from behind his heavy wood desk.

"Well, I was able to see Uncle Rulon, and he told me to follow my heart."

Uncle Fred grinned. "So, can I tell Warren that there has been a definite yes?"

"No!" I shot back in alarm. "I don't know. I won't, I can't. My heart—everything in me is just screaming no."

"Are you defying the prophet's words?"

"No, I'm not trying to defy the prophet, I am just trying to do what is best for me."

"Well, I just want you to know that if you turn down the prophet's offer, it's very likely you will never get married—"

"I cannot," I interrupted.

"And I could not have you welcome in this house anymore," Uncle Fred said.

Tears began to pour from my eyes. In all the times I had met with Fred since this mess started, I had always tried to maintain my composure, but now, exhausted, hungry, and defeated, I broke down in front of him. Seeing this opening, he took the chance to exploit it. I felt the world closing in on me. I hated Uncle Fred, and Uncle Warren, and even my mother for putting me in this position. I was fourteen years old with no money and nowhere to go. When my brothers and sister had tested the boundaries of rebellion, they had been shipped off to reform. While that was hard for them, at least it wasn't permanent. Marriage to Allen wasn't just permanent, it was infinite—a punishment that would continue through this life and into the next.

If I didn't marry him, I'd be left with no other options. For a fourteen-year-old girl with no family and no place to live, it might as well be a death sentence. I had always been an optimistic person, but as I stared the possibility of this bleak future in the face, I realized that even I was unwilling to push the limits of hope that far. I couldn't go to the local police; I feared they would just bring me back to Fred and report me to Warren. I contemplated going outside the community, but my fear of that evil world was overpowering. I thought back to all my mother's stories about law-enforcement officials chasing her in the middle of the night, trying to throw her father in jail. Who knew what the evil forces on the outside might do to me if I came to them with this story?

"Do you have a wedding dress made?" Uncle Fred asked, breaking the discomfiting sound of my quiet sobs.

"No!" I announced, rising to my feet. "Even if I was getting married, I would never wear a wedding dress. And I'm not going to get married, so I don't need a wedding dress."

When I returned to my mother's room, I found a draft of a letter that my mother had composed. In it, she'd begged her new husband, my new father, to be sensitive to my situation and realize that this was hard for me. She asked for a delay of two years and made it clear that if I married now, it would just create problems in the future. She'd even raised issues about Allen, explaining that he seemed to be a very immature person who didn't appear ready for a wife and reiterating that Allen and I were first cousins.

The letter surprised me. I'd been pleading with her to do something to prevent the marriage, and all along she'd seemed so sure that the situation would somehow work itself out on its own. Now finally she was trying to lobby on my behalf, but as a woman, Mom had no sway with Uncle Fred or the prophet. Still, it made me love my mother even more to know that she was listening to me when it seemed no one else was.

I collapsed into bed that night but couldn't fall asleep. I searched for reasons why Warren would contradict the words of the prophet. He'd been pushing the marriage as though the prophet had decided it for me, but I had heard the opposite from Uncle Rulon's mouth. I didn't know if this was truly the will of God.

On one hand it felt like I was being given to Allen for all the work he'd done for Uncle Fred, but on the other hand, it felt like there was a much larger reason, I just didn't know what it was. Uncle Fred could have asked the prophet to reward Allen with any of his daughters, but he'd chosen me, the young girl from the problem family, the girl whose brothers had all abandoned the priesthood. It was no secret that I had been close to my brothers, especially after the move to Uncle Fred's. Perhaps Uncle Fred and Warren felt the risk that I'd follow in their footsteps was too great.

Whereas the church was perfectly willing to let boys go, I can now see that the prospect of losing a girl was too much for them. If I left, I might bring other girls along, or get them to start questioning things. I know now that I was confident and I wasn't afraid to ask my questions. In short, I was a problem, and if they didn't solve it, they'd end up paying for it later.

The next day proved even more difficult. By the time I arrived at church that Sunday, deep melancholy had taken over my mind. Bouncing between prayer, sadness, hope, and fear over the past days had finally taken its toll on me. Choosing a seat in one of the rows, I tried to steady myself for the sermon. That was when I felt Allen's body next to mine. He was just a few inches away from me, and he didn't say a word. He didn't have to. I knew it was him.

"What in the hell are you doing?" I snapped at him.

Allen stumbled awkwardly over the words. "Uncle Fred told me to come sit by you."

My sadness turned to anger, and I sat seething. I couldn't believe Uncle Fred would do this to me in front of the entire community. My private struggle was now on display for all to see. Uncle Fred was taking advantage of me by having Allen sit there. Up until this point, few knew that I had been placed with Allen Steed for marriage, but seating us together in church served as a "silent" public announcement. Just having him this close to me felt like an attack.

Stepping out of the meetinghouse that Sunday, I was besieged by the gentle teasing of well-wishers calling me "Mrs. Steed." Now that the whole congregation knew that Uncle Rulon had had a revelation of marriage for me, any further attempts to get out of it would be publicly viewed as defying the word of the prophet. I could barely contain my fury at Uncle Fred's carefully crafted act. He'd effectively erased the privacy of my situation and foiled any remaining hope I had for a release from the marriage.

I stared past the happy crowd assembled around me at the majestic red mountains and thought about jumping off one of the sheer faces of rock. It wouldn't be hard to climb up there, and I was sure it was high enough that the jump would kill me. As hard as it was for me to accept, at fourteen, I was actually contemplating suicide.

It was in that moment that I should have realized that the priesthood made it impossible for a woman to make decisions about her life—even if she knew what was right for her. Marriage wasn't about God, or the prophet, or any of that. It was about controlling women, trapping them into believing that they didn't have any other options and the only way out was a leap into the arms of the Lord from hundreds of feet in the air. Yet, I still believed.

I hadn't spoken to my dad since I'd been removed from his home nearly two years before, but after church that day, my every moment was consumed by a vision of being rescued by Dad, Brad, and Caleb. They would come by in the middle of the night, and we would all escape under the cover of darkness. The only clues we'd leave behind would be our footsteps in the house and our tire tracks in the gravel. In the morning, people would wake up and gasp. I'd be condemned as a sinner and cursed by Warren and Fred. My mother and sisters would be devastated that I'd left them, but at least I would be alive. It made more sense to leave them alive than to die where I was. All I needed was for someone to save me, someone to give me a place to go.

But all this was just a fantasy. I had no way to contact Dad, Brad, and Caleb, and they didn't know about my impending marriage.

Just when I thought it couldn't get any worse, after arriving back home that afternoon, Uncle Fred directed me to go on a walk with Allen. There were people lingering nearby, and it was impossible for me to decline without appearing defiant to my priesthood father. Mom shot me a look. Earlier she had instructed me to be kind to Allen no matter what I was feeling inside, and with that passing glance she told me to remember those words.

The walk would be considered our "first date." While Lily and Nancy had had the luxury of a private afternoon drive with their spouses-to-be, I was being sent off walking into the mountains with every eye in the family watching.

Allen moved awkwardly beside me in his black suit. To some other girl in some other situation, Allen's sandy blond hair and blue eyes might have been attractive. He had a strong jaw and nice teeth, and there was nothing ugly or unkempt about him. Still, his face and his graceless demeanor made my skin crawl.

Hesitantly, we headed toward the mountains, where we were to go on a short hike. Allen was kind to me, but I couldn't return his attitude. I knew that I was being horrible, but I just couldn't convince myself to do anything differently. He kept trying to hold my hand, but I would brush his hand away every time.

I let out an exasperated sigh and declared, "I don't want you to touch me." At this point, a few tears pushed at the corners of his eyes.

"Why do you hate me so bad?" he asked, his strong masculine face looking momentarily boyish and lost.

"I'm sorry, but I just don't like you, and I cannot imagine an eternity with you."

He looked stunned by my response. Somehow not deterred, he gently nodded and said what any good priesthood man would: "God will change your feelings as long as you stay faithful. In time, you will feel differently."

I knew that would never happen, but I said nothing.

We remained mostly quiet for the rest of our "date," with me thinking over and over that I just couldn't wait for this hour to be over. A part of me wanted to give him a better explanation of how I felt, but my feelings couldn't be expressed in words. It was just an innate sense that God puts in each of us to see the difference between right and wrong. That inner voice was telling me that he was wrong for me on so many levels. Even before the marriage began, I was repulsed by him. He hadn't even held my hand, but he had already taken my innocence.

CHAPTER TWELVE

MAN AND WIFE

There's no force in this Celestial law. The prophet doesn't
force you to heaven. And when you enter into marriage,
you never have the right to think you have been forced
into a situation. You know better. Even my saying it to you,
you know it will be your choice when you say,
"I do" or "yes" to the prophet.
—WARREN JEFFS

The flowered clock on the wall read 4:30 A.M. as I stood in
front of the mirror in Mom's room blankly looking at my
reflection. The face that stared back was foreign to me. In
place of the young, spirited fourteen-year-old there stood an
empty-looking body with eyes that were swollen and irritated from hours of crying.

"So, this is what death is like," I whispered to myself.

I barely flinched as Mom straightened my shoulders,
which were rounded and heavy from the burden of the past
week. She was trying to correct my posture so that my sister
Kassandra could get an accurate measurement for the hem
of my wedding dress.

The night had been long and exhausting. After my terrible "first date" with Allen I had escaped to the comfort of
my own room, where my mother had found me. I had sensed
her hesitation even before she uttered a word.

"Lesie, maybe this is the right thing to do," she gently
prodded. "This must be the will of God and the prophet."

"Mom, I just can't do this," I replied in desperation.

"Everyone expects you to," Mom stated matter-of-factly.

She had watched as I'd gone back and forth between Uncle Fred and Uncle Warren in my attempts to halt the marriage or at least gain more time. But time and again, she'd found me crying in our room, frustrated over my inability to convince the powers that be that this was not my time.

"You have to do this," Mom admitted. "You have no other choice."

It was hard hearing those words from her. Her support from the previous week seemed to evaporate that night, and suddenly I felt hurt that she was giving in. I didn't understand what had caused the shift, and I was crushed to have the most important person in my life surrendering to Uncles Warren and Fred. At that moment, I felt angry at the whole world. What I didn't know then was that Mom had been secretly pulled aside and told that it was her responsibility to make sure that the marriage took place, as the prophet had directed. She'd been instructed to make it happen "or else."

So many people find it difficult to understand why I am no longer angry with my mother. It is hard for outsiders to comprehend the mind-set that came with our culture. We were taught that the priesthood and the prophet come before anything else, and Mom had already been forced to make this choice with six of her own children. It's hard to explain why she just didn't pack me up and take me away, but in her mind making that step would have damned us both. She was already a part God's chosen people and she didn't want to give up the utopia she believed she was already in.

To her, the outside world was like stepping into hell and nothing was worth trading that for. Because Fred and Warren were holding her accountable, if I failed to follow through with the marriage I would not only condemn myself, I would condemn her, too. Not only would she be risking eternal life, she would also be forced to choose a loss of home and community, and a relationship with the older and younger daughters she still had in the FLDS. As such, her feelings were rooted in a concern not just for my salvation, but for her own and for the safety of her two youngest daughters. Like so many FLDS members, Mom was a true follower.

She'd been taught to strictly conform to the priesthood. Knowing the strength of my mother's belief, I guess it never crossed her mind to question whether this church, this life, was right if it forced her fourteen-year-old daughter into marriage. If she did question that, she would have to face many other decisions she had made in her painful past.

Even then, I knew she had no "real" choice. The church was her home. It was all she'd ever known, and she, like thousands of others, couldn't leave or risk giving up her and her children's place among the faithful.

Ultimately, while it hurt to have her join the chorus of voices pushing me, I knew Fred and Warren were behind it; when I heard her say those words, it was as though they themselves were speaking. They were simply using her to get to me. And I knew that I had no choice but to listen to them.

I sat on Mom's bed for hours that night, silently watching as she and Kassandra hurriedly designed and pieced together the wedding dress. Mom had given up on getting the fabric at the store in St. George and had finally purchased some material at a small shop in Hildale. Perhaps she, too, had put off the inevitable in hopes of a miracle reprieve, but here we were just hours away from the actual ceremony and rushing to make an acceptable dress.

"How do you want the dress?" Kassandra asked, trying hard to elicit some input from me.

"I don't care," I told my sister. "Just make it simple." I didn't want anything fancy; there was nothing fanciful about what lay ahead for me.

"Elissa, I need you to hold still or I'm going to poke you with the pins," Kassandra announced, as sobs racked my body. These were tears of desperation and I could do nothing to keep them dammed up.

When the night of hurried preparations was over, the wedding day arrived. Dressed in a wedding gown, with my hair done up, I sat on my mother's bed totally exhausted.

"I know how hard this is for you, but I want you to feel beautiful," Kassandra said, placing a small box in my hands.

Through the clear plastic top, I could see a delicate tiara like the ones we'd admired during past shopping trips to St. George. Over the months that Kassandra and I had been together, we'd spent countless hours in prom-dress shops fawning over fancy gowns we knew we could never wear and dreaming up elaborate scenarios we knew would never happen as we tried on sparkly tiaras. Now my sister was giving me this beautiful representation of our shared fantasy. But while I loved the thought behind it, it only emphasized how far I was from my daydreams.

My sister and mother served as crutches, one on each side, as I descended the stairs of Fred Jessop's home. When I got downstairs, though, they sent me back up to change into an everyday dress so as not to attract attention to what we were about to do. Mom could barely steady me as I clutched her hand tightly and we stepped out to meet our waiting vehicles. Three vehicles were lined up in front of Uncle Fred's house that morning. Instinctively I followed Mom into the backseat of Uncle Fred's big Chevy Suburban and numbly fastened my seat belt when someone yelled out to me, "No, Elissa, you're riding with Allen."

I was crushed. I couldn't imagine driving with him and his family. All along, my mother had been by my side as my anchor, and I needed her desperately. This would be my fate for the rest of my life, wanting the comfort of home but being forced to be with a stranger.

In an attempt at chivalry, Allen tried to carry my bag, but I was rude to him, even in front of his parents. I knew my behavior was inappropriate and mean, but I didn't know how to act. I wanted to keep sweet and be happy, but something in me just knew this was all wrong. Nothing had prepared me for the huge step I was being asked to take, and I was a child in pain, lashing out in the only way I knew how. It probably wasn't easy for Allen either. I'd done little to hide my loathing for him. He, too, was being robbed of his perfect wedding, and neither of us had any power to halt the train.

After the three cars carrying the wedding party left Uncle

Fred's home, we briefly stopped at Uncle Rulon's compound in Hildale, where several cars joined our caravan heading out of town. We followed closely behind the vehicle carrying Uncle Warren and his father. My sister Rachel and a few of Uncle Rulon's other wives were with them; they had been asked to accompany their husband to tend to his ongoing needs. Sitting in the passenger seat next to Allen that morning, I felt like we were on the road for hours and hours, even though it was only a few.

Not wanting to even look at Allen, I stared at the car that contained Lily and Nancy. Mom and the mothers of the other girls getting married that day were in Uncle Fred's Suburban. We were supposed to consider ourselves lucky that Uncle Warren had allowed all of the brides' mothers to come along. With the recent scrutiny from law enforcement, many of the brides were forbidden to have even one family member present at the union, and usually it was only the father.

As we rode along the interstate, I took in the open expanses of the Utah horizon. It should have dawned on me that many aspects of the religion were based on revoking the rights of women. If a girl speaks her mind, get her married. Once she's married, get her pregnant. Once she has children, she's in for life—it's almost impossible for any FLDS woman to take her children if she leaves, and no mother wants to leave her children behind. At the time, I was still too young and blind to see the pattern. All I could think was that this land and these people were my home, but for me— and for most FLDS women—there is an unspoken yet enormous sense of entrapment. On the one hand, the landscape seemed to never end; on the other, all I could see were the walls closing in around me.

I wondered what Nancy and Lily were thinking. Lily seemed to be keeping sweet. From what I could tell Nancy was playing the role of the ideal FLDS bride, relishing every moment since the announcement was made. She saw it not as a sentence but as the beginning of our true path to heaven, our path by our husbands' side. As I looked at their car, I

was furious with myself for not being able to enjoy this occasion. Carrying out the prophet's will was supposed to fill
my heart with the love of God. My stepsisters looked happy,
and I, in turn, felt robbed of the joy I had always planned to
have on my wedding day.

Although I didn't know it when we set out, the plan was
to drive to Caliente, Nevada, just across the state line. One
of the FLDS men, Merril Jessop, owned a motel there. In the
past, weddings had been performed more in the open, at
least by FLDS standards, either at the prophet's compound
in Salt Lake City or at his compound in Hildale, with friends
and family allowed to attend. But by this time, all underaged
marriages occurred in secret. The young girls were driven
to remote locations outside of the jurisdictions of Utah and
Arizona, in order to evade the law. We went to Nevada,
where the laws were not so strict. There was to be no proof
of the ceremony, no unnecessary witnesses, and absolutely
no photographs or paperwork. In the past, the tradition was
to obtain state-approved marriage licenses when they were
legally possible, but with Rulon and Warren's frequent pre-
dictions that the end of the world was coming any day, there
was no need. Besides, some FLDS spiritual unions were
unlawful in the states' eyes, and there could be no marriage
licenses. All that mattered was the prophet's fulfillment of
the law of God.

Sad thoughts permeated my mind and put me in a somber
daze. We'd been traveling north along I-15 for about an hour
when our convoy pulled into a gas station in Cedar City,
Utah. My hand was already on the door handle before we
even slowed to a stop, and I leapt from the white Ford van as
soon as Allen put it into park. Mom must have seen me
through the window of Uncle Fred's Suburban and hurried
after me into the restroom.

"Mom, I can't do this!" I cried.

"Yes, you can. Yes, you can," she assured me, brushing
the tears from my cheeks.

"I can't even look at the guy, let alone touch him."

"It will all come in time," she told me. "This is what we

are told to do, so we have to live with it." Of course, she was trying to console me, but it was exactly what I did not want to hear.

Mom walked me back to the van where Allen and his family were waiting. I was nauseated and retreated into my thoughts. I felt so empty, as if there was nothing left to feel. Over the course of the previous night, all the rage and resentment inside me had given way to pain and sorrow, and now even those emotions were gone. I had fought my fight and lost. Despite how nice Allen's parents were being, and how excited his two mothers were as they sat side by side in the rear of the van chatting, it was hard for me to respond to them. Clearly the two women had spent time primping that morning. Since women and girls of the FLDS must adhere to such strict dress codes, there is little differentiation in style between formal and casual wear; most of the differences come from the fabrics used. Dresses for special occasions were often made of silks, satins, and fine materials. It was obvious Allen's mothers were draped in their best.

We'd traveled nearly 140 miles when a sign announced our arrival in Caliente, Nevada. I had no reaction. I just understood. It was like arriving in hell; my fate awaited me in this dust bowl whose name fittingly translates to "hot" in English.

The Hot Springs Motel was a seedy structure tucked into the side of a patchy, grass-and-dirt hill on Nevada State Road 93, hugging the highway just as it wound into Caliente. My heart sank as I surveyed the old white stucco building, with its garish green metal roof and a small sign that read OFFICE. Allen and his parents had been talking about how some of the rooms had hot tubs. Normally, a luxury like that would have piqued my interest, but today it was the farthest thing from my mind. I couldn't believe that they could be enjoying pleasant small talk while I was about to experience the most catastrophic event in my life. Slowly, I exited the car and awaited instruction. I had heard that some of Merril Jessop's wives worked at the motel and stayed there full-time, but that day Merril had sent one of his sons just to make sure that everything ran smoothly. We weren't to stay long; it seemed that they wanted us to get in and get out.

Some FLDS people came out to greet the prophet and our caravan. We were told to change clothes for the ceremonies in one of the motel rooms on the second floor. Instinct told me to run, but where? I stood frozen, not even realizing that Lily was right next to me, gathering me up to follow her and the other women inside. She knew I was suffering. Although she was only a few months older than I was, she possessed a composure I couldn't muster under the circumstances. While Lily didn't hate her husband-to-be like I hated mine, she, too, seemed to have second thoughts. Still, she had the physical and emotional resolve to guide me up the stairs alongside her. Holding my wedding dress with shaky hands, I looked into the whitewashed room and was repulsed. This was never how I'd imagined the scene of my wedding.

Tossing my things onto the bed with the ugly, multi-colored bedspread, I burst into tears. Lily pulled me into a hug and promised that everything would be okay. She and another of my stepsisters helped get me into my wedding dress and put me together.

"You know, girls, I really can't do this," I announced, as Lily pinned the dainty silver tiara Kassandra had given me in my hair. I'd always imagined that my wedding day would be magical, and I would be wearing a crown just like the princesses of the fairy tales I'd read as a child, but as Lily affixed the tiara to my hair, I felt nothing like a princess about to live happily ever after. "I can't go through with this," I uttered, tempted to rip the tiara from my head.

Nancy was disgusted with my continued disrespect. "I can't believe that you're turning down the prophet and defying God's will in your life. I just can't believe you're not being obedient," she said to me.

For a moment her words took me aback and made me

think, "You know, she's right." I was defying what they told me to do, but I was also tired of her criticism.

"Just because I care about my life doesn't mean I'm turning down the prophet," I replied coldly.

"Okay, I'll tell them that," she shot back over her shoulder before marching out of the room and down the stairs.

Lily and I exchanged looks and tried to comfort each other. In an attempt to make me laugh, she said, "There's a back door. We could just, like, run."

For that brief moment, we sat suspended in thought, each wondering if we could really pull off an escape.

"Well," she said reluctantly, "we better get down there. They're waiting for us."

Standing in the doorway, I took a deep breath and tried to steady myself in the white shoes that my sister had bought. Allen was standing at the foot of the stairs when I finally peered out of the room to answer the repeated calls to hurry down. At that moment, all I could think was "Please, just die." He reached out for my hand, but I couldn't bring myself to touch him.

"Oh, Lesie, you're beautiful!" Mom exclaimed, trying to be positive. This line, spoken by so many mothers to their daughters on countless wedding days throughout history, did nothing to comfort me or bring a smile to my face. Like Allen's mothers, mine had selected her finest dress and my favorite of hers—a gorgeous pale blue silk. Kassandra had styled Mom's long brown waves for the occasion, and even through my tears I could see that she looked lovely.

In a daze, I trailed the group to a covered patio off the main office, where I waited for my ceremony to begin. I was relieved that I didn't have to go first. My eyes scanned the space around me, falling inevitably on Allen. He tried talking to me, but I kept my lips firmly sealed.

"Mom," I urged again, "this is going to be the biggest mistake of my life. I can feel it and I know it." I didn't care that my sister Rachel was standing right there next to Mom. It pained me to see the two women with their bright smiles, even though I knew my mother's was fabricated.

"Just be strong," Mom said. "The Lord knows what he's doing." As Mom and Rachel exchanged pleasantries, I wondered what was going on behind the doors of the small side building where one couple had been taken. My thoughts were suddenly interrupted by the voice of Uncle Rulon's son Nephi summoning me: "They're ready for you," he said. "They're waiting."

I froze and he promptly asked, "Are you coming?"

The wobbly feeling I always got when I'd been summoned to Uncle Warren's office at Alta Academy suddenly returned tenfold, and I could barely make my legs work. The headache I had been nursing for days from all my crying grew more intense with every heavy step I took.

The building where the ceremony was to take place was set off from the rest of the motel. It had been cleared of its bed, and a few rows of chairs had been arranged for the weddings. I could almost feel my mother, worried that I might try to run, hovering right behind me as I tried to maneuver the gravelly terrain in my high heels and long, encumbering dress.

I paused in the threshold of the room to see what awaited me. Tears streamed from my eyes as I took in its tacky pink motif. It felt foreboding and grim. A thin layer of dirt covered the bottom edges of the walls, and every corner seemed to hide unfamiliar shadows. There were three short rows of seats for the wedding, two rows with three seats each and one with two. The two seats at the front were for Allen and me. My mother sat in the middle row alone with Allen's two mothers and his father directly behind her. Her face didn't offer me much comfort, but I was glad that she was there.

The prophet was at the center of the room, sitting in a big La-Z-Boy like the one Uncle Fred had in his living room. Uncle Rulon had the two next most powerful FLDS men on either side of him. Uncle Fred, serving as my father, sat to his left. Uncle Warren was on his right, signifying his role as Uncle Rulon's right-hand man.

While the prophet was just a few feet from where I was standing, I felt unsure I could walk the short distance to shake his hand, as was customary. I felt Uncle Warren's icy stare egging me on, and despite my urge to turn and flee, I managed to make my way over and greet them. Everyone was watching me as I moved from Uncle Rulon's outstretched hand to Uncle Warren's to Uncle Fred's.

Uncle Warren directed Allen and me to take our places in the front two seats. Feeling overwhelmed, I obeyed. After about a minute, Warren stood to receive the power to conduct our wedding from his father, who had authorized him to seal us in his name. He began reading a passage from *In Light and Truth: Raising Children in the Family Order of Heaven*. As he droned on, my mind raced, but Uncle Warren's stern directive startled me back to the present.

"Can we please have you stand?" he instructed, looking out over his glasses at me. I heard what he'd said, but I remained paralyzed in my seat. "So, will you please stand and take each other's hands," Uncle Warren continued.

Rising, I said, "Can't I just stand here?" That plea was ignored, and Allen took my limp hand in what is known as the "patriarchal grip." As Uncle Warren began the ceremony, I felt dizzy, like I might pass out. I knew that I should be paying attention to these sacred words, but I couldn't focus on them. My mind was still searching for an exit.

"Do you, Brother Allen Glade Steed, take Sister Elissa Jessop, by the right hand, and receive her unto yourself to be your lawful and wedded wife . . ."

Just like at my mother's wedding to Uncle Fred, I held my breath and desperately prayed that Uncle Warren would not seal me for time and all eternity.

". . . and you to be her lawful and wedded husband . . ."

I was praying that God would at least do this for me, that he wouldn't let Warren say those words, that he would let me be with someone else in heaven.

". . . for time and all eternity."

My heart dropped and tears slid down my cheeks. From this moment forward, my entire life would feel wrong; even in death I'd be miserable.

I wanted to run as Uncle Warren droned on with the

vows. "With a covenant and promise, on your part, that you will fulfill all the laws, rites, and ordinances pertaining to this holy bond of matrimony in the new and everlasting covenant, doing this in the presence of God, angels, and these witnesses, of your own free will and choice?"

Allen agreed promptly, "I do."

I could feel Uncle Warren's piercing gaze turn in my direction, and my heart began to race.

"Do you, Sister Elissa Jessop, take Brother Allen Glade Steed by the right hand and give yourself to him . . ." I was no longer hearing his words, for my mind was a jumble. Give myself to Allen? "No. Oh please, God, no!" my mind was screaming. I tried to focus on the words being said.

". . . of your own free will and choice?" he finished, waiting for my reply.

"My free will and choice?" I thought. Nothing about this day was my free will and choice. For the past week, I had desperately tried to tell the very man saying these words that I did not want this and had begged him to allow me to grow up first. He more than anyone else knew this was not my "free will and choice."

I couldn't say it. I felt the room fall silent as the words failed to find their way to my lips. Uncle Warren's stern gaze drilled a hole through me, and he looked so intimidating and powerful. I could feel everyone's stares as I stood there speechless. Time seemed to stand still as I searched the room for an answer. My gaze finally fell upon my mother, whose look of terrified agony said it all. If I denied myself and my family this moment, I would be going against everything that mattered to us. An overwhelming sense of defeat fell over me; as hard as I'd fought, it was all over now.

Warren's voice broke the silence. "Would the mother of the bride please stand and give her support?" Mom stood, grabbing my left hand. I could feel her hand trembling as she held mine. Stealing a look at her face, I could see that she was holding back tears.

"Do you, Sister Elissa, take Brother Allen, by the right hand, and give yourself to him to be his lawful and wedded wife for time and all eternity?" Warren repeated in a voice that made the question sound like a command. Even as the silence grew unbearable, I still couldn't bring myself to formulate the words. Suddenly, I felt my fingers being crushed by my Mom's death grip. It shocked me into the moment, reminding me that I had no choice but to respond.

"Okay," I said, almost in a whisper. "I do."

I could hear the collective sigh of relief rise up in the room. It was as if they'd all been holding their breaths in anticipation of what I was going to say, and were seemingly thankful that I had finally broken. In the last few moments, I had teetered on the edge of heaven and hell and ultimately had been forced to choose heaven, but for me, the bridle had been cinched tight and heaven would be my hell.

"In the name of the Lord Jesus Christ, and by the authority of the Holy Priesthood, I pronounce you legally and lawfully husband and wife, for time and all eternity . . ."

My soul was broken. I was now going to be Allen's wife for eternity, and there was nothing I could do about it.

"You may kiss the bride," Uncle Warren directed.

Reflexively, I backed away as Allen leaned in to kiss me.

The tears were falling freely, and I had to keep my shoulders from shaking. I lowered my head and shook it. "Please don't make me do this," I pleaded in my mind.

Uncle Warren looked at me pointedly, almost hissing the words: "Kiss Allen." All I could think of was the time in elementary school when Uncle Warren told me that I was to treat boys as poisonous snakes. To me, Allen was worse than that, and I could not bring myself to kiss him. Finally I gave in and pecked him on the lips. I was desperate to escape. I couldn't take it anymore. I turned to leave and was stopped when someone tugged on my hand.

At that moment, Uncle Warren took my hand and Allen's, putting them together in his, saying, "Now go forth and multiply and replenish the earth with good priesthood children."

I could barely see through my tears as I fled. I escaped into a separate room and dissolved. My mother followed me and I ran from her, locking myself in a bathroom. Crumpling to the floor, I was overtaken by sobs. I couldn't believe it. I had just gotten married.

Immediately, I could hear her soothing voice through the grain of the wooden door between us, almost begging, "Lesie, please let me in."

Mom was joined by my sister Rachel and Allen, who also tried unsuccessfully to get me to come out. I had been in there for several minutes when I heard a knock and the voice of one of the church elders, Uncle Wendell Neilson. I'd always liked Uncle Wendell and felt guilty and embarrassed that I was now avoiding him.

"I just want to be the first to congratulate the new Mrs. Steed," Uncle Wendell told me when I finally opened the bathroom door. I found momentary solace in his bear hug. "You know things will look up. Just remember to trust in God." He tried to cheer me up, saying that I would reap the rewards of obedience to the prophet. "Someday thousands will flock to hear your story of faith and courage." His words were kind and meant to be encouraging, but I didn't want my forced obedience to be an example to anyone. Both he and my mother tried to encourage me by reminding me that for a woman to take part in a spiritual marriage was the highest achievement she could reach. To them, I had been honored with this wonderful blessing.

After I came out of the bathroom, I was directed to go with the other brides to change for the luncheon. I had a hard time sitting next to Allen at the table. All through the lunch I could barely think, let alone eat. I was only ten minutes into it, and already my marriage was a nightmare.

CHAPTER THIRTEEN

ALL ALONE

The only true freedom of women is in the abiding of the
holy Celestial law of marriage, submitting herself to her
husband and head and living his law.
—RULON JEFFS

It was late afternoon when we loaded up into the cars for
our trip back to Hildale. The ride was long and quiet, and I
spent most of it in a daze, wondering where I'd be living
upon our return. Over the past few years, I had been moved
around so many times, and never with advance notice. Since
learning that I would be married, I had been so busy con-
testing the marriage that I hadn't thought about where we
would live when it was all over.

I was relieved when we pulled up to Uncle Fred's and saw
the large Jessop family outside to greet us. Everyone had
been excitedly awaiting our arrival, and some of the family
began snapping pictures as we stepped out of the car. No
pictures had been taken of the actual ceremonies because of
the risk that the documentation would fall into the wrong
hands, so these would be the first snapshots for our memory
books. Dozens of people were giving their congratulations
and posing us for our first husband-and-wife photos. Everyone was shouting at me to smile, and compliantly I did. I was
exhausted and could barely think straight. Numb, I did as

directed and tried hard to put forth my sweetest FLDS face.

Outside Uncle Fred's house, a horse-drawn carriage was waiting to take the newlywed couples for a ride around town. It belonged to a local FLDS member who had come up to Uncle Fred's for the afternoon to commemorate our wedding day. Without the strength to resist, I took Allen's outstretched hand and climbed aboard for the ride.

As soon as we returned to Fred's house, I stepped off and walked inside to avoid continued pressure to pose for more photos. My face was red and swollen from crying, and I refused to honor the repeated pleas to kiss Allen for the camera.

After the carriage ride and photos, we went to Allen's parents' home, where his entire family had assembled to welcome us. I smiled politely as Allen's mother greeted me with a bouquet of lilacs. One by one, I met his family, who all did their best to make me feel comfortable. Allen's mother had a small business sewing nightgowns and other sleep-wear. Ironically, she'd sewn my bridal trousseau, a white satin gown and pink satin robe with delicate flowers on it. They had been a gift from my mother, who'd had them made to order by Allen's mom before she even knew I was going to marry him.

That night, Uncle Fred had us to his home for dinner, which was followed by ice cream and cake. Still, I had no idea where we would be living; no announcement had been made.

At points during the evening, I was overcome by the ex-citement of the celebration, but inevitably, something would snap me back to the hard truth of my situation. I wanted so badly to be happy and enjoy this moment, but something inside just wouldn't let me. Later that evening I was pleas-antly surprised when my friend Natalie stopped by to wish me well. Though we no longer attended the same school, I'd been spending a lot of time with her. We had grown quite close, and she was one of the few people outside of Uncle

Fred's home whom I could trust and talk to. The morning of the wedding, Natalie's mother, Lavonda, had done my hair. Strangely, Natalie had been silent. I could see that it worried her to watch me prepare for my wedding. I'd been feeling self-conscious around her ever since I'd learned of my impending nuptials, and I noticed awkwardness on her part as well. She seemed to be afraid that being around me would call attention to her and bring her the same fate.

Now, here she was at Uncle Fred's house accompanied by several of her sisters to perform a song in honor of my wedding. The girls had beautiful voices and had produced some music CDs for the community. I was so touched that they would honor me with this lovely performance that I didn't think about what would happen when they left. Watching their eyes glow and hearing their voices glide over the notes, it never occurred to me that the day's events would change my life and friendship with Natalie. I was no longer a single fourteen-year-old like her. I was officially different; I was married. While she still had the freedom to act like a child, the standards for me had changed overnight. The sad truth was that after that day we no longer spent time together as close friends.

When everyone left Fred's home that evening, a horrible sense of abandonment crept up on me. One minute we were all celebrating, and the next everyone was saying goodbye. Right after prayer service that night, Uncle Fred excitedly led our procession up the stairs to our "new" bedroom, which was the same room that I had been sleeping in since I arrived at his home. He informed Allen and me that we were going to live in his home until the church assigned us a place of our own. The news that I would be close to my mother came as a relief. In anticipation of our arrival, he'd instructed some of the mothers to prepare the upstairs bedroom I'd been sharing with my two sisters as a honeymoon suite.

Just inside the door, a handmade banner reading "Honeymoon Hideout" hung across an archway. Peering into the room, I saw that the furniture was decidedly different from when I'd left that morning. The bunk bed my little sisters shared had been moved to my mother's room, along with all of their knickknacks. My twin bed had been replaced by a queen-sized one that I was expected to share with Allen, starting that very night. The bedspread had been decorated with dozens of Hershey's chocolate kisses arranged in the shape of a big heart. Homemade cookies and sparkling cider had been left for us. Also on the bed was a handmade sign with the words ALLEN AND ELISSA SEALED FOR TIME AND ALL ETERNITY, APRIL 23, 2001. As if hearing the words hadn't been enough, now I had to see them. I knew all of these gestures had been made with good intentions, but they only emphasized how wrong the whole thing felt.

The scene was surreal. Just a day earlier, this room had been a safe, comforting space, a sanctuary where I could escape the insanity about the pending wedding. Now its every corner had an air of foreboding, and the walls seemed to close in on me. I could barely look at it, let alone sleep there. As I tried to calm down, I was suddenly lifted into the air. Allen had taken me in his arms and was preparing to carry me over the threshold. I covered my face when I saw cameras poised and began to cry as he walked us into the room.

The cameras continued to snap outside of the Honeymoon Hideout, and my extended family pressed me to smile for the photos, saying that one day I would want to look back at this "happy" time. After what felt like an eternity in front of the camera, Uncle Fred congratulated us once again. He said that he was proud of me for doing what the prophet had told me to do, but pride from him felt tainted and ugly—nothing like it would have felt had I heard those special words from my real dad, after a wedding that I actually wanted.

Mom lingered in the hallway as long as she could to help me feel protected and loved. I had caught her crying back at the motel in Caliente, when I'd accidentally walked into the bathroom and found her in the arms of my sister Rachel. I knew this was difficult for her too, but there was no way for her to protect me now. After a few minutes, she finally declared, "I'm going to bed."

"No, Mom, you can't go," I pleaded. She didn't respond

with words, but her eyes spoke her pain. I had no idea what a wedding night entailed and I was horrified at the prospect and apprehensive to go into the room. I watched as Mom faded into her room, closing the door behind her. I wanted nothing more than to trail along like a little girl, but I knew that I couldn't.

Panic set in as Allen closed the door. I had never been alone with a man before, but here we were in a bedroom, of all places. I had no idea what to say, and an uncomfortable silence fell between us. Awkwardly, I sat down on the bed and cringed as he approached me. He sat down next to me and I quickly scooted over, grabbed my nightgown, and fled down the hall to the bathroom to change. As soon as I closed the door I collapsed, dropping to my knees with my back pressed against the door. I couldn't even cry anymore; I was out of tears.

I stayed in the bathroom for a long time, battling in my head. While part of me was angry that I'd lost the fight, there was the other side, the faithful priesthood girl side, that was consoled that I had done what I was told to do. I tried hard to convince myself that it was going to work out and that God was watching over the situation. I thought of how hard I'd fought and of all those people who had congratulated me, telling me I was going to be happy someday. All of a sudden, I felt the urge to vomit and bent over the sink in horror. When the nausea finally passed, I stared at myself in the mirror worrying what to do next.

I knew I had to open the door and return to the bedroom, but the only thing I wanted to do was run into my mother's room and hide in the corner.

"This is what the priesthood told me to do," I convinced myself. "I have no choice but to do it."

And with that thought, I took off my socks, shoes, and dress, but that was as far as I would go. I put my nightgown over my tights, my special church undergarments, slip, and even my bra and panties. On top of all this, I wrapped the new pink satin robe tightly around me. I wasn't thinking that Allen would try to touch me, I just felt safer with all the layers. Even with all my clothes on I still couldn't imagine being in a room by myself with a man.

It wasn't just that I was afraid of Allen, I was overwhelmed at the idea of being in bed with him. As a naïve fourteen-year-old girl, I had no idea that people did more than sleep in bed. The truth was that I knew nothing about sex. Absolutely nothing. I didn't even know that sex existed. It was a word not used in the FLDS culture, and what it described was never discussed before marriage. I didn't know husbands and wives did it. Growing up in the FLDS, I had no concept of where babies really came from. No one had ever taught me about boys except that they were "poisonous snakes." I had no idea what Allen expected of me now that I was his wife. All I knew was that I didn't want him to touch me, period.

Allen was sitting on the bed when I returned from the bathroom. I watched as he rose to go to the bathroom himself, and when I heard the shower running I felt relieved. "I just want to go to sleep before he gets out of the shower," I thought.

Closing my eyes, I heard him coming back into the room, and I lay perfectly still trying to pretend that I was fast asleep. All of a sudden, I felt him hovering over me, and then his hand on my shoulder shaking me. I clenched my eyes shut, and eventually he gave up, crawled in next to me, hugged me, and then rolled over and went to sleep. It was one of the longest nights of my life. I was drained but too scared to sleep, not knowing what might happen. I tried to fight it, but there were moments throughout the night when I drifted off from sheer exhaustion.

By dawn, I was back in my clothes and out on the terrace to watch the sun rise. Unsure of how to act when Allen woke up, I took off on foot down the road. I walked for hours, up into the dusty heights of the mountains, contemplating my situation. I had taken this rugged path many times before, and there was comfort in the familiarity of the well-worn trail. I hoped to find a resolution, but when I returned to Uncle Fred's house late that morning, none had appeared.

Mom and Allen were wondering what had happened to me. Mom took more pictures that morning. She wanted me to have photos for scrapbooking, and though she had the best of intentions, it was hard for me to pose next to Allen.

That afternoon Fred gathered the three newly married couples in his office to tell us that he was sending us all on a honeymoon and gave each man an envelope of money for the trip. The next morning, we would be joining him on his usual trip to Phoenix to shop for the community storehouse. The thought of going to Phoenix again left me momentarily excited. I'd been there before and enjoyed it. I assumed that this trip would actually result in me spending less time with Allen.

Though this gift was for everyone, it seemed clear that Uncle Fred hoped my spending some time away from the house with Allen would bring me closer to him. For much of the day, Allen tried to be cute and kind, but whenever he tried to hold my hand, I would pull away. When he moved over next to me in bed that night, I rolled to the edge, almost falling off.

I was too overwhelmed and too busy evading Allen's touch to check in and see how the other newlyweds were doing, but we all came together again for our departure. Everyone could tell that our relationship was not going as well as the others. This was on full display during the ride down to Phoenix, when both Nancy and Lily sat close to their new husbands in Uncle Fred's Suburban, while I made sure there was an empty seat in the second row between Allen and me.

When we arrived in Phoenix, Fred informed us that he'd gotten us each a hotel room, and the news terrified me. I had envisioned this trip much like the one I'd taken with Uncle Fred in the past, but now I realized that we would be on our own. After our night at the motel in Phoenix, we would be traveling in Texas, New Mexico, and Colorado, stopping in other motels along the way.

After checking into our room in Phoenix, I scurried to the bathroom for a long shower. My plan was simple: I would take as long as possible in the bathroom each night, hoping that Allen would be asleep when I returned. That first night, I had no such luck. When I came out of the bathroom, he was in his shorts. The only thing I could think was, "Put some pants on." I had never seen a man with so little clothing, except a few in swimming suits, and even that had made me uncomfortable. Now, seeing my husband in his underwear made me cringe.

Allen came over to my side of the bed and sat down beside me. Slowly, he began inching his hand up the back of my pajamas and unhooked my bra.

I whipped around instantly to face him with fire in my eyes. "Don't touch me."

"Well," he said, "we're gonna have to do it sooner or later."

I just looked at him blankly. I had no idea what "it" was. All I knew was that I didn't want anything to do with him.

I moved into the other double bed to sleep that night, but the same thing happened the next night, with Allen touching me even more. Petrified, I grabbed his hand as he slid it down to my lower body. "Please don't," I begged, my voice shaking with fear. I had never been touched like that by anyone, and there was nothing about what he was doing that seemed right. He tried to kiss me, and I avoided his lips as best I could.

The next day I continued to avoid Allen when we were out with the other couples. They teased us, trying to get me to kiss my new husband.

"If you kiss him, I'll give you one hundred dollars," Nancy's husband, Tim, offered one afternoon.

"No," I said firmly. "No, I'm not doing it."

Tim smiled. He'd been kind to me, and in some way, I felt he understood my hesitation. He was nothing like Lily's husband, Martin, who was constantly making fun of people. Even as I insisted that Allen not kiss me, my fellow honeymooners managed to snap off one or two shots of him seizing a hug. I hadn't been expecting Allen to grab onto me at that moment, as he suddenly pulled me toward him and pressed his lips to mine. Even now when I look at the photo it pains me to see how I had to block him with both arms. As he held me in his tight grip and forced me to kiss his sloppy lips, I fought to contain my anger. The only benefit of this disgusting and embarrassing kiss was that Tim considered it legitimate enough to give me a hundred dollars, which was the most money I had ever had at one time. But sadly, it wasn't mine for long. My "priesthood head" made me give it to him later during our honeymoon.

That forced kiss was the only time I kissed Allen during the honeymoon. I did my best to not even talk to him. To prevent Allen from holding my hand, I found a small paper bag and pencil and kept my hands busy by logging the trip's events on it. I almost felt bad when Allen started to cry from the teasing he was getting from Lily and Nancy over my reluctance to get near him, but the fact that he continued to touch me in spite of my protests prevented me from having compassion for him.

On the last night of our honeymoon, I woke up to the sensation of my skin being touched beneath my nightgown.

"What are you doing?" I demanded.

"I'm doing what I have a right to," Allen replied with an air of entitlement. "I'm your husband," he announced, as if that gave him rights to my body.

"Please don't touch me" was the only response I could muster. I had no idea why he insisted on feeling my most private areas. It was clear that I would have to be on alert, even at night when I was supposed to be asleep.

The next morning, while we cruised along the highway toward home, I overheard Nancy and Lily whispering and giggling about "physical relations" with their husbands. Even though Allen hadn't been shy about putting his hands on my body, I didn't know what they were talking about.

"So," Nancy whispered with a smile stretched across her face, "have you guys really done anything?"

"What? No," I replied, baffled.

"Well," she assured me, "maybe it could happen tonight. We could put a bug in Allen's ear."

I was a little frustrated, as the whole conversation flew

over my head, but later I would look back at my naïveté with longing.

I was relieved when we returned to Short Creek that Saturday and resumed living next to my mother. Although I had to be alone with Allen at night, I felt comforted knowing that Mom was nearby. I remained scared and couldn't shake the feeling that had set in when Allen said that he had a "right" to me, like I was his to claim, like someone had just handed me to him and now he could do whatever he wanted. I had no idea what he did want, but I knew that sooner or later, this thing he was trying to do with me was going to happen. And like most things that had happened in my life, there would be nothing I could do to stop it. But I wasn't about to give up without a fight.

A couple of weeks after our wedding, Allen's parents invited us to their home to celebrate his birthday. He would be turning twenty on May 12, and since we had planned a trip to Canada to visit other family members on that day, Allen's mothers had prepared a nice pre-birthday dinner for us. After dinner, Allen suggested that it would be nice for us to walk back to Fred's. He was clearly trying hard to make me feel comfortable, and I didn't know how to treat him, especially after the way he had been touching me. I didn't want to be with him, but I knew I had been acting mean and I felt bad. I told myself that I had to give this a shot. I was doing my best to fight the feelings of revulsion and find a way to accept Allen as my priesthood head, so I agreed.

We'd been walking for several minutes when Allen directed us to the small school grounds not far from Uncle Fred's home. There was a big grassy area with some swings, and he suggested that we stop there and talk for a while. We sat down on the grass looking up at the early-night sky.

"Do you love me?" he asked.

I was quiet. It felt okay, sitting on the ground staring up at the stars. It was a beautiful night, and I could see so many constellations. It didn't make me love him as I was supposed to, but it was the most effort he'd made toward romance since we were married.

I felt Allen get up beside me, and turning to look at him, I was shocked by what I saw: Allen stood in front of me, exposing himself.

"What are you doing? Put that away!" I demanded, closing my eyes tightly.

"This is what I look like," he announced matter-of-factly.

"I don't even want to see," I shouted, jumping up. I ran as fast I could toward home with Allen close on my tail. I'd never seen a man's penis before, except when changing baby diapers. Tears streamed from my eyes as I tried to understand what had just happened. I raced upstairs to Mom's room.

"What's wrong? What happened?" Mom asked.

I couldn't bring myself to tell her. I was too embarrassed, and I thought that she would think I was the most terrible, evil, disgusting person in the world. It was as though I had done something horribly wrong by seeing a man like that. We had always been taught that it was a sin to even touch a boy, let alone see him naked.

"I hate him," I blurted out. "I hate him! I hate him! I hate him!"

"Who?"

"Allen."

"Lesie, what happened?"

"I'm not going in that room. I'm not going to talk to him."

"Did he do something?" Mom asked.

I broke into sobs. Mom's attempts to calm me down were interrupted by a knock at the door.

"Elissa?" I heard Allen's voice summoning me.

"Go away!" I shouted.

"Lesie!" Mom admonished. She was desperate for me to stop acting so disrespectfully. I knew I was being immature, but I couldn't help it. What was happening was just too difficult, and I didn't have the tools to handle it.

I waited in Mom's room until two or three in the morning before returning to my bedroom. Turning the doorknob, I tried to be as quiet as I could, hoping not to wake Allen. But when I stepped inside, I found him in his underwear sprawled out on top of the bedspread. Reflexively, I backed away as he stood and came toward me. I was trembling as he reached for my buttons and began unfastening my dress.

"Don't touch me," I cried. "I don't want to have anything to do with you."

Suddenly, he pulled off his underwear and exposed himself to me again. Closing my eyes, I begged him, "Please don't do this. I don't want anything to do with this."

"This is what we're supposed to be doing," Allen announced. "This is what married people do."

"Well, I don't know what you're doing, so please don't."

Allen hesitated, "Don't you ever want to have a baby?" he asked.

"Not with you," I told him in a trembling voice.

"You know, I'm not going to hurt you," he explained as his hands worked the back of my dress. "This is what the prophet told me to do to you."

As the word *prophet* escaped his lips, I felt suddenly alarmed that I was not following what the priesthood had intended. Somehow it had never crossed my mind that the church wanted us to do whatever it was that Allen was doing. I tried to trust in what Allen was telling me, but the way he touched me was too unsettling and I hated how it made me feel. Panicked and unwilling to continue, I leaned close and whispered, "Please, just go to bed. Please, just get dressed." But the words had little effect on him. As he pulled off my dress, I began to cry.

"Stop it," Allen instructed. "Don't act like a baby. Do you know what I'm doing?"

"No," I said, recoiling. I watched as he circled behind me, and I felt his firm hand unfastening my bra. After he had removed my church undergarments, I grabbed the blanket from the bed and held it in front of me as a final layer of protection. He ripped the blanket from my grasp, exposing me completely. I stood trembling, feeling horribly ashamed.

He took a step back and his gaze crawled over my entire body. "I've always wanted to see a woman naked," he proclaimed.

I'd never felt as vulnerable as I did during those moments when he scrutinized every inch of me for the first time. I hadn't been naked in front of anyone since I was a little girl. Everything about me had been laid bare. Standing in front of Allen, I could feel his eyes taking in my body with a look that I did not trust, but I was too frightened to try and put my clothes back on. I was crying as he brought me over to the bed.

"Now do you know what I'm going to do to you?" he said in a weird way.

"No," I responded with a whimper. He began to tell me what he was planning to do, and it only made me confused. When he started to describe it, he got excited in a way I had never seen before, and the look on his face was almost animal. A sick feeling rose inside me, a scream bubbled up, and I was on my feet. Grabbing the blanket, I ran for the door, desperate for the protection of my mother's room. When I saw that Mom wasn't there, I flopped down on her bed and began to sob into her pillow.

My cries eventually woke my sister Ally, who crawled over and without saying a word put her arms around me.

"I'm sorry for waking you. Go back to sleep. It's a school night," I said.

"I'm just helping you cry."

Her response made me cry all the more, but that night, with my little sister curled up beside me, I slept peacefully in Mom's bed.

"All better?" Ally asked me when we woke up the next morning.

"Yes," I said with a smile, and she smiled back. Even though she was young, she knew I was not okay, but my answer was sufficient for her and she started to prepare for school.

I too had to get ready for school. I wanted to finish the ninth grade, because school was very important to me. As much as I disliked Uncle Fred's school, it was better than being home and having to face Allen. I was glad to be on my way that morning, but I hated how everyone treated me differently because I was married. It was like they refused to let me be a fourteen-year-old girl anymore. Marriage, it seemed, was more important for a girl than anything else—especially learning.

I was deep into my algebra exam that morning when I felt a hand on my shoulder. "There is someone at the door for you." My teacher's voice startled me from my math problem.

Looking up, I saw Allen standing in the hallway, peeking into the classroom.

"Can you tell him that I'm in the middle of a test?" I asked my teacher.

"I'm not gonna tell him anything," Mr. Richter informed me. He was one of the stricter teachers, and I knew he wouldn't help me.

Rising to my feet, I hesitantly made my way to the door. When I reached it, I saw that the school principal had accompanied Allen.

"I'm going to just take you for the day," Allen told me. "The principal said it's okay."

"But I have a test," I said, hoping the principal would insist that I stay to complete it. But since this was a priesthood school, neither Allen nor the principal saw the importance of my finishing the exam.

Following Allen to the parking lot, I got into the passenger seat. I was livid but held my tongue as we drove around Utah and Arizona. Allen was angry at how I'd acted the previous night, and with a raised voice, he related his frustration. I'd never seen him lose his cool, and his ill temper took me by surprise. In the FLDS, becoming angry was frowned upon.

"I just hate you," I told him. "And I hope you go to hell."

At first, he seemed as if he was about to melt into tears, but after a few minutes, he got so upset that he smashed his sunglasses on the steering wheel so hard that a piece of the wheel broke off and fell to the floor. "You didn't go and tell your mom, did you?" he demanded.

"Tell my mom what?"

"You didn't go and tell her about anything, did you?" I knew he was referring to what had happened in our bedroom the previous night.

"No."

"Well, you'd better not," he reprimanded. "She needs to stay out of our business completely. If it was up to me, we wouldn't even live by her."

That night, I refused to go to my room and stayed with my mother, but I didn't confide in her, despite her offer of support. The following morning I was summoned to Uncle Fred's office, where I found Allen with Fred. My stomach churned as Fred motioned for me to sit down.

"Allen tells me that you have been rebellious toward him," he began. "What's going on?"

I wanted to tell Uncle Fred the truth and how I was certain that Allen didn't deserve to be a priesthood man and have all the privileges that came along with it. Instead, I tried to save myself. "I'm doing the best I can," I told him.

I was furious that Allen had gone to him to complain that I wasn't being a submissive wife. And I hated the smug look he wore as Uncle Fred reprimanded me for disobedience.

"Lesie, you're not standing up to your vows," Fred said in a soft voice. I could tell by his tone that Uncle Fred was displeased with me and I shrank in the face of his reprimand. At the end of the meeting, Allen grabbed my hand and led me from the room. I waited until we were out of Uncle Fred's line of sight before I pulled my hand away from him and ran to find my mother.

A few days had passed when I decided I needed to speak with my mother about what Allen was doing in our bedroom. I was certain that he was telling me a tall tale when he said that it was his right. I couldn't imagine that it was okay, and I wanted to hear it from Mom.

"Mom, how do people have a baby?" I asked her straight out.

"Well," she stammered, "that is for Allen to tell you."

Her refusal to answer my question bothered me. If I had only known what was going on, I would have at least understood what Allen was trying to do. As it was, his actions only made me feel dirty. All she would have had to do was explain what had to happen for a woman to have children, but she didn't. She'd been admonished by Uncle Fred to stay out of our affairs, and she couldn't even tell me the one thing that I needed to know.

Days later, I was talking with one of the girls who'd been married with me. She could see I was very upset and needed a friend. Taking pity on me, she told me a little about "man/wife relations," but her explanation was terribly vague and a little scary and I walked away even more confused.

That night, I returned to my room to find Allen waiting up for me.

"It's time for you to be a wife and do your duty," he told me as I walked through the door.

"No," I said, breaking down in tears. "Please don't make me do anything. I don't want to have that kind of thing with you."

"Why?" Allen asked me.

"Because I don't like you," I said, unable to hold my feelings back. I could see that my words hurt him, and he looked upset. "It's just that the last thing I want to do is spend the rest of my life with you."

Allen's face grew red with anger. He grabbed me and, without saying another word, undressed both of us. I was frozen with fear and again asked him to please let me be. He pulled me over to the bed and pushed me down. With tears pouring out of my eyes, I tried to block it all out. My entire body was shaking and I was crying as he got on top of me.

"Please stop, I don't know what you're doing. I can't do this," I begged.

"It's okay," Allen told me as he touched me all over my

body. "You're going to learn that this is what's supposed to happen . . ."

And then it finally did happen. I just lay there in shock. It hurt so bad, and I thought, "God, please, let me die." As he put himself inside me, I wanted to scream for help, but there was no one to help me. I had nowhere to hide. My mother's room, my little sister's embrace, Uncle Fred, Uncle Warren, nothing and no one would save me, and so I lay there silently, staring at the cracks in the ceiling, watching a part of me die.

When it was all over, I curled into a ball and continued to cry. Allen rolled over and fell asleep, and I lay there feeling like I'd been left for dead. Rising from the bed, I went into the bathroom to clean up. I didn't want to go to my mom. I felt dirty and used, and I was worried that she would think I was a disgusting, evil person. Nothing could cleanse the soiled feeling I had inside. I felt sick and my thoughts turned to death. Rummaging through the medicine cabinet, I found a half-bottle of Tylenol. I poured the tablets into my palm and swallowed them. Convinced that they wouldn't be enough to kill me, I then grabbed a bottle of ibuprofen and swallowed what was left of those too. I collapsed in a heap next to the tub. I just wanted to die and not deal with Allen, Uncle Warren, or Uncle Fred again. I felt so hurt and betrayed by them all, including my mother.

Mom found me early the next morning on the floor of the bathroom, my head in the toilet, vomiting. Alarmed, she gathered me up and held me in her arms.

"What's wrong? Lesie," she cried as she brought me to her room. I couldn't bring myself to tell her what had happened with Allen or that I'd taken two bottles of pills in an attempt to escape from my life, only to have a sudden change of heart. I made myself throw up minutes after I'd taken the pills and had spent the last several hours desperately trying to purge them. As bad as my life had become, I had pulled myself back from the brink of self-destruction.

I had no idea how I was going to get out of this marriage or out of my life, but that night, I had realized that killing myself was not the answer. From then on, my goal was simple: to survive. I needed to survive in this marriage until I could figure out my next step. That morning, with my stomach weak from heaving all night and my body exhausted from sleep deprivation, I made a resolution. Somehow I would get through this; somehow I would survive.

PART TWO

Chapter Fourteen

SURVIVAL BEGINS

Give yourself mind, body, and soul.
—WARREN JEFFS

The second week in May, I traveled with Allen to the community in Canada to visit my sisters Teressa and Sabrina. We caught a ride to Bountiful, British Columbia, with one of Allen's brothers, who lived in Idaho just across the border. Teressa and her husband, Roy Blackmore, lived with Roy's father, Dwayne, and his family. Sabrina was married to Dwayne, which made her one of Teressa's mothers-in-law and also made it convenient for us to visit both of them.

Ever since Allen approved the trip, I had been anticipating it with some pleasure, but from the moment we arrived it was obvious that Allen and I were not a happy couple. My sisters tried hard to make the best of the visit by offering to take some nice photos of us, but I attempted to get out of any pictures that forced me to pose with Allen. My resistance to being near him was met with a bit of scolding, and my sisters reminded me to keep sweet.

Despite my hesitation, I put on my wedding dress and allowed Teressa to do my hair in a fancy updo. Both Teressa and Sabrina had a natural talent for photography, and they chose the perfect outdoor backdrop for our wedding poses. I knew I should be grateful for their kindness, and a voice in my head kept telling me that one day these pictures might mean something to me. But no matter how hard I tried, I couldn't fight the feeling of revulsion that came up every time I was close to Allen. I tried hard to fake it, but my body language screamed my reluctance.

Since that first night when Allen had violated me, he had forced himself on me several more times. I didn't know what to do or how to stop him. I hadn't told anyone anything about it. I'd been begging him to not to do it, but all he did was assure me that it was okay. Night after night, he insisted that this was supposed to happen and it was what we needed to do. My only option was to lie there in distress, even though it hurt me so much in every way. It had gotten to the point where each night I knew it was coming. My repeated refusals made no difference. I'd close my eyes and try to imagine myself someplace else or see how high I could count. I just wanted it to be over, and I knew if I fought him, it would just end up stretching out the agony.

With our trip to Canada, I hoped to get a reprieve from this pain by spending as much time as I could with my sisters, but I still had to go to sleep at night, and Allen was always there, ready and waiting for me. Even at my sisters' home, he was adamant that we do it. When it was over and he rolled over to close his eyes, I quickly redressed and tip-toed downstairs to the kitchen to get a drink.

It was late, and the whole house was quiet. With tears pooling up in my eyes, I sat down on the back stairs that led to the kitchen, unable to find a place for the pain that had been building up inside me. I was startled by my sister Teressa, who appeared in the doorway. She'd been in the kitchen when she heard my sobs and immediately came to investigate. She'd never liked Allen, and she couldn't believe that I had been forced to marry him. Nonetheless, she had been willing to give him a chance.

"What's wrong?" she asked.

"Oh, I can't really talk now," I said, embarrassed that she'd caught me like this.

"Yes, you can. You can talk to me," she said, stroking my head.

It was very hard for me to reveal what was going on in the bedroom with my new husband, and I faltered as I tried to explain it. Finally Teressa's gentle reassurances allowed me to reveal my horrible secret. I told her a little about what Allen had been doing to me at night.

"What's he doing to me?" I asked her, alarmed by the fury rising in her eyes.

"You are having marital relations with Allen," she told me. "Do you know what that is?"

"What's that?" I asked her not sure what she was referring to.

Because *sex* is not a word that's used in the FLDS culture, Teressa told me the basics of "man-wife" or marital relations. I was still confused because Allen was doing a lot more to me than what she explained. I told her how I felt like an evil, disgusting person, and she assured me I wasn't and that none of it was my fault.

"Elissa, he doesn't have to be doing that to you. You need to go and tell him that you don't want to do this."

"I have told him. I have told him from the very start that I don't want him to touch me. And I don't want to do or see anything. I don't even want to kiss him."

"This is wrong. Maybe you should go talk to Uncle Rulon and Uncle Warren about this, because they need to know how Allen is treating you."

Teressa's words resonated with me, and it was good to hear that maybe I was right. Maybe this wasn't supposed to be happening. Maybe we weren't doing what was proper. All I knew was that I just couldn't continue doing what Allen wanted me to. I was surprised when Teressa expressed disappointment with our mother because she hadn't told me what was going to happen after the marriage. But she was angry that Allen was forcing me to have relations with him, because I was so young. She had wanted him to wait.

By the end of our trip, I realized that Teressa must have spoken to someone else about my situation because the tension in the house began to mount and Allen wanted to get out of there. I was reluctant to say good-bye to my sisters, yet I was returning home with a sense of relief that I'd been able to share the truth with Teressa, and that she'd confirmed that what was happening was wrong.

"You do not let him do something to you that does not feel good," Teressa instructed before our departure. "If he does, you tell somebody. You go to Uncle Fred and tell him what is going on." Teressa wanted to tell him herself, but as an FLDS woman, she was forbidden to meddle in my marital affairs. As I stood there talking to her that day, I saw the same defiant spark in her eyes that I had always admired when I was growing up. Her certainty and her strength gave me hope. She was determined, and I took courage in her words.

On the way back from Canada, I learned that Lily had run away from her husband, Martin, and from the FLDS. Underneath her effort to keep sweet, she'd apparently been quite unhappy in her marriage and had escaped from Uncle Fred's home soon after I'd left for Canada. Everyone was looking for her, and the priesthood was panicked. Some of Lily's older brothers and sisters had left the FLDS Church, and everyone speculated that she had run off to be with them. People were fearful that the apostate part of her family would convince her to go public about her underage marriage, and by the time we arrived in Hildale, Lily's disappearance was all anyone could talk about.

In the coming weeks, Allen resumed his work for Uncle Fred, helping with the care of the zoo. He was paid a small stipend, which he used for our living expenses. We didn't have to pay room and board at Uncle Fred's, but Allen needed money for gas and other miscellaneous things. Meanwhile, I tried my best to complete the ninth grade, but with the wedding, the honeymoon, and our trip to Canada, I had missed nearly a month of school, and in the end I failed my final exam.

Soon after our return, I set up an appointment with Uncle Warren. I was encouraged by Teressa's advice and Lily's bold move. I didn't want to leave the FLDS—I just wanted to leave my marriage. I knew that if I left the religion, I would be forbidden to see my mother and younger sisters, and worse, I would lose my chance to go to heaven. Besides, where would I go? All I wanted was a solution that would allow me to remain with the little family I had left and in the only community I had ever known.

The more I thought about it, the more I believed that Uncle Warren would put an end to Allen's activities. Everyone knew that he'd basically taken over for the ailing prophet. Trusting that he had the power to make Allen stop, I placed a call to Uncle Rulon's compound. Uncle Warren's brother Nephi, who acted as one of Warren's scheduling secretaries, answered the phone. I told him that I needed to see Uncle Warren right away, but Nephi wouldn't let me speak to him over the phone. "Well, what's this concerning?" he asked.

"I just want to see him," I replied, unwilling to provide any more information. Finally, I was given an appointment.

On the designated day, I was feeling optimistic as I stepped into the waiting room, but the looks I received from people coming in and out of the prophet's office immediately unnerved me. Everybody knew that something big was happening if you were there to see Uncle Warren. Since I'd just gotten married, people cast curious glances in my direction, eager to know what could be going on so soon after the wedding.

"Elissa," Uncle Warren greeted me with a handshake and a smile. "How are you doing? Where's Allen?" he asked, surprised to see that I'd come on my own, without my priesthood head. "Does he know you're here?"

"No" I replied, a little scared of how he would respond.

"Are you going behind Allen's back?"

"I wanted to see you alone," I told him, noting the harsh look on his face.

Following him into the prophet's office, I felt more at ease. His manner seemed kind, and I was certain that he was concerned for my well-being. While I knew that my family had had difficulties with Warren in the past, I had been taught to trust him, yet as the prophet's mouthpiece he also inspired fear.

"I'm not doing very good," I told him as he took a seat in the swivel chair across from me. "I can't do this."

"Why not?" he asked me, looking puzzled.

"I just can't be Allen's wife. I don't want to be here, and I never wanted to be here."

"Well, you will learn to love him," he assured me.

"But he touches me and does things to me that I am not comfortable with and that I don't think are right or fully understand." I was sure that once he heard that, he would understand what was happening, and like Teressa had said, he would put a stop to Allen's behavior, but I was shocked by his reply.

"Well, that is not for you to decide. Your husband is a priesthood man," he said in his slow, hypnotic way. "You are to be obedient and submissive to your priesthood head."

"But Uncle Warren," I implored, "I don't know what he's doing to me. And he touches me in my private parts and touches me in ways that I don't like."

Warren knew without a doubt what I was talking about, even though I had no idea how to talk about such personal, secret things with the most powerful man in our community. I didn't even know words such as *sex* or *rape,* but I communicated to Warren the only way I could, and I knew that he understood.

"Allen is your priesthood head, and he knows what is right for you."

I could feel the tears welling up and a thick, dry ball forming in the back of my throat.

"A woman's role is to be obedient without question to her husband," he continued, his narrow, black eyes boring a hole into me. "He is your priesthood head and will later lead you to the Celestial Kingdom, but only if he considers you a good priesthood obedient, submissive wife."

"I'm sorry I failed this test that the prophet and God have given me," I said. "Will you please just let me be separated from him? Please, I want a release," I begged. A "release" in the FLDS is like a divorce. There is no such thing as a legal divorce. No member would think of going to court first, even if the marriage was legal. Only the prophet can grant a release, and it is extremely rare for a couple to request a release from a marriage that was revealed by God through the prophet. Just by asking, I was taking a great risk.

"I just can't do this," I said. "I'm sorry. I just, I beg you to please let me out—"

"You are doing insane things that will lead you to be unfaithful," Uncle Warren firmly interrupted. "Sometimes in our lives, we are told to do things that we don't feel are right. Because the Lord and the prophet tell us to, then they are right. You need to put your heart and feelings in line. You need to go and repent. You are not living up to your vows. You are not being obedient and submissive to your priesthood head. And that is your problem.

"You need to go home and repent and give yourself mind, body, and soul to Allen because he is your priesthood head and obey him without question because he knows what's best for you. He will be directed by the priesthood and the spirit of God to know how to handle you."

Clearly, Uncle Warren had not been listening to me. I had explained that Allen was touching me in private areas in ways I hated, and Warren didn't flinch. He was completely unmoved. The only response Warren had was for me to go home, repent, and obey. I had no idea what I was supposed to repent for, and the only thing I could think of was being obedient to Allen. Somehow, all of this was my fault, because I wasn't doing my duty in the eyes of the priesthood.

"Well, can you at least talk to Allen?" I asked.

Rising from his chair, Warren crossed the room to the bookshelf just behind me. Removing a volume of *In Light and Truth,* he sat back down by the desk. Skimming the pages, he marked a few that he felt were relevant to my situation. I knew the book well; it was the one that he had used to teach us at Alta Academy.

"I want you to go home and read the marriage covenant

every day. And I want you to remember the covenants you have made to God and yourself," he instructed, handing me the book. He also made it clear that I needed to stop confiding in my mother or anyone else about what was going on in my marriage.

"Can I come back and see you and let you know how things are going and maybe just get some words of comfort from you?"

"Well, you need to set that up through your husband," Uncle Warren said, rising from his chair to show me out. "He needs to be here when you come in. And I don't want you to come in here without him."

Any hope for a release faded away as I heard Uncle Warren's instructions. Not only had he denied me a release, he was sending me home to repent and submit my mind, body, and soul. Stepping out into the hot afternoon sun, I felt hollow and frozen, believing myself to be a very wicked person. What I was doing with Allen felt wrong, and I felt unclean for being part of it. As hard as I tried, I couldn't stop my tears.

"What happened?" Kassandra asked me when I emerged from the prophet's home that afternoon. She'd seen me go in to speak with Warren and had been watching from the kitchen window, waiting for me to come out. As soon as she saw me leave, she dashed over to meet me.

"Kassandra, I can't talk to you," I said, trying to hide my tears. "I'm not supposed to talk to any of my sisters or anyone about it. I'm supposed to go home and obey my husband."

Allen was upset when he learned that I'd gone to Uncle Warren, but it didn't stop him from continuing to touch me and force himself on me. He justified his actions by saying that this was what needed to happen for us to have a baby; it was what the prophet had intended for us. Each night that we had relations, he held my salvation hostage. What made it even harder was that he'd make me watch him touch himself, and left me feeling even more embarrassed and impure. Worse, he'd taken to manipulating me and my ignorance about sex, telling me that a man could become very ill if he didn't have relations at least every few days.

I found it almost impossible to be obedient and do what Uncle Warren had directed. I couldn't just submit to the will of my husband, but my resistance left me feeling like I was failing in the eyes of God. When I resisted Allen's advances, he would condemn me for not obeying the prophet. When I gave in to him, as soon as he was done, he'd tell me that I was wicked for giving in to my mortal desires. Either way I was evil, and these mind games confused me terribly. Later I sensed that after he'd gotten what he wanted, he felt guilty, knowing that he'd violated me not just for the purpose of conceiving children. He absolved himself by passing his guilt on to me.

Somehow, I had gotten to the point where I could survive the abuse, but now I also had to deal with these mental games. Allen would continually use my emotions to free himself of his wrongdoing. While he was extremely soft-spoken and meek in public, behind closed doors I saw another side of him. Privately, he was calculating and controlling. Sometimes he would lose his temper.

As time wore on, Allen confided some of his fantasies and I was so turned off, I would shut my eyes and plug my ears. In addition, I came to see that he routinely painted his fingernails with clear polish, which was the only color that FLDS girls dared use. He told me that he liked his nails to look neat and clean, but the behavior struck me as very off-putting in a man.

After a while, I just became numb to the whole charade. I had to continually remind myself that I was doing this for my salvation in heaven, and that my goal in the meantime was to survive. I was willing to sacrifice happiness on earth for happiness in my next life, convinced that either Allen would change once we got to heaven or God would fix the situation.

It felt like we were having marital relations all the time, at least once or twice a week. Sometimes I would sleep in my mother's room just to avoid it. While I didn't want to give in to Allen, Uncle Warren had put my eternal salvation at risk and I had no choice but to surrender. While Warren Jeffs did not actually use the words "have sexual intercourse" when telling me what to do with my husband, his directives to "submit" and "give myself mind, body, and soul" to my husband meant just that. If Warren hadn't intended me to have sexual relations with Allen, he never would have required me to marry him with the commandment to "go forth and multiply and replenish the earth with good priesthood children." In a matter of weeks, my act of survival often became an act of submission.

The coming of summer helped to raise my spirits. That June we celebrated Uncle Roy's birthday, marking the beginning of the annual summer festivities. The community was beginning to prepare for the Pioneer Day parade, but sadly this year would not include the dancing girls. In the fall of 1999, Uncle Warren had banned performances and theatrical productions—especially dancing. With no TV or movies, this effectively put a stop to all forms of entertainment. He did so on the grounds that the end of the world was once again upon us, and we needed to focus on praying rather than lighthearted pleasures.

As Warren tightened his grip on the community, Kassandra grew more and more frustrated. Having the opportunity to help with various productions and the dancing girls had been one of her few outlets from Uncle Rulon's home and a source of fulfillment. My sister had earned quite a reputation for her creative choreography, and her work as a dance instructor had touched the lives of young members.

Kassandra was just nineteen when she married the eighty-three-year-old prophet, and it had become increasingly difficult for her to cope with the restrictions that came with being one of his many wives. After years of encouraging Rulon's wives to separate themselves from their families, Warren had recently commanded them to sever all their ties with the rest of the FLDS people. This way they would be at home under Warren's watchful eye. To Kassandra it seemed odd that Warren continued to marry his father to so many young, pretty girls, despite the fact that Rulon was far too infirm to be much of a husband.

In Kassandra's eyes, she was not a wife, she was just a number. She secretly longed just to hold the hand of a man she loved and take a quiet walk alone with him. But the longer she was married to the ailing Rulon, the more painfully obvious it became that she would never realize this kind of simple joy.

As Warren's newest set of regulations began to set in, Kassandra's frustration boiled over. She could see how Warren was manipulating and controlling his father's family, and this made it hard for her to obey his directives. Just like most of the Wall kids, Kassandra had always had a freer spirit than many FLDS people, and she began to push back against the oppressive force that was bottling her up. While our sister Rachel, who was also married to Rulon, tried hard to obey Warren and remain at home, Kassandra couldn't take the pressure. She continued to escape the constricting home environment by spending more time with our family and friends. Her desire to have an outlet and friendship, especially with some of the young men in the community, did not escape Uncle Warren's notice, and he admonished her for not being at home with her husband. However, Kassandra was determined to find a sliver of companionship, and she continued to act out.

I'd been married for just under three months when I celebrated my fifteenth birthday. As I turned a year older, I resolved to try to do a better job of following Uncle Warren's directives and doing everything that the prophet expected of me. But in order to do this, I knew I would have to bury many of my instincts; if I let them shine through, I would never make it. My only choice was to put on a different act, to persuade other people that I was happily doing my duty. If I convinced others, I might even be able to convince myself.

Allen took me horseback riding in the mountains to celebrate my special day, and his kindness made me wonder if
eventually I could grow to love him. His brother and sister-
in-law joined us for my birthday ride. I actually caught myself
enjoying time with the small group of people. That night, at
Uncle Fred's, the family had a birthday cake for me. As we
gathered for prayer afterward, Uncle Fred surprised me with
an "encouragement box." It was a big gift-wrapped box that
contained many smaller wrapped items that a woman would
need for a new home. There were measuring cups, utensils,
and tablecloths. At the very bottom, I found a small box containing a tiny wooden crib with a plastic baby doll wrapped
in a blue blanket.

"That's just a little encouragement to show you what you
can have," Uncle Fred said with a big smile.

We'd been having a good time. Everyone was laughing as
I opened each of the gifts, and a little unsure how to react, I
laughed along with them. I was touched by the thoughtful
present and by the family's taking a few minutes to honor
my birthday. When I got to the baby, though, I felt suddenly
pressured by the clear reminder that I was supposed to start
having children. The gift seemed like another directive.

Soon I started to feel like I had less and less time to think
about my own problems. About a month after my birthday, Uncle Fred assigned me the role of keeping Lily encouraged about life. Lily had returned to Hildale earlier in
the summer, lured back not by responsibility to her marriage
but by the boy who had won her heart before her arranged
marriage to Martin. I was told that prior to her return, she
had taken refuge at the home of her brother, who had also
left the FLDS, and the boy she liked had been instructed by
Warren and Fred to find Lily and convince her to return.
While it was not clear whether the boy made any promises
of a life together, he made Lily feel that he wanted her back
in the FLDS. In the end, the draw of his words was too much
for Lily to resist and she returned to Hildale, only to find out

I was my mother's eleventh child of her eventual fourteen, and we were close from the moment I was born.

As I grew up, Dad started calling me Goldilocks because of my long blond hair and how I skipped around the house.

Though I had many older sisters, the closest in age was seven years older than me. As a result, I grew up spending a lot of my time with my brothers.

Our annual camping trips offered a chance for many of my siblings to spend time together. In the vast spaces of the wilderness, we could roam freely without the secrecy of our normal lives.

My parents always tried to expose us to classical music even though we were in the FLDS. Here I am performing with my brothers and sisters in a violin recital in Salt Lake City.

FLDS members must wear church-sanctioned clothes at all times, even in warmer weather. The Utah summers could be brutal in our ankle-length Pioneer dresses, and for the boys constantly running around in collared shirts was incredibly uncomfortable. I'm in the front row on the left.

This photo of Dad, his three wives, and his younger children was taken in 1996. My mother stands behind Dad.

This photo was taken on Pioneer Day down in Short Creek when some of my sisters and I were in the Dancing Girls troop. I'm standing second from the right.

This picture of me and my father was taken at Alta Academy shortly before I was baptized in its basement "baptismal vault."

Warren often went on school excursions with us. He was our principal and was highly respected, so posing with him for a photo was considered special.

Here my brother is walking toward the highway on the day that Dad ordered him out of the house. In his hand is his sign that read DENVER. My mom later told me that leaving him on the highway that day was one of the hardest things she ever had to do.

I was staying with my sisters at the prophet's home in Hildale when I was invited to take a picture with the prophet Uncle Rulon. It was an incredible honor to have your picture taken with the prophet, and for years I cherished this photo.

When we were taken down to the Steed ranch, we were surrounded by our extended family and there were so many of us that we had to eat in shifts. Here my siblings and I stand with many of our cousins.

While we were at the Steed ranch, Dad and Mom were remarried. Here Dad and Mom are with Warren and Rulon in Rulon's living room, where the ceremony was performed.

Even today, Alta Academy still looks like an ordinary house, but it's a massive structure that stretches far away from the road. Abandoned and slated for demolition, it holds many memories from my younger years in Salt Lake.

One of Alta's secret cubby holes where women and children could hide if there was an unexpected raid by authorities.

Cryptic writing scrawled inside a secret hiding spot in Alta. Though they were never substantiated, rumors often circulated that the crawl spaces, which had locks on the outside, were used to correct disobedient children and wives.

Though our lives in Salt Lake were never perfect,
it was the only home I knew, and the only place I wanted to be.

When we arrived down in Short Creek, the landscape was quite
different from what I was used to. At first I found the inescapable red
rocks overpowering, but in time I grew to appreciate its beauty.

From the start, life at Uncle Fred's was difficult with so many kids from different families thrown together. Suddenly I was surrounded by a large group of girls aged twelve to eighteen, and at times the cliques that formed could be vicious. Here is a large group of my stepsisters outside of Uncle Fred's house. It was common for girls of the same family to make matching dresses, as seen here.

The move down to Uncle Fred's was hard on all of us and it grew even more difficult after Fred married Mom. As a result, we all grew incredibly close, relying on each other to get us through the tough times.

GRADE 2000

Celebrating my eighth-grade graduation with my mom. I was so proud when I graduated, but later that summer Warren would order all FLDS members to leave the Colorado City public school. Eighth grade would be the last I would complete.

The morning of my wedding day, the worst day of my life.
My face is so red from all the crying I'd been doing.

Here I am with Allen on our wedding day. My stepsisters and the other mothers at Fred's house worked for hours to turn my old bedroom into a "Honeymoon Hideout." It was a nice gesture, but their effort only emphasized the darkness I felt inside.

This picture was snapped right as Allen picked me up to carry me across the threshold. I covered my face to hide my tears.

"Allen and Elissa sealed for time and all eternity."

Several weeks after my wedding I received an encouragement box from Fred for my fifteenth birthday. Inside was a baby doll, and though no one said a word, the message was clear: the pressure was on for me to have children.

I often took refuge from Allen with my sisters and my mom, staying with them whenever I could so that I would not have to see him.

This photo of me and my sister was taken on my sixteenth birthday.

Here I am in my Ford Ranger truck driving around some of my
stepsisters and some other girls. Eventually that truck would
become my home, and I would spend my nights there
to avoid sharing a bed with Allen.

By my seventeenth birthday, things with Allen had grown
increasingly unstable. While my mom tried to cheer me up,
little could distract me from my problems.

My first Christmas morning shared with Lamont in Oregon.

The last time I saw my mother was the day after Fred's funeral,
where she met and spent a few stolen moments with her grandchild.
This photo was taken a few short months after I left the FLDS.

This picture, taken with Lamont and our two children,
was snapped not long before Warren's trial began.

Though Warren and his
defense attorney Tara
Isaacson made for an
intimidating pair, I did
my best to retain my
composure. As she put her
hand on his shoulder,
she said the words
"This man is innocent."

During his testimony at trial Allen asked the judge if he could stand.
While I was not surprised by this outlandish request,
it caused a great many whispers in the courthouse.

When the verdict had been delivered, I decided to break my silence
with the press and make a public statement. The journey to
that point had been a struggle, but for the first time in months,
I breathed a sigh of relief.

I carried this photo of Sherrie (left) and Ally (right) in my purse every day of the trial to give me strength when I felt weak.
Even now, I still bring it with me wherever I go to remind myself of what I am fighting for.

Today Lamont and I live with our two children. It has been a difficult road, but together we're building a better future for our kids and praying to God to help us get there.

the whole situation had been a cruel trap that had used her heart as bait.

Now I can see that Uncle Fred and Uncle Warren had been behind the whole thing. It was contradictory to see how they had enlisted a boy she wasn't even supposed to like to convince her to come back, and she was sickened that they had used her emotions against her. This heartbreaking betrayal and being back in her unhappy marriage pushed Lily closer to the edge, causing her to try, once again, to take her own life with an overdose of pills. Like her first attempt, this too was unsuccessful, and her behavior from then on was strictly regimented by one of Fred's wives.

If this wasn't bad enough, Lily had also been shunned for her attempt to get out, and she had few friends left in the community. During her short time on the outside, she'd cut her hair to just below her shoulders and given herself bangs. FLDS women are forbidden from cutting their hair or even wearing it loose; to do so was considered disobedient to the prophet. Getting a haircut was what the very few girls who did leave did, since it was a show of defiance against the church. Now, though, her haircut only marked her as an outcast, and no matter where she went people identified her as trouble.

Given the extent of her isolation, I wanted to reach out to Lily. At the time, I was also finding myself increasingly isolated. Natalie and I had all but lost touch. As a married woman, I no longer fit in with my old friends, who were part of the young teenage group. I also didn't fit in with the older adult married group. I was a fifteen-year-old bride, stuck in the middle. But I did have Lily.

Uncle Fred told me I would be held accountable for any of her missteps, and I became consumed by setting a good example. To encourage Lily, Uncle Fred sent the two of us on a camping trip with our husbands, and our stepbrother Jonathan and his wife, Jennie, came along. We did our best to enjoy ourselves, and for the most part we succeeded. Martin brought a four-wheeler, and we all went for rides. Jennie had a bubbly personality and brightened our trip. I really enjoyed spending time with her, and we became friends during our time in the wilderness. I was excited to find a "married" friend.

As part of my survival strategy, I had taken Warren's words to heart, and by the time of that trip, I had stopped fighting Allen when he tried to have relations with me, realizing that it was something I just had to do. At times it also got me things I needed. I hated to have to ask Allen for money, but it was a lot easier to do if he was happy with me. Life was more bearable when he wasn't angry, and I preferred getting the sex over with rather than being forced to watch him masturbate, or worse, having him put his fingers inside me to get him turned on.

On the camping trip, I tried to fit in and behave like any other married woman—talking and laughing when I could, trying to feel free and have some fun. It was easier to cut loose and relax away from the confines of Short Creek. This trip more than any other time proved to me that I could maintain the appearance of happiness for Allen and everyone else. I was keeping sweet just like they'd always told me to, and in the process I started to forget some of the doubts that I'd had about the FLDS as my wedding approached. For the first time in months, the questions I'd been asking myself about why God forced us to marry and broke families apart began to subside. Finally I was learning how to smile for the camera.

Still, there was always a lingering doubt about how sustainable the strategy was. A general fear resided in my stomach, a feeling that unhappiness was just around the corner. To survive, I had managed to trick myself into making an intolerable situation seem tolerable, but I had no idea how long I could keep it up. It was hard work, suppressing the real me, the loud voice that didn't want to be with Allen and didn't want to be married. I couldn't keep that part of me silent forever. Eventually the chorus that I had quieted would start to escape. The question was not if it would happen, but when.

CHAPTER FIFTEEN

THE DESTRUCTION IS UPON US

The judgments are coming very soon and our only
survival is to keep sweet and obey what God tells us to do.
—RULON JEFFS

As 2002 rapidly approached, Uncle Warren again began proclaiming the coming of Zion. He delivered ominous sermons warning about the mass destructions that were imminent and commanded all faithful members to waste no time in relocating to Short Creek.

I never knew how to feel about these supposed life-altering orations. "The wicked on this land are about to be destroyed," Uncle Warren declared during one church meeting. "This is the land where the new city, the city of Zion, will be built. This land must be swept clean first. After the Great Destructions, everybody's going to be wiped off, except for the priesthood people, under President Jeffs, who have kept sweet."

I knew that as a good priesthood girl I should heed these cautionary statements, but my fifteen-year-old questioning mind couldn't grasp a concept so ominous. For months Warren had been directing the priesthood people to congregate in southern Utah for the destructions. The 2002 Winter Olympic Games were coming to Salt Lake City that February, and people from all over the world would be gathering.

Warren told us God was luring them to Salt Lake for the destructions, and all the FLDS followers still living in the Salt Lake Valley were directed to sell their homes and move to the twin cities to be with the priesthood people for the coming of Zion. A flood of followers overwhelmed the twin cities of Colorado City and Hildale. With no homes, they were instructed to move in with members already living in the area until they were assigned homes by the priesthood. But the influx was so great that some folks ended up camping out on the properties of others. Those who did find accommodations were living crammed two and three families to a home.

I didn't know it at the time, but my father and Mother Audrey were among the throngs of people from Salt Lake who'd packed up their lives and headed south to be in place for the ascent to heaven. About a month after we'd been taken away from him, Dad had been rebaptized into the priesthood, but by that point, we had already been reassigned and he was not allowed to contact us. He had continued to live with Audrey at the Claybourne Avenue house for the next couple of years, and over time, Justin, Jacob, Brad, and Caleb had joined him there.

Brad was seventeen when Warren directed Dad and Audrey to Short Creek, and trying desperately to finish high school. While he'd been in foster care for some of the time after his escape from Uncle Fred's, he'd recently left his foster home and been forced to find another living arrangement. Dad had offered to let him stay temporarily, and Brad had only been at the house for a short time when Dad announced the move to southern Utah.

Warren made it clear that while Dad and Audrey were welcome, my brothers were not. He did not want what he perceived as their rebellious influence anywhere near Short Creek. As far as the priesthood was concerned, parents were required to abandon "unworthy" children, and soon the practice became commonplace. At the prophet's request, FLDS fathers drove problem children to neighboring towns, dropped them off, and told them never to contact their family again. Though I'm sure Dad didn't want to abandon his sons, his devotion to the priesthood, like that of hundreds of other parents, was blind and absolute. He followed Warren's command and told all of his sons that they could not join him and Audrey in Short Creek.

Because they were nineteen, Justin and Jacob were able to find a place of their own, but they struggled to make ends meet, since neither of them had a high school education. Brad again had to find a place to live, and finally a friend offered him a room to rent. Brad worked hard to keep a full-time job and stay in school so that he could complete the twelfth grade. In the months to come, we'd learn that he had become deathly ill and was hospitalized. Though he recovered, his illness put him out of a job and kept him from graduating high school. Soon he was homeless, living out of his car and barely able to buy food. Eventually he began to call Mom. Although she was upset, there was nothing she would do to help him since she was entwined in the FLDS culture and frame of mind.

As for Caleb, the prospect of leaving him behind was not as simple. He was in seventh grade at the public school, nowhere near an age where he could take care of himself, and it was obvious that Dad felt obligated to figure out a more responsible plan for him. The answer came from a former FLDS couple named Ron and Jamie Barlow, who lived in Hurricane, about twenty minutes outside St. George. Dad agreed to pay them to take care of Caleb. The Barlows were eager to return to the religion and had been repenting at the prophet's directive to regain their standing in the church. They had not yet been given permission to move back to the community, but they hoped that taking care of Caleb would show their loyalty and faith.

It was a couple of months before I learned that my father was in Colorado City. When I finally saw him, our brief reunion was filled with mixed emotions. He and Audrey were living in a little camper on someone's front lawn. The move had taken them from a spacious, beautiful home to almost no home at all. Dad wanted to build something, but as the owner of all the land in Short Creek, the church said he couldn't because time was too short.

Seeing Dad was a joyful moment but it was also painful. Knowing that the priesthood wouldn't allow me to view him as my father made our meeting awkward and I didn't know how to react, other than with a hug. Our past was filled with so much hurt that it was hard for me when the conversation turned in that direction. He told me he'd only recently learned of my marriage to Allen and expressed his frustration at having not been there to try to stop it even though it probably wouldn't have done any good. When he asked me how I was, I simply said I was fine. It was inappropriate to complain, and I was doing my best to keep sweet.

In the end, I was so caught up with what was going on in my own life that I didn't have the time or energy to be angry with my father. I had larger issues to confront. In early 2002, I began to suspect that I was pregnant. Terrified, I purchased four pregnancy tests during a shopping trip to St. George with my mother. I was still afraid to tell her what was happening in my marriage and hid them from her by having her wait in the car while I went inside to buy the groceries. As soon as I got home, I locked myself in the bathroom to learn my fate. Carefully, I read the instructions over and over. Each test was slightly different, and I was getting myself very confused. When the first one revealed a positive result, I moved on to the next, horrified to see a plus sign pop up again on the applicator's screen. Unconvinced, I used all four tests and was momentarily heartened when one seemed to come up with a negative result. But upon rereading the directions, I realized that I had made a mistake and a sinking feeling took root in my stomach.

I sat frozen for a long time, staring at the four tests lined up along the linoleum of the bathroom floor. Two months earlier, one of the mothers in Fred's home had shown a video to Lily and me explaining the facts of life and what happens to a woman's body when she is pregnant. Now that video was my life. My fate had been decided for me again.

Disposing of the four tests, I kept the results to myself and went about my routine, never telling Allen that he was going to be a father. For weeks I kept my secret, contemplating how I was going to overcome this new hurdle and frightened by how it would affect my life. One night in the spring, I was awakened by a horrible pain in my abdomen and raced to the bathroom to vomit. I barely made it down the hall before I started throwing up, and I realized that blood was running down my leg. I honestly thought I was dying, that God was killing me for my disobedience to the prophet and Allen. The only place I could think to go was to my mother's room, where she was asleep. I wanted desperately to wake her, but I was too scared I'd get her into trouble. She'd been warned to stay out of my business, and I knew that she'd need to abide by that directive.

I sat in the bathtub for nearly four hours, bleeding and cramping. I couldn't bring myself to go to my mother—I couldn't burden her. Finally, when the pain began to subside, I took a shower to clean myself up and figured out that I had lost the baby. My first thought was to call Kassandra and tell her what had happened, but I blamed myself for the miscarriage. At the time, I believed that miscarriages happened because God believed the mother was unworthy. I was sure that I had been punished for being wicked, and I didn't want anyone else to know.

For the next four days, I could barely gather the strength to get out of bed, and I refused to mention a word to anyone about what had happened. All I wanted was to sleep forever. Kassandra stopped by several times and finally got fed up with my apparent laziness because I was in bed with no excuse. Despite her pleas to explain what was wrong, I couldn't summon the words. All I could do was lie there in silence.

That winter, Uncle Fred eagerly informed Allen and me that we would be moving to a new home on church land, a two-bedroom trailer in a small trailer park across the state line in Colorado City, just next door to one of Audrey's sons. The trailer would be Uncle Fred's gift to us, and we could decorate it however we wanted.

Young elders in the FLDS often received property during one of the many priesthood meetings held throughout the year or during a private meeting with the bishop. Young men who had been deemed worthy participated in a lottery in which a hat containing the addresses of available plots of land in the community was literally passed around. Whichever plot a man picked was where he was allowed to build his home. The twin towns were a self-contained community where we would barter services amongst ourselves. Usually homes were built using this barter system, and labor was often donated as part of the church's Saturday work projects.

Allen was electrified over the prospect of having his own space, but I couldn't stand the thought of moving away from my mother. Worse was the idea of being alone with Allen in a trailer every night. Although the trailer was little, it had a decent-sized living room, dining room, and kitchen combo: and the two bedrooms were separated by a bathroom. Luckily for me, it wasn't ready to be lived in yet, and Allen enthusiastically took to the project of refinishing the inside. Whenever he wasn't working at his job, he spent time fixing up the trailer. I was glad to have him so preoccupied, as it gave me a break from him and allowed me to spend more time with my mom and sisters. Having a goal seemed to take some of Allen's focus off of me for once, and I was grateful that the project went very slowly.

Though I was not looking forward to moving in with him, I focused on enjoying the little things about life. For many months, I suppressed my feelings as best I could and tried to make the situation livable. Almost daily, I tried to convince myself that this was going to work out and that someday I would feel different about him, but I was still hesitant and extremely uncomfortable about having man-wife relations with him.

Early that spring, some of Allen's family helped us work on the trailer. We spent the evening roasting marshmallows and hot dogs over an open fire in the yard. When they left for home and I waved good-bye, I thought how pleasant the day had been. But like everything with Allen, this good moment would become tainted.

I was just finishing cleaning up when he came behind me whispering in my ear that we should stay the night and christen the trailer by making it ours.

"You're crazy," I replied, not wanting to sleep with him at all, let alone in an empty trailer with no power, no furniture, and no heat. I was still dealing with the emotional fallout from my miscarriage and was not interested in doing anything intimate. But he insisted.

"It'll be fun," he coaxed.

Shaking my head, I looked at the sparse surroundings and the still-wet paint on the walls. This was not a home yet, and the space seemed awkward and cold. We were standing in the bedroom, where he had blown up an air mattress and thrown a sleeping bag over it. Even the sight of the makeshift bed was too much for me, and as I turned to leave, I felt Allen's firm grip on my arm. I protested, and he pulled me back into the room. The sexual encounters between Allen and me were often overpowering, with him in control, but on this night I felt absolutely helpless. Even though during this period I was trying to set my feelings aside and submit to him, he would still disrespect me and force me even when I said no.

I struggled to get away, but he pulled me close and pushed me down on the mattress. I rolled off onto the floor, telling him, "I don't want to have anything to do with you tonight." Relentless, he grabbed at my clothes and pressed me back on the bed. I was trapped—not just physically but mentally. Allen was on top of me, ignoring my pleas to stop. The smell of fresh paint enveloped me as I started to count in my head; soon it would be over.

With our one-year anniversary approaching, I started sewing a special dress in my favorite shade of pink to try and get excited for the day. On the morning of April 23, I was taking extra time to perfect my hairstyle and get ready. All of a sudden, one of the mothers called upstairs to me, informing me that Uncle Fred wanted to see me at once.

I didn't even have my shoes on when I raced downstairs to find a uniformed Colorado City police officer standing next to Uncle Fred. He was Rodney Holm, the same officer who'd plagued my brothers and taken Caleb from Fred's house after the mix-up about Fred's tapes.

"I want you to go get some shoes on and go with this officer," Uncle Fred instructed. Momentarily shocked I felt my heart race as I tried to figure out what I had done wrong, but no one would give me an answer.

"Rodney, can you please tell me why I'm going with you?" I asked. When he didn't respond, I grew frustrated and told him that he didn't have a right to take me without an explanation. But Uncle Fred insisted I get my shoes and go with him.

My fear and frustration turned to tears as I ran to my room. Nobody seemed to care what was happening, and Mom wasn't at home. She'd been working for a local woman, caring for her handicapped infant, and was out of the house during the day. I called Kassandra in desperation. She was with Mom at the babysitting job, and the two were frantic when I told them what was going on, but there was nothing they could do to help me.

As soon as I went back downstairs, I was handcuffed and escorted to the police car that waited outside as the entire Jessop family looked on. By the time we pulled up to the station I was in hysterics. Rodney left me in the car while he went inside, and after a few minutes he emerged and told me he had to take me to the Mark Twain, a restaurant in town. I had no idea why. When we got there, Rodney paraded me inside, still in handcuffs, and that was when I saw Allen. I felt myself being handcuffed to him and heard laughter. I turned to see Uncle Fred with two of his wives, and Lily and Nancy and their husbands. All I could do was stand there embarrassed with tear-stained cheeks in the dress that I had worked so hard to sew.

Everyone had been in on the joke. While I smiled during the party, inside I was seething. I was humilated and deeply hurt. Allen knew how I felt about the local police, after the way they'd treated my brothers and me. But he just didn't get it. After the lunch, he was grinning as he helped me into his car. "Do you like what I did for you?" he asked.

I exploded. "Do you know what that was like for me?" I shouted in his face. "You take me to my mother's work right now! I hate your guts."

Later, I was able to see that Allen had intended it to be a funny surprise for me, but the fact that he would have me arrested as a joke only proved that he was completely out of touch with me and my feelings. When he saw how upset I was, he showed up with a handful of roses, but I couldn't get past it. Included in the bouquet was a handwritten note: "Dear Elissa, you are the flower of my life. Love, Al." But there was no apology.

Even though I knew the card was motivated by good intentions, I didn't believe his words. In his attempt to live up to his priesthood responsibilities to teach and train me to be a "better" wife, he'd repeatedly hurt me physically and emotionally to the core of my soul. In a loving marriage, actions such as this note should have been special and warmed my heart, but instead it felt like Allen was trying to make me forget the past. While he'd said he was sorry for countless things during our marriage, he never said it for the reason that mattered most. I resented the way he made me feel like he had a right to my body just because I had been given to him as a wife. For this he never asked forgiveness, or seemed the least bit sorry.

Our first anniversary marked a turning point for me. After that moment when Rodney handcuffed me to Allen, I wondered if I had the energy to try to make the marriage function anymore. Any illusion that I had used to convince myself that it was going to work out was shattered, and all the bottled-up heartache that I'd been trying to ignore came rushing to the surface.

Allen still seemed to allow himself to believe that things were going okay. He continued to send me notes and letters. "Carry this card with you always to remind you just how special you are to me," read one of the pre-printed greetings. "Knowing you are a part of my life makes me smile at the craziest times. I would rather spend time with you than any-one else. You are the love of my life and this card will re-mind you about how much I'll always care about you. Love, Allen G. Steed."

That he would sign his full name to such a note only con-firmed how contradictory his words and actions were. We were still strangers to each other. As hard as I had tried, I couldn't make myself love him, and more than ever I was convinced I never would. No matter how many times he pro-fessed his love for me, I knew that you don't hurt people that you love. The way he was treating me I felt like he viewed me not as a partner and equal, but as a possession. Some-thing deep in my heart knew that no man, woman, or child should be anyone's chattel and be robbed of their God-given free will.

Over the next few weeks, I was able to gain some dis-tance from Allen. I had been working two jobs, one as a health aide to the handicapped infant that my mother cared for. Another was as a dressmaker. I had befriended the owner of the local fabric shop, and she and her daughters had agreed to sell my creations on consignment in her Hildale boutique. I'd always had a talent for sewing and had begun putting it to good use making dresses for girls. My profits were about twenty dollars apiece. Soon I was getting special orders, and I was grateful to be less dependent on Allen for money.

When Teressa arrived from Canada for a visit in late spring of 2002, she could see how upset I was. Without hope about my marriage, I felt dark, empty, and lifeless.

Teressa knew that something needed to change, and she insisted to both my mother and me that I speak to Uncle Warren again.

In the coming weeks, I set up another appointment, but when Uncle Warren stepped out into the waiting room, he was unhappy to see that Allen wasn't with me. I had brought my mother instead.

"I want to speak to you without Allen present," I told him nervously, relieved when he agreed to hear me.

"How are you doing?" he asked as Mom and I took a seat, and we began to engage in small talk. But Uncle Warren was direct and quickly moved the conversation along. "What do you need?"

I outlined the reason for my visit. "Well, it's been an entire year, and I have tried to be obedient and submit to Allen. But I am still nowhere, and I don't trust Allen and I most definitely don't love him. I don't feel like I can continue to be his wife, let alone have his children."

After a long pause, Uncle Warren asked me about my mother. "What is your relationship like with your mother?"

"Well," I said, smiling and looking over at Mom, "she's my best friend and confidante. I love her so much. And she has helped me through this."

"Have you been saying your prayers and taking actions to stay obedient and keeping your faith up?"

"Oh, yes, yes I have," I told Uncle Warren, eager to show him how hard I had been trying. "I have been doing everything I know how to do to make this work. I have given myself to Allen totally and completely. And I tried so hard to be submissive and obedient to him even though I didn't agree with anything that he wanted."

Believing that I had proven myself a worthy wife and done all I could to try to make my marriage work, I felt optimistic that Warren would see that I was not at fault for what was happening between Allen and me and would release me from the marriage.

He crossed his legs and took a breath before speaking. "You need to break off your relationship with your mother," he began. "To break away from the tight close bond that you two have. You need to put your loyalties in your husband, not your mother." He turned to address Mom. "You are being a meddling mother, and you need to let your daughter go and do what she is told to do by Allen even though neither of you agree with what is going on."

I was stunned and confused by Uncle Warren's directive. "Well, Uncle Warren, I don't know what else to do. I have done everything I know how to do."

"You go back and be obedient. And you give yourself mind, body, and soul to that man because he's your priesthood head. The prophet and I have confidence that he will do what he is told to do. We don't question what the priesthood does. We remember that the priesthood is again on earth. And the prophet is again on earth. And whatever he directs to be done is to be done without question. If you are not careful," he cautioned, "you will lose your faith and fall away. You will lose the opportunity that you have to establish a salvation and a place in the kingdom of heaven. Allen will lead you to the Celestial Kingdom, and if you are not worthy, you will not have a place there. You need to spend more time at home with your husband."

"But Uncle Warren," I said, "I hate having husband-wife relations with him."

"You are being very selfish. You need to set aside your feelings and do what you are told to do," he said without sympathy.

His response flattened me. "I don't know what to do because you've got to do something," I said. "It is impossible for me to love this man."

"You know, you have no right to feel that way," Warren told me, his tone growing hostile. I was speechless as he continued to lecture my mother and me until he concluded the meeting.

In the weeks that followed, I did little to change my behavior toward Mom, but following Uncle Warren's directive, she became less and less accessible. I'd long been avoiding moving into the trailer with Allen, but Mom and Rachel were instructed to move all of my stuff for me, and all at once I was out of Fred's house. My mother was trying to follow Uncle Warren's instructions and stay out of my marriage, but that also meant staying away from me. Kassandra, too, was being directed to stay at home and pray. Uncle Rulon was not well and Warren wanted his dozens of wives close by and focusing solely on the prophet.

Relegated to the house, Kassandra did her best to keep her spirits up. In a later conversation with Kassandra, she told me of a very disturbing incident that had happened in the prophet's home. One day she was in the dining room with several other wives and Rulon's sons Isaac and Nephi, waiting to pray over the noon meal. Uncle Rulon came in and sat down for lunch. He was very quiet and said nothing for a few moments. Then he leaned forward as if he was about to say something important, and pounding his fist on the table once, twice, three times, he announced, "I want my job back!"

Everyone at the table sat looking at one another, not knowing how to respond. Rulon's mind was not always there, and no one could really tell if his thoughts were running away from him or if this was something else altogether. Kassandra sat watching as some of the prophet's wives tried to calm him down. They assured him that he still had his job, but he was adamant.

"No, I don't," he shouted. "I want to take care of my people!"

As the sound of his fists on the wooden table hung in the air, people assumed Uncle Rulon was experiencing a moment of dementia. On the contrary, this was a display of lucidity. While it was never really clear what level of involvement he'd actually had in governing the people since his first stroke back in 1998, there was no question that the church had grown increasingly strict with Warren speaking for the prophet. Now, in this one dramatic moment, it seemed Rulon realized what had been taken away from him. But it was too late for him to get it back.

Uncle Warren was immediately summoned. He arrived to find his father edgy and inconsolable.

"I want my job back!" the prophet told his son.

"But Father, I'm just helping you," Warren insisted, assuring Rulon that he was still in charge and that he had never lost his position. On this day it seemed that he did not believe his son—and neither did Kassandra.

CHAPTER SIXTEEN

DEATH COMES TO SHORT CREEK

"He Shall Be Renewed"
—TITLE OF SONG BY WARREN JEFFS

When the Winter Olympics passed without the end of the world coming, Warren made us all feel that we had again been "exceedingly blessed" with more time to repent and purify ourselves. The Lord wanted a perfect people, and he didn't feel that he had that in us yet.

As a part of his mission to make us more perfect, it appeared that Warren started to use any excuse he could find to tighten his grip on the church, ostracizing various male members—even high-level officials—and often directing them to leave FLDS property. Such was the case with Winston Blackmore, the bishop in Bountiful, whom Warren began to aggressively "handle" in the summer of 2002.

For weeks Uncle Warren had been hinting that something would happen and saying that he had "a very important message from Father." He told us to "prepare" ourselves because the news would "rock" us to our very core, but he never elaborated on the details. Once he felt confident that he had laid the proper foundation, he made the proclamation. We were all assembled in the meetinghouse when Uncle Warren assumed his position at the podium. On the stage behind him, Uncle Rulon sat in his designated chair beside Uncle Fred and several other church elders. Warren had taken steps to make sure that the message was going out to all of the faithful. The meeting was also being piped through phone lines to the worshippers in Canada eleven hundred miles away. While Warren always started his orations with a reminder that his words were coming from the prophet, Uncle Rulon himself rarely spoke aside from the usual "Brother Warren speaks for me."

Now Uncle Warren primed us again for the impending news. In his slow monotone, he delivered the bombshell. "Winston Blackmore has been aspiring to position," he said. "He is pushing his own words beyond that of the prophet. He is seeking power and aspiring to power and is in need of serious reprimand." Warren then instructed the people to destroy or turn in any tapes or writings produced by Uncle Winston, in particular any stories of priesthood history.

Everyone was stunned into silence. Known affectionately to the extended FLDS congregation as Uncle Wink, Winston Blackmore was a well-respected member of the church who held an enormous amount of influence. He had been ordained as a bishop by the previous prophet, Leroy Johnson, and during his tenure he proved to be a kind and reasonable man. Many of the people held more love and respect for Winston than Warren, who was feared more than loved.

"Brother Winston is offered the hand of repentance, but he has been handled by the prophet," Warren declared.

Uncle Rulon was next given a microphone. The prophet could no longer stand easily and remained seated for the announcement. In the past, Uncle Rulon had spoken to the people, but recently he would ramble and repeat himself until Uncle Warren stepped in to take the microphone. On this day, his voice was weak and at times inaudible. The entire congregation, and particularly those assembled in Canada, strained to hear what he was about to tell us.

"If you people in Canada just stand behind Elder Winston Blackmore, it will be okay," Uncle Rulon uttered thinly over the speaker system.

Uncle Warren quickly bent down to correct his father. Congregants in the front rows overheard him whispering, "No, Father, that is not right."

The prophet looked at his son as if confused and then implored, "Oh yes, do what Brother Warren has told you."

Warren interrupted, booming into the microphone, "Give your loyalties to the prophet."

With that, the meeting abruptly ended and questions immediately swirled over what had happened to make Uncle Winston a target of reprimand. It appeared Winston's beliefs had been more in line with those of former prophet Leroy Johnson than those of the Jeffses. Like Uncle Roy, Winston seemed to believe that there was room in the church for people to make mistakes and be human. His stance on purity was not nearly as vigorous as either Warren's or his father's, and he had produced teaching materials, but his beliefs were nothing new and didn't seem to be cause for such a dramatic dismissal.

When the fallout from the announcement began to subside, it was quietly whispered that Winston's punishment came about because he had been questioning the extreme direction in which Warren had been taking the church. It was rumored that Warren and Winston had had many confrontations in the days and weeks before Warren went public. People said Winston saw that Warren was being dishonest in his communications with his father concerning the people and the church and manipulating him and decisions being made. They disagreed on how Warren was treating members that he deemed unredeemable; he sent them away, while Winston often refused to give up on them. I also heard that Warren went so far as to send Winston a list of people that he wanted cut off from the church completely, but reportedly Winston resisted.

The select few who were in the front seats the day of the announcement had taken note that the prophet's original words were at odds with what Uncle Warren had said.

Looking back, I see that Warren timed the announcement perfectly. Rulon's health had been in rapid decline, and

Winston Blackmore was one of the few men whose influence could turn people against Warren. If Warren waited until after Rulon's death to make such an accusation against Winston, people would have questioned his motives and doubted the directive, but having Uncle Rulon onstage and "supporting" Warren's claims made it unquestionable.

Warren used the community's sincere belief that the prophet would continue to live for hundreds of years to justify his commands and teachings. For much of my life, Uncle Rulon and Warren had been preaching that Rulon would be the last prophet on earth. They taught that he would never die; rather he would be "renewed"; once again he would be a man in his twenties who would continue on as the prophet living with his sixty-plus wives. In his renewed state, Rulon would lead us to Zion after the destructions and live for three hundred years. This idea was regularly discussed and universally accepted in the FLDS. We embraced this prophecy with all our hearts and the song that Uncle Warren wrote late that summer, narrating the glories of Rulon's renewal. I'll never forget the intense emotion in the meetinghouse as the people raised their voices in unison to the chorus of this song:

> For he shall run and leap on Zion's streets of gold.
> Eye hath not seen nor ear hath heard the glory
>   he shall know.
> We love him so
> His body will then be renewed, restored as in his youth
> His handmaidens shall be increased and great will be
>   his seed
> His people shall rejoice in him
> The story tell again
> The Lord has worked a miracle
> Our prophet has been healed.

Some of Rulon's wives had even been given baby cribs to keep in their rooms as an incentive to stay pure for Uncle

Rulon's imminent rebirth, when he would begin to create offspring again.

Until that could happen, Uncle Warren had been standing in and assuming the care of Uncle Rulon's family. For years, Uncle Rulon's wives had been conditioned to go to Warren—not their husband—with any and all concerns. Whether it was about the household or even their own personal feelings and life, they were required to check in with Warren regularly and keep him apprised of what they were doing and where they were going. Some of the women had even confided in Warren about female medical concerns such as endometriosis. They were required to spell out in detail everything that they were experiencing, before they could be granted Warren's permission to see a doctor.

These intrusions by Warren only alienated Kassandra further from him. She told me that she and Warren never saw eye to eye, and she used every opportunity to circumvent him and deal directly with Uncle Rulon. When she wanted permission for something, she tried to ask her husband and not Warren. Her actions aggravated Warren, and he never missed a chance to reprimand her. As Rulon grew feebler, Warren's invasions only escalated, eventually becoming unavoidable and impacting her life in frustrating ways. Whereas before he'd been a nuisance, now his interest was inescapable and his constant monitoring and control followed her wherever she went. In response, Kassandra grew more independent, frequently disobeying many things, including the curfew that Warren had imposed on all the wives.

With Rulon's health failing, most of the prophet's young wives spent the summer of 2002 at home praying for his renewal. They all dreamed of the days when they could start to produce children with Rulon—even going so far as to sew baby clothes in anticipation. But Kassandra wanted nothing to do with that. She continued to leave the compound whenever possible, and she'd been caught sneaking out on several occasions. Unbeknownst to Uncle Warren, Kassandra had begun a friendship with a young FLDS member named Ryan Musser, who was actually one of Rulon's grandsons. They shared a close, secret bond, and her trust in him gave her an outlet for her bottled-up emotions. Ryan was the one person whom she felt she could confide in without the threat of her words being reported back to Warren.

As fall approached, a rift grew as some people— particularly those in Canada—disagreed with Warren's ac- cusations about Uncle Wink. Meanwhile, Winston appeared unwilling to back down, and simply continued to do what he had always done. Warren had sent messages to the people in Canada, telling them, "You are either with the prophet or against him," making it very hard for people to pick a side. A division opened up, and with questions of loyalty and power looming overhead, no one knew how the priesthood would resolve it.

On Sunday, September 8, I walked with my mother into the meetinghouse for church. Upon our arrival, I noticed that the rows of chairs where Rulon's wives usually sat were empty. Immediately I sensed that something was wrong, and my suspicion only grew when I noticed that Uncle War- ren's family was also absent from their seats just behind the prophet's family. Sitting with my mother and sisters in our usual spot, I overheard whispers that Uncle Rulon had been taken to the hospital.

The meeting began with Uncle Fred presiding. He stood at the pulpit and solemnly informed the congregation that the prophet was very ill and had been rushed to the hospital. Everything proceeded as usual with the opening prayer and each and every member exerting faith for the prophet's re- newal. Several minutes into the meeting, Uncle Warren's voice boomed over the PA system. He was calling from the hospital, where he was holding vigil by his father's bedside. "The prophet has had surgery," Warren reported in his usual monotone. "He is doing fine."

An eerie silence fell over the room as we all prayed to

God on Uncle Rulon's behalf. About forty-five minutes passed before Uncle Warren came over the speakers with a second, devastating announcement. "The prophet has passed away," he related in a somber tone. "Say your prayers."

A solemn hush blanketed the meeting hall. I sat waiting for Uncle Warren to call back to tell us that God had performed a miracle and Uncle Rulon had been renewed. But the service ended, and in bewilderment, I followed the rest of the members out of the church.

Shortly after Rulon's death, Warren informed us that the prophet's renewal would now be much like that of Jesus Christ, except that Uncle Rulon would stay among us mortals as our leader. While we all expected that Uncle Rulon would soon reappear in his renewed form, the church began planning his funeral, to be held on September 12. The people tried to understand God's design in taking the prophet in death. The only way we could find comfort was to have enough faith that we would witness a great miracle.

On the day of Uncle Rulon's funeral, the program informed us that the prophet was presiding over his own service and remained the highest priesthood authority in attendance. Warren consoled us by saying that his father was "in the next room" and could hear and see all that was unfolding. To members of the FLDS, the term "in the next room" means that a person has crossed the thin veil into the spirit world. Uncle Warren, as the prophet's ordained first counselor, was there simply to administer his father's will. As the organ played, my eyes traveled to the casket in the center of the room. The prophet was inside, and I was afraid he had no way out.

During the viewing, I had kept waiting for him to sit up and address the people. I would later learn that I wasn't alone in that misguided belief that day. But no one dared to say anything; we just waited as we'd been instructed. We looked on through our tears as the prophet's wives sang him one last song: "He Has Been Renewed." Reading ahead in the program, I noticed that Uncle Warren would be speaking soon. He had listed himself as "Elder Warren S. Jeffs for

President Rulon T. Jeffs." Remembering that moment now, I see clearly that he was silently assuming the prophet's position by designating himself the continued spokesperson of his father.

Looking up, I saw that Uncle Warren was no longer at the podium. His brother Isaac had begun delivering the benediction. As the service drew to a close, everyone was on pins and needles waiting to see what would happen. We'd all had our chance to pay our respects to the prophet, but now the coffin was closed and the ceremony was winding down.

Our hearts were even heavier when the sad truth became evident, Uncle Rulon was to be buried in the ground and Uncle Warren would be delivering the graveside dedication. Not only was his casket closed, but it also was going to be covered beneath six feet of earth. I stood paralyzed in fear, worrying that by burying the prophet, he would never be able to get out. And looking around at the distraught mourners I was certain that I was not alone in my concern. Nevertheless, we were made to believe that he would soon be among us again and we were to wait. As the casket was lowered and the final benediction delivered, the entire community stood in expectation until Uncle Fred finally instructed us to go home.

The Monday following the prophet's funeral, Warren assembled the congregation, declaring in his sermon, "I say to the people, hands off the prophet's family." This made it clear to us all his father's wives would not be married off. And he would continue to supervise them. In the days after the former prophet Leroy S. Johnson's death, men in the community put pressure on Uncle Rulon to marry off his young wives. I had heard that those women had effectively been put on the "auction block" for some of the prominent FLDS men. Standing in front of the whole congregation, Warren assured us that this would not happen to Uncle Rulon's wives. The statement confused many of us because we believed the prophet would be coming back. If the prophet was indeed returning, there was no need to reassign his wives.

As the days stretched into weeks, the hushed speculation about the prophet's renewal and return began to fade, and to our eventual realization, we remained on earth without our prophet.

CHAPTER SEVENTEEN

FALSE PROPHET

Your only real family are [sic] the members
of the priesthood who are faithful to our prophet.
—WARREN JEFFS

The weeks after the prophet's passing were an uneasy time for the FLDS. The prophet was never supposed to die, and now that he had, Warren did his best to maintain control. Confused and desperate to know what was next, everybody attended all three of our weekly church meetings. In the past, only the Sunday service was mandatory, with Saturday's work project attended mostly by the men of the community and the Monday-morning meeting, a lighter service of song and prayer, attracting fewer people.

Even I attended the Saturday meeting on September 22, hoping to gain new information that might help to restore my sense of security. Warren was at the pulpit as he'd been for several years, but on this day, his message subtly started to change.

"I pray the Lord will honor our prophet's prayer," he began. "This is the word of God, and I yearn to give Father's message."

He started preaching that his father actually had been "lifted up and renewed," but that it hadn't happened in the physical sense as it had always been predicted. It had been a spiritual renewal. As the weeks went on, Warren continued to imply that the prophet was always around even though his body was nowhere to be seen.

"Can you feel the prophet's love?" Warren asked us at another meeting. "Father is just in the next room," he again assured us. "I can feel him close. He is speaking through me. Live as though he is still walking among us. He is among the people and working with us still." To these words of comfort he added: "There are experiences ahead of us. Tests and judgments that only the pure in heart will be able to endure."

At the time, I was far too indoctrinated to recognize that Uncle Warren was priming us for his formal succession. Although he had always vehemently taught the beliefs of our faith and the prophecies of our future, I think he must have known the truth: his father was a mortal man who would remain buried just like everyone else. Thus he had to reprogram the people to accept a new interpretation of the prophet's death, an interpretation that would allow him to take full control of everything. Looking back on it now, I see that the crazy explanation of the prophet's renewal should have shown us that he was manipulating the situation to serve his own purposes. But none of us who had been born and raised in the FLDS Church could see his actions objectively. The repetition of Warren's extreme ideas had effectively conditioned us, and fear had rendered us unable to express any feelings of doubt.

At the October 13 meeting, Uncle Warren offered us our first glimpse into the plan he had been crafting behind the scenes. In order to receive our full trust and attention, he continuously reminded us throughout the speech that he was serving as a conduit of his dead father's wishes. His voice was even-toned and soft despite the arresting quality of his words. "I am here to do the will of the prophet," he started. "He desires us to be more fervent and faithful. The time is short." Again he insinuated that our faith would soon be tested. He pointed to the Book of Job from the Old Testament, in which God challenges Job's faith with a series of difficult and painful tests. "You may not understand it," Warren remarked. "But soon we will be tested to see who will be the 'wise virgins' and who will be prepared. Only the pure at heart will be able to endure."

Warren was referring us to the parable of the ten virgins from Matthew 25, in which ten virgins set out under the cover of darkness to meet their bridegroom. On their journey, a split occurs between the "wise" virgins, who have brought extra oil for their lamps, and the "foolish" virgins, who have not. Though all ten are believers, the rift between those who are prepared and those who are not is clear. Warren wanted to determine where that split in faith existed in our church and dispose of our "foolish virgins" while there was still time.

But before the foolish virgins could be separated from the wise ones, a leader would need to be established.

To our surprise, that day Warren invited a respected elder from the congregation to the podium. The congregant had become a close devotee of Warren's in recent years. That Saturday, we sat in the meetinghouse in rapt silence as the elder recalled an event from earlier that week, when Uncle Warren had dedicated a church farm, the land, the water, and its workers. It was imperative to receive this special blessing before establishing a home or a business. The church elder said that watching Warren perform the important ritual was like "watching Jesus Christ walk through the masses and bless the water, the fish, and the bread."

"He's just as holy, he's just as pure," the elder said of Warren. "He is the Lord's servant. He is as his father. He does lead and guide us through him. Warren Jeffs is our leader."

This devoted follower was the first man to stand up and declare this. Since he was a well-regarded elder, it was no surprise that Warren used him to deliver the first statement. As I sat in the meetinghouse that day, I struggled to take it in. "This is a test," I repeated over and over in my head. I couldn't believe that Warren Jeffs would be the next prophet. Only a few weeks prior, Warren had insisted that he had no such aspirations and that Uncle Rulon would continue to lead us.

The following week, there were more puzzling declarations in church. This time, Warren's brother Isaac stood up and affirmed the elder's proclamation. He told us that his father had "confidence" in Warren and wanted him to be his successor. There was a feeling of mystery circulating among the people that only grew as the weeks went by. While Warren had publicly declared that none of Uncle Rulon's wives would be remarried, he started to arrive at church surrounded by several of them. Normally, this would indicate that the women were either sealed to him or were about to be placed by his side. The suspicion went unconfirmed, as no one dared ask about it.

I worried what this would mean for Kassandra. Before Issac's speech, she confided in me that Uncle Warren was secretly marrying some of his father's wives, and she was terrified that she would be next. Despite Warren's public claims that nothing would happen to her, it seemed less and less likely that he would uphold what he had promised.

Several days after Issac's testimony, Kassandra called me to ask if I could give her a hand moving some of her things from the prophet's home. She said she was getting married and she wanted to make sure that she was ready when her day arrived. The news came as a surprise, but she assured me that her marriage would not be to Warren.

"Who are you marrying?" I asked, confused yet intrigued.

"I can't really talk about that now," Kassandra replied with an air of mystery. She just told me that she needed to be prepared. "I've seen some of the other girls married, and if they don't have their stuff together, then they don't get to take it with them."

Eager to help, I drove over to Uncle Rulon's and met Kassandra outside. Her room was on the lower level, with a door just down the hall that led out to the back of the compound. I couldn't understand why she was in such a rush, or why she kept looking both ways before stepping out into the hall-way. "Let's hurry. Get it out," she implored, referring to the furnishings we were carrying. She had me nearly sprinting from the house with each trip we made to my Ford Ranger truck. Finally we headed to my trailer. Kassandra wanted to store her belongings in our shed. I didn't really think much of it, and more than anything else, I was glad that her life was taking this enlivening turn.

A few days later, on November 2, I arrived home from work to find an unfamiliar truck parked on the gravel drive in front of my trailer. Suddenly, I saw Kassandra emerging from the storage shed.

"What are you doing here?" I asked, surprised to see her so late in the day.

"I'm just coming to get some of my stuff."

"Are you getting married?" I inquired.

"Not yet, but I will soon."

"Well, whose truck is that?"

A slight breeze swept through the trailer park and Kas-sandra hesitated, appearing nervous. "I don't know. I got dropped off," she said. "It was here when I arrived."

It didn't make sense that she would move her things with-out a vehicle. I could tell that something wasn't right, and I attempted to follow Kassandra back into the storage shed, but she prevented me from entering. "What's going on?" I asked her with a flare of frustration.

She was growing visibly anxious. As I pressed her for details, Ryan Musser emerged from the shed, and in a flash everything came together.

"We're leaving," Kassandra announced.

Her statement shook me to the core. My heart sank and I started to cry. "You lied to me."

"I had to get you to help me," Kassandra said.

"You used me!" I shouted. "How can you do this? How can you leave Mom and the girls? How can you leave us here?"

For weeks, Kassandra had been borrowing my cell phone and my truck. I never asked her any questions. But now, faced with news that she was leaving the community, I was angry over the deception and terrified that I would never see her again. Aside from Mother and my two young sisters, she was all I had left. As members of the prophet's family, Rachel and Michelle were all but removed from my daily existence. My contact with both of them rarely went beyond the superficial "Hello, how are you? I love you." Without Kassandra, I'd be completely lost. She had become my lifeline and one of my greatest reliefs from my problems with Allen.

"You are horrible for taking her away," I declared to Ryan.

At sixteen, I was too young and faithful to understand why she was doing this, and I believed that she was making a big mistake. Sensing that I was going to try to stop her, Kassandra reached out and grabbed my cell phone and car keys.

"What are you doing?" I said in desperation. I wasn't going to let her go without a fight, and she knew it. I wanted to call Mom to see if she could talk her out of it, and she refused to return my phone and keys until she and Ryan were safely on their way. I stood in tears as they finished packing up and, over my continuous protests and sobs, started up the engine.

"Please stay," I begged. "You can't leave us. Don't just abandon everything."

I knew that things were bad for Kassandra; they were bad for me too. But I couldn't imagine abandoning my mother and sisters like I'd been abandoned. I'd seen it happen too many times. It only caused more pain.

I clung to her like a child when she embraced me for our final good-bye. Stepping up into the passenger seat, she tossed me my cell phone and car keys. The dust from the truck's spinning tires blew into my face as she and Ryan drove off down the road. Heartbroken, I nearly collapsed. By the time I reached my mother's, I was inconsolable.

"What's wrong, Lesie?" Mom asked softly, stroking my hair and trying to calm me down. I was so upset I couldn't speak and at first just stood before her, my shoulders shaking uncontrollably and tears rolling off my cheeks.

"Kassandra's gone," I finally told her. Both Sherrie and Ally were in the room when I blurted out the news, but I was too numb to relate any more of the story and could hardly react when Ally fell apart. We hadn't lost a sibling since Caleb left two years before, and all the pain that had been lying dormant came flooding back. Once again our family had been torn apart; once again I had been left alone.

I didn't tell Allen about Kassandra, but this kind of news traveled fast and he heard it from someone else. He said he was sorry but expressed concern about the influence that Kassandra's departure might have on me.

"She is a wicked example," he told me. "And I hope she doesn't wear off on you."

In the days following Kassandra's departure, the shakedown was intense. Uncle Fred began with my mother, interrogating her for hours, wanting to know where Kassandra was, what had happened, and how. Mom was directed to write a letter of explanation to Uncle Warren outlining all she knew about the circumstances surrounding her daughter's defection. My interrogation was even more rigorous. Kassandra had used my cell phone, and she and I had been captured removing her belongings on the video system that monitored the perimeter of the prophet's compound. My unwitting role in Kassandra's flight was now on tape and being used as evidence of my alleged involvement in her defiant act of betrayal.

It felt like I had just committed murder or a bank robbery with the way Uncle Warren and Fred questioned me for hours. Fred demanded to see my cell phone, and he almost confiscated it for good after he learned that Kassandra had used it to make calls in the days leading up to her escape.

"I had no idea," I insisted. "I had no clue that Kassandra was doing anything other than what she told me. I trusted her. She told me she was preparing to be married, and I believed her."

But Fred didn't believe a word I said. He was certain that

I had purposely moved my sister's stuff from the prophet's home and had acted as an accomplice by storing it in my shed. While I loved my sister, I grew furious at her for what she had done. I felt she had thrown Mom, Sherrie, Ally, and me to the wolves, seemingly without a thought about what impact her actions would have on us. I had thought she was my best friend and my closest confidante, but she had been hiding the truth from me. She had forced us to answer for her, but the only answer we could give the priesthood was "I don't know."

The pain and betrayal I felt were only compounded by the silent unease hovering over the community at large. The testimonies of the church elder and Issac Jeffs had stirred some confusion over who would lead us, and while no one dared question out loud, there were many who clung to the diminishing hope that Uncle Rulon would return.

Then, at a service on December 1, our community was shocked again when Warren stood at the podium and said, "Unbeknownst to me, Father had prepared witnesses for this time. May we now hear from Sister Mother Naomi."

Naomi Jeffs was a wife of Uncle Rulon, and the daughter of Merril Jessop, the church elder who owned the motel in Caliente where my wedding ceremony took place. She was barely twenty when she was sealed to the prophet in 1993 and was very well regarded in the community. Her angelic beauty promoted a communal belief that she possessed an exceptionally pure heart. Even though her reputation was impeccable, I was in utter shock during the service as I watched Naomi step up to the microphone in her long pink dress with the white lace trim. It was highly irregular for a woman to speak in church. In fact, it rarely ever happened.

"I pray for Father's spirit and for Father to be near me," Naomi began in a sweet, soft voice. "That he will speak through me. And I will only say that which he wants me to say.

"I first ask, 'Do we really believe in Uncle Rulon?' If we do, then we believe that Warren Jeffs is the prophet at this time."

Naomi's opening remarks were disquieting, but what she would soon reveal would send a ripple through our congregation. "I am so grateful to be married to our prophet," she told us, admitting that she had been sealed to Warren. It turned out that Naomi was among the first of seven of Rulon's wives who had married Uncle Warren in a secret ceremony on October 8. I thought back to the conversation I had with Kassandra in the days before she left. This was clearly what she was referring to, and I started to understand why she had fled. Although I still felt hurt and abandoned by her, part of me—a part I dared not express—couldn't help but be grateful that she had left before being married to Warren.

As we all digested the startling information, Naomi recounted a series of anecdotes that proved Warren's natural place as our prophet. We'd always known that Uncle Rulon would return as a young man to carry out his mission, but we'd imagined that he would be renewed in his own skin. Now Naomi was implying that the transformation had been more subtle: Uncle Rulon had returned to us in the form of his son.

Now that I no longer belong to the FLDS, I can understand how an outsider would find all of this ludicrous. But having spent my entire life listening only to this powerful rhetoric, to the constant repetition of these extreme beliefs, I was completely conditioned to believe whatever I was told by the people I believed to be God's messengers. Though the FLDS are understandably offended by the word *brainwashed,* the truth is, I was, and I could not access, let alone act on, my inherent doubts.

Naomi's testimony was met with absolute silence as we all sat riveted, listening to her recount her private conversations with Uncle Rulon. "He told me many times before and after his stroke that I would be called as a witness, and he told me many other things that are too sacred to repeat. Just before his death, he told me, 'Stay close. I need you. I won't be here much longer. I'm going away, but I will be close.'"

She recalled an instance in which she, Warren, and another of Uncle Rulon's wives, Mary, were in Rulon's room.

The prophet was sick. "Warren walked out into the hall and I looked upon him and I saw Father's holy light shine on him. I felt the same feeling on Warren that I had felt on Father. The majesty of his priesthood was shining through him. The brilliance of Warren's countenance overpowered me and a surge went through my body. At that moment, I knew.

"I bear witness that Warren Jeffs is the prophet," Naomi declared, her delicate voice resonating through the meeting hall. "I bear testimony that Father kept Warren close for this very reason. Father is closely guiding Warren and will only have him do the Lord's will." This carefully orchestrated presentation, along with the testimonies of the church elder and Issac Jeffs, solidified Warren's position as our new prophet. It had been almost three months since the death of our prophet, and while Warren had assured us that he was not aspiring to any position, he'd continued to lead all of the meetings and prayer services. In fact, several of his staunch supporters had taken to standing outside of the meeting-house before services to poll male congregants on where their allegiance lay. "Do you support Uncle Warren?" they'd ask, refusing admittance to those who didn't answer affirmatively. Many of us who now sat listening to Naomi Jeffs's oration had been screened before entering this life-altering meeting.

There were no dissenters among us to dispute Naomi's claims. We all robotically absorbed her words. To those assembled that day, her testimony dictated that our prophet had intended to continue his work through his son. While some of us silently hoped that Uncle Fred would take over instead of Warren, Fred, the man who had held the bishopship of the twin cities for so many decades, remained eerily silent. From that day forward, the people of the FLDS would look unwaveringly to Warren Jeffs as the prophet.

CHAPTER EIGHTEEN

REFUGE IN CANADA

Perfect obedience produces perfect faith.
—FLDS PARABLE

In the confusion after Rulon's death, many people came down from the community in Canada to pay their respects to him. This meant there were lots of vehicles making the return trip, and I was hoping to catch a ride to Bountiful in one.

I'd already been feeling hopeless about my marriage after the ill-fated first year anniversary, but our move to the trailer around my sixteenth birthday the previous summer had only made things worse. Becoming sixteen had been a turning point for me in some ways. It had enabled me to get a job on the books and a valid driver's license. Although I had access to a vehicle and like most FLDS teens had been driving in the Crik since I was fourteen, the license afforded me a new sense of security. I no longer had to worry every time I saw an out-of-town police car, and I could now legally drive in St. George, away from the scrutiny of home. Allen was working regularly for Reliance Electric, installing light fixtures, and had a second vehicle, the brown Ford Ranger that he let me use.

Being legally allowed to work enabled me to earn a more

significant income. Along with my jobs as an aide for the disabled infant and dressmaker, I had agreed to work under another woman in the FLDS as a direct seller for Salad-master. I went door-to-door selling pots and pans and also prepared meals for families in their homes as a way to demonstrate the products. I'd always been good in the kitchen, and this was a new way for me to use my culinary skills. This work became quite lucrative for a girl my age, and I was earning a lot more than I was turning over to Allen each week. In the FLDS, a woman is expected to hand over her entire paycheck to her husband, and he is to handle all of the finances and provide for her. It frustrated Allen that I wasn't following those rules, and it only added to the strain of the marriage, even though I was giving him enough money for the use of his truck.

What Allen didn't know was that some of my reasons for not turning over more money were that I was anxious to make sure my family members were provided for. I felt responsible for them. Mom had to go to Uncle Fred when she needed money for shoes, fabric, or other necessities for her and my younger sisters, but she felt uncomfortable because she always had to produce convincing reasons for the things she needed. She was also too proud to ask for assistance, and it felt as though she held a lower status in Uncle Fred's home than many of the other wives, although it was never spoken aloud.

In addition to the responsibility to my mother and little sisters, I also felt compelled to help Caleb, who was still living with the Barlows in Hurricane but was basically on his own. He'd started eighth grade at Hurricane Middle School and had joined the football team. I would sneak down whenever I could to watch his games and take him to dinner. Understandably, Caleb seemed to be hurt about being abruptly left at the Barlows' by our parents. I did my best to make sure he knew he still had family that cared, but as hard as I tried, I could not alleviate his pain. I could see that it was so difficult for Caleb to know that his biological mother and father were just thirty minutes up the road and they weren't taking care of him. No matter what I did, my presence in his life would never make up for being without his parents.

As if all this weren't enough, I was also keeping an eye on my older brother Justin, who had recently come to southern Utah. In the months after Dad and Audrey moved from Salt Lake, he and his twin, Jacob, parted ways. Jacob remained in Salt Lake City, but Justin had come down to Hurricane and was rooming with a bunch of boys who had been expelled from the FLDS community. Since his arrival, I had been doing my best to help Justin out, and whenever I was in Hurricane, I would visit him as well as Caleb. Sometimes, Justin would go without food for days at a stretch, and he was often sick.

Over time, shouldering all these responsibilities and managing my deteriorating home life began to take its toll. Technically, I was living with Allen in our trailer, but I spent as much time as possible with my mother and sisters up at Uncle Fred's. Although I loved being with my mom, Uncle Fred's home was a tense place for me. Allen was often reporting to Fred about my disobedience, so I had to be careful in my comings and goings there. Even though I was still in a desperate situation, I did my best to keep my mother sheltered from the truth. She had Sherrie and Ally to worry about. I didn't want her to know how Allen was using me sexually. And I certainly didn't want her to know about the miscarriage that I'd had that past spring, or a second one that I suffered in the late summer of 2002. The second was not nearly as severe as the first, but still, I was traumatized.

The result of all this was that on the nights when I was with Allen I found it more difficult to maintain a "sweet" composure in the face of his constant advances. One experience in particular that fall pushed me to become desperate to get away from him. Eager to get some time alone, I had called Uncle Warren in October to ask if we could meet.

"No," he'd said firmly. "You need to come in here with Allen."

"Well, can I just ask you over the phone what I need?"

Pleased when he didn't hang up, I proceeded to tell him that I wanted his permission to travel to Canada to visit my sisters.

"Well, that is between you and Allen," he told me. "You need to bring it up with him."

"Well, I have," I explained. "I've asked Allen if I could go, and he said no. I . . . I just need a break. I need some time separate from Allen so that I can gather my thoughts and regenerate."

"Pray, and just remember what your mission in life is," Warren said before hanging up that day. He hadn't given me permission to go.

By December 2002, I had become so depressed that I was struggling to get out of bed in the morning. A glimmer of hope was rekindled in me when my sister Teressa and her husband, Roy, arrived from Canada to pay respects to Uncle Rulon and visit his grave. Spending time with them immediately raised my spirits, and from the moment Teressa saw me, she knew I needed to return to Bountiful with her. Despite my continued pleas, Allen refused to let me go.

"I'm not going to do anything," I told him. "I just want to see my family and have a break."

Allen knew that our marriage was falling apart, but he refused to let me go. "Your place is by my side," he said. "You need to be here."

At one point during Teressa's stay, I accompanied her and Roy to an appointment that they'd set up with Uncle Warren. Since he was now officially our prophet, they needed to check in and seek his guidance before returning to Canada. Warren did not seem pleased that I was with them, and I was very nervous. Teressa maintained that she needed my help with her new baby and raised the issue of me accompanying them back to Bountiful. She and Roy had three children, and Teressa made it seem like with Roy out of the house for much of the workday, she would need an extra set of hands to help out.

I also tried to explain it myself, telling Warren again, "I

don't feel like I'm in a good place right now. I need to have some space from Allen and to gather my thoughts."

Warren couldn't understand why I was bringing up the same problem again. "I've already told you that you need to speak with Allen about this," he reminded me. "You need to do what Allen tells you. If you are not careful," he admonished, "you will follow in the footsteps of your sister Kassandra and you will lose your faith the way she has. She has been given every opportunity to have salvation, and she has given that up. She is damned to hell."

Teressa jumped in to support me. "We'll take really good care of Elissa and keep her encouraged."

My downward spiral had alarmed her greatly, and while she didn't say anything to me, the fact that she'd been willing to allow me to attend this meeting with Uncle Warren showed how seriously she took my condition. Uncle Warren was not particularly fond of Teressa. She did not have a high standing in the FLDS and was considered trouble because of her strong will. So at first Uncle Warren was resistant. He had told me that I needed to go home and learn to obey Allen. But my sister and I persisted, and eventually Warren agreed to call Allen and hear his position over the speakerphone.

"I just don't feel like she should go," Allen said. His denial infuriated me, and I wanted to shake him through the phone. But I tried to keep sweet, hoping that Teressa and Roy could help to persuade him.

"I have either got to have time or space to go and regenerate, or else I can't do this anymore and I want out," I said, directing my comments at Uncle Warren. "I just want out."

After more back-and-forth, Uncle Warren finally conceded, saying that if it was all right with Allen, I could go. Allen sighed. He was obviously unhappy with Warren's words, but he had enough sense not to push any harder. Reluctantly he agreed, but before I could get too caught up in celebrating, Warren reminded me that I needed to remember my duties and the commitments that I had made. I happily accepted.

I could hardly contain my joy as I packed my clothing

and readied myself for the trip. What I hadn't told Allen was that I was pregnant for the third time. If he'd known, there was no way that he would have agreed to let me go. I didn't know how or when I would eventually break the news, but it didn't matter. I was on my way to Canada.

We hurriedly left town before Allen could change his mind, but what I didn't realize when we left was that our ride to Bountiful would turn into a family reunion of sorts. Unbeknownst to me there had been a lot of contact among my family members. Both Kassandra and Teressa had been in touch with our brother Craig over the past month.

It had all started when, out of the blue, Craig called Kassandra at the prophet's compound in the days before her escape. A while back, Kassandra had obtained Craig's address and secretly sent him a care package that included her direct phone number at Uncle Rulon's house. More than a year passed before he finally called her in late October 2002. He'd learned of Rulon's death and felt compelled to get in touch with Kassandra to see how she was faring. It was a miracle that she was still in the same room with the same phone number, since it was common for the prophet's wives to be moved around and their phone numbers to be changed.

This was the first time that anyone in our family had spoken to Craig since he left in 1996. He was upset when he later heard about all of the difficult times our family had been through. He had no idea that Mom and her youngest kids had been taken away from Dad and that she'd been reassigned to Uncle Fred. The news of my marriage to Allen also infuriated him. Craig encouraged Kassandra to stay strong and not give in to pressure to remarry. While Craig was committed to helping those of us still in the FLDS, he saw Justin's situation as the most urgent.

I didn't know it when we set out for Bountiful, but my older siblings had hatched a plan to move Justin to Oregon, where Craig and now Kassandra were living, so Craig could help him. They decided that we would pick up Justin and drive him to a mutually agreed upon place, from which Kassandra and Ryan would take him the rest of the way to Craig's house.

Before we even got to Kassandra though, we would see yet another old family member. Our first stop would be in Salt Lake City to catch up with my brother Jacob, whom I hadn't seen since we moved to Hildale for good in 1999. We were all eager to see him after so much time and meet his new baby. He'd met a girl shortly after he moved out of Dad's home on Claybourne Avenue. The two had now moved in together and were raising an infant daughter. Although visits to my "apostate" siblings were strictly forbidden, like Teressa I was willing to take the risk.

The moment we drove into the Salt Lake Valley, homesickness enveloped me. A fresh snow had fallen, and the majestic Wasatch mountains were blanketed in white powder. The wintry scene was a welcome relief from the red clay that dominated the landscape of Short Creek. Even though I'd come to appreciate the rugged panorama of arid land, I missed this place that I had once called home.

Being back in Salt Lake reminded me of all the good times I'd shared with my family, the snowball fights with my brothers in our front yard, sledding in the mountains with Dad, and skating on the homemade ice rink we created every winter from packed snow and a garden hose in our backyard. The crisp sound of blades on ice rang clearly in my mind as we drove the city streets en route to my brother's apartment. I couldn't help but wish that I could go back in time to when things made sense and Dad was there to love and protect me, and I wondered whether I would be married and pregnant at sixteen if the priesthood hadn't split us up. I was sure that Dad never would have let this happen, that I'd be at home sipping a cup of hot chocolate and enjoying my true family instead of desperately trying to get space from the husband I didn't love.

As we made our way to Jacob's house, I wondered how it would be for me to meet his girlfriend, Whitney. The mother of his child was African-American. Hearing this came as a huge shock to me, although today I am embarrassed to admit it. All I could think of were Warren's words from Alta Academy that nonwhite people were the most evil of all outsiders. His racist remarks and hate-filled bigotry were a routine part of the classroom experience at Alta Academy, and from them, I had developed a prejudice about anyone whose skin looked different from my own. I had been told that my brother was damned to hell for even associating with Whitney.

When I met Whitney that day, it was the first time I'd ever been introduced to an African-American. I didn't know what to expect or whether Warren's words would be true, but within minutes, my unease dissipated as I instantly liked Whitney and their baby. Whitney was so different from what I had pictured in my mind. She was clearly not the evil person that Uncle Warren had described. She was kind and welcoming to my siblings and me, despite our differences. She even let us hold the baby. Jacob had named his daughter after our sister Michelle, whom he'd loved as much as I had. Their baby was gorgeous and—like her mother—different from anyone I'd ever seen. She had milky caramel skin and exotic bright brown eyes. Even though she was only a few months old, I could tell that she would grow into a radiant beauty.

As I sat there talking to Whitney, I found myself thinking that all it took was contact with the outside world and the barriers of fear that Warren had constructed came tumbling down. It was becoming much harder for me to view outsiders as evil when they were my family. Jacob was a good person and he was creating a good family. I could not stomach the idea that he, his wife, or his daughter were somehow wicked just because they were not a part of our church.

I was happy to see my twin brothers reunited. As for me, I was overcome with a mix of emotions when I climbed back into the car for the next leg of our journey north. Being back in Salt Lake City and seeing this unit of my family gathered together reminded me that there was a whole world out there beyond Short Creek that I had all but forgotten.

We traveled a less direct route than we normally took in order to meet Kassandra at a convenient spot for her and Ryan. My sisters had agreed upon the parking lot of the Red Lion Hotel in southern Oregon. I hadn't heard a word from Kassandra since she'd left the previous month, and I was still upset with her for leaving, not to mention all the trouble she'd gotten me in. Though I missed her immensely, I acted distant during our meeting. I felt severely abandoned, and the load that I felt she'd forced me to carry on my own was starting to crush me. She looked happy with Ryan but very different from how I remembered her—her hair was cut short and she wore worldly clothes of slacks and a blouse.

I hung back as Kassandra and Teressa caught up on things but tuned in when the topic turned to Craig. He'd embarked on a great journey since leaving our home in 1996. He'd bounced around a bit but now was living near the coast in Oregon. I was happy to hear that he was okay but a little disappointed that I wouldn't get to see him. I remained withdrawn for much of the meeting, staying close to Justin as my two sisters spoke in hushed tones so that I couldn't hear. It bugged me that they were whispering right in front of me like I was too young to participate in their "adult" conversation. Every time I moved in closer, they would stop speaking, and by the end of the afternoon I was offended by their slights.

With Justin safely dropped off, we pulled onto the road for the last leg of our trip, and I was relieved we were almost there. Before we left Hildale, I hadn't told Teressa that I was "with child," even though I was already close to four months along and suffering from terrible morning sickness. Because my two previous pregnancies had ended in miscarriages, I was scared that this too would have an unfortunate end. The thought of my miscarriages made me feel horribly guilty, and I was certain that God was punishing me for my disobedience. Even as my third pregnancy had passed the two- and three-month mark, I couldn't bring myself to seek medical care at the women's clinic at Uncle Fred's house. I was nervous that within hours of my appointment the entire community would know that I was pregnant. Pregnancy was proof of what Allen and I had been doing, and the thought of such a private, unclean matter becoming public gossip felt dirty.

When we got to Bountiful, almost instantly I felt a change in myself. At last, I was able to relax. Letting my guard down a bit, I finally told Teressa about the baby growing inside me as well as the others I'd lost. She was kind and compassionate, and helped me to feel good about myself. She brought me to see the FLDS midwife, Jane Blackmore. I had heard that Jane was in the process of leaving her husband Uncle Wink, the former bishop for the community in Canada, as part of a broader move on her part to leave the FLDS altogether. She'd recently moved to a location about twenty minutes outside of the community but kept her birthing center in Bountiful, where Teressa took me for my first-ever prenatal examination. Jane immediately set me at ease with her gentle manner, and she agreed not to tell anyone about my pregnancy. I knew that if word got back to Allen, I would be ordered to return to Hildale. After some routine tests, she searched my belly for a heartbeat. It was at that moment that the magnitude of my circumstances crystallized. Hearing the heartbeat made my pregnancy real, and overcome by my situation, I burst into tears.

Jane understood; she made me feel safe and like it was going to be okay. I confided in her about my previous miscarriages, and she promised to take care of me. She did not approve of my underage marriage, and she knew what lay ahead for me both in the delivery room and as a new mother. I was still a child, and Jane appeared upset that a person so young should be put in this difficult and emotionally trying position.

She encouraged me to go into the hospital in the neighboring town of Creston for an ultrasound, but I had no medical insurance. Not to mention that it was a huge risk for me to seek care at a real medical facility. I had no money and was not a legal resident of Canada. Medical personnel would have wanted to know where my parents were. If they learned my age, they might learn of my marriage, which could be a huge problem. Seeking help ran the risk of shining a spotlight on the FLDS, and I feared the repercussions.

My checkups with Jane did a lot to ease my apprehension about the pregnancy. That winter, I rang in 2003 surrounded by the warmth of my sisters and their families. Teressa assured me that I was welcome to stay with her and Roy for as long as I wanted. "I'll take care of you," she vowed.

Of course, the occasional thought of Hildale only made my anxiety return. Everything was unsettled back there: my marriage to Allen, the situation with my family, and the leadership of our people under Warren. I'd begun to wonder about the way things were developing. I took great risk in silently questioning whether Warren's behavior was right. He'd told us that none of the prophet's wives were going to be married, and he'd also said that he wasn't going to be the next prophet. It didn't make sense to me because neither of these assurances had happened as he'd said they would. In Canada, I saw the fallout from Warren's declaration about Winston Blackmore. A new bishop had been assigned to the Canadian community in the wake of what we thought was Uncle Rulon's decision to strip Winston of his position. Bountiful was now divided over where to pledge its allegiance.

By early February, I was almost six months pregnant. I'd been to the midwife for two examinations, and everything seemed to be progressing well. When I next saw Jane on February 20, I expressed concern. I hadn't felt the baby move in a couple of days, and I was feeling very weird. I'd begun experiencing a burning sensation in my stomach as well. The next night, I awoke to a sharp pain in my side and spotting. I kept trying to tell myself it was probably nothing to worry about, that I'd just been to the midwife. I tried to go back to sleep but was too uncomfortable. The next morning, I was speaking with my sister Sabrina in her bedroom when suddenly blood began gushing down my leg.

She raced me to the bathtub and immediately summoned Teressa, who called Jane for instructions.

"Bring her in right now!" she told my sister. I hardly had time to think as my siblings gathered me up and bundled me into the car. By the time we arrived at Jane's, I had lost a lot of blood. I was terrified as Jane quickly started an IV and checked me over. I was hemorrhaging badly, and she couldn't find a heartbeat. The baby had died, and my body was going into labor to expel the fetus. I would actually have to deliver the baby, with no anesthetic. I was sicker than ever before, and barely able to stand. My condition frightened Jane, but she was helpless because I was not a Canadian citizen, and due to my situation, I didn't have access to Canadian health care. She was so concerned for me that after the initial crisis she took me to her house outside the community to keep me close.

I'd gone through labor to produce a stillborn child. The trauma was overwhelming. Jane tried to console me, reassuring me that it was not my fault. But it wasn't easy for me to put behind me. I felt like I was to blame, and it took me a long time to get over the suffering. Part of me was relieved and part of me was devastated. This stillbirth only reinforced my belief that God was punishing me. I reviewed the last two or three years of my life, and all the things I'd done and how I hadn't been a submissive wife. I wondered if this was why God was bringing this on me. Still, Allen had not made it easy for me, and it had been at his insistence that we have children in the first place.

At age sixteen, I'd been married for less than two years and already I'd had two miscarriages and a stillbirth. I couldn't prevent what was happening to me, and I didn't know what was wrong. Was it God warning or testing me? Was it that I was impure? It wasn't just the miscarriage; I started to worry that my body was somehow just wrong. Consumed with guilt, I begged everyone to keep what had happened a secret, fearing that if Allen found out, he would surely make me come home.

In the end, it didn't matter whether or not Allen knew. I'd been dodging his calls for a while, but not long after my miscarriage, my priesthood responsibility knocked at my door and I could no longer ignore him. He wanted me back in Short Creek, and he called to let me know that Uncle Warren was instructing me to come home. Uncle Fred, too, had said that it was time for me to return. I'd been gone much of the winter—nearly three months.

"I'm not coming back," I told my husband.

"I've changed," Allen insisted. "Everything is going to be okay."

"I can't," I told him. "I don't love you and I don't think I ever will."

Allen began to send cards and letters in an attempt to sway me, and when his efforts failed to bring me back, I later learned Uncle Warren telephoned my sisters' husbands and told them that I could not stay with them any longer. Teressa wanted to keep me with her, and she'd tried to do everything she could, but she had zero influence. Even her husband could not sway Uncle Warren. Everyone was afraid to go against his power. Not long after Warren's call, Allen informed me that he was going to drive up to Canada to see me.

I felt like a deflated balloon when I saw him step out of his truck that first day of March, a bouquet of flowers in his hand. He said he'd missed me so much, but I couldn't say the same. There was pressure from every direction, and the decision to stay in the marriage was not mine to make. Uncle Warren, Uncle Fred, and even my mother were urging me to come back to Hildale to carry out my responsibilities as Allen's wife. It was as though I was being pushed into this marriage all over again, and I didn't want to succumb. I knew that if I agreed to get into his truck that day, there might not be another chance to get away from Allen. I had fought hard, but here I was again, back at square one.

I could feel that familiar lump forming in the back of my throat as I fastened myself into the passenger seat and waved farewell.

"It's going to be okay," Allen assured me as he turned the key in the ignition. "I'm not going to hurt you."

From the first few moments of the drive, I could see that he was making a huge effort, trying to start over and make me fall in love with him. I decided that the only way it was going to work was if I was completely honest, so I told him what I'd been keeping from him for so many months.

"I was pregnant, and I had a miscarriage," I announced, as we drove south along the highway. "And it wasn't the only one."

"Why didn't you tell me?" he asked in a soft voice, slowing the truck to look in my direction.

"I didn't want you to know. I was having such a hard time being pregnant in the first place, and I didn't want you to know or Mom or anyone."

It was clear that Allen was hurt, even though he managed to maintain his composure. But his sadness was not for what I'd been through; it was for himself and the fact that he was not going to be a father. The way he spoke only heightened the guilt that I already felt, as if he was trying to make me see that I'd done something bad. As I sat there listening to him place responsibility for the miscarriages solely on me, I felt upset that he wasn't taking time to understand how I was feeling. The only thing he wanted to do was blame me for them. The conversation slowly shifted away from this painful topic as I sat silently in the passenger seat watching the mile markers fly by.

Allen had set his mind on making our drive back to Hildale a kind of second honeymoon, and he promised that he would try harder to respect my feelings. I wanted to believe that he meant it. We'd been on the road for a while when we exited the highway in Lava Hot Springs, a riverside resort town in southeast Idaho, halfway between Salt Lake City and Bountiful. He had booked a room at the Lava Hot Springs Inn, where we would spend the night. The rooms, some of which had jaw-dropping views of the Portneuf River, had comfy big beds and huge bathtubs.

The emotional drama of the day had worn me out, and I dressed for bed the minute we returned to our room from dinner that night. After a few short minutes I dozed off to sleep, but when I woke up I knew something was not right. Dazed, I realized that I was in bed next to Allen and he was undressing me. In spite of all his promises, here I was just a few hours reunited with him and already he was going back on his word. Catching him beside me unfastening my nightgown brought back a flood of old feelings. I loathed him and I hated what he was doing to me. It was an instant reminder of how many times it had happened and how he'd refused to stop even as I begged him to. I'd just confided the harrowing events of the past few weeks, and the fact that he would even think of pushing himself on me in this way only proved to me how little he thought of me. To him I was merely an object of sexual desire. There was no me, just a body.

"This is going to be the exact same thing all over again," I blurted out. "All your promises, they mean nothing. Nothing has changed."

"I'm doing it out of love," Allen declared. Everything he did was a contradiction, and before I knew it he was playing the guilt card again. As he continued to put his hands all over me, I just froze.

"Okay, fine," I uttered. "Get it over with."

CHAPTER NINETEEN

NOWHERE TO RUN

Had the people gathered together and anointed one
of their number to be a prophet, he would have been
accountable to the people; but in as much as he is
called a God, he is accountable only to God.
—BRIGHAM YOUNG

Returning to life in Short Creek was not easy. In the months
that had passed since I went to Canada, things had become increasingly oppressive under Uncle Warren. While
he'd only been officially the prophet for a short time, years
of his influence had already had a huge impact. What had
once been a community of industrious people who lived by
the motto "Love thy neighbor as thyself" had slowly shifted
to become a society of paranoid and fearful souls. Everyone was looking over his shoulder to see what his neighbor
was doing, and Warren was encouraging people to report
any wrongdoings. It seemed his goal was to rid the society
of those he deemed unworthy and who would prevent the
rest of us from being lifted up at the end of the world.

Our new prophet's teachings became more severe and
apocalyptic. "Soon the Lord is going to cleanse the people,"
he warned. "And it will be revealed to the prophet those who
are halfhearted, and they will be weeded out." The mood in
Short Creek continued to grow more sullen and uneasy.
Life had become all about "perfection" and watching your

neighbor and turning him in if deemed necessary to prove "perfect obedience."

During a church meeting the previous February, Warren had shocked the congregation when he announced that Jethro Barlow, an FLDS member, had been expelled from Short Creek. Warren singled out Barlow as "unfaithful" and ordered him to "repent from afar." The news was quite unexpected, since ostracizing usually occurred in private. It was something you'd hear about after the fact, usually in whispers. From what I could recall the only time an announcement like this had been made to the whole church was when it had happened to Winston Blackmore a year earlier. In my life this marked the first time that somebody had been publicly disciplined in this way, and no one knew how to react.

Jethro Barlow was the son of one of the church's founding elders, George, and taught religious school. That Uncle Warren had deemed a son of George "unworthy" came as a total surprise to many of us. George was one of the community's ordained patriarchs and was regularly called on to teach the people.

"He has led some young people to be unfaithful," Warren said of the junior Barlow. "The Lord is dealing with him severely."

The seeds of this banishment had been sown a few months earlier, when Jethro learned that he was on the "blacklist" of unworthy FLDS members that Warren had been compiling. For months Jethro had attempted to meet with Warren to find out what he had done to be placed on the list, but Warren had refused to even speak with him. Later I found out that Jethro himself didn't even know he would be cast out that morning. He only heard the news when Warren's helpers would not let him enter the church meeting.

I wish I could have seen back then that Jethro Barlow was merely a test case for Warren. It presented a chance for him to see how the people of Short Creek would react to such a display of absolute power. If there had been a public outcry, he might have thought twice about making such a bold move again, but no one said a word on Jethro's behalf. We were all too afraid. It set a dangerous precedent. At this very same meeting, Warren also completely "cut off" Winston, meaning that he could no longer be a member of the FLDS. He declared there was no bishopric in Canada. The people were to look to Warren for counsel and leadership. We were now to treat Uncle Wink as an apostate. The divide that had begun to open up the previous summer when Winston had been publicly handled was now made permanent with the people forced to chose a side with some going with Winston and others following Warren.

It was in this unsettling environment that Allen and I were trying to get our marriage on track. Shortly after I returned from Canada, Teressa informed my mother about my miscarriages. She also told her about the difficulties that I'd had with Allen from the beginning, and how he had been forcing himself on me. When Mom finally confronted me about it, she fought to contain her emotion. "Why didn't you come to me?" she asked, breaking into sobs.

"I was trying to protect you from this pain," I told her, my heart in my stomach as I watched her tears fall. We'd become so close, and the fact that I hadn't shared this with her cut her deeply. "I didn't want you to know how hard it is for me because you already have enough to worry about. You have these two little girls, and you need to make sure that this doesn't happen to them."

"I won't," Mom vowed. "I won't let this happen to them."

She sounded sincere, but I had a hard time believing that there was anything she could do to stop it from happening to Sherrie and Ally—not unless she was willing to forego her eternal salvation and leave the religion with my two little sisters.

Nevertheless, she did do her best to help me. She spoke to Allen and asked him to start respecting my needs.

From that point on I noticed a change in how he treated me, and my outlook shifted as well. I didn't want confrontation with Allen. I knew that I had a responsibility to my priest-hood head, and I wanted to fulfill the vows that I had been forced to make. God had placed me here for time and all eternity, and on a deep level, I believed that he would reward me for following his will.

As part of Allen's renewed attempts to improve our marriage, he decided to celebrate our second wedding anniversary with a trip to Lake Powell. He planned an overnight at a fancy hotel to try and make up for the last few years.

On our first night there, I surprised him by wearing one of my newest outfits, a straight denim skirt to the ankle and a long-sleeved blouse. Like some of my peers back in Hildale, I'd started to wear clothing that was considered rebellious by the more traditional members of our society. It had become something of a trend among the FLDS teenage girls, and I excitedly bought into it. It felt good to be a little defiant, and I wasn't as self-conscious when I was out in public. Not only was my skirt straighter than our normal styles, but it had a tiny slit up the back that revealed the two pairs of thick tights I was wearing to hide my church undergarments. In addition, I'd taken to styling my hair with a single pouf in the front, having decided that the signature FLDS wave, which was similar to the 1940s wave only much poufier and much taller, was just not my style. Allen didn't seem to notice my bold new outfit at first. As I lingered in the room, waiting and wondering when we'd be leaving for dinner, I realized that he was totally entranced by the television and had lost track of the time. Finally I spoke up, reminding him that it was getting late.

I could see the panic on his face when he realized what time it was. Grabbing my hand, he hurried us out of the room and down to the resort restaurant. But the door to the fancy Rainbow Room was already closed, and Allen grew quietly upset. He'd wanted to make this a special night for us, and he was feeling like he'd blown it. I was so embarrassed when he started knocking on the door of the restaurant, pleading with the hostess to let us come in and have a meal. His polite request was denied, and we ended up sharing our second-anniversary dinner at a local Denny's. I was more amused than upset. I guess being a bit older made it easier for me to understand what it was that he'd been trying to do. I also knew how easy it was to get caught up in the novelty of television, since it was strictly forbidden in our community.

The next day, I did catch Allen's attention by wearing a pair of pants that I'd purchased during a shopping trip to St. George with Kassandra before she fled. When I put them on, he cautiously asked me, "Why are you wearing those?"

"Because I want to wear them out here on the beach," I said with an air of defiance. I was certain that my pants were not the only articles of clothing Allen was objecting to. I was also wearing a short-sleeved pink T-shirt that revealed the skin on my arms. Clothing such as pants and shirts for women were strictly forbidden. But he saved his comment about the shirt until our ride home that afternoon. "Please don't wear it again," he requested as he steered his truck north along the highway.

After that anniversary, Allen continued to try to follow my mother's advice and pressured me less, but it was just a matter of weeks before his old behavior returned. For my part, I was trying to obey him as best I could. While I understood his efforts to be more considerate of my needs, nothing could change the fact that I didn't love him. I still slept at Uncle Fred's when I could, and I still tried to minimize the amount of time I spent with Allen. When I was home, all that I gave to him was my physical presence. We were living together, but emotionally we were separate. There seemed to be no connection except for his continued sexual advances. When I returned to the trailer, I always knew what was going to happen and I tried to prepare myself. My goal was to avoid conflict with him, but he grew more frustrated by the day, angry that his change in attitude had failed to sway my heart.

Eventually, his frustration would boil over, making many

of our disagreements heated and severe. Over the course of a few weeks, his kind demeanor crumbled and his assumed authority as my priesthood leader returned with a vengeance. I did my best to fight him off, but there were times I had no choice but to submit. Some of our arguments culminated in physical struggles. He'd slap me or push me up against the wall. I didn't understand why he was behaving that way. One minute he would threaten me, the next he was trying to hug me. Once he even hurled a lamp in my direction. Luckily, I didn't get hurt. It frustrated me that no one could see the Allen that I saw behind closed doors. People would reprimand me for my unaffectionate attitude toward him, but they didn't understand how he treated me when no one was watching.

To protect myself, I'd grown more stubborn in my unwillingness to do as he wished. I wanted to move my things into the other bedroom and take a break from him. He was furious and lost his temper. He chased after me, and I ran into the second bedroom and tried to close the door behind me. But Allen kicked it in, and the door struck me in the eye. I woke up the next morning with a shiner.

This was not the only time that I'd sustained a bodily injury. My five feet two inches and 145 pounds were no match for his broad frame. At just below six feet, Allen towered over me, and he weighed more than 220 pounds. There was little I could do to stop him once he'd set his mind to having things his way—especially when it came to sex. In the bedroom he'd get rough sometimes, and though I tried hard to fight him off, I was rarely able to stop him once he got going.

What made things worse was how I was manipulated. His mind games were a constant. Most of what he said was to coerce me in one way or another. He'd tell me that if I wasn't one with him as the priesthood taught us, then our afterlife in heaven was in jeopardy. In retrospect, it's easy to dismiss his words, but at the time I sincerely believed that he and this arranged marriage were my keys to eternal salvation. Because of all the pressure I was receiving from him, the priesthood, and the community, I had no choice but to obey him.

By June, Allen was fed up with the way our marriage was going, and worried about the possible consequences, he initiated a meeting with Uncle Warren. He felt he had tried everything and no matter what he did it was met by my resistance. He refused to see that his version of kind and respectful behavior was not seen that way by me. In his eyes, everything had the same result: I wouldn't become the submissive, obedient wife that I should be. I was grateful that Allen had been the one to initiate this meeting with Uncle Warren. Perhaps now the prophet would take the situation more seriously and grant me the release I had been asking for. Warren was happy to see us. "How are you doing?" he asked us when he stepped out into the waiting room. He was still operating out of Uncle Rulon's office, but now that he was the prophet, it was officially his headquarters.

Allen and I sat side by side. "I don't feel like things are going very well," Allen said in his humble, obliging way. "It's been two years, and Elissa is still having problems with obedience. She does not trust me, or allow me to direct her in what she's doing and what friends she should have. I think she needs some counseling because I feel like she's being a little rebellious."

Turning to me, the prophet asked, "Elissa, how do you feel?"

"I have told you so many times how I feel. Honestly, I just can't trust this man. I don't love him. I don't know if I'll ever love him. And I don't feel comfortable around him. Things have happened between us that I don't agree with and that I don't like or ever want."

Warren began to ask us questions, trying to determine why we didn't yet have any children. "Because when you have children, your responsibility changes," Warren explained. "You are not selfish. It's not all about you. It's about children and raising them up to be good, obedient, faithful priesthood children. Sometimes, having children changes everything. And it makes people fall in love because they have another life on earth together."

I sat silently in my chair staring at the flowers sprouting from the garden just outside. I didn't want to have children with Allen. I was certain of that. But I wasn't prepared to say it aloud. We'd already had a number of heated discussions over it, and they'd all ended badly. Listening to Warren speak, all I could think of was a time when Allen had said very much the same thing, insisting that if we just had a baby together, I would love him. When I disagreed, Allen grew forceful, telling me that we needed to start a family immediately. That's when he'd forced himself on me.

Directing his gaze at me, Uncle Warren told me how I was failing in my mission, "because you are not being obedient." It was always the woman's fault. If the marriage wasn't working, it was because she wasn't faithful enough. "I have given you so many opportunities to change your actions and allow yourself to accept what you have chosen to do. You need to remember your vows. You still need to give yourself over to Allen, mind, body, and soul. You need not to question him."

Warren's words seemed so hypocritical. He was saying that I had chosen this when I really had had no choice at all. It was nothing I hadn't heard from him before. I couldn't see how this marriage was going to improve. But I sat silently with my hands folded in my lap, listening to Warren's directives.

"Your problem is that you are questioning Allen and the priesthood itself," he declared. "And when you question the priesthood and your priesthood head, you are questioning God."

Just when I thought it couldn't get any worse, Warren asked me again about my relationship with my mother. And when I answered, he reminded me that I needed to change my loyalties to my husband. "You need to make sure you are at home in the trailer, under your husband's roof, at night," he instructed. Clearly he intended to go to Uncle Fred about my absences at night. "You need to be very careful about what you do because you will lose your faith," he warned. It was Warren's way of telling me that my disobedience was leading me to apostasy. "You, like some of your family members, are a little spirited," he admonished, locking eyes with me.

Turning toward Allen, he told him to have a "strong, firm hand" with me and remember he was a priesthood man. "Allen, you need to live up to your priesthood commitments, and you need to be careful how you conduct yourself."

Upon hearing this, my ears perked up for the first time in the meeting. The significance of Warren's warning Allen was not lost on either of us. From now on, any complaining that Allen did to Warren or Fred about me would be seen not just as my failure to obey but also as Allen's failure to control me. If Allen could not enforce his authority over me, he might not be worthy to hold the priesthood.

Rising to his feet, Warren imparted his final words of encouragement. "You both need to remember to keep sweet and keep the spirit of God about you. This is both of your missions and your callings, and you need to do this so that you can grow in love and have a life together."

Early that summer, in my attempts to gain more space from Allen, I accepted a job as a waitress at Mark Twain's, the family-style FLDS restaurant just off the highway at the entrance to town. Mark Twain's would supplement my already busy schedule working for Saladmaster and doing some part-time child care, and I started immediately. My niece Meg soon joined me there as a cook.

With Kassandra gone, in the months before I'd left for Canada I'd grown exceptionally close to Meg, who was the daughter of one of Mother Audrey's daughters. Even though I was technically her aunt, I was only eighteen days older than she and we'd known each other our whole lives. We'd strengthened our friendship the months before I'd left for Bountiful, and we'd stayed in touch by phone during my visit with Teressa and her family. Meg knew how unhappy I was in my marriage. It was hard for her to imagine what it was like to have a husband at our age, but of all the teenagers I knew, she was one of the few who didn't treat me like an outcast because I was married. Though she couldn't understand what I was going through, she was there for me as a friend and confidante. My friendship with Meg was deep because we were the same age and curious about many of the same things. I was secretly envious of her lack of restrictions. She was free to enjoy her teenage years without the responsibility of a husband, a home, and bills, while I was struggling to make my way in this very adult world.

From the start I enjoyed the Mark Twain, and the clientele quickly came to like me. This job also allowed me to interact with a lot more kids my own age and encouraged me to participate in normal teenage activities that both the church and Allen would have forbidden if they had known. Some nights after work, I secretly joined Meg and some of the other employees in "the Sticks" area of the desert. There we would build a fire, turn on music, drink beer, and basically act like typical teenagers. In our culture this was terribly taboo and we were running the risk of a severe reprimand. We'd usually gather near the huge pale limestone boulders that, through some miracle of nature, had risen up from the red clay in various parts of the landscape. We'd sit for hours on those piles of rock talking and watching the sun set over the desert. I had never done anything like this before, and just being around kids my own age was a huge relief.

Sometimes Meg snuck out of her parents' house at night, and she and I just drove around for hours, cruising along the back roads of the Arizona strip with the forbidden car radio blasting. For those few hours every week, it was like we were totally free, as close to normal teenagers as we'd ever get. Our favorite bands were Bon Jovi and the Backstreet Boys, and I even started to buy some banned CDs during my shopping trips into St. George. Sometimes we'd drive into Hurricane in the evenings, even though everything was closed. Other times, we'd sneak into town and see a movie. One of our first was *Pirates of the Caribbean*. I hadn't been to the movies since childhood. We were so scared we couldn't even eat our popcorn, but we loved every minute of it. I'd never had an experience like that, and it was a big moment for me.

Allen knew that I wasn't sleeping at home much and that bothered him, but he had little clue about what I was doing. He probably just assumed I was spending time with my mother. I went to great lengths to hide my rule-breaking from him for fear of what he would do if he found out. My goal wasn't to confront him with my disobedience; it was to keep it as quiet as possible so that he couldn't take my freedom away.

In the end, my time with Meg was less about rebelling against Allen or the church and more about me. It was about enjoying my life and starting to live on my terms. Being married, I was literally supposed to be an adult. I'd never been able to be a teenager before, to break the rules and do the kind of things that teenagers do. What we considered breaking the rules was actually pretty tame, but it made me feel liberated. With the truck winding down the darkened roads and the music playing at full volume, I was no longer Allen's wife, I was myself.

But I couldn't drive around forever. Eventually I had to go home. The second I would walk through the trailer door, the person I was with Meg suddenly disappeared, and once again, I was miserable.

CHAPTER TWENTY

A PAIR OF HEADLIGHTS

According to your faith, so shall it be.
—WARREN JEFFS

August began with yet another devastating blow from Warren that brought the morale in Short Creek to new lows. This time it was a community event that sparked Uncle Warren's wrath.

It had begun a few months earlier when Shirley Barlow, a former wife of our prophet Leroy Johnson, began assembling a slide show to commemorate the fiftieth anniversary of the 1953 raid on Short Creek. As Shirley collected various photographs and artifacts from that time, many other community members became involved. So much material was gathered that the slide show evolved into a three-part film. The first of these was scheduled to be shown during our annual celebration of Uncle Roy's birthday in June, and the last installment was to be aired on the eve of the raid's anniversary.

Then Warren announced that this year we would not be celebrating Uncle Roy's birthday. Though Uncle Roy had begun this tradition himself, and it had been carried on for years, Warren declared that the event was not what Uncle Roy would have wanted. This came as a huge shock to the

community, who looked forward to the event as the beginning of our summer celebrations.

For much of July, Warren was away. He was gone for
days at a time and would not tell the people where he was or
when he would be back. Still, he found time to put an end to
our July 4 festivities as well as our Pioneer Day celebration.
July 4 he took away because he said it was celebrating the
government, which was against us, but there was no real
reason given for ending Pioneer Day. Though it was a tradition that went back decades, Warren didn't attempt to justify
himself; as the prophet he needed no explanation.

At first Warren allowed the anniversary slide show to
move forward as scheduled, even attending the first viewing
himself. The community proceeded to honor the fiftieth anniversary of the raid in his absence. Believing that he would
be pleased and that we had his approval, we went ahead and
aired the final installment on the night of July 24. A section
of the library in Colorado City was cleared for the display of
all the pictures, since it was on that spot that authorities had
first found the people congregated in prayer that fateful day.
There were also artifacts such as baby blankets and shoes that
had been left by the children who'd been taken from their
mothers.

At the center of town, some of the church elders erected a
monument to Uncle Roy and the raid, and the unveiling was
held on July 26, with Mayor Dan Barlow leading us in the
dedication. Some of the local craftsmen had engraved the
monument with these special words: "The Prophet Leroy S.
Johnson stood on this site with the people and met the raid-
ing police officers. He later declared the deliverance of the
people in 1953 was one of the greatest miracles of all time."

On the day of the dedication, Warren was away on one of
his mysterious trips, but when he returned in early August
and learned what had been done in his absence, he was livid.
On Sunday, August 10, he stood up in church and chastised
the people of Short Creek, accusing us of being like the people in Moses' day, worshipping the golden calf as he was
receiving the Ten Commandments from God. He told us

that he'd received a revelation from God and commanded the destruction of the monument. "Verily I say unto you my servant Warren, my people have sinned a very grievous sin before me, in that they have raised up monuments to man and have not glorified me," Warren related to us the terrifying revelation. Never before had he dictated a revelation directly to the people, and hearing how angry the Lord was with us for partaking in "idolatry" struck fear into our hearts.

Warren accused the people of being unworthy of future blessings and declared there would be no more meetings held, neither priesthood nor Sunday meetings. He also commanded that there would be no more marriages, baptisms, or confirmations. But he said the people would continue to pay tithing to him and support the FLDS storehouse.

Raising his hand in the air, our prophet told us that the land of Short Creek would now be "cursed."

"I want that monument plowed to the ground, broken into pieces, and scattered in the hills where no one can find them," he commanded, "and all the pictures and stories put in the church archives and forgotten."

Terrified, several church elders jumped to their feet and raced out of the meetinghouse to follow his directive, bulldozing the monument that very afternoon. As time went on, we would see that Warren's tirade had been prompted by jealousy. The monument and slide show had honored another time and another prophet. There was little mention of either Jeffs.

That day, Uncle Warren officially put an end to what had become a way of life for the people of the FLDS. He delivered a message from God, informing us that because of what we had done there would be no more socials, no more school, and no Harvest Fest. He had effectively ended Short Creek social life. We were to repent and pray privately that the Lord would forgive us.

For many, losing the right to marry was the severest punishment. It was unclear how long the ban would be in effect or if it would ever be lifted. Those men with fewer than three wives worried that they would never attain eternal salvation, while unmarried women feared that they would not gain entrance to heaven unless they were placed beside a man.

It was the harshest punishment Warren had ever issued, and it set off a frenzy of anxiety. Our salvation was at stake, and it was looking less and less likely that we would all be saved together. If Warren's words held true, some of us would be saved, but most of us would not.

On August 31 my mom and I decided to quietly phone Kassandra to wish her a happy birthday. When I called, Ryan picked up the phone, and after I asked to speak with Kassandra, he informed me that she was in labor. I was shocked. I didn't know she was pregnant. When Kassandra finally phoned us back, we learned that she and Ryan were living together, and they now had a newborn son. As Kassandra shared her exciting news, I began to understand things that had been confusing me for months: the mysterious whispers with Teressa when we dropped off Justin; Kassandra's hesitance toward me. These were because of the coming baby, and understandably she hadn't wanted me to know about it.

With the baby safely delivered, Kassandra began to open up more about her situation. She was living in Oregon near my brother Craig, who by then had taken both Justin and later Caleb under his wing. In a follow-up call in September, Kassandra expressed an interest in becoming a sales representative for Saladmaster because she needed money and knew how lucrative the business had been for me. When I spoke to my boss in Colorado City about bringing Kassandra on board, she saw a company benefit, and even though she was FLDS, she was eager for me to fly out and sign Kassandra on. She would receive a commission from Kassandra's sales, and she provided me with the pots and pans that Kassandra would need to get started.

The only problem was Allen. Since our meeting with

Warren, little in our routine had changed. I continued to split my nights between Uncle Fred's and our trailer, but the nights out with Meg had led me to find a new bedroom: my truck. It had begun during the warm nights of the summer, when it made sense to sleep in my truck rather than going home to Allen. But as the season moved into fall, I was not eager to give up my new refuge and I was still spending a couple of nights there.

I'd wait until it was late and then park in a quiet spot up by the reservoir above the twin towns where my mother and I liked to go walking. Sometimes I'd be startled awake by a knock on my window, or the beam of a flashlight being shone in my face by a Colorado City police officer. While the police appeared to be in the business of strictly enforcing our religious laws, crimes against children seemed to go uninvestigated and unpunished. To my amazement, these policemen never seemed alarmed to see a teenage girl sleeping alone in her truck. Finding me there night after night never prompted any questions. There was never an investigation into the possibility of trouble or abuse. I was simply ordered to go home, precisely the place I was trying to escape.

When I approached Allen about going to Oregon, I didn't ask for his permission; instead I just told him that this trip was essential for my job. While he was reluctant to have me leave, he was scared of what Uncle Warren would do to him if he explained the truth. Ever since our meeting with Warren in June, he had been hesitant to complain about me. Besides, Warren was scarcely around in those days, as his trend of being strangely absent from Short Creek had continued.

If Allen had made this a big issue, I would have had no choice but to stay. Even though I was testing my limits, defying him on this would have been too disobedient. It had been less than a year earlier when his refusal to allow me to go to Canada had led us to a large-scale confrontation involving the prophet. Although staying with my apostate sister was far more unacceptable behavior on my part, Allen didn't seem to have the stomach for another protracted fight. In the end, he said that I could go.

With $2,500 in the bank from months at my various jobs, I was able to buy my own plane ticket, but shortly before I left in early October, I discovered something that was becoming all too regular: I was pregnant again. Though my stays in Allen's bed were getting more infrequent, when I was there he would often push me into having sex. Once more, I was unwilling to tell Allen. Not only would he make me stay, he would blame me if something happened to the child. So I kept it to myself.

On the day of my flight, my boss drove me to the airport in Las Vegas, where I boarded a plane for Portland. As a youngster I'd flown a handful of times, but this was the first time I was completely on my own. When I landed in Oregon, I leapt from the plane and began running through the airport to find Kassandra. I nearly tripped over the young woman who stepped out into my path, and I couldn't understand why she wouldn't let go of me when I tried to continue on my way.

"Lesie," the woman said.

I was surprised that she knew my name. Focusing my attention on this attractive brunette, I realized it was Kassandra. She looked nothing like the girl I knew in Hildale. This Kassandra was wearing flip-flops and capri pants. Her hair was loose and fell to just below her shoulders. Long, pretty earrings dangled from her ears, and makeup highlighted her beautiful blue eyes. Sure enough, it was Kassandra. As she enveloped me in a warm hug, I relaxed immediately. For months everyone in Short Creek had been calling her evil, but all at once I recognized that this couldn't be further from the truth. She was the same kind and caring person she always had been, and now she had a beautiful infant son.

I'd only been at Kassandra's small apartment for a day when Craig called, wanting to see me. Reluctantly, I took the phone and heard his upbeat voice boom into my ear. "Be ready early in the morning," he told me.

As promised, my brother arrived at 6:00 A.M. the next

day. He looked older and more mature than he had the last time we'd seen each other, almost seven years earlier. He was very masculine and handsome, with a strong jaw and fair blond hair like mine, cut close to his head. His deep blue eyes shone with a glow I hadn't seen before.

"Oh my God, you're all grown up," he said, smiling.

"Yeah," I retorted, not sure what to say. I knew that he'd made the long journey away on his own, but I had worried for his safety and felt hurt that he'd left our lives so completely.

Craig produced a jogging suit for me to wear, informing me that we would take a sunrise walk on the beach together. I had never seen the ocean and was excited by the prospect of getting my first look at the big waves. Changing out of my long dress into a pair of soft, comfortable pants was a thrill too. My brother and I walked way out onto the breakers in the fading gray mist of morning. Standing there as the waves crashed on the rocks beneath us was unlike anything I'd experienced.

"You abandoned Mom," I told him, my pent-up anger suddenly unleashed.

Craig let my words hang in the air for a moment. Then he responded with a question, asking me why I continued to stay in the community. He was patient with me, and cautiously explained some of the journey that he had taken thus far.

He told me he'd gone to Colorado to get some space from the confines of the religion so he could think with a clearer mind and begin to do some research. He was convinced that there was no divine revelation behind our teachings. It was Craig's firm belief that a group of old men had been dictating the lives of everyone else. It was earth-shattering to him at the time to such a point that he became deathly ill. Listening to him tell it now, I was upset as well. But Craig was sensitive to where I was in my life and knew that I wasn't ready to absorb what he'd come to believe. He treaded lightly and did not try to sway my beliefs. Instead, he prepared me with thought-provoking questions in an attempt to understand where I stood. It was clear that the priesthood still had a great hold over me and that I was not at all ready to dismiss all that I had been taught.

I returned to Kassandra and Ryan's apartment feeling refreshed and—even so many miles away—somehow at home. That morning was the beginning of what would prove to be an incredibly eye-opening trip during which I started to ask inner questions of my religion that I had never before dared to ask. Watching Kassandra's little family and seeing joy on the faces of three of my brothers was a necessary lesson for me. My siblings had fallen from grace in the eyes of the priesthood, and they had supposedly signed themselves up for hell. However, being in their company confirmed the suspicion that I'd had all those years ago at Bear Lake: people on the outside are not wicked at all. They might live in a world of Hallmark holidays, cropped pants, and haircuts, but they are nothing like the demons that Warren spoke of.

This was my first solid look at life beyond the high walls of Short Creek, and it impacted my entire view of the world. In a bold move, I cut some of my hair in the front, making chic bangs. I also started wearing capris and some of the other modern styles Kassandra was into. One day, I joined Kassandra on a trip to the supermarket, donning my new pants, a pair of flip-flops, and a stylish short-sleeved top. As we walked from aisle to aisle, no one stared at me. It was the first time I'd been outside Short Creek without people noticing me. I felt unbelievably free. No one raised an eyebrow or tried to stifle laughter when I walked by. I looked just like everybody else.

The outing to the market was electrifying, but it couldn't compare with the pure joy I experienced when I spent Halloween with my siblings. Caleb and Justin both came over to Kassandra's to celebrate with us, and we had a blast carving pumpkins and decorating the house. In homage to my newfound adoration for *Pirates of the Caribbean,* I wore a white ruffled shirt, a pirate's hat, and britches in the form of cropped denim pants. I loved waiting for the doorbell to ring and jumped off the couch each time it did to see the cute neighborhood children in their wild costumes. Handing out packaged candy to little kids dressed as witches, princesses, and superheroes served as one more cherished taste of what life in the rest of the world could be like.

In retrospect I understand that my siblings—Kassandra and Craig especially—were laying the groundwork for what they knew I needed to do. They were not only exposing me to the simple joys of the real world but also zeroing in on me with thought-provoking questions and remarks about my life at home. I ate sushi for the first time and went out late-night bowling. Everything I did reminded me of my time with Meg, and I did things that I never could have dreamed of back in Short Creek. I was hungry for life, and everywhere I looked things were glossy and new.

At one point, I had a chance to sit down with Kassandra and learn what had really happened in the wake of Rulon's death that prompted her to leave the FLDS. The day Uncle Rulon died, his wives were in mourning, but they took heart in Warren's declaration that none of them would be married. This was followed by his similar statement to the whole congregation. But just one month later, he'd gathered all of his father's "ladies" together to announce his secret marriages to seven of them. Among them was Naomi, who would later stand before the community to deliver the message to the people that Warren was the next prophet and admit her union with him. These seven women were the first of Rulon's many young wives who would be reassigned.

I was shocked to hear about what had been going on inside the prophet's home. In the days after Warren married those first seven women, he'd begun to arrange for the marriages of some of Rulon's other young wives. He declared it their new mission in life to be married, explaining that this was the "next step" that Father wanted them to take. Kassandra told me of her panic as she watched her sister wives being given to the men that Warren deemed worthy, among them his brothers Isaac, Nephi, and Seth. Warren had even gone so far as to present her with a list of "worthy" men that she could marry. Suddenly, her escape made a lot more sense, and I felt bad about carrying around my anger over her unexplained departure.

The joy of my trip was momentarily halted when I received a call from my boss accusing me of having stolen merchandise. In the weeks before I left, a sales rep from California had come to Utah and was pushing to have me removed from the company. I was hurt to be shunned by my employer after a productive relationship with her. After hearing what was going on, Kassandra no longer wanted to represent Saladmaster. Her decision created even more trouble for me when my employer insisted that Kassandra pay for all the pots and pans I'd lugged to Oregon. It took a few days to resolve, but in the end I no longer had a job with Saladmaster.

Though the business aspect of my trip no longer mattered, I chose to extend my stay in Oregon. One of my last nights was celebrated with a picnic on the beach. We built a fire and roasted a chicken, all huddled together in the slightly chilly breeze of early evening. As we sat laughing and munching on the delicious food, the conversation shifted from light to deep. My siblings put me on the spot, questioning me about why I remained in the FLDS and trying to convince me to leave.

"Do you honestly believe in Warren?"

I had no answer.

"Why are you still there?" they pushed.

"I have to take care of Ally and Sherrie!" I retorted, the sting of abandonment still remembered in my heart. At the time I thought that neither Kassandra nor Craig had any idea what it had felt like to be deserted. It had happened to me six times, and the thought of inflicting that kind of a wound on Sherrie and Ally was deplorable.

It was a hard conversation, but in the end it was helpful for all of us. I finally felt free to confront Kassandra about the pain she had put me through when she fled. "I feel like you just left me."

She understood how I had felt and told me how sorry she was that she couldn't be there for me at that time. We hugged in reconciliation and I was relieved to be free of the weighty and difficult feelings of betrayal that I'd been carrying with me all this time. Then they told me something that was important for me to hear.

"You would not be an evil person if you left," Craig told me firmly. "You are whatever you decide to be."

The sun had long since disappeared over the glittering ocean, leaving us with only the flickering light from our fire to see by. I felt so warm and comforted beside them even with the new unsettling thoughts that swam around in my mind. I had been in Oregon for what felt like a short time, but already something in me was changing. I wasn't ready to take the big leap, and I appreciated that my brothers and sister could see that. Nonetheless, my eyes were opening to a new and different world, one that would allow me to be anyone I wanted.

After that night, the cell phone calls from Allen, which had been coming in throughout my stay in Oregon, became unavoidable. It had been almost three weeks since I'd left him, and his messages were getting more flustered and impatient every day. When I finally picked up, he sounded furious: "You come home right now." I knew that if I continued to ignore him and didn't go home right away, I would get into major trouble. Mom also phoned me, asking me to return.

"Lesie, come back, please," she said softly, almost pleading. "I can't lose you, too. I need you here, and these two little girls need you."

My taste of freedom and real life had been a thrilling adventure, but I knew my time in Oregon was over. My belief system had begun to fray at the edges, but it was far from gone, and my obligation to Mom and the girls weighed heavily on my mind. Quietly I still wondered: If I left, would I really be okay? Or would doomsday arrive and leave my wasted body behind while the righteous were lifted up to heaven?

I boarded a plane in my long, drab FLDS skirt and top, a far cry from the comfortable and stylish clothes I'd been loving in Oregon. Allen was waiting for me when I arrived in Vegas, wearing a look of frustrated disdain. I could see he was irritated with me and berated me during the trip home. "I'm your priesthood head!" he exclaimed, exasperated. "I am done sitting by and excusing your terrible behavior."

After a while I just stopped listening. I was shocked and amused to discover that all I could think to myself was, "I don't care."

Since I was no longer an employee of Saladmaster, I put myself on the schedule for some double shifts at the Mark Twain restaurant to make up for the drop in my income. I'd report in for my first shift around 11:00 A.M. and then stay on through closing after 10:00 P.M. In addition to bringing in extra money, this routine allowed me to spend a good part of the night away from home. Even though the restaurant closed at ten on weekdays and eleven on weekends, I would often stay until midnight to clean up and close it down. I was a good waitress, and customers seemed to enjoy me, and since I was making consistent money, I didn't have to ask Allen for anything. But I still had no place to sleep at night. Mom's room was mostly off-limits now, and I was tired of fighting with Allen.

I once again took to sleeping in my truck, only now that it was November, it was much more difficult. Fearful of being turned over to Uncle Warren by the police, I began to drive out of the FLDS community at night and park my truck in the desert. I equipped my vehicle with everything I would need to pass the night—a fuzzy blanket, a small pillow, a cooler filled with drinks, granola bars, and a small heater that I could plug in to my lighter. The desert gets cold fast at night, and with no cement to hold in the heat, I felt the chill of the autumn air. I'd purchased a small CD player to distract myself. My mind would just go insane if it was quiet. I was trying to be this tough girl, but inside I felt lost in the dark. Once I awoke to find a family of coyotes surrounding my truck. We'd long been told that the lands surrounding the Creek were haunted by the spirits of those who'd once walked "here" back in biblical days. The area had once been a thriving city, and God had destroyed it to cleanse the land. But the possibility of being confronted by a spirit was just another terrifying thought that permeated my imagination as I reclined in the driver's seat and tried to settle in for the night. While the eerie sounds of the coyotes and other nocturnal creatures frightened me, I preferred them to being at home with my husband. Part of the problem though was that I kept having to move farther into the desert because the Colorado City police kept finding me. Where once I'd been just on the edge of the barren lands, now I was deep into them, nearly two miles outside of town.

I would usually stay out there until 5:00 A.M., when I would slowly make my way back to the trailer, hoping that Allen would be gone to work for the day. He was working his same job at Reliance and had to leave early in the mornings. Once inside, I'd shower and then fall asleep until my next work shift. It had gotten to the point where I was spending just one or two nights a week with my husband. But even these brief times together landed me in trouble.

By mid-November our relationship had reached a new low. He was particularly upset with how much I was away from the trailer in light of the fact that I'd just gotten home from Oregon. I was already more than two months pregnant, but he still had no idea. After one argument in which he hit me, I began to feel that familiar cramping in my abdomen. Fearing the worst, I raced to the bathroom and was greeted by the worrisome sign of a miscarriage: I was bleeding. Desperate to get away from Allen, I ran out of the trailer without even stopping to grab a pair of shoes or my coat. Jumping into my truck, I headed for the desert. I was cramping so badly I had to stop at the gas station on the edge of town to use the facilities. I was passing blood clots, but with nowhere to go, I had to ride out the miscarriage in the restroom. A knock on the door startled me, and I was horrified when a man's voice informed me that the station was closing up for the night.

I cleaned up as best I could, got back into my truck, and headed for my usual spot in the desert. My truck slid to and fro as I tried to maneuver it up the small hill off the dirt road where I'd been parking at night. It had been raining for nearly a week, and the parched land had turned into a carpet of mud.

I tried to steer past a juniper tree when my tires began to sink into the wet terrain. It started to snow, and I could barely see where I was going. I pressed hard on the gas, but the truck wasn't moving. Not only was it muddy, I now had a flat tire.

Exasperated and in pain, I climbed out of the truck and reached into the back for my jack. I'd been on my own for some time and was familiar with changing tires, but I felt weak as I attempted to raise the front of the truck. Suddenly, I felt it slipping, and the next thing I remember I was lying on the ground beside the front fender.

That was when I saw the pair of headlights.

I immediately assumed it was the police. I was freezing, in the middle of a miscarriage, and I didn't even have shoes on. Now there was the possibility that I was going to be arrested for being out past curfew.

"Is everything all right?" I heard a man's voice ring out through the darkness.

All I could see was the outline of a person standing over me. "I'm fine," I blurted out, hoping that whoever it was would just go away.

"You don't look fine," the man pressed, moving in closer to where I lay covered in mud. I could tell by the way he stared down at me that he didn't believe me.

"Here, let me help you with that tire," he said gently. I hovered over him as he worked to put the front end of my Ford Ranger back on the jack. My body involuntarily shivered as I stood watching him. "You're freezing," he said. "Why don't you just go and sit in my truck while I fix your tire?"

"I can do it myself," I insisted, not wanting to put him out and involve him in my predicament.

"I'm sure you can," the man said, smiling, as he led me to his truck.

I felt so foolish sitting in the passenger seat as this stranger set about changing my tire. The air blowing from the car's heater began to warm me, and I tried to calm myself down. I grew worried as the man lowered my truck to the earth and then turned to get in beside me.

"Why are you out here?" he asked. His face looked remotely familiar, but I couldn't place it. He was not much older than Allen, maybe about twenty-five or so. I knew he was just trying to be kind, but I could get into a heap of trouble even talking to a strange man. All I could think of was getting out of there and fast. I knew he was waiting for an answer to his question, and I provided none.

"Are you okay?" he continued. "It looks like you have a black eye."

"Yeah, I'm fine," I quickly replied, looking down at my feet. I felt embarrassed that he had noticed my bruise from a recent argument with Allen.

"I'm Lamont Barlow," he told me. At that moment, I realized how I knew him. He was a friend of Meg's sister and for a while Meg had had a crush on him. She'd even borrowed his four-wheeler a couple of times that past summer.

"Oh," I replied, unwilling to tell him my name. After a few minutes, it became clear that I wasn't going to offer any more information.

"Well, here's my phone number," Lamont said, handing me a piece of paper he'd torn from a pad. "If you ever need anything—"

"I don't think I will," I cut in politely, and reaching for the door handle I climbed out of his truck. I felt incredibly weak, and the cramping in my stomach was intense. But I put on my best face and started toward my truck. "Thanks a bunch for helping me," I said, waving and straining to smile.

"Do you need a ride home? I don't think it's a good idea for you to drive," Lamont yelled after me.

"No," I shouted back, assuring him I was fine. Home was the last place I wanted to go at that moment. "Well, I'm just gonna follow you out to make sure you're okay. You have my cell number if you feel dizzy or can't drive. Call me and I'll pull over."

I watched in my rearview mirror as we crawled along in the muck toward the highway. As soon as I hit the paved road, I floored it. I didn't want him to know anything about me. I was certain he was going to turn me in to Uncle Warren.

I could not have been more wrong.

CHAPTER TWENTY-ONE

PROMISE NOT
TO TELL

Trust in God. He works in mysterious ways.
—SHARON WALL

Day was breaking as I steered my truck back toward town. All I could think of was getting to my mother. Pulling up in front of Uncle Fred's, I called up to my mom's room to have her buzz open the gate. Through the large windows of the back door, I could see my mother in her bathrobe, hurrying down the stairs toward me. Her face grew flushed with concern when she took in my mud-streaked clothes and my wet hair that was plastered to my tired face.

"Lesie!" she gasped. "What's wrong?"

"I'm having a miscarriage, Mom," I said in a lifeless voice, the words barely audible from my stooped position.

A pained look spread across Mom's face as she placed an arm around my shoulders, leading me upstairs to her new room in the north wing of the house.

"Do you need to see the midwives?" she asked.

"No! That's the last thing I want to do now," I told her. She was worried, but I was too delirious to care about anything.

"I am sorry this is happening again," Mom said with a mix of anger and sadness in her voice. "It's going to be okay."

My mother's reassuring words were the final thing I heard as I dozed off in her comfortable queen bed that morning. Over the next few days, Mom watched over me, which set my mind at ease. Her tenderness filled me with nostalgia; I was catapulted back to childhood, when skinned knees and bruises could be magically healed by my mom's touch. It felt so good to finally let her in after trying to keep my pain from her for so long. In this moment, I could be the little girl and let my Mom share some of the burden I'd been carrying alone. At least I wouldn't have to deal with Allen in this condition. My body was so worn out. Between my nights with Allen and in my truck, I'd barely been getting sleep. That exhaustion, combined with the physical trauma of yet another failed pregnancy, had taken its toll on me.

By this point, Allen didn't have much contact with my mother, but when he phoned to find out if I was there, I overheard Mom telling him that I was really sick. The tone in her voice telegraphed her anger. She also called the restaurant to alert my manager that I would be out for a few days. It was a relief to be back under Mom's protective wing, and I snuggled deep under the covers content to be free of Allen for the moment. But periodically, one worry would surface in my mind: the stranger who had helped me with my tire. I worried about who he would tell and what they would say. With paranoia so rampant in our community, I knew he would say something. It was only a matter of time.

I was at my mother's for several days before I finally had the strength to get up, and I knew I needed to get back to work. Looking in the mirror I saw that my eye was still bruised, but luckily I'd perfected the art of concealing my bruises with makeup, even though we weren't supposed to have it.

Meg had been worried about me and was happy to see me back at the restaurant. I'd barely made it through the door before she rushed over to find out how I was doing. I'd told her about the miscarriage, my tire, and the man who'd helped me on the dirt road in the desert that night. Meg assured me that Lamont Barlow wouldn't tattle on me to

Warren. She'd known him for a while and believed that he was a good guy.

My friend had her own pent-up drama from her days without me, and it came spilling out once she was sure that I was okay. For the last several months she had been in love with a boy from Short Creek named Jason, and they'd been sneaking off together until he left the FLDS. It was a risky situation, but she was worried that he'd forget her now that he was gone for good. I could tell that she really liked him, and often when we were driving together, she'd beg me to circle the block around his house, hoping to catch a glimpse of him. We acted so silly, giggling when we saw him out on the lawn or through a front window. We'd always duck down, hoping that he wouldn't see us. At night sometimes I'd drive her to secret rendezvous points where they could steal a few minutes together while I waited in the car.

A part of me worried that she would find herself in a situation much like my stepsister Lily's. I didn't want her to end up in a loveless marriage like mine, but I didn't really know what to say to her to make her feel better. As long as she was a member of the FLDS, she could never live out her dream of being with Jason.

It didn't take long for the lunch rush to hit. I was taking an order when I heard the bell on the front door ring, alerting us to more customers. Glancing over at the entrance, I spotted the sandy brown hair and the toothy smile of Lamont Barlow, the young man who'd helped me in the desert. He was there with several other men waiting to be seated. I quickly finished taking orders and dashed back into the kitchen to avoid being seen by him. Peering out from behind a corner, I watched as the hostess led his group to a table in my section. I raced back to the kitchen to talk to Meg, who was the cook. Even though it had been pitch-black and lightly snowing that night, I was certain that he would immediately recognize me if I waited on him. Though Meg assured me he wouldn't turn me over to Warren, I couldn't be sure. I begged the other waitress on duty to take my table. But she was already overloaded with customers.

I began to panic. "Meg," I whispered over the sizzle of burgers on the grill. "Help! I can't go back out there. The guy from the desert is here."

Peeking into the main dining area, she let out a giggle. "I've already told you, nothing is going to happen. He won't tell on you," she assured.

"I know, I know," I said in a low tone, wishing that he would just get up and leave. I was also feeling guilty that he'd given me his phone number. It was highly improper for me to have the number of a man other than my priesthood husband.

I walked shyly over to the corner booth, where he sat engaged in conversation with his friends. Pulling out my order pad, I greeted them, told them about our lunch specials, and asked, "What can I get for you today?" With my eyes fixed on my notepad, I tried not to look up for fear of making eye contact with him. It seemed like the longest shift of my life, but I managed to make it through without ever meeting Lamont's gaze.

Later on, I was at the register cashing out another customer when I felt someone staring at me. "I won't tell if you won't," I heard a man's voice whisper. I glanced up to see Lamont standing before me with his lunch check. Ordinarily that would not be enough to make me trust someone—such was the hysteria that Warren had introduced to all of us. But there was something in his smile that set me at ease. I smiled back at him as he settled his bill, but I didn't want to tell him anything about me.

Lamont turned up at Mark Twain's several more times that week. I didn't know how to react then or later when he came in having secured a job as a cook. I had no idea that Lamont had begun to ask questions about me. After our meeting in the desert, he was curious about me and began investigating. He knew I was Meg's friend, and he tried to find out from her why I had a black eye. It infuriated him to think that someone would strike a woman, and he grew even more upset when he heard that I was in an unhappy marriage.

It turned out that he'd seen me a couple of times over the

few months before we met in the desert; he even remembered me from a Pioneer Day parade some years back. I had
been one of the dancing girls, and he was marching just
ahead of us as a platoon leader for the Sons of Helaman. He
later confided that he'd been so taken with me that day that
he'd turned in the wrong direction when the church elder
called out his group's marching orders.

As the days turned to weeks, my timidity around Lamont
evaporated. The more I saw, the more I realized that he was
not out to get me into trouble, and we began to forge a
friendship. Lamont was living at his father's house in Hildale
at the time, but things at home were not going well for him.
At first I didn't know the full story, but from what I gathered
he'd had some trouble with Warren and was trying to recon-
cile his complex emotions about our faith with the residual
desire to reach heaven.

Later that month I met Meg and Jason at Brian Head Resort for a secret day of snowboarding. Jason had driven down
from Salt Lake, and I was surprised when Lamont showed up
to join us. They had a great group of friends, and their enthusiasm was infectious. Though he was a bit older, Lamont
had a fun and vibrant personality that lit me up. In the days
after our outing, I found myself wondering about him.

"What do you know about him?" I asked Meg as we
drove through town in my truck.

"Well," she said with a sigh, "he's had a rough life. His
mom died and growing into adulthood had been tough for
him."

I shook my head in quiet sadness. I thought of my love for
my own mother—that desperate, clinging love that held us
together. It was hard to imagine life without her, and I was
sure that Lamont had suffered a great deal from the loss.
Maybe wanting to protect Lamont's privacy, and also probably because she didn't know the whole story, Meg stopped
there and we moved on to other topics.

Meg and I continued to spend hours driving around, talking about life, and avoiding our homes. One of my favorite
things about my truck equipment was a tiny television with

a built-in VCR I had bought in secret. In the summer months and into the early fall, Meg and I had rented movies or borrowed them from Meg's older sister and driven out to the desert to watch them in the bed of the truck out under the stars. But winter's biting winds prompted us to simply hook up the TV between us on the dashboard and watch the movies side by side in the truck cabin.

Despite the fun that I had with Meg, my fourth failed pregnancy brought a renewed sense of desperation. My sporadic appearances at the trailer became even less frequent. Allen didn't like that I was away so much, but by that point there wasn't much he could do about it. I had been treating him with disregard ever since he'd forced himself on me after a fireside get-together in the foothills of the Vermillion Cliffs.

Before that gathering, I hadn't been spending much time with him, and I worried that I might get into trouble if I didn't agree to join him. We'd roasted marshmallows and enjoyed a few hours of fun with members of Allen's family and friends. When it began to grow dark, Allen asked me if I wanted to drive and talk for a while.

"Okay," I said, a little reluctant, but knowing I still had a responsibility as his wife. We circled around until Allen stopped the truck at a field that had a scenic overview of the twin towns. In his awkward way, Allen was trying to alleviate some of the dissension between us. At one point, he asked me if I ever wanted to have children. I didn't know how to answer. I didn't want to have children with him, but I knew he would view me as defiant if I told him the truth.

He opened the tailgate of the truck, and we sat with legs dangling, enjoying the twinkling lights of the sleeping towns and the sound of the crickets. Allen asked me why I was distant and hostile toward him. In the past, I had realized that my feelings didn't matter, but in this moment, I summoned the courage to again tell him the truth he didn't want to hear. Since my last miscarriage, the space I'd taken from Allen had allowed me to look at him and our relationship more closely. What I saw was that Allen and I were never supposed to be together, and it was never going to be anything other than what it was: a forced, ugly union. "You know, Allen, I just don't trust you," I said. "I just don't love you and I don't want to be here."

I waited to hear Allen's response, but there was none. A heavy silence fell between us as I blurted out what I had been holding in for so long. "Things you've done in the past have hurt me, and I just can't trust you anymore," I said. "I don't know how much longer I can do this."

"Well, if you just have a baby with me, things will change. You'll learn to love me," Allen replied in a desperate tone.

"No, I won't." It worried me to see that my words were making Allen frustrated. He reminded me that my salvation depended on my obedience to not just him but the prophet.

"The prophet has put you here," he reminded me. As I searched my mind for a response, I could feel Allen's hand on the back of my neck and his wet lips coming for mine.

"Don't do this," I told him. I knew his pattern. A kiss was just step one for him. It always led to more, and I was unwilling to go there. "Don't touch me. If you truly want to try and make this work, you are going to leave me alone."

"Well, you are my wife, and I am your priesthood head," he snapped back.

As I felt his hands move to my shoulders, I issued another warning. "Don't do this," I said. We were like two armies coming to battle, and I didn't want to give in. "If you do this, you will pay the consequences, and things will never be the same."

I tried to rise to my feet, but his strong grip was pushing me back into the camper shell. "We just need to have children and you'll feel different" were the last words I heard from his lips. Once again, Allen had me trapped. I had no vehicle to drive away from him.

"Do what you're going to do and just bring me home," I said. "I just want you to know it will never be the same."

That night I promised myself that I would never allow myself to be in that situation again. It was a promise that I kept. If I couldn't get a release from Allen, I would at least stand and protect myself.

While Mom had been able to get me into Uncle Fred's on some nights, it had become increasingly difficult to visit there without being noticed. In addition to the security gate that required a pass code, cameras had been strategically placed to survey the perimeter. On some nights my sister Ally would sneak down to let me in after everyone had gone to bed, but that wouldn't work every night.

When I couldn't stay with my mom, I went back to sleeping in the desert in my truck, but with winter fast approaching, my little plug-in heater was no longer sufficient to keep me warm. I figured out that if I turned the heater on for eleven minutes, it would warm the truck for at least an hour. I had to be careful not to fall asleep while the heater was on because it might drain the battery.

One day in December I was at the Twain, as we affectionately nicknamed our restaurant, chatting with Lamont, who'd stopped in for a meal. He told me that he had a movie he wanted to lend to me, and I could feel my cheeks grow instantly pink. My little television adapter and my "wild" nights with Meg watching films were rebellious enough by FLDS standards. To borrow a film from a boy would be a huge taboo. At first I reflexively declined Lamont's offer, but after I thought about it some more, I decided to take him up on it.

We agreed to meet out in the desert so he could lend me the movie without us being caught. When I approached, I noticed his truck immediately. It was a stunning gold Ford F-350 jacked up on huge tires. In Short Creek, a boy's truck was his baby, and Lamont's was gorgeous. So I was absolutely shocked when he insisted that I take it for a drive. "No way!" I declared, smiling.

Lamont's soft blue eyes lit up and his white teeth shone in a large grin. "Come on, now," he said, "How often do you get to drive a truck like this?"

He was right and we both knew it. I shifted my weight from one foot to the other, contemplating what to do. "Well, okay," I agreed, trying to stifle my excitement. I was nervous as heck when I climbed up into the driver's seat and shifted into gear. What if I crashed his truck? What if we got caught? My mind raced too quickly for me to catch up.

Gently, Lamont teased, "Give it a little more gas than that, Elissa." He laughed. And I did too. Slowly, I pushed my foot down a little farther and off we went, kicking up dust and careening around the desert landscape like two kids.

As the drive came to an end Lamont and I found ourselves talking, unable to stop. He asked me where I'd grown up, and I told him that I was from Salt Lake City. He had noticed my surname, Wall, because legally this was still my name and I needed to use it at work.

"I haven't known many Walls," he said, "but I am a friend of Travis."

I smiled at the mention of Travis, missing all of my brothers fiercely at once. Lamont had spent some time in Salt Lake, where he had linked up with Travis, who I hadn't seen since Mom moved us to Hildale in 1999. I eagerly soaked up the stories about him and how cool Lamont thought he was. For years my family had worn a black mark. It was refreshing to hear someone speak with respect and admiration for one of my siblings, especially one of my brothers whom I loved and missed so deeply.

When Lamont told me that his mother had died after falling into a coma, I was shaken to the core. Tears clouded his blue eyes as he briefly detailed the story for me.

"I am so sorry," I said almost in a whisper. Yet it felt comforting to have someone trust me with such a personal story. I had never had a man outside of my family confide in me like this, and for the first time ever, I had the sense that I was connecting with a member of the opposite sex.

The days wore on, and my friendship with Lamont deepened. One day he called Meg and asked for her help, explaining that he was suffering a bout of lymphedema. I asked Meg about his condition, and she explained that

Lamont's lymph nodes were prone to infection; if one shut off, the others would back up. The infections caused him high fevers and discomfort that could only be treated with antibiotics. I was upset to hear that Lamont was sick and I wanted to comfort him without being overbearing, so I sent him a text message saying, "I hope you get feeling better."

Meg had offered to drive to Hurricane to pick up his prescription, so we hopped into my truck and were on our way. Of course, there was a pharmacy closer to home, but if we got caught there, we would be chastised. We couldn't let people know that we were associating with a man who wasn't our priesthood head. Meg dialed Lamont's cell phone, and he was able to drag his fevered body out of bed long enough to meet us in the Sticks, where we could secretly hand over his meds. I worried quietly about him for the next two days, but I didn't want to disturb him. Finally, he texted me and thanked me for what I'd done, saying he hoped we could keep our friendship in the future. I was ecstatic but a little scared. I enjoyed Lamont's company more than that of any other man I'd met. Already our friendship had broken the rules of the church, and I didn't know where things might go.

Just a few days after our trip to Hurricane, Meg and I were both working the dinner shift, and I could tell that something was up. Her typical carefree look was not there when she climbed into the passenger seat that night for the drive home.

"Lesie," she said, tears filling her eyes, "I have to go." The words came out almost in a whisper as Meg told me that Jason was coming to get her the very next day. They were heading to Salt Lake City together. "I need your help," Meg pleaded. "Please."

That familiar feeling of being left behind came crashing back, but I didn't let it get the better of me. Though the loss would be monumental, I had to help my friend. She was opening up to me the way that I had wanted Kassandra to, and I could not bring myself to try and convince her to stay. When Kassandra left, I thought she was damning herself to hell, but now I knew this wasn't true. I didn't want Meg to end up by the side of some old man or, worse, with a man she didn't love. Jason cared for her and she for him. That was enough for me.

Solemnly, I nodded. "Of course I'll help you." We shared a long hug, and I tried to control my sobs. When we finally let go of each other, I shifted the truck into drive, wanting to make the most of our last night. Together, we rode through the encroaching darkness of night, blasting our Bon Jovi and Bad Boys Blue CDs and belting out verses in a final hurrah.

We saw each other the following day, had lunch, and even snuck off to one last movie. That night, I arrived beneath Meg's window to help her escape. I softly called out to her, and almost immediately one of her bags was thrust in my direction. With only starlight to guide us, we ran down the road to where I had discreetly parked my truck. A passing car nearly spoiled everything—you never knew who could be out making the rounds to get people into trouble—but we hid and continued on our way unnoticed. We reached my vehicle and hopped in, then drove to a gas station several miles outside of town, where Jason had arranged to meet us.

I handed Meg her half of a crystal friendship pendant on a chain that I had ordered for us only a week before. The necklaces did not interlock in the traditional way to form a heart, but when they were laid one on top of the other, the light created a heart within them. "I want you to wear this," I said, "and know that you are always in my heart."

Tears streamed down both our cheeks as Meg promised, "I will always be with you." We shared one final embrace. Meg took her belongings and headed for Jason's car, waving once before getting inside. Frozen behind the steering wheel, I watched them drive away until the taillights disappeared.

The days after Meg left were agonizing, and Lamont sent me a text message saying that if I ever needed anything, I could call him. I didn't want to plague Mom and the girls with my problems, so I took him up on his offer, finding refuge in long phone conversations with him. His soft and affirming friendship kept me afloat. The sweet taste of Oregon had not gone away, and I tried to remember all that I had learned from that trip. It was difficult without Meg, and with all the tumult in the past two years I had become like a body with no soul. But through the storm, although I couldn't see it then, the clouds were beginning to part, and I found friendship in Lamont. I could feel the chemistry growing between us, but fear prevented me from saying a word to anyone about it. Besides, there was no one left to talk to.

CHAPTER TWENTY-TWO

A STORY LIKE MINE

Always strive to be a better parent to your children
than your parents were to you.
—DALEEN BATEMAN BARLOW

As my friendship with Lamont strengthened, my family
life continued to take unpredictable turns, only this time
it was not my marriage that caused upheaval, it was my
mom's. One night in late December, Uncle Fred mysteriously
vanished. Under the cover of darkness, an ambulance arrived at the Jessop house to collect the bishop. I would later
hear that a few of Fred's daughters actually saw several men
enter the house and load Fred onto a stretcher. Beyond those
eyewitness accounts, no one knew anything else; Warren
did not say a word about it to anyone in public.

It wasn't until two days after Fred's sudden removal that I
learned additional details from Mom. She and the other
members of the Jessop family were shocked when church
elder William T. Jessop gave them the fateful news. William
was the son of one of Uncle Fred's wives, and like mine, his
mother had been reassigned to Uncle Fred. Though technically by priesthood standards his last name was Jessop, I
always thought of him as William Timpson, just as I thought
of myself as Elissa Wall.

"Uncle Fred is gone," William Timpson told members of

the Jessop family that morning. "I have been assigned to be your new caretaker."

He did not elaborate. In fact he offered little consolation to the group of anxious wives and children who had no choice but to watch in stunned silence as William Timpson and members of his family moved into Fred's house over the next few days and assumed control. With no concrete information as to the whereabouts of Uncle Fred, rumors began to circulate throughout the household. Some of the wives speculated that Uncle Fred was so worthy that he'd been taken to Zion. It was unclear how many of his wives had gone with him the night he was taken away, which heightened the concern among those who remained. Over the weeks, a consensus set in that the wives who'd been left behind were not worthy enough to move on and would remain in Hildale for now.

I could sense Mom was terrified at the prospect of never reaching Zion, and she quietly fretted over her uncertain future. Once again, she was losing a husband due to the prophet's decision. And as a believer, she didn't want to have sacrificed so much just to lose it all.

It would be more than two weeks before the prophet publicly addressed us about Fred's disappearance, and his words did little to assuage Mom's heightened anxiety. "I have released Uncle Fred from his duties as bishop," Warren told us during a meeting in early January. "I assure all of you that Uncle Fred is in full agreement with this decision."

Memories of Winston Blackmore surfaced in our heads, and Warren's declaration immediately raised suspicions for some of us. Fred's leaving was too sudden and mysterious to be explained with such a simple statement. The fact that his wives didn't know what was going on created an even greater air of secrecy. Without Uncle Fred there to confirm Warren's statement, there was no way to know what had really happened to him, but no one dared to question Warren's vague account. In the days that followed, some quietly claimed that Warren had sent Fred to an FLDS compound in Colorado or Texas.

During this same meeting, Warren announced that William Timpson Jessop would replace Fred as bishop of Short Creek. To see such a youthful man in such a highly regarded position was strange. William was in his mid-forties, and there were many other men in our community who were more prepared for this key role. But his appointment had come from the prophet, and that was all that mattered.

Again, another New Year had come and gone and the Great Destructions had not covered the lands. The pressure on the people was even greater now to be perfect and pure, as we were told the end would be coming any day. The following week saw another shake-up. It was early in the morning of January 10, 2004, and we were all assembled in the meetinghouse for the Saturday work project. Uncle Warren had stopped Sunday church meetings but not the Saturday work meetings. He wanted the men to work and the people to continue to turn their money over to the priesthood.

"I seek unto the Lord that only his will and purpose be done this day," Warren began in his persuasive monotone. "The Lord has placed upon me the mission to search for the pure in heart. Whom the Lord loves he chastises and grooms. I come with a message of correction and an invitation of repentance."

Whereas in past meetings Warren had delivered his sermons in strong, self-assured fashion, this day his voice was shaky and he continuously cleared his throat. It seemed he was not entirely comfortable with what he was about to do, but he forged ahead. He praised the "good work" of church elders and prophets John Y. Barlow and his own father, Rulon. Then he made a startling announcement. He read eight names from a list—four were sons of Barlow, four were sons of Rulon, Warren's own blood brothers. He denounced each of these individuals as "master deceivers" and ordered them out of the community.

Just as he had eliminated the threat of Winston Blackmore in the months before his father's death, now it seemed he had purposely removed Uncle Fred in the weeks before executing this very public expulsion of respected and beloved church members. He knew that Uncle Fred was the only person who could and would protest such an outrageous decree.

"Verily, verily, thus sayeth the Lord to this people, all those who join with these deceivers and hypocrites will be darkened and will have to be cast out," Warren affirmed.

Too fearful to utter a word, congregants sat like drones listening to these unbelievable declarations, too afraid to look over at those men who were seated among us. Many of them were longtime friends of these men, and a good number were their relatives and descendants. One of the names mentioned was George, the respected patriarch and Lamont's grandfather, but not a word was spoken in his or anyone else's defense.

Addressing the four Barlow men directly, Warren offered these vague reasons. "You judged and criticized legitimate authority," he said, before turning his focus to their wives. "All you ladies married to these men are released from them and will remove yourselves immediately from their presence. If you don't, I will have to let you go."

In that moment Mom and I swapped disbelieving glances, but before any whispers could be exchanged, Uncle Warren delivered yet another blow. Thirteen additional men were to be exiled, including nine who had wives and families and four who were the sons of upstanding church members.

Nothing like this had ever occurred in the church. A banishment on this scale, and in this public manner, was unprecedented. What had begun with Jethro Barlow's exile the previous year came to fruition that day. It was a slippery slope that Warren was bringing us down, and few of us had the courage to say anything about it.

"The work of God is a benevolent dictatorship. It is not a democracy." We all sat frozen as he addressed those now standing and elicited votes on their own fates. "If you go along with this, raise your hand," he said, watching as twenty-one hands went up in unison.

Uncle Warren next called upon the people of the congregation to raise their hands in favor of the will of God. He watched carefully to see if there were any dissenters among the hundreds of raised hands. I felt horrible as fear forced me to lift my own hand in the air to be counted.

"Does anyone oppose?" Warren asked. "Raise your hand and stand up if you do."

Looking back, I wish that I and the other members had shown the courage to stand to defend these men. But as we exchanged terrified glances, everyone cowered; no one wanted to be the only one.

"I am calling for a fast for the next two days," Warren instructed. "All of the families are to keep to themselves."

Warren brought the meeting to a close, asking the entire congregation to kneel as he gave a lengthy prayer. As we recited "Amen" in unison, a sudden movement on the pulpit caught my attention, and I looked up to see Uncle Warren literally racing from the stage. It was not clear why he was in such a hurry, but in retrospect I have wondered whether it was fear of an uprising. Whatever dissent there may have been in the hearts of the people, they bit their tongues and said nothing.

I hadn't been out of the meeting for more than an hour when a text message popped up on my phone. It was Lamont asking that I call him. When I reached him later that day, it was the first time I'd ever heard him sound so angry. "What the hell is going on?" he asked me. "If my grandfather is screwed, then I'm screwed." Lamont hadn't been at the meeting that day, but one of his relatives was and he had immediately called Lamont to tell him what had happened. Lamont told me how he'd arrived at his grandfather's house feeling like this whole thing was his fault, and he tried not to be seen as he listened to his grandfather address his family.

"He was weeping and destroyed," Lamont told me. "He told his family to turn to the prophet. He said he was submitting to the will of the prophet. He had a testimony and was going to prove his faithfulness during this test."

Lamont knew that something wasn't right. Warren's

words came as a shock, but his motives had been in place long before. This latest action, however, pushed things too far. It was hard to believe that such a drastic and unprecedented step was actually the will of God. I could hear frustration and anguish with Warren and the FLDS way of life hiding in Lamont's voice that day.

In the months since Lamont and I first met, I had been slowly learning that he possessed a history of challenging the priesthood that was as colorful and fraught as my own. Like me, Lamont had been raised in an FLDS home that was marked with turmoil and dissent. Like me, he had asked some difficult questions with difficult answers. Like me, his road to our meeting in the desert had been paved with hardship and doubt.

He was the oldest of eight children and grew up aware of problems in his parents' marriage. His mother, Daleen, was just sixteen when she was placed by the side of Lamont's father, Grant Barlow, a staunch FLDS follower who had been raised to respect and abide by the teachings of the priesthood by his father, George. Their union went smoothly at first. They were both very young and had enjoyed many good times together. But aspects of the religion began to challenge their love. Daleen was not the kind of woman to submit when she felt she was in the right. Broad and big-boned, she was unwilling to blindly follow things she did not wholeheartedly agree with. Because of her "rebellious" attitude, she often found herself being marched up to the home of her father-in-law for a reprimand. Daleen was aware that George was a patriarch of their church and wielded a lot of clout, however, not even his influence could lead her to "correct" her insubordinate streak. She resented having a man who wasn't even her husband tell her how to raise her children, run her home, and handle her marriage.

Complicating matters was the fact that Grant frequently struggled to feed his growing family. He had been instructed by his father and the former prophet Leroy Johnson to work for his uncle in their sheet-metal shop, but he rarely received any compensation for his work. As a result the family barely had enough food to survive and Daleen was forced to watch her children go hungry, unable to do anything about it. Grant's lack of care for his children created a rift in their marriage that deepened over time. The two were often at odds over the extent to which the church's teachings would be upheld in their home, and their arguments were heated.

Finally Lamont's father found the courage to go against the advice of the elders and find a job that provided an actual paycheck, but eventually new problems took root in the marriage. The Split in the church at the end of Uncle Roy's days caused a division between Lamont's parents, as many members of Daleen's family decided to leave the FLDS. Lamont's mother sided with her relatives, and it got to the point where Grant forbade his wife from associating with some of her sisters because of their apostate status.

But Daleen didn't feel it was right to have to choose between her family and her church, and she had the courage to eventually leave the FLDS and take her kids with her.

On July 3, 1992, Daleen summoned her eight children to the front yard. She had told them they were going somewhere, but they had no idea where. Lamont told me that he and his siblings were at first excited at the prospect of an adventure but became a little bit apprehensive when one of their mother's sisters pulled up in a van. The big Fourth of July celebration was to be the next day, and they worried they wouldn't be back to partake in the fun.

"Get in," his mother instructed. She'd directed the kids to pack as much stuff as they could fit in a suitcase, and she loaded up the car. Lamont hesitantly obeyed, but when he realized what his mother was doing, he was furious. Though he knew things were difficult at home, Lamont had never expected her to flee and he had no interest in leaving the community. When it became clear that his mother didn't intend to return, Lamont worried about seeing his friends and family again.

As the eldest child, he tried to put on a brave face for his younger brothers and sisters who cried furiously as the van wound its way along Highway 59 to St. George. His mother took them to stay with one of her sisters, who'd left the FLDS many years before. But her trailer was hardly big enough to accommodate his mom and her eight children, which made things difficult for everyone. At school, Lamont fared little better, fighting to adjust to the new way of life. Back in Short Creek, he had been popular among his peers and loved the community, but public school in St. George was a different story. His classmates teased him mercilessly for being a member of the FLDS and for the way he dressed. The family was so poor that Lamont had just two pairs of pants, one that was too short and another that he couldn't button around his waist.

Lamont did his best to keep his complaints to himself. Life on the outside had saved his mother, and he began to see a side of her he'd never encountered before. She went out in the evenings with her sisters. She smiled and laughed and even met a man whom she felt deeply in love with. Daleen lit up when he was around, and over the next few months Lamont and his siblings came to know and like him, too. But the romance ended abruptly when Daleen became pregnant with his child.

Then one day in late 1992, less than six months after he and his siblings had left the FLDS, Lamont's aunt returned home to the trailer in tears. His mother had suffered a rupture in her uterus and, in pain, collapsed to the ground, striking her head extremely hard on the tile floor. She was bleeding internally and sustained some brain damage as a result of her fall. By the time the ambulance arrived she was in a coma, and there was no indication of whether she would ever come out of it.

With Daleen incapacitated, Grant quickly tried to repossess his children. To avoid him, Lamont's aunts would load Lamont and his siblings into a car and drive them furiously around St. George. His mother's relatives would lecture him and his siblings about how evil their father was. Lamont had always loved and respected his father, and these stories made him confused and unsure what to believe. The resentment that he'd felt toward his mother for taking them out of

Short Creek began to fade, and for the first time he started to have a more balanced sense of what had really gone on at their home.

Every second that he could, Lamont, was holding vigil by his mom's bedside, but by late December she'd been moved to a long-term-care facility. It was ten in the morning on December 30, 1992, when Lamont received the devastating news that his mother had passed away.

As if losing her wasn't hard enough, that night his grandfather came to him and directed that he and his siblings not attend a funeral service in St. George that her family was planning. "They are apostates," George told his grandson.

Already, the priesthood leaders had denied his mother the right to a proper funeral service in the FLDS Church. All they would allow was a graveside, closed-casket ceremony. In their eyes she was a wicked woman who died because she'd left the priesthood. To further inflame Lamont's already conflicted feelings, he was told that the prophet, Rulon Jeffs, had held a prayer circle with Lamont's father and grandfather to pray that God intervene on Grant's behalf. They'd put a photo of Lamont's mother at the center of their circle and "placed her in the hands of God." As Lamont understood it, they'd asked for God to take her life so that Grant could get his children back.

The fact that this group of men would wish harm upon her for making the choice she felt was right for her family presented huge doubts in Lamont's mind that something was wrong with his father and the church. Leaving Short Creek had been challenging for Lamont, but he had never wished for his return to happen like this. In the coming years, Lamont said he'd discovered a respect and admiration for his mother's strength. He celebrated her ability to do what was right in her eyes and not blindly follow one man's word. Her death only reinforced the importance of the role that she had played in his life, magnifying her legacy even then to the point where Lamont abhorred his father's views and the church that had created them.

It was with these thoughts in mind that Lamont and two

of his brothers snuck out of the community and attended his mother's funeral in St. George. When his father arrived in town later in the day to take the boys home, Lamont refused to get into the car. Buoyed by his many aunts and uncles, Lamont grew indignant as his father fought with him to get in.

"This is your choice," Grant Barlow told his son before driving off that day.

It was a choice that Lamont soon regretted. While his many aunts and uncles had wanted him and his siblings to remain with their mother, none were prepared to take on the guardianship of a rebellious, angry, and grieving fifteen-year-old. In the end, he went to Salt Lake City, where he lived with one of his mother's sisters who, ironically, was still a member of the FLDS.

For the next two years he struggled in Salt Lake, attending Alta Academy under Warren's watchful eye. Lamont had a terrible time adjusting and being accepted by his aunt's family. He felt extremely misunderstood and because of all the confusion he'd been experiencing, he often found himself on the receiving end of harsh punishments. He was a teenage boy who'd lost his mother and his community, and much like my own brothers, he didn't have anyone to understand him or to confide in. Lost and searching to find his way, Lamont finally broke down and telephoned his dad in 1995 to ask if he could return home.

It felt so good to be back in Short Creek, but soon he was battling a host of issues stemming from the fact that he had been unable to mourn his mother's loss properly. He fell in with a rough crowd and got into trouble. Methamphetamines were being smuggled into the FLDS community with some regularity and Lamont began using. It was not long before his reckless behavior landed him kicked out of his father's house, and later in the hospital. An overdose of pills and complications of his lymphedema nearly claimed his life.

Under these dire circumstances, Grant came to Lamont's bedside one afternoon and asked his son to come back home.

"Lamont, why don't you just come home and be my son?" he said in a humble, soft tone. In the months before his overdose, Lamont had been living in an old converted school bus with a mattress for a bed. His father's words brought him to tears, and when Lamont left the hospital, he prayed to the Lord to help him be strong and never touch drugs again.

Once back in Short Creek, Lamont became a dedicated member of the church. He attended services often and donated as much time as he could to the various work church projects. He was so happy to be welcomed back into the priesthood and even more excited when his grandfather took a personal interest in him. George Barlow told Lamont how proud he was of his hard work, and he spent a fair amount of time encouraging his grandson to follow the priesthood. As time wore on, though, Lamont started to wonder if he would ever be able to shake off the stigma of his unruly past. Several of his birthdays went by with no mention of a possible marriage for him. In the FLDS, the pressure for men to marry is just as intense as it is for the women. Men are expected to marry quickly after receiving the priesthood, and those that the prophet passes over are usually viewed as tainted. Men who reach the age of twenty-five without a wife are considered a menace to society. The older Lamont got, the less chance there was that he would have a bride.

Just as Warren kept close watch on the girls as they got older, so he did with the boys. He had long known that Lamont was a potential source of contention, given his mother's escape and death. In addition, Warren would have boys in the FLDS write letters of "confession" in which they were forced to disclose some of their most personal secrets in order to repent. Using these letters and other information, Warren branded troublesome boys from an early age, just as he did difficult girls. The only difference was the solution. Problem girls were married as soon as possible. Problem boys didn't get married at all.

There were a host of reasons why Rulon and Warren would pass a man over for marriage, but in Lamont's case the reason seemed obvious: he had strayed too far, too young. His open conflict with the religion and his strong feelings for his apostate mother were not to be trusted. It didn't matter that his refreshed vigor for the church was genuine. All that mattered was whether the prophet could trust him.

Because of Lamont's renewed faith, he desperately wanted a family so that he could teach the invigorating power of the priesthood, but as for all members of the FLDS, his fate was not his own. Lamont expressed his concern to his grandfather. Already, three of his four sisters had been married, and he was the oldest child of the family. His grandfather assured him that his time would soon arrive. When his twenty-third birthday came and went, his worry increased. Later that year, he was passed over for marriage again. This time, Warren selected his younger brother Steve to receive a wife. The union was performed in secret, but Steve quietly took Lamont aside to inform him of it, knowing that he would be hurt if he found out some other way. Each time he and his brothers had gone to see Uncle Warren, the messages he'd imparted to the boys were different. While he'd tell Lamont's younger brothers that they "needed to prepare for marriage," to Lamont he'd say, "You need to learn to love the truth."

It was a riddle, and Lamont couldn't decipher it. He persevered with the support of his grandfather, but all that ended in late 2002 when Lamont's next youngest brother, Mike, was assigned a wife. While he was happy for his brother, it was at this moment that Lamont realized that he had no future with the FLDS. His only remaining unmarried brother was handicapped, which meant that he had been passed over by the prophet for marriage intentionally. With Warren as the prophet, he would never be assigned a wife. To compound his confusion and frustration, Lamont had started a concrete company with two of his cousins, and was beginning to plant its footprint when disaster struck. After the expulsion of Lamont's uncle Jethro he'd agreed to help him move his things from the community. But word got around that Lamont was fraternizing with apostates and his partners turned on him, thus pushing him out and dissolving the company, leaving Lamont financially destroyed. It seemed that in an instant, the priesthood had again taken everything from him. His company was destitute and he'd been again passed over for a wife. Even though his mind and heart were still true to the religion, he'd lost all hope.

The following morning he paid his grandfather a visit and in a tearful exchange explained why he was leaving the church. George Barlow did his best to try to persuade him to stay and even followed Lamont to Salt Lake City to convince him to come home. In Salt Lake, Lamont was living with some other friends who had just left the church, but in less than two months, he was out of money and sleeping in his truck. Word of his failed business precluded him from finding work, as potential employers in the Salt Lake Valley who'd once been affiliated with the FLDS were swayed by the rumors that Lamont was to blame for his business' failure and declined to hire him. While his efforts to get on his feet had been valiant, he'd repeatedly been turned down wherever he went. He hadn't eaten in days and his cell phone was about to be shut off. That's when his grandfather came to him with an offer of redemption. Grandfather Barlow told him that there was still a chance for him to come back and make a life for himself in Colorado City. All he had to do was follow the will of the prophet, and the will of the prophet was for him to sign a paper in order to prove his faithfulness to the church.

Apparently, the wife of a prominent FLDS member had fled the community with her children and had sought refuge with Lamont's aunt in Salt Lake City. During his time in Salt Lake, he had seen the woman over at his aunt's house, and now his grandfather wanted him to sign a court affidavit listing a number of accusations to help the woman's husband, a leading church elder, fight to obtain custody of their children. In return, Lamont would have the opportunity for a life in the FLDS and be reunited with his family. Since it was the prophet making this request, chances were excellent that if he complied, Lamont would gain Warren's good favor and be allowed to come back to Colorado City and perhaps have a chance at the future he'd been working so hard toward.

Destitute and longing for his family and friends, Lamont agreed. Short Creek was the only place where he'd ever felt useful, and the idea of returning home filled him with joy. Five hundred dollars in cash was suddenly placed in his hand.

"Warren said you're going to need this," his grandfather told him.

It was the prophet's wish that Lamont check in to a hotel in St. George where he was to remain for one week. He was to use the money for the room and board and stay inside, have no contact with anyone except his grandfather, and write a letter of confession to the prophet. Determined to prove his worthiness, Lamont didn't even turn on the television set for the entire week. But at the end of those seven days there was still no word from Warren.

His grandfather came to see him every day and offered him support.

Lamont took strength in his grandfather's encouraging words, but he was worried. He had run out of money and the hotel was asking him to leave. Grandfather Barlow instructed him to return to his father's house and contact Uncle Warren's as soon as he could.

It took several tries before Lamont finally reached the prophet.

"How are you, Lamont?" Warren asked. "I got your letter of confession." Lamont held his breath, hoping the prophet approved of what he'd written. "Did you sign the document?" Warren asked, referring to the court affidavit.

"Yes, I have," Lamont answered politely.

For a moment, there was dead silence on the other end of the line. "Well, you can move back into your father's house," Warren instructed.

"Oh, I'm already at Father's," Lamont said.

"You are?" Warren asked, sounding surprised.

"Yes, Grandfather instructed me to move in."

"I see," Warren said, pausing again before delivering the decision that would seal Lamont's fate. "Well, you've lost your priesthood. You will need to be rebaptized. Keep the spirit of God."

Lamont's heart sank as he heard the click on the other end of the line. The conversation had lasted less than thirty seconds. He'd done everything the prophet had asked. He'd stayed at the hotel. He'd written the letter of confession. He'd even signed that horrible paper to help Warren bring back the woman who'd escaped with her kids. The guilt from that was overwhelming, and still he was being punished.

When Lamont had first looked at the legal document, he'd felt torn. On the one hand, he was defeated and he'd lost his business and his family, and he just wanted to go home to a place that was familiar. On the other hand, he knew that by signing the paper he would be making enemies with the only family that he had outside the FLDS Church, not to mention that he would let down this young woman who was trying to protect her children. I sensed there were issues that Lamont had with his family in Salt Lake, and while he didn't want to burden me with them, I could tell that he'd been deeply hurt.

Signing that paper had been wrong on so many levels, and it was clear from how Lamont spoke that it was the greatest regret of his life. In that one phone call to Warren, all of his hopes of getting a family and living his faith were dashed. His sacrifices were deemed irrelevant, and he was back at square one. The prophet had given him no indication of when he could expect to be baptized, especially since Warren had discontinued the practice as part of the community's punishment for erecting the monument to Uncle Roy. Lamont feared he would never rejoin the priesthood, let alone have the chance to marry, but he didn't want to be homeless again. Unwelcome in Salt Lake City, he had no other choice but to stay at his father's house for the time being.

He hung up the phone with Warren, realizing he may have made the biggest mistake of his life for nothing. For months he just existed in the community, not sure how he would ever prove faithful or worthy. That fall, he received more devastating news. Warren had sent a message to say that he had lost a future in the priesthood and there was no hope for him. Lamont had done nothing to provoke this latest retribution. He had stayed under the radar, but his usefulness to Warren was done and it was apparent more than ever that his desperate desires to be a faithful member of the community had been used. He had been nothing more than a pawn and Warren had waited for the legal case to which they had tied Lamont's name to die down to deliver this final blow. Climbing into his truck, Lamont set off for the barren lands of the Arizona strip. The wide-open desert was the one place where he found peace and could think things through. It was late November and a chill had set in, but Lamont was too distraught to notice. A war raged inside him as he fought the urge to just end it all. While there had been several times in the past when he'd entertained the idea of taking his own life, on this night he felt particularly melancholy. He couldn't imagine again moving on and having his family disown him once more, but the thought of growing old alone in a society where marriage is everything was too painful. As he pressed on the gas pedal, a light snow began to fall over the desert. Cranking up the radio, he steered along the muddy route toward the radio tower, about two miles in from the road. Suddenly, headlights caught his sight and he steered over to see if he could lend a hand. It appeared that someone had gotten stuck in the mud and was struggling to get a car out.

Jumping from the cab of his truck, he saw a young girl lying on the ground beneath the front end of her vehicle. She seemed to be in pain, and he asked if he could help.

It was fitting that Lamont found me when he did. In a strange way, Warren really had controlled our fate: had he not revoked Lamont's priesthood when he did, Lamont never would have gone driving and never would have found me in my sorry state. Likewise, if I hadn't been on the run from

Allen, I would never have been out in the desert. Our chance encounter had been born out of our individual hardships, circumstances colliding to change everything.

For the first months of our friendship, Lamont did his best to conceal his difficult past, but it had come out in bits and pieces. Now, with the exile of his grandfather, his fear became palpable. He worried that his grandfather's banishment was his fault, and he feared that it would not be long until Warren removed him as well. If Warren was purging the ranks of even the most pure, like Lamont's grandfather, then a pariah like Lamont who'd lost the priesthood would not be far behind.

Talking to him on the phone after his grandfather's banishment, I could hear the uncertainty in his voice, but I could also sense something else—an excitement to talk to me and a reassurance that the only thing comforting him now was the sound of my voice. By the time we got off the phone, he was no longer frantic. He was still concerned, but our conversation had relaxed him. I'd provided the support that he'd needed.

That night, hours after we'd hung up, the importance of that conversation began to come into focus for me. The dependence forming between us had grown dangerous. Our closeness had become something else as we relied on each other for sanctuary from our difficult situations. I didn't know what was happening. But I didn't want to stop it.

CHAPTER TWENTY-THREE

LOVE AT LAST

Happiness is the object and design of our existence.
—JOSEPH SMITH

Despite the growing strength of my friendship with Lamont, Meg's absence from Short Creek was painful. She'd reached out to me in the weeks after she and Jason fled to Salt Lake City to let me know that they were doing fine and she missed me, but beyond that our conversations had been infrequent.

One day Meg called and told me about a trip to Las Vegas that she and Jason were planning to celebrate Valentine's Day. Worldly holidays such as this one were strictly forbidden in the FLDS, and their special overnight adventure sounded romantic. I couldn't imagine doing something like that with Allen. I was surprised when Meg begged me to join them in Vegas.

"Come on, Lesie, it will be so fun," she insisted.

The idea of spending a whole weekend hanging out with my best friend was enticing, but in the wake of Uncle Warren's recent punishments, I was nervous about breaking any rules and the potential repercussions of getting caught. I wracked my brain trying to come up with ways to escape to Vegas, but it was terrifying. I couldn't think of a legitimate excuse to use if someone asked where I was going. Finally, I just decided to do it.

"I'm going to Vegas with Meg and Jason this weekend," I confided in Lamont one night in early February.

He threw his head back in laughter. "Wow, you're pretty brave," he said.

Hearing the words from his mouth made me believe that they might actually be true. If anyone found out that I was even thinking of doing such a thing without my husband, I could be severely punished. But I wanted to see Meg, and Las Vegas was only a two-hour drive from St. George.

I wasn't even thinking about Allen as I packed my overnight bag an hour before hitting the road. I was worried about what I would tell Mom if she called. I knew she would be in touch to see what I was up to and where I would be sleeping that night, and I wasn't certain I could bring myself to lie to her. Suddenly my phone rang. It was Lamont. "Hey, I think I'm gonna join you guys in Vegas," he declared.

At first I didn't know what to say. "You won't get in trouble?" I asked, concerned yet excited at the prospect of having him join us.

"No, I'll be okay," Lamont assured. "I really want to see Meg and Jason."

I knew how much Lamont liked Jason. They had been friends for many years, and it had been hard on him since he and Meg had left town. I eagerly steered my truck south along I-15 en route to Nevada. It was the same road that I'd taken to my marriage ceremony, only this time, instead of feeling petrified, I was exhilarated. As I watched the landscape rush by me, I giggled aloud, thinking of how much I'd changed since then. Back when I got married, I never would have taken a risk like this. Not only was I making a spontaneous decision, my decision was extremely taboo.

My hotel room was right next door to Meg and Jason's, and Lamont's was down the hall. The minute I arrived in Vegas, I traded my ankle-length skirt and ugly blouse in favor of a pair of brown slacks and a cute pink T-shirt. Ever since my trip to Oregon, I felt more comfortable being in public with "normal" people when I wasn't in those FLDS-approved garments, and with my long hair swept back in a simple ponytail, I was ready to enjoy the weekend.

During the day, we walked up and down the strip, popping in and out of shops and stopping to enjoy cheap eats at lively, casual restaurants. We even rode the loopy roller-coaster at the New York-New York Hotel and Casino. At first I was afraid to ride it, but grabbing Lamont's outstretched hand, I decided to take a chance. We rose toward the sky, taking in the incredible view before we plummeted at breakneck speed down the 144-foot drop. Lamont was laughing and the warm Vegas sun reflected in his blue eyes. As the speed picked up, the ride felt reckless and dangerous, but it also made me feel free.

On solid ground, I turned to Lamont, consumed by my first real taste of romantic love. A fluttery sensation took root in my stomach, and all at once I was giddy in a way that I never had been before. I had spent much of the weekend watching Meg and Jason fawn over each other. Seeing them together, I came to realize the difference between real love and the emotion that Allen professed to feel for me, but it also made me understand the true weight of my feelings for Lamont. I had always known what it was to love my family, but the passion I felt for Lamont was something entirely different. It was invigorating but perilous, and it did not take long for guilt and a sense of wickedness to grab hold of me.

That night we ate dinner at the Stratosphere Hotel in a restaurant situated eight hundred feet off the ground. There were views of all Las Vegas, and taking in the expansive scene, I appreciated how far I was from Hildale in every way. Somewhere out in the distance my mom, Sherrie, and Ally were sitting down for dinner. Allen was probably returning home to find the trailer empty again. Meanwhile I was suspended in midair, hanging above the bright lights of Vegas and looking out at my future.

While we were eating dinner that evening, a photographer for the restaurant came around and offered to take a souvenir photo for us at the top of the Stratosphere. Our

small group huddled together with our arms over one another's shoulders in a friendly embrace. Lamont stood next
to me with his arm around me. It was an innocent gesture
for an innocent moment, and the photo perfectly summed up
our weekend together.

After we returned, Lamont confided in me that he had
officially left the FLDS, and now he was renting a room at
his friend T.R.'s house. The prophet of the Centennial Group
had offered him work and welcomed him with open arms.
Lamont had been hesitant to tell me that he was officially an
apostate, but he was relieved that I didn't spurn him. Encouraged by my reaction, he even invited me to come by and
meet his friends Leysiy and T.R. Even though every FLDS
teaching inside me said that I shouldn't go, I went.

One night in March, Lamont and I decided to secretly see
a film, and afterward he drove me back to my truck. We
lingered for a few minutes talking.

"I can't keep this inside any longer," Lamont said, looking at me intently. "I love you."

My breath was caught in my chest. I couldn't believe
what I was hearing. Of course, Allen had spoken those
words to me before, scribbling them in cards or uttering
them aloud because he thought he should, but Allen's words
didn't sound at all like Lamont's. Lamont was so sweet and
his emotion so pure. I loved him too, but I was too afraid to
say it. Unable to muster up even a sound, I sat paralyzed in
the passenger seat for a very long while.

My silence terrified him. "Elissa, are you okay? What's
wrong? Why aren't you saying anything? Please, speak to
me."

I could hear Lamont addressing me, but I was unable to
respond. I'd spent my entire life wishing and praying to love
someone, but each time I'd given my heart, it had been torn
apart. I'd loved Dad, and he was taken away from me. I'd
loved my brothers, and they, too, were out of my reach. My
love for Kassandra and later Meg had also been genuine, but

again, I'd ended up feeling used and left behind. Now that the moment was finally here for me, I was too overwhelmed to own it. If I told Lamont I loved him, I would be giving him my heart and committing myself to him. I wanted to do this, but Allen's presence in my life couldn't be denied.

I had the urge to flee. Grabbing the door handle, I jumped out of the truck, leaving Lamont with no explanation as I got into my vehicle and drove off. The following day I pulled out my cell phone and called him. At first we were quiet and a little awkward, but then I blurted out, "What you said last night . . ." trailing off.

"I shouldn't have said it," Lamont said softly into the phone. "I'm sorry. I just—"

"Whoa!" I stopped him. "Honestly, I love you too." But then I choked up and snapped my phone closed.

I sat there watching the phone vibrating on my bed as Lamont called me back ten or more times. I didn't know what else to say, and I wanted so badly to pick up, but I was frozen. Finally, I dialed my voice mail and listened to his message: "I am so happy, Elissa. I want to talk to you about this more. Call me back."

Knowing that Lamont loved me was a powerful and frightening thing. I had been so cheapened and tarnished by my relationship with Allen. I didn't really think that I deserved to be loved, especially by someone as engaging and kind as Lamont. I was sure that I loved him and I wanted to be with him more than anything, but rather than making things clearer, this thought only made them more confusing.

The day after he confessed his love for me, I finally returned Lamont's voice messages and agreed to meet him later that day at the big white rocks in the desert where Meg and I had watched movies. It was a safe and private spot, filled with memories for me. I arrived a little early and got out of my truck to wander and think.

The very beginnings of sunset were stretching across the vast Utah sky as Lamont's truck pulled up, and he rushed over to collect me in a big hug. Looking at him that day was different than it had ever been before. Somehow, being in touch with our true feelings and sharing them had changed everything. We climbed into his truck to talk things out. At first the conversation was a little awkward, but then I looked into his eyes and with tears rolling down my cheeks said, "I love you too."

"Then what's wrong?" he asked.

"This is just so new for me." The words came out without my planning them. I just let out everything I was feeling inside. "To tell a man I love him and mean it is just . . ."

Lamont nodded in understanding. "I know," he said softly.

We sat quietly for a few minutes staring out at the rapidly disappearing sun. Finally I asked, "What do I do now?"

"That's something you have to decide for yourself," he said. "I love you and I would be the luckiest guy in the world to have you." His voice wavered as he continued. "The person you are with doesn't have a right to be with you," he explained. "I don't care who told you to do this. Whether it was God, the prophet, your parents, or anybody else. No man should treat anybody how he treats you. I'm not going to force you to be with me; only you can make that decision. But I'm here and I'm not going anywhere."

I was struck by his honesty. We talked about how to proceed. I was nervous about what my fate would be if I left. "Is the Devil going to be waiting for me?" I asked.

"I've had the same struggle. I left, came back, and left again," Lamont said. "It's hard because once you question one thing, you start to question everything. And this whole life you know and all this suffering hasn't all been for nothing. You have to always remember one thing," he explained, recalling Joseph Smith, the founder of the religion we were a part of. "Joseph Smith said that 'happiness is the object and design of our existence.' God would not want you to throw your life away now for some unknown future."

"If I leave Allen, can I still go to heaven?" I asked, probably sounding somewhat like a scared young child.

"All I know," he said, "is that you have to make a choice

in your own heart, and I believe that your heart will tell you right whatever it is."

The next couple of weeks were a confusing yet happy time. Just to know that someone out there loved me was empowering. Nevertheless, doubts swarmed my mind as I began to scrutinize the FLDS with a fresh intensity. I knew what was going on in our church was unjust—from Warren to the marriage to plural marriage—but I couldn't have those thoughts without thinking that I would be damned to hell.

I didn't know how to make this giant leap into the unknown. Each time I pictured my future on the outside, images of my mother and sisters flooded into my mind. I knew all too well the feelings of abandonment that Sherrie and Ally would experience, and I didn't want to subject them to that. If I wasn't there, who would protect them from being married off when they were still kids? I had already seen that Mom didn't have the ability to stand up for them. There was nothing I feared more than the girls experiencing my fate.

Mixed with these emotions was a new feeling. I started to recognize that I needed to take care of myself, too. Being with Lamont was one of the only times I felt safe, and if I turned down that comfort, I might never get it back. This wasn't just about my mom and my sisters; it was about me.

When I could, I would drive out to visit Lamont at T.R.'s house. One night, I stayed late socializing with T.R. and his wife while Lamont was in Durango on business. Weary from a long day and dreading the options of sleeping in my car in the desert or being confined to the trailer with Allen, I decided to stay the night in Lamont's room. Over the next couple of months, I continued to find respite in the safety of the guest room that Lamont was renting in T.R.'s home, but I only stayed there on the weekdays when Lamont was away at a job site.

I wasn't comfortable sharing a room with Lamont yet,

and I worried that he would grow impatient with me for not sleeping with him. That moment never arrived. On the contrary, Lamont assured me that any romantic overtures would have to come from me. He would not partake in any intimate contact unless I initiated it. For the first time since I'd married Allen, I didn't feel as though somebody wanted something from me. Lamont's putting me in control of the situation was a powerful gesture. Knowing that he had no intention of coming on to me made it easier to let my guard down and allow him to see who I really was.

I will never forget our first kiss. We were sitting in the truck by the white rocks, and I told him that I had finally made up my mind. "I want to be with you," I declared. "I want to be happy with you. And to . . . have a life." Images flashed in my mind of what life with Lamont could be like—babies and birthdays and unrestricted love. My heart and mind were ready to take this leap forward, and on this night I was ready to kiss him for the first time. I hadn't planned it; it just came over me as I looked at the face I had grown to love so much. I leaned in and he followed suit. The kiss was brief but magical—soft, passionate, and absolutely nothing like Allen.

"It's going to take some time for me to leave," I explained. "I'm scared to leave my mom and the girls behind." Lamont knew that the tiny remaining family I had in Hildale relied heavily on me to make sure they had clean clothes, socks, and everything else. Mom had just had foot surgery and was laid up in bed recuperating. Although Ally and Sherrie looked out for each other, they were both too young to adequately help Mom or see to their own daily needs. Sherrie was now thirteen, and Ally was ten. I would have to give them up completely if I left the FLDS, and the thought was too much for me to handle.

"I understand," Lamont said. "I really do."

Over the next few months, Lamont and I grew more and more in love by the day, while my relationship with Allen dwindled to nothing except for the fact that we technically shared a "home." People in the community viewed us as married, and no one knew the truth about my absences. Fear of Warren had kept Allen's complaints to a minimum, and so all I had to do was stay out of Allen's way. I always remembered the promise I had made to myself months earlier never to be Allen's victim again. The only way to make sure I kept that promise was to avoid him, so that's what I did. What I really wanted to do was scream out to the world that there wasn't even a piece of me that still belonged to Allen, but lifting that veil would have risked everything. It hurt to deceive the people I cared for most, but my position was impossible. It was either my family or my heart.

Lamont's love had cocooned me, and by April, my apprehension about sharing a bed with him evaporated. Being with him felt so natural, and I no longer wanted us to be apart. However, this change renewed my concerns about expectations for any physical component of our relationship.

"I'm a virgin," he confided. Smiling, he again reassured me, "I've waited twenty-five years. What's a few more? I don't want you for your body. I'm not here for that. I care about you."

Upon hearing those words, I found myself even more drawn to him. Shortly thereafter, we began to plan our future together. Still, for all of our optimism, I was not ready to take the leap of faith and leave the FLDS.

I was alone in Lamont's room one day in May when a knock at the door startled me. I knew he was on his way back to town, but he wasn't supposed to be arriving this early. Fixing my hair, I opened the door to find a deliveryman holding an enormous bouquet of flowers, and ripping open the card, I savored Lamont's words. When Lamont arrived several hours later, he was clutching a second, even more enormous bouquet. The plastic wrap that encircled the flowers crinkled as we fell together in a hug, and later on that night I prepared a special prime-rib dinner that I had brought home from work.

"Lamont, I love you so much," I blurted out as we sipped the sparkling cider he'd brought home. For the first time ever, I longed to be intimate with a man. I snuggled up close and whispered that I was ready to give myself to him. Being with him was not at all like being with Allen. The softness of Lamont's touch, the warmth of his body next to mine, and the incredible connection I felt to him was more than I could have ever hoped for. I had always known that Allen and I were never meant to be together. Now I know that God had sent Lamont to save me.

Spring turned to summer and life continued to change rapidly. I was still working at the Twain, saving pennies toward a bright future. I was excited and apprehensive as my eighteenth birthday rolled around on July 7. My period was late and I went to the drugstore to grab a pregnancy test. It was a process I knew all too well, but I had always experienced this moment with a sense of dread and panic. This time as I watched the two positive lines appear on the stick, I wasn't sure how to react. To my amazement. I didn't feel guilty—only excited.

Not wanting to keep the news a total secret, I phoned Meg to tell her. I had been confiding in her about my relationship with Lamont, and now I squealed into my cell that I was pregnant. Meg was thrilled by the news, and then she told me that she was pregnant, too.

"Just leave, Lesie," Meg instructed. "Leave and be happy with him. He'll take care of you."

I knew Meg was right. Ever since I'd decided that I wanted to be with Lamont, it was as if I'd been waiting for the right moment, the right reason, to present itself. Now I was pregnant with his baby; if this wasn't the right moment, then there probably would not be one.

Lamont called my cell phone that day and said that he had something to give me for my birthday. I wanted to see him so badly, but I was a little nervous too. I knew that I would have to tell him about the pregnancy, but I didn't want to scare him off. I was scared myself. This was a big step, and despite my excitement, I worried how it would affect our lives. This would be the first true test of our commitment to each other. When my shift ended, I hurriedly drove out to meet him at T.R.'s house.

I walked into his room, and Lamont greeted me with a single, red rose, an embrace, and a kiss. I was nervous, wondering if he somehow suspected the pregnancy. As if the flowers weren't romantic enough, he walked across the room to put on some soft music for us. Then he came back over to me, kneeling down on one knee.

At first, I didn't understand what was happening. "Why are you on your knee?" I asked, laughing a little bit at his silly pose. In the FLDS there is no such thing as an engagement or a proposal, and there never has been. This romantic tradition was something I had only encountered in the handful of movies and television shows I'd seen. I felt my heart beating faster as Lamont slowly pulled a ring from his pocket.

"You don't have to answer right now," he said cautiously. "But I want you to know that even if the whole world chases us away, I love you and nothing is going to change that."

I placed my hand in his and allowed him to put the beautiful ring on my finger. It had belonged to his mother, which made it all the more special.

"I have news for you," I said, smiling between kisses.

"Oh?" he said, still laughing with the joy of the moment.

"Um . . . I'm pregnant," I said, hoping that he would be as thrilled as I was. I'd been betrayed so many times by the men in my life. And while I believed that Lamont was different, I still worried that this very serious situation might scare him off. "We're going to have a baby."

Lamont's laughter subsided. "Say that again."

"I'm pregnant," I repeated.

The confusion in his face turned into a big grin. Lamont had been dreaming of becoming a father for years. Everything about the moment felt right, and in my mind I was completely ready to rid myself of the church, Warren, and

Allen. Despite his happiness, I could see Lamont was also concerned about me. He knew my history with pregnancies, and we both knew what it would mean to leave the FLDS for real. It always would have been difficult, but now it would be necessary. It was time for me to stop talking about leaving and actually do it.

CHAPTER TWENTY-FOUR

CHOOSING
MY FUTURE

An apostate from this Work is the
most dark person on earth.
—WARREN JEFFS

For the next several months I struggled with my inevitable decision to leave. I knew I couldn't ride the fence and have a foot in both worlds. Eventually I would have to make that leap, but until that point, I could not bring myself to say a final good-bye. Though I'd begun to disagree with aspects of our religion, the thought of Mom, Sherrie, and Ally thinking of me as wicked was too painful.

The longer I stayed, the more I risked conflicts and confrontation with Allen. While I'd been avoiding him for the better part of a year, he was growing increasingly upset that I never called and never came back to the trailer in the evenings. It had been many months since I'd last stayed the night, and it seemed the only remaining thing that connected us was the priesthood's title of marriage, which I didn't feel obligated to honor. I felt in my heart there had never been a marriage; it had been a sham.

As the weeks passed that summer, Allen's hostility escalated. He'd begun leaving me dozens of messages, saying things like "You either choose me or else." All of them went unreturned. He couldn't bully me into submission as he'd done in the past, and my unwillingness to engage only frustrated him further.

Once, when he'd seen me at Uncle Fred's house with Mom, Sherrie, and Ally, he'd actually confronted me about his suspicions that I was spending time with people outside of the FLDS. "Why are you fraternizing with apostates?" he asked me.

"Well, they're only apostates in some people's minds," I told him.

"Well, I want it stopped!" Allen commanded.

I just stared at him blankly. He no longer had a hold on me, and my indifference only made him angrier.

On another occasion in late summer, Allen returned to the trailer to find me there gathering up some of my clothes. "Why don't you come home and be a wife?" he asked.

"Because you lost your chance," I retorted. "You have used and abused me, and I will not keep myself in these shoes."

Our conversation grew heated, and when I blurted out a smart-aleck remark, I felt the sting of Allen's hand across my cheek. A ripple of fury swept through me. "You will never, ever, lay another hand on me, ever!" I yelled.

"What are you trying to tell me?" Allen snapped. "You're done?"

"That's right," I replied, shooting him a venomous look. "Go to Warren, go to William, I just don't care anymore!"

I wasn't surprised when Mom called a few days later to inform me that William Timpson, the bishop, had told her I was not welcome at Fred's anymore. While he was in charge of Fred's family, to me it was still Uncle Fred's home and William Timpson was simply the family's caretaker.

"Whatever, Mom," I responded, tired of it all.

She just told me to "calm down," saying things like "You'd be much happier if you would just allow yourself to follow the prophet." But I was well past that stage, and in her heart, I think she knew it.

Even though I'd been banned from Fred's, no one ever tried to stop me when I visited Mom and the girls. Deep down, I think they all knew that what had happened to me was wrong, and with all the changes going on in Short Creek, my presence in the home was the last thing on their minds.

"You look different," Mom told me during a subsequent visit. "You look happy."

I wanted so badly to tell her about Lamont and the pregnancy, and there are still days even now when I wish I had, but as I stood before her that afternoon, I said nothing. Instead I just smiled, pleased that she'd noticed the change in me.

Things went on like this for much of September, and my inability to cut my ties eventually began to frustrate Lamont. Since I'd accepted his proposal and told him about the baby, he'd been eager for us to begin a life together. He was tired of sneaking around and hiding our relationship. He believed that keeping our love a secret made it appear as though we were admitting that what we were doing was wrong. But my inability to let go of my mother and sisters began to wear on our relationship and there came a time when Lamont and I almost called it quits.

Having lost his mother, he understood what I was grappling with and how difficult it was to make the break. But he also believed that I had a right to be happy and to live a life without the restrictions that the church demanded. I knew that he was right, but my love for my mother and my lifetime of religious conditioning continued to hold me back. It was hard for me to explain how I felt, and I was still learning to communicate with a man. It pained me that I would have to hurt so many people just to have a chance at happiness. That I was not performing my "duties" as a wife to Allen, and ignoring William Timpson's words to stay away from Fred's home were bound to get me into trouble sooner or later.

It all started on the night of October 12, 2005—Lamont's twenty-sixth birthday. I wanted to do something extra special for him, and he was out of town on a job, which gave me plenty of time to set up for the big birthday bash I'd been planning. I'd invited a bunch of his friends, and we intended to surprise him when he came home that evening. T.R. had donated the use of his enormous living room and cleared an area to serve as a giant dance floor. We covered the furnishings and the floors in plastic, and I painstakingly decorated the space with balloons, streamers, and tons of lights.

I was so excited when Lamont finally arrived and we all shouted, "Surprise!" But not long into the party, one of the guests found me chatting with some girls.

"There's a guy outside who wants to see you," she told me.

Alarmed, I asked, "Oh yeah, who is it?"

"He says his name is Allen."

I could feel the blood rushing from my face, and I must have looked awful because within seconds Lamont was by my side.

"What's wrong?" he asked.

"Allen's here," I stammered.

That's when Lamont took over the situation. "I'll take care of this."

Over recent weeks, Lamont and I had become aware that Allen had taken it upon himself to play detective. He had started to trail me and had also put his brothers on shifts to follow me around. By this point, I no longer felt that I needed to hide what I was doing. I was not at all ashamed of the choice I'd made. Part of me wanted to make a clear statement to Allen that I was no longer under his control, but I also didn't want to make it public that I had defied him as a wife and cut myself off from my mothers and sisters.

Lamont rounded up of a bunch of his friends to go outside and confront Allen. For months Lamont had been holding in his aggression toward Allen at my request for secrecy but finally Allen had gone too far.

"How many are they?" I heard Lamont asking one of the people who'd seen Allen in the driveway.

"Four guys," he was told.

I stayed inside as Lamont and his posse made their way to the driveway. Allen sat behind the steering wheel, his window barely cracked, when Lamont and his eleven friends approached the vehicle.

"What can I do for you?" Lamont asked.

"I'm here to get my wife," Allen replied meekly.

"Your wife," Lamont repeated coolly, a surge of anger rising in him as he confronted the man who'd been abusing me since I was fourteen. "Are you talking about the one that you masturbated in front of? The wife you raped and beat up? You mean that wife?"

Allen shrunk down in the driver's seat. Nobody, including Allen's friends in the car, had been aware of what he had been doing to me all this time. But even with this public humiliation, Allen did not back down. He and Lamont stared at each other without saying a word. "Well, I want to at least get my car," Allen finally uttered.

"She'll bring that to you at a later date," Lamont said crisply. "Now you put your truck in gear and you leave."

I could hear the crunch of tires backing up over the tiny pebbles that dotted T.R.'s driveway. It was a relief to see Lamont walk through the door, but I knew that the problem was far from over.

When my mom contacted me that November. I sensed that something was wrong the moment I answered the phone.

"Lesie, they've found a picture of you and another man," she said, breathless. "William wants to talk to you about it."

There was a long pause and I held off on saying anything. Allen had returned to the trailer that night after confronting Lamont and gone through all of my belongings. Until that night, I'd been keeping my stuff locked up in the second bedroom, but he'd kicked the door in and torn through all of my possessions. For months, I'd been careful about leaving things around, but it appeared that he'd found one thing, a photograph, that was now creating a stir.

"Lesie?" Mom's soft voice cut the silence. "Is it true?"

"Is what true?" My heart was racing.

"Is it true what they say about the picture?"

"Mom, I know that you are not going to understand my

choice. But no matter what anyone tells you, I am a good person and I love you very much."

I was furious as I hung up the phone. Allen had found a photograph of me with Lamont in Las Vegas. The picture was a way to get rid of me, a concrete piece of evidence they could use to illustrate to the people, and to my mom and sisters, that I was the worst type of apostate.

I was instructed to meet William Timpson at an office in the center of town. But first I had to go and see Mom. She'd begged me to come and meet her at the trailer. In retrospect, I realize that Mom knew this could very well be our last moment together and had some important items to give me. She was sobbing when she got out of the car, and seeing her this way, I broke out in tears, too.

"Trust in God," she told me. "He works in very mysterious ways."

That afternoon she gave me an envelope. Inside there were letters from her and both of my younger sisters, each professing their love. Mom also gave me a tape recording of an original song for piano that Sherrie had composed for me. "Keep encouraged," Mom said in parting. Leaving Mom that afternoon made it even harder to face the upcoming battle.

When I arrived at William Timson's office, Allen was already there, wearing a smug look on his face as he sat in a corner of the room.

"What are you trying to do?" I asked him.

"Well, that's for the prophet to decide," he answered in a self-righteous tone.

As I took a seat, the bishop dialed the phone and clicked it into speaker mode. I could feel myself cringing as Warren's methodic voice rang out from the desk. "Are we all here?" he asked. The fact that he wasn't in the room was not surprising. His absence from the community had been accepted for months, and whatever he was doing away from Short Creek was far more important than dealing with me in person. In the months since Lamont's grandfather and the twenty other men were ostracized by Warren, the mystery about Warren's behavior had only grown. Over the summer, more individuals and families had started to disappear almost overnight. One day a man would be there, the next he and his family were gone. We started to call them "poofers" because like a magic trick they went "poof" and were no longer there. It was as though Short Creek and all the people in it were eroding right in front of our eyes. No one knew for sure what was happening, but rumor was that the worthiest families were being taken to Zion and leaving the rest of us behind. But it didn't make any sense. How could the prophet and those worthy people have gone to Zion when there hadn't been any destructions?

The meeting got under way with William Timpson confronting me with the souvenir photo of me with Lamont, Meg, and Jason at the Stratosphere Hotel—the four of us standing with a panoramic view of Vegas in the background and our arms around one another's shoulders. There was nothing suggestive or romantic about the picture, but the fact that I was in Vegas with apostates and dressed in slacks and a T-shirt made the image pretty risqué. "Is that you?" the bishop asked, pointing me out in the lineup.

"Yes, that's me," I replied indignantly, certain that he had expected me to admit wrongdoing and plead for forgiveness.

"Elissa, you need to tell us what is going on and why Allen has these concerns and accusations," William asked.

I was surprised when Allen spoke up. "She's involved with someone else," he began. "And she's associating with apostates and no longer being an honest, truthful wife."

"What is your relationship with this gentleman?" Warren's voice chimed in. Even though Warren was physically absent, his scolding manner permeated every word that he spoke over the phone.

"Yes," I said back to him. "I am in a relationship with this gentleman. I met him a while ago."

"Have you ever betrayed your marriage commitments with this man?" Warren's disembodied voice filled the small room.

I could feel myself growing flushed as I sat in my chair,

unwilling to provide an answer. I knew why he wanted to know, he wanted to humiliate me by prodding for salacious details. There was a long pause before Warren spoke again. "Have you ever had relations with this man?"

His question repulsed me and I refused to answer him.

"Has any part of him ever been inside you?"

Now I was infuriated. He had no right to know and even less of a right to inquire about such a personal thing. But Warren continued in this vein for several more minutes. "Well, I will take your unwillingness to answer the questions as a yes," he said. "William, I want you to end the marriage."

In one moment, what I'd been asking for since the very beginning had been granted. Not because of all my begging and pleading. Not because I'd complained about the terrible things that Allen had done to me. Not because I'd endured three years with a man I didn't love and Warren had taken pity on me. I had been forced to suffer with no hope of it ever stopping. And now that I'd finally taken a step toward my own happiness, I was being punished and labeled a sinner.

"Do you realize that adultery is a cardinal sin?" Warren asked me. "And that the only way that someone can repent from a cardinal sin is to be destroyed in the flesh?"

I sat dumbfounded. Uncle Warren was telling me that I literally had to be destroyed, *killed,* in order for God to forgive me. In my short life, I had heard teachings of the doctrine that Warren was referring to. I had always felt petrified when I'd heard whispers of the ritual called blood atonement. If deemed necessary, an FLDS believer who was wanting forgiveness from the priesthood and God for a sin must willingly turn himself over and allow his blood to be "spilt upon the ground." While I'd never known if it had been practiced in my day, there were stories of people succumbing to this bone-chilling act in earlier times. The way it was supposedly carried out was in a secret ceremony in a special room dedicated by the priesthood where the "sinner" would lie upon an altar and agree to be bound while a specially ordained elder took his life. And he who took the life would be guiltless before God.

I couldn't believe the direction this meeting was going. Here I had gone to Warren multiple times, begging for help with things I felt were wrong, and in an instant he was judging me and telling me that I may have sinned so greatly that I was eligible for destruction. He continued to probe me for information. But I was so enraged that I burst into tears.

"I want you to write a letter of confession for all the things that have transpired between you and this gentleman," Warren directed, seeming to take joy in my sobs. "And I want you to know that you are no longer welcome to see your mother or be in Fred's home. You're to treat your mother and your sisters as though they are dead to you."

Now I broke into hysterics. What I had feared for months had finally come to pass. Warren had enough power to take from me everything that I held dear in that community. I would never be allowed to see my mother or my little sisters again. All these years of pain and suffering had been for absolutely nothing. The only reason I had endured for so long with Allen was to be close to my mother and sisters. Now I would have to live without them. It was the harshest verdict he could have delivered, but then he drove the dagger even further.

"Allen," Warren's voice boomed. "Job well done." Warren was commending him for his role as husband in the marriage he had placed him in.

I had to summon all my strength not to rise to my feet and rip the phone from the wall. As he sat there lavishing praise on Allen for having his way with me and intimidating me for nearly three years, the rage that had been simmering inside me for so long boiled to the surface. I wanted to scream out so that all of Hildale could hear me. "I did everything I could, and I have only tried to do what you have told me to do!" I yelled at the phone. "And I asked to be out long before it came to this point."

Just as he'd done all along, Warren ignored me and continued condemning me for my wickedness. What he could no longer do was condemn me to a life with Allen. "You held up your end of the bargain," he told the man who had used my salvation to hold me prisoner. "You are relieved of her as your wife."

Warren next addressed the bishop, instructing William Timpson to bring me to my father's house in Colorado City until he could decide what to do about me. Dad had finally been given a vacant home that he and Audrey had renovated. There was a certain irony to his pronouncement, that now after all these years, I was going back to my real father. For the past eight years, all I'd ever wanted was to be my father's daughter and to have my family returned to me. Leaving him that day in 1999 had triggered a chain of events that was only ending this day in the office of William Timpson. I had finally come full circle. Before releasing me back to my father, Warren reminded me that I had failed in my mission to God, but I stopped listening to his words. I didn't want to know the God of Warren Jeffs. I didn't want to know a God who would willingly break apart families. I didn't want to know a God who forced girls to get married. The God I knew, who I believed in and who I still believe in to this day, was real, but he had nothing to do with Warren Jeffs.

Warren adjourned the meeting with the words "The Lord's will be done."

I left the room with tears streaming down my cheeks. The men were still inside talking, so I waited in the hallway quietly. When Allen was finished, he came out and walked straight past me like I was air, to his truck.

William Timpson then came into the hall to follow me in his car to my dad's. Taking a long look at my tear-stained face and bloodshot eyes, he said, "Trust in God, Elissa."

"What God do you want me to trust in?" I asked, my voice wavering. "The one who put me here and is telling me that I'm a wicked person?"

William didn't try to respond in any way; we just walked quietly outside. I could feel a quiet ambivalence on his part toward his weighty new position as bishop. Unlike the older men of the church, he had not yet developed a stern and controlling style. He never would have admitted it, but I could almost feel sympathy coming from him.

On the way over to my dad's house, I felt both betrayal and relief. No matter how it had occurred, I was forever free of Allen. There had been countless times that I'd wondered if any of this would have happened if we hadn't been taken away from Dad, but I also recognized that it was too late for him to do anything. I wasn't a little girl anymore, and I had a lot of healing to do. Four years ago he might have been able to help, but now the die had already been cast.

We arrived at Dad and Audrey's house and William walked me to the door. When my dad answered it, his expression was soft but questioning.

"This is your daughter and you need to take care of her," William asserted.

"She will always have a place in my home," Dad said, looking at me with a nod. I walked through the threshold and into my father's arms. Mother Audrey, too, was kind and welcoming. They didn't ask me any questions as they cleared out a bedroom for me to stay in and busied themselves getting the house in order. Dad looked me in the eye and said, "I am so grateful you're away from Allen." Protective tears welled up in his eyes, but his voice remained steady and soft. "I want you to know I love you, and no matter what, this will all be okay."

"You know what, Dad?" I said, trying to be as strong as he was. "It *will* be okay." And I actually started to believe the words as I said them.

Warren may have been the prophet, but I was the one who could see my future. He could no longer tell me how to live my life. I would decide, and I was choosing happiness with Lamont Barlow.

Dad and Audrey showed me into the bedroom that they had set up for me, and after kissing them good night, I shut the door.

When I knew I was alone, I poked around the room looking for some paper on which to compose a letter to my father. I found a yellow legal pad in a corner of the closet and sat down to write. As tempted as I was to stay there, Dad and Audrey were still fighting to remain in the church. They were too intricately connected to the world I needed to leave behind. In the letter, I told Dad that Mom, Ally, and Sherrie were the only reasons I had remained here all this time. If I couldn't be with them, then I didn't want to stay—although a part of me wanted to live with him. Trying to set his mind at ease, I asked him not to worry; I'd be safe. I'd call when I could; all he'd have to do was pick up the phone. Leaving the letter on the bed, I tiptoed out of the room and down the hall, where I slipped out the front door and into the car.

I drove with the headlights off until I reached the end of the street, and when I knew I was safe, I called Lamont. "Please come get me. I'm in town." I told him.

"I'm on my way," he promised.

A few minutes later we met in the parking lot of the post office. I wasn't about to take Allen's car, so I left it and got into Lamont's. Sliding into the passenger seat, I kissed Lamont and placed a hand on my belly. Inside a baby was growing, a baby my mother would never know. The thought of raising a child without my mother's beautiful singing voice and her loving gaze was almost too much, and again I broke down crying. I was making this choice to leave, not just for me and not just for Lamont, but for our child. I was making this choice so that our child, be it a girl or a boy, could grow up in a world without the walls and boundaries of the priesthood, a world where God and faith are instruments of hope, not tools of manipulation. I was making the choice that my mother had been unable to make for me and my siblings. I was choosing to give my child the power of choice.

PART THREE

PART THREE

CHAPTER TWENTY-FIVE

NEW BEGINNINGS

Take the first step in faith. You don't have to see
the whole staircase, just the first step.
—REV. MARTIN LUTHER KING, JR.

I'd felt as though I'd leapt across the Grand Canyon as I lay
down beside Lamont that first night. I think both of us had
naïvely hoped that this giant step would be our final hurdle
and from this point forward we would live a fairy-tale life.
I'd always known that leaving would be hard. There was no
way I could live in a closed community for eighteen years and
suddenly emerge ready to live in the world beyond it. But
nothing could have prepared me for the initial difficulty of
life on the outside.

When I awoke that first morning after leaving my father's
house, I was paralyzed by fear and regret. "What if they're
right?" I worried. "What if I've made a mistake and I really
am going to hell?"

For the first few days I was devastated, and while Lamont
did his best to comfort me, I just couldn't seem to stop crying. It took three days for me to calm down enough to tell
him what had happened in my final meeting with Warren,
Allen, and William Timpson, and even then the information
had to trickle out in pieces. Leaving the FLDS had drained

me of strength and left me emotional, washed up, and exhausted. It was as if all of the pain, loss, and uncertainty that I'd tried to "put on a shelf" over the past eight years suddenly fell on top of me.

I finally mustered the strength to venture out of our house, but it was unsettling to feel so out of touch with my surroundings. In all of my thinking about leaving the FLDS, I had focused so exclusively on my mom and sisters that I hadn't considered many of the other things that would make the transition hard. Everything about our new life was strange and unfamiliar. From the moment we woke up to the moment we fell asleep we were both plagued by an entirely new set of insecurities that had come with our new lives. The tiny house that Lamont rented for us in Hurricane was on a quiet street inhabited by "normal" families, who shot us confused glances because of how we dressed.

I tried to conquer this awkwardness by dressing differently, but it wasn't that simple. Each new day brought with it the anxiety of not being able to "look the part." My attempts to blend in only made me stand out more as I wore unusual combinations, such as T-shirts with my long skirts and thick FLDS tights, thinking that it made me look normal. I'd always wanted to wear normal clothes and had done so on occasion as part of my attempt to test my individuality, but with nothing familiar to cling to, I sought refuge in my old FLDS wardrobe.

My hair, too, was a huge source of worry for me. Because FLDS women were all raised to keep their hair long, I'd never had a haircut aside from a few wispy bangs, and now my thick, blond locks fell down past my waist. I had mastered my hair as a member of the FLDS and I knew how to sweep it up and back, pin it properly, and construct the tight braids that were all the rage in our society. But now I found it impossible to get in step with the styles of this new world I was in, leaving me no other option than a French braid that looked ridiculously out of place in the streets of Hurricane and St. George. It was too long and I felt completely uncomfortable with it loose. Seeing strangers with their hair in shoulder-length blunt cuts or easy, free curls made me long to look like them, but I just didn't know how.

Part of what made our transition so difficult was that we barely had the financial resources to cover our bills, let alone acquire new clothes. In Colorado City there is no such thing as a mortgage or rent payment. A church-run trust called the United Effort Plan or UEP owns the land on which the people reside, and lots are awarded to worthy members of the priesthood to build on with the expectation of a monthly donation to the church of 10 percent of a man's income. Of course, members are encouraged to donate as much as they can, and many contribute significantly more. A portion of the monthly tithing is used to fund the communal storehouse where we purchased some of our food, paper goods, and other necessities at a very low cost. We had lived our lives in big families and the shopping was done for us and usually in bulk at stores like Costco.

As a result, we'd never had to think about everyday money issues. Lamont and I were now confronting the jaw-dropping prices at the local grocery stores. To make matters worse, Lamont had taken an unpaid leave of absence from his job as a field operations manager for a local construction company that first week to help me make the initial adjustment, but my uncontrollable crying scared and confused him. He was worried that I regretted my choice to be with him. While his support during those days was invaluable, the loss of income left us unable to make our rent that month, creating a hole that we then had to dig ourselves out of.

The financial pressures would have been hard for anyone, but we knew absolutely nothing about money management. Financial planning was not part of any curriculum either of us had been taught, and because we'd been raised to think that the end of the world was imminent, we had always learned that personal credit was of no value to us. With little credit history to speak of, we both struggled with employers and banks that demanded such information.

During this time I was also undergoing the hormonal struggles that most pregnant women endure, which made me unpredictably emotional and particularly weepy. I had secretly seen a midwife before my departure from Short Creek, and because of my complicated history with pregnancies she advised me to see an ob-gyn. I was already in my twenty-fourth week, and the doctor recommended that because of my Rh-negative blood, I should have injections of Rh immunoglobulin (RhIg) to suppress my body's ability to react to Rh-positive red cells. While he couldn't say for sure, he believed that this could have been a part of the problem with my earlier pregnancies.

It was reassuring to know that a precaution could be taken to prevent losing another baby. The idea that there was an explanation for my miscarriages and that God had not been punishing me after all gave me comfort. I took good care of myself, but Lamont and I still worried a great deal. Though he knew about my miscarriages, I'd never told him about the stillbirth. Originally it had been too emotionally painful to describe or even bring up, but now I didn't want to make him more concerned than he already was. Not sharing this with him didn't make it go away, and often I worried that I would end up in another pregnancy nightmare.

While these problems of fitting in, money, and my pregnancy brought my anxiety to new heights in the first weeks, what weighed heaviest on me was the fact that I might never see my mother and little sisters again. I longed for Ally's infectious smile and the sound of Sherrie on the piano. Mom had secretly called me in those first days to make sure I was okay. It was healing for me to confront the issues that I had with her because of my marriage to Allen. Tearfully, she told me how sorry she was and that if she could turn back time, she'd change the outcome. Still, she held out hope that I would come back and repent, so that we could remain a family.

Like so many things about the FLDS, her words were one big contradiction. While she was genuinely sorry about how my life had turned out, it seemed she couldn't see that there was any way other than that of the church. She'd lived her entire life in the FLDS, and she didn't have the mental capacity to question beyond its walls. This conversation was one of the rare times I'd ever heard her express doubts. Her willingness to actually raise questions made me cautiously optimistic that she would continue on this road, but only time would tell if she would actually be able to change her beliefs. At fifty-four, this would be a monumental feat, to reverse a lifetime of conditioning. I knew that Mom loved me, and in the only way she knew how, she was trying to communicate that to me. It was with this understanding that I was able to begin the process of letting go.

Though Lamont and I remained in love and hopeful that we would adjust, those first weeks offered a frustrating overall picture of our new reality. Gone was our vision of escaping and simply starting anew. It would be an arduous road, but it was one that we needed to travel. It seemed like everyone we came into contact with during that time had left the FLDS with dreams of starting a new life only to end up penniless and drug- or alcohol-dependent with no place to turn. I thought back to all the times when I'd seen my older brothers go through the same struggles that I was now experiencing. I wish I could have known the mental battle that had to be waged.

Getting out wasn't just about starting a fresh routine, it was about establishing a totally new way of thinking. When you leave the FLDS, your whole foundation crumbles. You have to start from scratch and think about large, far-reaching questions, like What do I believe in? What about heaven? What are morals? What will I fight for? We had gained freedom and each other, but we had lost the ground beneath our feet. It made it even harder when our thoughts turned to the families we'd both lost. While I was now without my mom and sisters, Lamont too had lost his family.

Despite everything that had happened to me, I continued to talk to God as if he were my friend, and I begged him to give me the strength to find myself. I wanted to believe that God loved me, even though I had made such drastic changes and abandoned the FLDS. Still, I wasn't sure if he would listen to me. Years and years of intense religious conditioning led me to second-guess everything about my new life. It was truly a godsend when my friend Natalie's older sister, Sarah, turned up at my front door in Hurricane one afternoon with a boxful of maternity clothes and the new mother's "bible," *What to Expect When You're Expecting*. I'd run into Sarah at a party in the weeks before I'd left Short Creek and was surprised to learn she'd left the FLDS after meeting a local boy and falling in love. During our conversation, it became apparent that she was terribly lonely as she tried to navigate her strange new surroundings and the joys and worries of a first pregnancy with no family around to support her. Knowing that I was in her shoes, she'd come to impart friendship and her knowledge on me. I was extremely grateful, and Sarah quickly became my lifeline. I'd never imagined just how difficult my transition would be, and even now, I look back with wonderment at how I managed.

We'd been out just about three weeks when Dad phoned to say that he was going to be in Hurricane and wanted to meet for dinner. After finding my note on the bed that night, he'd called my cell phone a few times to check in and make sure I was okay. While I'd told him where Lamont and I were living, I hadn't told him that I was pregnant. I'd been able to conceal my pregnancy straight through my last days in the FLDS, but in early December I suddenly popped, and now I was nervous about how he would react. Still, I was hungry for any family and was looking forward to seeing him.

He was seated at a far table at J.B.'s restaurant when Lamont and I walked through the door. Lamont panicked as we approached, seeing my Dad sternly looking us up and down. He'd never met Lamont, and Lamont was worried about how my father would react to the man who'd taken his daughter from the FLDS and was expecting a baby with her.

When we reached the table, Dad stood up, pointed his large, tanned finger at Lamont, and said, "I only have one thing to say to you."

Lamont recoiled in fear, waiting to be told off.

Holding my breath, I watched as Dad's scowl softened

and he declared, "I'm getting the check for dinner." For a moment we both stood there not sure if we had heard right, but then Dad broke into a grin and gathered me in a big bear hug. His words put us at ease, and the rest of the meal was lively and pleasant. When we were ready to say our good-byes, we stood up and Dad embraced each of us.

"I don't care what your decision is, Elissa. I'm just glad that you are no longer with Allen." To experience this kind of love and approval from a parent, with no questions asked and no judgments made, was invigorating. It was the first time in my life that I'd made a weighty decision on my own and received approval for it. All that mattered to him was my happiness. I knew that his allegiance still lay in the priesthood, but I was comforted that he was not going to abandon me just because I had finally chosen for myself.

In those early weeks, Lamont also tried to reach out to his family. Eventually, he hunted his grandfather down and got him to agree to meet for dinner. The two of them went to an Applebee's in St. George to eat and talk about everything that had transpired. Lamont was troubled by the way that George appeared a mere shell of his former self. Having lived as a well-respected patriarch for much of his adult life, he'd now been forced to take a room in a home shared by several other men. Isolated from everyone he knew and loved, he appeared to have been doing a lot of internal searching to try and determine where he'd gone wrong and why he'd been removed from the church.

"Lamont," George said, his face strained by grief, "Leroy S. Johnson once told me there are only two things a man can do to lose his priesthood. One is adultery; the other betrayal of God. I did neither of these things, so I just don't understand what it could be." His voice broke as he held back tears.

Seeing this old man who had once been a strong and influential figure reduced to a lonely creature was difficult for Lamont, but it reinforced to us how Warren's rule had created victims of all ages and sexes. His grandfather was just one more example of the pain that had been inflicted in the name of God.

* * *

That December, I celebrated my first-ever Christmas in Oregon with Kassandra. Craig, Justin, and Caleb had recently moved to Hawaii, and though she and Ryan were preparing for a move to Idaho, Kassandra was still on the West Coast. I arrived in Portland alone in the second week of December. Because we couldn't afford to have Lamont miss even an hour of work, the plan was for him to meet me there on Christmas Eve.

From the moment I arrived, Kassandra offered me a great deal of relief. We talked about our experiences leaving the FLDS, and she assured me that everything was going to work out. We also talked about Mom and the few telephone conversations that we'd each had with her since I left. Mom had become more bold in speaking to her kids on the outside. She'd even taken calls from Craig, and my brother had opened a dialogue with her that included some talk about religion. We'd all grown hopeful when Mom raised questions and didn't immediately dismiss Craig's thought-provoking conversations. She'd even wondered aloud about some of the things that had been going on in Short Creek and why everything had become so secretive. "It just doesn't feel right," Mom had said during one call with me, but our conversation was too short to delve any deeper.

It had been particularly painful speaking with Ally and Sherrie. My heart broke when Ally asked that I come and get her. While Sherrie was the older of the two girls, she was also more compliant, much like our sister Michelle. Ally was more like me, stubborn and sassy, and at just eleven years of age, she was not afraid to express her desire to leave Short Creek right in front of Mom. "Please, come and get me," she'd begged, and I wanted nothing more than to go and pick her up that minute.

Her longing to be rescued weighed heavily on me. Mom later asked that Kassandra and I "encourage Ally to stay." After hearing those glimmers of doubt in Mom's voice a few weeks earlier, we were disappointed that she remained stuck in the FLDS mindset. I would have honored Ally's request to leave in a heartbeat, but I knew that it was too risky at this point. I was six months pregnant and barely scraping together enough money to get by each month. As much as it pained me to admit it, there was no way that Lamont and I could support an eleven-year-old girl. I thoroughly intended to go back in and get them as soon as possible, not realizing the chance would never come.

Kassandra and I commiserated about how frustrating it was not to be able to help more. She had already been out for nearly two years and was much further along in the process that I was just beginning. As a result, she had begun to entertain thoughts of involving law enforcement, an idea that intimidated me. I'd only been out for six weeks and still held my deep-rooted fear of police and all government officials.

While thoughts of Mom and the girls preoccupied me in Oregon, I was excited to be with family for my first Christmas. And now that I was on the outside, Kassandra was eager to help me through my transformation. Our first stop was to the mall to get my hair cut. I had agreed to take off five inches, but Kassandra must have secretly told the stylist to bring it up over my waistline. I watched nervously as she pulled it back in her hands and was shocked when she cut off seventeen inches of my flaxen locks.

"Do you want to donate it or save it?" she asked me.

I was too traumatized to speak. It needed to come off, but it was hard to part with. Back in Short Creek, my hair had been my one beauty accessory, and all my life I had been taught to value it. Still, I realized I needed the haircut to feel more "normal."

As Christmas neared, Kassandra and I began talking about the tree we would have. When the time came, we scoured the nursery forever, looking for the "perfect" one. It had to be the right height, with no holes, and it had to smell good. The poor man tending to us grew exhausted from cutting away the mesh bundling and displaying our various choices as we scrutinized each tree carefully. "This is my very first Christmas," I said, smiling apologetically, and any hint of sourness on his face dissolved.

After lugging our tree home, we stayed up until 3 A.M., laughing, talking, decorating, and sipping hot chocolate. I stood back, admiring our creation. Growing up in Salt Lake, we'd drive past outsiders' houses and see their trees glistening through their living room windows. Now I was no longer seeing it from a distance. Christmas had come into my life, and I felt myself beginning to enjoy my new world for the first time.

As planned, Lamont arrived on Christmas Eve, and I was overjoyed to see him. That night it was difficult to fall asleep, and in the morning my anticipation got the better of me. I was probably the first "kid" in America awake that day, out of bed by 5:00 A.M. and hoping someone else would soon join me. When no one did, I began preparing a huge breakfast, desperate to get the festivities started. If they smell it, they'll wake up, I reasoned, but by 7:00 A.M., I was still waiting. Finally I ran in to wake up Lamont. "It's Christmas morning!" I announced. "It's time to open the presents."

Lamont loved the maroon-and-white blanket I had made for him. And he burst into laughter as I squealed aloud tearing at the wrapping paper of the digital camera he'd put under the tree for me.

We had a wonderful celebration and stayed in Oregon to ring in the New Year with Kassandra and Ryan. For the first time since I could remember, I celebrated the coming New Year without fear that the world was going to end. Instead I watched the ball drop in Times Square on Kassandra's twenty-five-inch TV and looked forward to 2005 with the hope that it would bring bigger and better things into our lives.

Our return to Hurricane in early January was dampened by the discovery that a letter I'd written to Ally had been returned to me. I tried to call Mom, but there was no answer on her private line. Days passed and my repeated calls found no one home. Reluctantly, I phoned the main house at Fred's. They told me that Mom and the girls were not there, but that was as much information as I could glean. Finally, I was told that Mother Sharon was gone and she was not coming back. The news sent me into a tailspin, and I immediately reached out to the family for help.

Kassandra and Craig decided it was time to involve law enforcement. We all had worried that Mom's phone at Uncle Fred's house might have been monitored and her conversations with her children overheard. Now we feared they had moved Mom to keep her from us and hold onto future brides in Sherrie and Ally. Knowing that the Colorado City Police Department would offer no help, Kassandra phoned the neighboring Washington County Police, who encouraged her to file a missing-persons report on Mom and both of my sisters. Craig, meanwhile, called prominent church elders trying to find Mom. His interest caused a stir in Short Creek, with followers complaining that the Walls were causing trouble once again.

While we all worried about Mom, life marched forward, and on February 18, 2005, I was in labor. That day, Kassandra came down to St. George with her young son to lend a hand and fill the role my mother no longer could. Like every young girl, I had always imagined the birth of my first child with my mother by my side, but Kassandra did a terrific job, and she was there to welcome my son, Tyler, into the world.

Everything changed for me the moment I held my son in my arms. Looking at Tyler's little face, I was in awe of him. He didn't belong to the prophet or the priesthood. He was mine, and no one could take him from me or make me abandon him. Up until the minute I saw him, I hadn't even imagined how much I could love this baby, and I could tell that Lamont shared my sentiments. I knew how much he wanted to be a father, and seeing him holding our child in his arms was among the happiest moments of my life. He was entranced, staring joyfully into our little boy's blue eyes. In that moment I realized that I was finally free. Free to make my own choices, free to send my child to school, and to college, and to let him experience all the world had to offer us. It didn't matter anymore that a single man had condemned me to hell or that the people I had known and loved upheld his words. I made a deal with God and myself that I would leave that judgment up to him. I knew that he would never send this precious baby to me if he felt I was a sinner.

Tyler was less than a month old when I got news that Uncle Fred had died on March 15 and a funeral was being held in Hildale later that week. There was still little news about Fred's disappearance, and no one seemed to know the truth about where he had been. I was told that he was in Colorado when he died, and I started to wonder if perhaps Mom was there as well.

That same day, my phone rang. It was Kassandra telling me to hurry down to the police station in Colorado City. "They're going to clear up Mom's missing-persons report," my sister blurted into the phone. "Mom's going down to the police station, and you've got to get there to meet her."

Bundling up the baby, I jumped into my car and headed for Highway 59 into Short Creek. I hadn't been back there since my departure the previous November, and I was a petrified about how I would be received. But I was desperate to see Mom and confirm that she was okay. I arrived to find that she'd already been there and gone. Filled with disappointment, I was walking back outside to my car when my cell phone rang. It was Mom.

"I'm in town right now," she told me. "William Timpson said that if you want to, we can set up a meeting and I can see you for a few minutes." Tears filled my eyes at the sound of her warm voice. Back in December I'd told her I was pregnant, and now I informed her that her new grandson had been born. She was thrilled to meet him, and we scheduled a rendezvous for the following morning. I called Kassandra as soon as I hung up. She was already planning to come down for Uncle Fred's funeral, and when I told her about the meeting with Mom she put a rush on her trip.

It was pouring rain the next day when Kassandra and I drove in her blue Ford Focus to the meeting spot. Mom was already there waiting for us, and with no shelter, we all jumped into the backseat of Kassandra's car. The first few minutes were pleasant as Mom expressed her love for us and gushed over the baby, but our joy was instantly cut short when the conversation turned to the missing-persons report that Kassandra had filed. Mom was hurt that her children had gone against the priesthood like that and asked that we not do it again. I was alarmed to see how agitated Mom appeared, and even more disturbed by the big white truck that was parked along the street when we arrived. We all knew that inside were members of the FLDS who'd been sent to keep watch over Mom.

The conversation turned awkward as Kassandra pressed Mom, and I silently wished she would stop. It was all still fresh enough for me to remember what it felt like to be a true believer. All Mom was asking was to be able to live her beliefs without us fighting them, and I didn't yet have the perspective to understand what my sister was trying to do. We wanted to know why Mom hadn't brought Ally and Sherrie along that day.

"We didn't want a problem," Mom explained, and it was clear from her tone that "we" referred to the priesthood elders, who feared that Kassandra and I might try to take the girls with us. She declined to tell us where she and the girls were now living and implored us not to stir up any more trouble. I was certain that leaving the girls behind was a calculated tool on the elders' part to ensure that Mom returned for them. Otherwise, the risk would have been too great that Kassandra and I would persuade her to leave and take our sisters with her.

"What are you going to do when Sherrie faces the same thing that Elissa did?" Kassandra asked Mom. Sherrie was now thirteen and quickly approaching the age at which I was placed with Allen.

Mom was indignant. "I'll do something," she replied.

My sister stared over me at Mom. "I don't feel like you have the power to stop something from happening to those girls. I don't feel like you have the power to protect them."

"Yes, I do," Mom insisted. It was sad to hear her trying to convince herself of that. I knew how much she loved those girls, and that she would never want any harm to come to them. But the ominous sight of the white truck with the tinted windows was an ugly reminder of what lengths these people would go to to keep a hold on their followers.

"No you don't," Kassandra shot back. "You didn't have it when it happened to Lesie, and you won't have it when it happens to those girls."

"Well, that's just something I'll just have to put on a shelf," Mom said, referring to her inability to halt my marriage to Allen. It seemed that no difficult conversation with Mom had ever been complete without this line.

"I'd rather see you die than fight the priesthood," Mom said. Her words were a hard slap on the face. Everything Mom had ever done had been influenced by her loyalty to the church above all else, but to hear her phrase it in such indisputable terms was upsetting.

"I'm not trying to fight you," Kassandra assured her. "I'm not trying to fight anybody. I'll tell you what. If we can go to the funeral tomorrow and I hear something that puts our minds at ease, then we will leave this alone." Mom agreed, and before departing she told us to pray for an answer from the Lord. Later that day, she orchestrated a phone call between William Timpson and me, in which he welcomed Kassandra and me to Fred's funeral. "I give you my personal permission," he told me.

The next morning, Kassandra and I set off for Hildale. We'd spent an hour or so styling our hair in the FLDS updo and selecting dresses to fit in with the crowd. More than three thousand mourners turned out for the funeral service that was held in the large meetinghouse at the center of town. Several men guarded the door, and we were greeted by a few. Before granting us entrance, we were asked if we were carrying cell phones. Kassandra offered to turn hers over but was told to just take it to the car. That's when we were confronted by church elder Willy Jessop. He had a reputation for being gruff and unkind, and though he probably knew the answer, he asked who we were. The church elders who had been involved in our conversation all stepped back as Willy confronted Kassandra and me. When we identified ourselves, he told us that we were not welcome.

"We have a personal invitation from William Timpson," I told him, growing upset. It was exceptionally cold outside and had started to lightly snow, a rare event in sunny Hildale. I had Tyler bundled in my arms, and he was just six weeks old, but Willy didn't care about that.

Kassandra and I were not allowed inside for the entire three-hour service, and we sat through most of it in Kassandra's car. We waited for the procession to come out and positioned ourselves so that we would be at the front of the line, that way, when we reached Fred's grave we would be close to where Mom would be standing as one of Fred's wives.

I was desperate to see her again, and I knew this might be our last chance. I rocked the baby in my arms and tried to keep every inch of his tiny body sheltered from the icy air. When the service was finally over, scores of congregants came pouring out the large double doors. Standing by Fred's grave site clutching my infant to my chest, I was aware that I was the latest scandal in town, and I was joined by my apostate sister. Everywhere around us there was a wall of silence, as people we'd known for years dismissed us with a glance. To them, I was no longer important, worthy, or loved. I was just one more lost soul who had no right to be standing on their sacred land.

Mom joined us at the end of the burial.

"See? Wasn't that beautiful?" she said, smiling contentedly.

"They wouldn't let us in," I told her. I knew what was going to happen now, and I silently wished that we'd just been granted entrance to stop the inevitable confrontation.

"Oh, Kassandra, it must have been a mistake," Mom nervously replied.

"No, it wasn't a mistake," my sister told her. "This was God's answer."

Again, I found myself in the middle of my mom and my

sister. Our conversation was cut short when Mom was hurried away with the rest of Fred's wives.

I was relieved to receive a call from her that night. She'd gone to William Timpson about how we'd been restricted from the service. Willy Jessop had told the bishop that we'd been confrontational. The misunderstanding led to William's decision to grant us permission to visit with Mom again the following day at Cottonwood Park. When we arrived Mom was already there waiting for us, and so was the same big white truck with the FLDS men inside, observing our entire visit from behind the tinted windows.

We spent three hours together, and snapped plenty of photographs, many of which are in frames displayed around my house today. I brought Lamont along so that he could meet my mother. She was kind and accepting to him and our son. Mom pushed Kassandra's son on the swing and cradled Tyler in her arms. As I watched Mom playing with her grandchildren, I was overcome by a sense of grief that they would have to grow up without her. With tears in the corners of my eyes, I asked, "Mom, are we ever going to see you again?"

"I don't know," she replied, shaking her head softly. There was a long pause. "I wish I could be a grandmother to my grandchildren," she said in a wistful tone.

"Mom, you still could," I urged. "We would love to have you in our lives." A quick flash of images came into my mind—possibilities that would never come to pass—of Ally, Sherrie, and Mom getting out and starting over with us. Mom continued to press me not to involve the authorities again, bringing it up several times. Her words were unexpected and there was something about them that seemed forced, as though perhaps this meeting had been about more than just seeing her grandchildren.

Eventually we had to say good-bye. With a distant look in her eyes, Mom walked toward the two men who'd been watching over us and disappeared into their truck.

Kassandra and I looked at each other, devastated. As much as we didn't want to believe it, inside we both knew this would be the last time we'd ever see our mother.

CHAPTER TWENTY-SIX

COMING FORWARD

Evil flourishes when good men do nothing.
—SHARON WALL, QUOTING EDMUND BURKE

After that last meeting with Mom, we lost contact with her for a second time, and I began receiving pressure from Kassandra and Craig to help them do something about it. In her efforts to locate Mom and the girls, Kassandra began speaking with law enforcement, and during those conversations, she briefly told authorities what had happened to me. Though I'd specifically asked her not to say too much, she came away from those exploratory calls with the impression that, if I didn't come forward to authorities by what would have been my fourth anniversary to Allen that April, the criminal statute of limitations would run out on possible charges being pressed.

Kassandra and Craig were pushing hard for me to present my story to authorities, hoping that it could help gain Sherrie and Ally's freedom. While I wanted nothing more than to help my younger sisters, I was not interested in speaking to police. I had not lost my fear of law enforcement, and I worried about what the priesthood would do to me if I talked to the police about my life. I also didn't want to hurt Mom.

Nevertheless, as April approached, the pressure on me

intensified. In addition to Kassandra and Craig, Lamont's uncle Jethro Barlow, the man who'd been publicly expelled from the FLDS, contacted Lamont with some information about a law-enforcement investigation that had been launched into my relationship to Allen. He raised the possibility of a subpoena, and I was terrified. During his short reign as prophet, Warren had expelled a lot of people, and some of them had come together on the outside. They were working hard to remove Warren from power, and I was viewed as someone who could help them.

There were already a number of lawsuits in the works that were designed to challenge Warren's abuse. Shem Fischer, an expelled FLDS member, had been one of the first to find the courage to file lawsuits against Warren Jeffs and the FLDS. His actions blazed the way for others, and he eventually became a valuable tool for law enforcement in their efforts to address the abuse of minors in the FLDS. The group of FLDS exiles known as "the Lost Boys" later also filed a civil suit against Warren and the FLDS Church seeking compensation for "unlawfully banishing them from their homes and their families."

Warren's nephew Brent Jeffs had also accused him and others of repeated acts of sexual abuse when he was just a boy of about five or six attending Alta Academy. The Utah Attorney General's Office declined to press criminal charges on Brent's behalf, but that didn't stop him from filing a civil suit. Brent Jeffs told the press that he'd decided to come forward after his brother Clayne committed suicide. Medical records revealed that Clayne had also been sexually abused.

A lawyer for Warren Jeffs denied the charges, calling the action "part of a continuing effort by enemies of the church to defame it and its institutions."

Lamont and I were appalled by this information about Warren's behavior. Warren had always held himself up to be the most righteous and had demanded perfection from us all. Even masturbation was considered a sin, and Warren punished and often exiled boys who admitted to such an "evil" activity. Lamont told me that Warren instructed boys to confess in painstaking detail, describing what they'd done and how it made them feel. Thinking back to how often Allen had done this in front of me, I found myself even more furious at what I'd been forced to endure.

With this gathering storm against Warren, Lamont and I began to understand Warren's mysterious absences since at least the summer of 2004. That was when the first of these lawsuits was filed against him. Outside of Short Creek, there was a lot of public speculation that he was giving up on the southern Utah community to evade the lawsuits piling up against him and the church. The media began to explore a new FLDS settlement in Texas, one that Warren had been building for a couple of years. YFZ (Yearn for Zion) Ranch was the walled-in community being constructed in a remote location outside of El Dorado, Texas, on 1,697 acres for use as a "hunting retreat."

By late January 2005, a massive footprint of a building began to take shape, and in late March a temple rose up from the landscape. The enormous structure soared ninety feet above the ground, and as April neared, news reports claimed that workmen were busy applying a coat of primer to its exterior. There were reports that Warren wanted the construction to be complete by April 6, the date of the annual priesthood conference. Not only would the FLDS temple be a place to get closer to heaven, but it could also be a place where rituals such as blood atonement could be performed. I'd always been taught that this ritual could only be performed in a temple. Members of law enforcement quietly prepared themselves in case Warren was planning something more ominous for the temple's completion date.

As the April 23 deadline to file charges loomed, Kassandra and Craig increasingly encouraged me to come forward. While I fretted over the possibility that one day I might regret not speaking out, I was not prepared to make such a leap. All I wanted was to close the door on that chapter of my life, to put the past behind me and settle into my role as a new mother. It was fun to focus my attention on the little things like what outfit I would dress my baby in and how I would comb his thick shock of dark brown hair. It would be weeks before his fair blond locks would come in and months before he would utter his first sounds, but I was eager to soak in all that motherhood had to offer me. Lamont and I had started to make some friends in Hurricane. We'd moved to a nicer house that had a swimming pool in the backyard, and I was excited at the prospect of enjoying summer barbecues with friends like "normal" people do.

I finally told my siblings I just couldn't do it. April 23, 2005, passed like any other day, and I breathed a sigh of relief, believing that I was ready to move on to the next phase of my life. My optimism, however, was misplaced.

Lamont returned home one day to report that an investigator from the Mohave County Sheriff's Office in Arizona had unexpectedly joined him and his friend for breakfast. Apparently, there was great interest in my story and this investigator was eager to speak with me about my marriage to Allen. From what Lamont told me, Kassandra and Craig had been misinformed when they were told that the statute of limitations would run out for me that past April. There was still plenty of time for them to file charges against Warren based on what happened to me, and even without my cooperation, this investigator could subpoena me and force me to testify against my will.

The more I heard, the more I came to see that somehow I was going to get sucked into this once again, and the possibility frightened me to no end. Lamont was also scared, and neither of us was prepared to take on the priesthood. We had family members and friends still there, and going up against the priesthood was like going against them.

My determination to stay out of the spotlight grew firmer as I watched another young FLDS woman get thrown to the wolves that spring. Like me, she'd been driven across state lines to Caliente, where at age sixteen she was sealed by Warren to a man twelve years her senior who already had a wife and four children. Like me, she'd been unable to bear her marriage, but when she escaped the community she eventually went to the police. Authorities in Mohave County

convinced her to bring rape charges against her FLDS husband and Warren, and she testified before a grand jury. But
before they could hold Warren accountable in a court of law,
her name was leaked to the press. Her family members who
were still in the FLDS hunted her down and "loved her" out
of testifying. Soon after that, she disappeared for a long
stretch.

Because they'd lost their only other accuser, the investigator from Mohave County redoubled his efforts to convince
Lamont to have me come forward. They'd lost their star witness, and they were eager to recruit me in her place. I, however, was unwilling to be that girl, and Lamont made it clear
that they should leave me alone.

My panic only heightened when a lawyer from Salt Lake
City began calling Lamont in early May. Roger Hoole was
representing "the Lost Boys" and Brent Jeffs in their civil
suits against Warren Jeffs and the church and its financial
arm, the UEP Trust. They'd won a victory in Utah, with the
state court agreeing to take control of the UEP Trust away
from Warren and his cronies and assign it to a court-
appointed trustee. But everyone knew that this was not
enough to completely stop the FLDS prophet from controlling the lives and homes of the people. They needed a witness to file criminal charges against Warren, and that, they
hoped, was where I would come in.

Though Roger was also interested in bringing Warren to
justice, his methods were more relaxed than those of the
Mohave County investigators. He wanted to help me come
forward on my terms, without the pressure of Utah and Arizona on my shoulders. In a series of calls, he told Lamont
that he believed he could protect me from being called to
testify against my will. He was already representing a number of former FLDS members and had gained their trust. I
continuously declined to speak with him, but as the days
passed, I grew anxious about the possibility that Arizona
prosecutors would subpoena me.

Eventually I became tired of hearing everything second-
and thirdhand, so in mid-June I picked up the phone and

dialed Roger Hoole. "Roger," I began as soon as I heard a man's voice on the other end of the line. "This is Elissa Wall. If you guys want to know about me, then you should talk to me directly." I could sense that I had caught him completely off guard, and there was a momentary pause before he answered me.

"Well, hello there," he replied in a kind tone. It sounded as though he was smiling when he said, "Well, all right then."

That conversation was the first of many. I quickly learned that Roger was very disarming, and he listened intently to my concerns. While there was intense interest in me by members of law enforcement, no one really knew my full story, and he was willing to let me talk at my own pace. Listening to him discuss his other clients, I was encouraged to see that some of the people who'd taken legal action against the church were okay, and God had not struck them down with lightning. Despite his reassurances, I remained extremely fearful of what could happen to me if I decided to speak with police. After several meetings with Roger, he raised the idea of having me speak with an attorney in Baltimore named Joanne Suder. Suder had made a name for herself representing alleged victims of clergy sexual abuse in the Catholic Church's Baltimore archdiocese and had initiated the lawsuits for the Lost Boys and Brent Jeffs.

One weekend in early July, I agreed to fly to the East Coast to meet with her on the condition that Kassandra and Lamont could accompany me. I had never spoken to anyone about what had transpired in my marriage, and the idea of telling a total stranger worried me, but from the start of our first meeting, she set me at ease. While I didn't reveal much, my answers to her questions provided enough information to indicate that crimes had been committed.

I would later be accused of seeking Joanne Suder's counsel to initiate a civil action for monetary gain but the idea of taking money from the church had never crossed my mind. All I knew about Joanne was that she was an attorney. I had no idea what kind of law she practiced, and at that point I was too uneducated about the legal system to understand that there were different kinds of lawyers for different issues.

I was relieved when our meeting ended, and over the next few days Lamont and I debated whether I should take my case to the next level. The ease of the weekend faded almost as soon as we got back to Utah and heard that the investigator from Mohave County was attempting to locate me to serve me with papers.

Frantic, I telephoned Roger.

Roger was careful not to push me. He knew I had to come around on my own, and he'd seen what had happened to the other female FLDS witness who'd come forward. Neither of us wanted to see me go down her path, but at the same time, a small voice inside was telling me that coming forward might be the right thing to do.

Finally, one day, I met with Roger and asked him straight out, "Am I going to end up in a court?"

"Do you want me to be honest?"

"Yes," I replied, looking up at him. I had come to trust Roger, and I was certain he would be straight with me.

"Yes, Elissa, sooner or later, you are going to end up in a courtroom testifying."

It was at that moment that I put my fate in Roger's hands. He'd been working against child abuse perpetuated against the FLDS people. He had outlined a plan to help the people of the church, and on that day I became a part of it. I put my trust in Roger that he could help me in knowing the right thing to do. He'd already helped to accomplish the removal of the UEP Trust from the control of Warren Jeffs, so it could no longer be used as a tool to force parents to kick out their boys or marry off their girls.

I started to see the important role I could play, but I needed it to be on my terms. With that in mind, Roger arranged a dinner meeting with the district attorney of Washington County, Utah. I was terrified at the prospect of sitting down across the table from this kind of person. I had already formulated an opinion of what such a man would be like and I was uncertain if I wanted to attend the meeting.

Lamont and I sat in his truck outside the restaurant in St. George for nearly twenty minutes as I agonized over whether I would go in. Roger would do what he could to make sure that I would not be slapped with a subpoena. I was trembling as I followed Lamont inside with Tyler in my arms. As we neared the table, I could see that Roger was seated next to a slender man with wire-rimmed glasses. He stood and smiled at me, his eyes were kind. During the course of our meal, I studied him. He was soft-spoken and very respectful. Here I had expected a brash, boastful man, but he was nothing at all like what I'd anticipated. Brock Belnap erased all of my prejudices about prosecutors, government, lawyers, and law enforcement, and by the end of the meal I began to relax in his company.

Brock told me that what had happened to me was criminal, and if I decided to press charges, his office was willing to go forward. His voice exuded patience, and I was surprised by how attentive he was to my concerns. I didn't want my name getting out there, and I needed assurance that that wouldn't happen. I could never forgive myself if something happened to my infant son, and I needed to know that both he and my family would be protected.

Though Mohave County prosecutors were still interested in using me as their witness, there were compelling reasons for proceeding with Brock and prosecuting in Utah first. The penalties for what Warren had done were harsher in Utah, and Brock seemed more willing to prevent my name from being exposed to the public until it was necessary. While it would be several more months before I officially sat down with detectives, that night the wheels of justice began to turn against Warren Jeffs. The Washington County District Attorney's Office agreed to enter into a confidentiality and cooperation agreement with me that would shield my identity and allow me to back out at any time if it became too much for me. To protect my identity, Brock Belnap also agreed to hold off on charging Allen until after Warren, who at the time was hiding, had been arrested. He also agreed not to pursue incest charges, because that could have helped give me away. This agreement was signed in early November.

"We will never push you into anything," the district attorney assured me. It was a promise he would uphold. That day, we searched our calendars for a time for me to meet with detectives. With Christmas upon us and my family gathering at my home in St. George, we put it off until the first of the year.

As I understood more about my situation, I came to see that criminal proceedings against Warren were only one of the options at my disposal. I could file civil charges against him as well to help ratchet up the pressure. Though I wasn't eager to spend any more time in the court system than I needed to, I didn't want to pull any punches in my efforts against Warren. I carefully weighed my options and decided that if I was going to do this, I wanted to go all the way. I hoped the criminal proceedings would be a useful tool to elicit justice, but the civil trial could be an effective counterpoint.

On December 13, 2005, I filed a civil suit in neighboring Iron County against Warren Jeffs and the FLDS Church seeking monetary damages in "an amount to be determined by the jury." The following spring, I would add the UEP Trust as a defendant. Pursuing the trust, which had been used by the priesthood to control me, presented other opportunities for me to make a real difference. I wanted to find a way to make resources available to young girls and women trying to leave the FLDS, and believed the civil suit could help. The suit alleged that Warren had forced me into an underage marriage with an older man and that I'd suffered as a result. Fearing repercussions, I decided to file the suit under a pseudonym, the initials M.J. Bringing this case in Iron County and using those initials would help divert attention from me.

With the civil suit filed, I refocused my attention on the

criminal investigation. On New Year's Day I navigated the walkway to the Children's Justice Center in St. George. Dressed in a pair of dark slacks and a blouse, I followed Roger and his brother Greg, who was also co-counsel, into the converted residence that now housed this child-friendly office. Brock Belnap from the Washington County DA's office, and two of his associates were waiting for me and escorted me to a meeting room. My nerves were on edge as the reality of what I was about to do hit home. I was going to talk to someone. I was going to tell that person as much as I could about what had happened to me.

That person turned out to be two people: County Sheriff's Detective Shauna Jones and Ryan Shaum, an assistant district attorney for Washington County, and that meeting was the most challenging of my life. I broke down countless times over the four hours I was there, recalling, as best I could, what I had tried to forget: my marriage to Allen and the horrible abuse I endured during the three years I spent as his wife. At times I felt as if I couldn't breathe, and I had to stop the interview to be comforted. I was so nervous that I just kept blurting out details in random order, unable to stop my mind from racing. It was as if I'd opened my own Pandora's Box. The moment the lid was lifted, it all came pouring out and there was nothing I could do to stop it. It was painful, but in the end, it served as a critical turning point for me because I had to begin facing what I had tried so hard to bury in the past. Shauna Jones was a pro and knew how to gently draw me out of my shell. Even though I was older than most of the victims she usually interviewed, I was still very childlike. What came out of this meeting for me was the realization that what had happened to me was wrong in the eyes of the world.

Leaving the interview I felt a measure of relief that I'd unloaded some of my pain, but I didn't have the tools to deal with all of my emotions. Over the next several days, I suffered terrible nightmares and anxiety attacks. At times I became so breathless, I thought I was going to die. As the months progressed, however, my anxiety began to fade.

That March, I returned for a second interview, and later a third.

On April 5, 2006, the Washington Country District Attorney's Office held a press conference to announce that they were charging Warren Jeffs with two counts of rape as an accomplice, a first-degree felony, for forcing a teenage girl into a marriage to an older man. That teenage girl was known only as Jane Doe IV, to throw off the priesthood and lead them to believe that Jane Doe IV was one of a number of victims coming forward. Only a handful of people knew that M.J. and Jane Doe IV were both me, and that secret was closely guarded.

As I sat in my living room in St. George watching the evening news that night, I realized that I had to overcome my fears and forge ahead. Having the charges announced publicly meant there was no turning back. At that moment, it became painfully real to me that I was going to have to again face Warren Jeffs.

Chapter Twenty-seven

CAPTURED

The work of justice could not be destroyed;
if so God would cease to be God.
—BOOK OF MORMON

The very same day that criminal charges against Warren Jeffs were announced, the Washington County District Attorney's Office issued a warrant for his arrest. Prior attempts to locate the FLDS prophet in connection with other pending legal matters had failed, and I doubted he'd ever be caught. Being part of such a closeted community, he had thousands of people willing to help him and tons of money at his disposal. It was quite possible he could remain under the radar forever.

When a month passed and efforts to bring Warren to justice continued to yield no results, federal prosecutors filed a charge of unlawful flight to avoid prosecution, and Warren was officially listed as a fugitive from justice. That May, his name was added to the FBI's Most Wanted list and a reward of $10,000 was offered for information leading to his arrest. With his face plastered on posters around the state, people in our circle began to suspect who had come forward against him, and Lamont and I both began to experience the pressure from what I'd done.

At the time, Lamont was working as a construction-site

manager, and many of his subcontractors were active FLDS members. Allen was on some of his jobs.

"No friend of mine is going to fight Warren Jeffs," one man said within earshot of Lamont. Lamont heard the message loud and clear. By June, men were walking off a job if Lamont was on it. I felt terrible about how he was being treated, but I wasn't ready to pull out from my commitment.

Incidents like this created concern for our safety among my attorneys, Roger and his brother Greg, as well as the prosecutors in Washington County, and they reached out to me in early June. Agents from the Utah office of the FBI offered us protection. Brock and others thought it might be a good idea. A meeting was organized to discuss the possibility of Lamont and me entering the Federal Witness Protection Program, which would entail us literally disappearing from our lives, receiving new identities, and relocating.

"I've barely put my family back together," I said, growing emotional. "I'm not going to leave them now."

A long debate ensued and alternative plans were entertained. It was decided that we'd enter a less severe witness protection program, which included being relocated and going into hiding. None of us were comfortable with the arrangement, but I was six months pregnant with our second child, and Lamont and I feared for the safety of our small, growing family. There seemed to be little choice. I was distraught as we packed up our house that July for our big move north. We'd been living in a rental on a quiet cul-de-sac in Hurricane, and my friend Sarah and her husband, Terril, were now our neighbors. We'd grown close over the months and had begun to socialize with other families on our street. It was fun to be like "regular" people and do things like host barbecues in our backyard. That summer had marked another historic event for me. Ten of my family members had reunited for a Wall family camping trip. I had finally been able to reopen communication with my family. Justin, Jacob, Travis, Kassandra, Teressa, Caleb, Brad, Dad and Audrey, and one of their sons, spent three days in the mountains learning to be a family again. All of us had experienced so much hurt and pain from the past. Still, we realized that no matter what it had taken for us to survive, there was one thing that could not be taken from us: our bond as a family.

Once in Salt Lake City, Lamont and I put our few worldly belongings into storage and headed for the motel where we'd be staying until appropriate housing could be secured. With fall rapidly approaching, I grew lonely and desperately missed my life in southern Utah. Lamont and I were to keep a low profile, and neither one of us could get work because we were in the process of getting new identities. We were living our days in the small hotel room, trying to make do, but with a one-and-a-half-year-old who'd just begun to walk and a baby on the way, it wasn't easy.

As August drew to a close, Warren had been on the run from the criminal charges for more than four months, and authorities had been looking for him in connection with other legal matters for nearly a year. Already, several of his supporters had been arrested, and one, his brother Seth, was even thrown into jail for refusing to divulge his whereabouts. Seth had been picked up the previous October during a routine traffic stop in Colorado when police mistook him for Warren. Once they realized who he was, they demanded information about his brother's whereabouts. When Seth refused to cooperate, he was placed under arrest. According to news accounts at the time, during a search of his vehicle, police found $140,000 in cash, prepaid phone cards, and a bag of letters addressed to the prophet. Authorities later informed us that one of those letters was from the police chief of Colorado City, asking Warren's advice on how to handle the missing-persons report that Kassandra had filed on Mom and the girls back in February 2005.

It was three o'clock in the morning on August 29, 2006, when the phone in our hotel room startled me awake. It was Brock Belnap from the district attorney's office in Washington County. "Warren's been caught," his soft voice informed me. "In Nevada."

A shiver ran through my body. "Warren's been caught,"

I whispered to Lamont, hoping not to wake up my sleeping son.

Lamont and I spent most of the day in front of the TV transfixed by the news. A mix of fascination and trepidation filled me as I listened to the Nevada state trooper who'd taken Warren into custody being interviewed for the cameras. He said he'd pulled over the shiny red Cadillac Escalade because the vehicle's temporary Colorado license tags were partially obscured and grew immediately suspicious when he saw how strangely the occupants were acting. Warren's brother Isaac was at the wheel, and Warren was munching on a salad in the backseat, wearing a T-shirt and shorts. He was acting extremely nervous and wouldn't make eye contact. The vein in his neck—the carotid artery—was visibly pulsing, which immediately tipped the officer off. In the way back of the truck sat Naomi Jeffs, the former wife of Rulon and current wife of Warren, whose convincing testimony to all of us had helped make Warren the prophet.

The trooper explained that what had given the men away was their conflicting stories when separated and questioned individually. Warren told the officer they were en route to Denver, while Isaac said they were heading for Utah. The officer radioed for backup, and later the FBI. He was incredulous when Warren provided him with the fictitious name of John Findlay, then produced a receipt for a pair of contact lenses that had been purchased in Florida as proof of his identity. As other officers arrived on the scene, one of them recognized Warren. Eventually, when members of the FBI arrived, Warren realized that the jig was up and admitted who he was.

In the red Cadillac, officials confiscated twenty-seven stacks of $100 bills worth $2,500 each, totaling $54,000, fifteen cell phones, walkie-talkies, two GPS units, a police scanner, a radar detector, laptop computers, several knives, some CDs, two female wigs, one blond and one brunette, women's dresses, sunglasses, three iPods, three watches, a stack of credit cards, seven sets of keys, a photograph of

Warren and Rulon, a Bible, and a Book of Mormon. Authorities also found a duffel bag stuffed with unopened envelopes and suspected they might contain even more cash.

It turned out that the envelopes were tithing letters from the FLDS people. They had been opened just enough to extract the money inside but not enough to have read the letters. All Warren wanted was their money; he didn't even care enough to read their letters. We'd heard about one from a five-year-old boy, telling Warren that he and his mother only had the five dollars that he'd enclosed but he prayed it would be enough to send back his father, who had apparently lost the priesthood and had had his family taken away. It broke my heart to think of Warren so callously ignoring a young child's plea, but it didn't surprise me.

Attempts to question Warren proved futile. FBI agents reported that he was "cordial" but "uncooperative," insisting that he was being subjected to "religious persecution." As I sat on the edge of the bed in our small hotel room that day, isolated from my friends and family, I thought how ironic it was that Warren had been arrested and taken into custody in Nevada, the very state in which he'd committed his first crime against me.

The thought of Warren in the Clark County Jail in Las Vegas gave me a certain amount of pleasure. For nearly four years, I'd been held prisoner in a marriage that I didn't want to a man I didn't love. Just as he had decided my fate, now others would decide his.

A few days later they moved him from Nevada to Utah, and he learned that I was the one bringing criminal charges against him. It was his constitutional right to know. To ensure my continued safety, the Washington County District Attorney's Office stepped up security, installing cameras outside our place of residence and at the law offices of Roger and Greg Hoole, where I was spending a good chunk of my time. All at once, I faced the notion that the people I grew up with were going to learn to hate me. I was going against their prophet and going against my mom's wishes.

It had been nearly eighteen months since I'd last heard from my mother, and I knew that she might try to contact me in the coming days. Now that Warren knew my identity, there were concerns that church elders would encourage her to dissuade me from testifying against Warren. The forewarning came to fruition just seven days after Warren's arrest. My sister Kassandra called to alert me that Mom had just contacted her; Kassandra was certain that I'd be next. "They know who you are, and they are going to be looking for you," she cautioned.

I could see the concern on Roger's face, but I was committed to not taking Mom's calls. I was in the middle of a legal meeting at his office when my cell phone ring. The room fell silent as I pulled it from my purse and placed it on the conference table. We all knew who it was; Mom's calls always showed up as "unknown caller." Watching my cell vibrate on the conference table, I felt lured to answer it. But I fought the urge and let it go to voice mail.

Dialing in to retrieve the message, I pushed the speaker button and placed the phone on the table.

"Hey, Elissa," Mom's voice rang out. "This is your mother. I just wanted to call to say hello." Listening was extremely painful, and my stomach twisted, but along with my anxiety was my anger at Mom for letting a year and a half go by without getting in touch. All eyes were upon me as I tried not to cry, but I was unable to hold back once the voice of my baby sister came on the line.

"Elissa, I love you and miss you," Ally said. At that moment, I realized that there was no way that I could talk to them. I knew what Mom was going to say if I phoned her back. She'd use my heart against me, and I wasn't sure I could stay that strong.

Over the next seven days Mom continued to test my willpower. It was difficult to ignore her repeated calls, and at the end of the week I allowed Roger to change my phone number. The timing of the calls was particularly awkward. That week, I was preparing for my wedding to Lamont. A bishop from the mainstream Mormon Church had agreed to marry us, and while it sounds bizarre, the only people who could attend the ceremony were members of law enforcement and lawyers.

I was very pregnant at the time and did my best to look the part of a blushing bride in a white blouse and skirt that Greg's wife helped me put together. Brock and his associate Jerry Jaeger from the Washington County District Attorney's Office drove up for the ceremony. I later learned that Brock and Jerry had spent the morning driving to jewelry stores with Lamont and Roger to find me a wedding ring. In the end the three lawyers helped Lamont pick out a ring that I absolutely loved. So many people had gone out of their way to make this a special day for us, but it was hard and lonely not to have family there. Still, there was something noteworthy about having all of these attorneys who were now my trusted friends at my wedding. I'd been taught to fear people like them my whole life, but in such a short time all that had changed.

Chapter Twenty-eight

FACING WARREN

I am not the prophet.
—WARREN JEFFS

As November rolled around, the prospect of testifying at the preliminary hearing on the twenty-first loomed large on the horizon. Over the weeks I'd had at least five attorneys offering explanations of how the legal system worked, and what the defense attorneys would be allowed to do. I was nervous, and made more so by the fact that my due date was just two weeks away, and I feared I was going to go into labor in the middle of my testimony. It wasn't just the typical anxiety and settling into a new system that most newlyweds experience. Lamont and I struggled with our son's loneliness as he was forced to say good-bye to his friends from home. We also had doubts about how to proceed and wondered if we were making the right choice for our family and our future.

I was still having moments when I doubted whether I could go through with it at all. In early October, I'd learned that the sexual abuse I'd suffered at the hands of Allen hadn't been the first time I'd been taken advantage of by a man. Fearing that in Warren's lawyers' efforts to dig up my past a dirty family secret would surface, Kassandra revealed that I had been molested when I was two years old by a young man who was a friend of the family and an FLDS member.

Kassandra said that no one suspected there was an ulterior motive behind his desire to hold me until my sister Michelle walked in on him and he dropped me to the floor. As she ran to pick me up, she discovered that I was without my panties and asked me where they were. Even though I was only two, I could speak well enough to answer her question, and told her that the young man had them. The horrible reality hit my sister when she found the panties in the driveway where the man's car had been parked.

My parents were incensed and Dad immediately telephoned the prophet's home to alert him to the man's behavior and that he was intending to press formal charges. He was told that the priesthood would take care of it and was not to go to the authorities because it would cast a bad light on the people. Of course, we heard that the young man's parents had been informed of the incident, but from all accounts nothing else was ever done.

Rage filled me as Kassandra described how Mom and Dad had assembled those who knew and instructed them never to speak of the incident unless I raised it first. Kassandra recalled that Mom felt that it was better to leave it unmentioned and hope that I was too young to remember it later. I telephoned my father, and I was outraged when he confirmed Kassandra's story. I couldn't believe that my family had kept the truth from me, but that was a typical response of FLDS families when unpleasant things occur. I grew even more furious when I learned that there had been other allegations of child sexual abuse and domestic violence lodged against this man later on in his life. Had someone done something to stop him back then, perhaps those other victims would have been spared.

Difficult as this new information was, it shed a new light on so much of my emotional past. Suddenly things that had never made sense to me began to gel in my mind, like why my attacker's name was always spoken as if it were a curse word and why I'd always had a creepy uncomfortable feeling when I saw him around. I wasn't sure how this knowledge would have changed my life, but I speculated about whether my severe reaction to Allen's touch was the subconscious result of this early victimization. I couldn't help but wonder what might have been different if Mom had only told me about this when I first asked her about man/woman relations in the early days of my marriage.

While this secret was psychologically burdensome, in the end it served to cement my dedication to eliminating the silence that surrounded the sexual practices of the FLDS. It was no mystery to members of the closed community that child abuse was rampant and often went unpunished. The way these crimes were being buried had to stop. I wanted to ensure that the children still living in that community would be safe. From the start, Sherrie and Ally were a major part of this larger purpose behind my agreeing to testify, and now they became even more crucial.

Every night I would pin up an old photograph of my little sisters next to whichever new bed I found myself in to remind myself that I was doing this for a good reason. In the photo, their dresses are bland and floral-patterned, their hair coiffed expertly as good little priesthood girls, but their smiles are radiant—one thing each of them could own. Waking up each morning, I looked at that picture and saw what I was fighting for. People, girls, were still being put in my position, and I needed to stand up and make it right. To fight for those who still hadn't found their voice. I brought that photograph with me everywhere, knowing that a little piece of Ally and Sherrie would be right in my hands whenever I needed to remember. Those girls were my purpose. I knew I had the strength; I just had to remember it as I moved forward.

The sight of reporters and satellite trucks lining the street in front of St. George's Fifth Judicial District Courthouse on the morning of the preliminary hearing unnerved me, and I was glad that Brock Belnap and Jerry Jaeger had arranged for us to enter the building through a rear door. The case against Warren was creating quite a buzz in Utah, and the story was all over the news. Television reports were calling this the biggest criminal case in Utah's legal history, and somehow I was caught in the center of it. I was terrified of having my picture taken and plastered across the newspapers, but prosecutors assured me that as a victim of sexual abuse I would have my public identity protected.

It was such a relief to have the support of Teressa and Kassandra, who were also testifying for the prosecution that day. In the summer weeks before Warren was captured, I'd asked my sisters for their permission to allow investigators from the Washington County Attorneys Office to contact them. I was grateful when they'd both agreed to speak out.

Teressa had left the FLDS just a few months earlier and was living with her children at Kassandra and Ryan's house in northern Idaho. Like so many women, she'd grown weary of Warren's ongoing involvement in her marriage. Her troubles began when she'd returned to Canada after a visit with Kassandra to find that Warren was upset because she'd missed three church services in a row. He told her she'd "lost her testimony" and was not "worthy enough to be a wife." He even banned her from engaging in sexual relations with her husband until she agreed to write a letter pledging her allegiance to him. When she refused, members of the community shunned her. The impact of their scorn played out one afternoon when Teressa's daughter cut herself severely and my sister didn't have a phone to call for help. Grabbing her bleeding child, she raced to a neighbor, and the family refused to let her in.

Her husband begged her to just write the letter so they could go back to living as husband and wife, and Teressa finally relented. But the letter wasn't satisfactory to Warren— he wanted another in which she pledged her undying allegiance to him. This seemed to be Warren's way of getting back at her for her past disobedience, and showing her the amount of control he had. He seemed to take pleasure in making her life harder. But Teressa couldn't bring herself to pledge her allegiance to Warren and chose to take her children and leave her husband and the religion instead. She'd been living with Kassandra in Idaho ever since.

Holding my breath, I marched through the back door of the courthouse and followed prosecutors to the courtroom where the hearing would soon begin. My husband, sisters, and I were directed to take seats in the jury box. Court officials were expecting a full house, and with only three rows of seats for spectators, admission was going to be on a first-come, first-served basis. It was a simple-enough setup, with rows of folding chairs for all the onlookers and fluorescent lights flickering overheard. It didn't look at all like TV courtrooms with shiny mahogany and large windows that let in the sun. As the room began to fill up, the sight of all the reporters scribbling on notepads in the two front rows unnerved me, but I tried to take comfort in having Lamont and my sisters by my side.

Everyone rose as the Honorable Judge James L. Shumate entered and took his place at the elevated wood desk in the front of the courtroom. Peering out at me through rimless eyeglasses, he acknowledged my presence with a nod. His kind, round face was partially covered with a light, mostly gray beard. I'd been told that he had a reputation for being fair and reasonable.

Two court officers suddenly entered the room through a side door, and my heart nearly jumped into my throat. The keys on their belts clanged a metallic rhythm as they led Warren into the courtroom. He looked gaunt. His funeral-black suit hung loosely on his frame, emphasizing his pale complexion.

I watched the man I'd once regarded as God's mouthpiece on earth walk to the defense table, where three lawyers, two male and one female, sat waiting for him. Everything came crashing in on me at once, and I started to panic. I felt dizzy and wobbly, but I couldn't look away. Warren was staring directly at us, and I was resolved to return his gaze. "I have to do this," I told myself, settling back into the cushioned seat.

I was glad that Kassandra and Teressa would testify before me. I had no idea what to expect and I hoped that watching my older sisters handle the lawyers' questions would empower me. They had been instructed to leave the courtroom before and after their testimonies as the court enforced the exclusionary rule, and aside from Kassandra's husband, Ryan, I had no family inside from whom to draw strength.

Kassandra was the first witness called, and she remained poised as she walked to the witness box, wearing a tailored black pants suit with a red camisole peeking out from beneath her jacket. Remembering Rulon and Warren's ban on the color red, she'd chosen a red garment as an act of defiance. While he remained stone-faced as she settled into the wood armchair, I was certain her rebellious gesture was not lost on Warren.

Brock Belnap smiled at me from the prosecutor's table. He'd come to court that day with assistant district attorney Ryan Shaum, who, Brock had explained, was more experienced in this criminal courtroom setting.

"What type of relationships did Mr. Jeffs teach the girls they could have with a young man as they were growing up and going into their teenage years?" the diminutive Shaum asked my sister.

Kassandra paused, a delicious grin parting her thin red lips. "He would use a phrase," she explained. "For the boys to treat the girls like snakes and the girls likewise. . . . You got in a lot of trouble if the boys started to talk to a girl in high school or in any of the grades, because they felt like that, you know, that was improper in their society."

"Did Warren teach or discuss with the girls whether or not they could date at any point in time?"

"He discussed it. And it was absolutely not," Kassandra said.

"What did he say about it?"

"That the reason they did not date was because God

would talk to the prophet and tell the prophet who that girl belonged to. . . . He said, if any girl did get involved with a boy, that they were clouding that revelation to the prophet, that God would not, because they had sinned by that, that God would not reveal to the prophet who they belonged to."

"Did you ever have an opportunity to talk to Mr. Jeffs about what Allen was doing and the way he was treating Elissa sexually?" Ryan Shaum asked Kassandra. I leaned in to hear her response. I'd never heard the details of this conversation that my sister had with Warren.

"One time, he had called me into his office—"

"Can we have foundation?" the lawyer Wally Bugden called out from the defense table. Warren sat beside him, unfazed and looking directly at my sister.

"When was this meeting?" Shaum asked to establish a time frame for the court. Kassandra told the court the conversation with Warren had occurred during the summer of 2002.

"Okay, and what caused you to go to Warren at that time, do you recall?"

"I had got in a lot of trouble because we, Rulon's wives, had been told to cut off all ties and communications with anyone outside his family, to cut off all ties with our parents, our mother. And I spent a lot of time with Mom and my sisters. And I was told, he particularly called me into his office to tell me that I was being rebellious and I was not being submissive to my husband.

"And he reprimanded me quite sharply. And then he told me that I was being a bad example for my sister and I needed to straighten up so that she would see what a good wife does and is submissive. And he said you cannot blame a man for finding out about himself, his life. And they need to work things out between themselves. She doesn't need to be talking to you about intimate matters, and to keep sacred things sacred. And that was between her and her husband. And if she was even to mention something to me, to say, no, you need to go to talk to Allen about this."

There it was, plain as day. As far as I was concerned,

Warren knew full well what was happening in the bedroom with Allen and me. When the questioning was turned over to the defense, I was amazed at how well my big sister was able to hold her own. She went toe to toe with the defense attorney, who at one point grew visibly annoyed at his inability to corner her and accused her of being a "hostile witness."

"First of all, I am not a hostile witness," Kassandra snapped back.

He went after her a second time, portraying her as negligent for failing to go to authorities when I was first placed for marriage to Allen.

"Now, you didn't contact the Washington County Sheriff's Office when Elissa was getting into a marriage that you believed that she didn't want to get into?"

"No, I didn't."

"But you did contact the police in the summer of 2005; is that right?"

"That is correct," my sister replied.

"And you told police at that time that you believed that there might be a sexual-abuse case involving your sister Elissa; is that right?"

"May I define the difference? When my sister was married, I was married to Rulon."

Her retort could not have been better scripted, and Bugden snarled in futility. When it was Teressa's turn, she smiled back at me as she strode to the witness stand, her long blond curls falling just past her shoulders. I remained alert, studying how she responded to the questions. After establishing my sister's particulars, Shaum asked what Warren taught about our role as women of the FLDS.

"What did he say was your role as a woman, particularly related to your husband or your future husband?"

Teressa hesitated. "That he was basically God to us and your husband is your way to heaven. You were to do what he tells you. He's your priesthood head."

When the prosecutor asked her about my state of mind during my marriage to Allen, she told the truth. "There was never a time she was ever happy about the marriage, ever."

Like Kassandra, Teressa stayed composed during the defense attorney's cross-examination. But Wally Bugden only asked her six questions.

"State calls Elissa Wall, Your Honor." Brock Belnap's soft voice summoning me to the front of the courtroom elicited an intense fear in me that only grew worse as I stumbled down the steps of the jury box. Not only was I extremely nervous, I was also unsteady on my feet as a result of the extra weight I was carrying with my pregnancy. Over the months, I'd grown to trust Brock, and in the days before the hearing, I confided that I would prefer that he conduct my questioning. While I'd come to know Ryan as a thoughtful, polished lawyer, I felt more comfortable with Brock.

"How are you feeling, Elissa?" he asked, smiling at me from the podium to the right of the judge's desk.

"Pretty good," I told Brock, focusing exclusively on his reassuring face. "A little nervous," I blurted out suddenly.

"Looks like you're pregnant," he said.

"Very, very pregnant," I answered, trying to get comfortable in front of all these people who'd come to hear my story.

"Now, do you know the defendant in this case?"

"I do," I said, glancing at the defense table.

"This gentleman here?" Brock asked me. "Who is he?"

"He is Warren Jeffs," I said, clearing my throat and trying to adjust my very pregnant frame in the hard wooden chair.

It was at this moment that our eyes locked. As I looked hard at his small, round eyes, an odd sense of tranquility fell over me, as if I suddenly understood that this man no longer had any power over me. Our gaze remained fixed for what seemed a minute, with Warren working to intimidate me with his "death stare," trying to make it look like it was the glare of God. The entire courtroom fell silent, with neither one of us willing to back down. After several more seconds, Warren shook his head slightly and finally looked away. I was no longer his victim, and with that realization I was liberated.

I tried to remember what the lawyers had told me—listen

to the question and pay attention to what is being asked of me. After a few minutes, I could feel myself settling down, and with Brock's gentle voice guiding me, I answered as best I could. When the state's questions came to a close, I worked to mentally prepare myself for Bugden's attack, but when it came time for the cross-examination, it was defense attorney Tara Isaacson who rose to her feet and strode toward me. Slender and standing nearly six feet tall in her three-inch heels, she towered over the two male defense attorneys.

"Ms. Wall, I think you said that your wedding day was the worst day of your life; is that right?"

"Yes, it was," I replied tentatively.

"That day, or that time in your life, was the darkest time of your life?"

"That is correct."

"You didn't want to do it."

"No, I did not."

"You were miserable? Is that fair to say? You didn't want to go anywhere near Allen; is that right? You were miserable all day and night?"

"Yes," I replied.

"Of the day of your wedding?"

"Yes."

She began to ask me about a photograph taken the day after our wedding of Allen and me reclining on the ground. We were both smiling, a fact that she made sure to point out to the court. I was unsure what she was trying to do, and my confusion mounted as she did the same thing with several more photographs taken the evening of the wedding to Allen, and the following morning.

"So, after your night of misery with Allen in the bed, where both of you, you said, were tossing and turning—is that right?"

"I was, yes."

"Okay, and you had a bouquet of flowers in your arm . . . and he has his arm around you."

"Yes, he does."

"And it looks like your arm is around him?"

"It's actually not."

"You hid it behind him?"

"Yeah."

"So, you are both smiling, right?"

"Yeah, but it wasn't by choice."

"So, you are being forced to smile in this picture?"

I didn't like where this was going, but I had no way of stopping it, and over the next hour, she pressed me to respond to countless questions intended to show that I'd been untruthful in what I'd said about Allen and Warren. It was hard for me to hear a woman doubting that my pain was real, and after a while I started to tear up. I felt so embarrassed showing weakness and crying in front of all these strangers. But her relentless attempts to discredit me and my claims began to wear me down.

"Okay, so let me just see if you agree with me. Allen's got his arms around your waist. And you are holding on to a tree. And it looks like he's trying to pull you into a creek or something?" Isaacson asked about another photograph she was offering into evidence.

"Yes," I replied, my voice growing timid.

"And are you laughing, smiling?"

"In disgust, yes," I said, trying to defend myself against this onslaught.

I was so relieved when the judge called a recess after almost two hours of testimony, but when we returned to the courtroom, it was more of the same. Isaacson was relentless, and the way she muddied up the facts made me angry. I did my best to rebut her attempts to paint me a liar and make Allen and Warren appear blameless. I could not allow her to twist the truth.

After I'd been on the stand for nearly four hours, Judge Shumate instructed the lawyers to finish. He openly reminded the attorneys of my very pregnant state, and expressed concern about the length of time I'd been sitting before the court. I was unaccustomed to this type of sympathy and respect from an authority figure. Over the course of the day,

I had come to see the court not as simply a blunt-force in-
strument of the state, a callous machine, but as a complicated tool carefully designed to implement justice. Here I
was two weeks from delivery, hormonal and exhausted, and
every effort was being made to make me feel comfortable
and confirm that my voice was heard.

Yet I couldn't deny the toll that the gruelling day had
taken on me. The questions from Isaacson had been intense,
and over the following months I would use them as a model
to prepare for what would be in store for me in the actual
trial. That first day at the preliminary hearing, I was still too
green to understand the connection that her questions were
trying to draw and refute her attempt to show that a smile in
a photo implied happiness—a point that I could have easily
countered if I'd had a better grasp of what was happening. It
was a clever approach, and I had been unready for it. That
would not happen again.

Less than a month later, in December 2006, I gave birth to
my daughter, Emily. I had been out of the FLDS for a
little more than a year, and even though I'd shaken free of
most of the mental shackles, it was still hurtful to hear that
followers of the priesthood were being told to pray that I be
destroyed in the flesh during childbirth. I took comfort in
my faith that God was watching over me, and had once
again blessed me with a beautiful baby.

I did my best to savor the sweet beginnings of my daughter's
life in the middle of this strenuous legal process. The defense
filed a motion to drop the charges, making a fairly persuasive
argument that Warren Jeffs was simply a religious leader doing his job. But word came in late January that Judge
Shumate had found sufficient evidence to bind Warren over
for trial with two counts of rape as an accomplice, and ordered that Warren remain in jail without bail pending trial.
Fittingly, he was housed in a facility called Purgatory Flats.

If I harbored any lingering doubts about going forward

with the trial, they were washed away when Lamont and I were invited to view a startling confession that Warren made on January 25, 2007, which had been caught on videotape in Purgatory. A split screen popped up, with Warren in his jail-issued green-and-white striped jumpsuit on the right and his brother Nephi on the left—each on the phone on either side of the Plexiglas barrier. The two men looked eerily similar, with the same thick glasses and mousy brown hair parted to the side.

In the beginning of their visit, Warren instructed his brother to have someone deliver a blessing to a sick girl in the community and sent a message of support and love to his followers. Since his incarceration, he'd been phoning in from the jail and had lots of privileges afforded him. The previous day, the jail had even recorded several phone calls in which Warren admitted to having lost the priesthood thirty-one years earlier for being "immoral" with a sister and a daughter.

Despite this grim disclosure, he seemed in good spirits when the meeting with Nephi commenced. The video was grainy, and it was strange to watch Warren in so private a moment. Half an hour in, it appeared the conversation was over and Warren went to hang up the jailhouse visiting phone, but then he had something further to say. Both men picked up their phones, and for nearly six full minutes Warren said nothing, while his brother waited patiently. Warren stared blankly and seemed to listen intently, almost as though he was receiving a revelation from God.

Warren broke the silence by instructing his brother to take dictation, and Nephi compliantly pulled out his notepad.

"I'm not the prophet," Warren began.

The words blew me away, and I turned to look at Lamont. We both sat riveted as the man we'd long been told was God on earth delivered a message neither of us ever could have predicted.

"I never was the prophet, and I have been deceived by the powers of evil, and brother William T. Jessop has been the prophet since Father's passing, since the passing of my father."

He continued, "I have been the most wicked man in this dispensation in the eyes of God. And taking charge of my father's family when the Lord his God told him not to because he could not hear him, could not hear his voice, because I did not hold priesthood. I direct my former family to look to Brother William T. Jessop, and I will not be calling today or ever again.

"Write this down also," Warren directed Nephi, who sat hunched over the small overhang he was using as a desk. "As far as I possibly can be, I am sorry from the bottom of my heart."

In response to this stunning announcement, Nephi remained silent, seeming unmoved, as he followed Warren's directions. "And write this," Warren continued. "The Lord God of Heaven came to my prison cell two days ago, to test and detect me. And he saw I would rather defy him than obey him because of the weaknesses of my flesh. I am hesitating while I am giving this message as the Lord dictates these words to my mind and heart. The Lord whispers to me, to have you, Nephi, send this message everywhere you can among the priesthood people and get a copy of this video and let anyone see it who desires to see it. They will see that I voice these words myself.

"I ask, write this down, the Lord told me to say and I yearn for everyone's forgiveness for my aspiring and selfish way of life, in deceiving the elect, breaking the new and everlasting covenant, and being the most wicked man on the face of the earth in this last dispensation."

Warren's voice cracked with emotion as he concluded his message. "I ask for everyone's forgiveness and say farewell forever, you who are worthy for Zion, for I will not be there."

I felt a bit sorry for Nephi, who now choked back tears and assured Warren that he would make it to Zion. Overwhelmed, Nephi clutched the receiver, unable to move as Warren hung up and turned to leave the room. It had taken

Warren almost an hour to deliver these few words. We could see by his actions that he'd wrestled with himself, hanging up the phone, then picking it back up again several times, even at the very end, when Nephi tried to console him.

"This is a test. You are the prophet," Nephi said, his voice shaking.

Warren again took the receiver. "This is not a test; this is a revelation from the Lord, God of Heaven, through his former servant—who was never his servant—who is dictating these words at this time, that you may know, this is not a test."

Finally, after remaining paralyzed by the reality of his own admission, Warren knocked on the door of the visitors area to alert guards that he was ready to return to his cell. He exited the room, and Nephi remained behind, looking shattered by the new possibility that everything he'd believed in his life was a lie. I recognized the look on his face, for I had felt that way once before. Tears gathered in his eyes and he remained as if glued, with his back pressed up against the wall, for almost five full minutes, perhaps waiting for Warren to come back and tell him it was all just a test. But that didn't happen.

Lamont and I were beside ourselves. We'd long known Warren's devious nature, but to hear him openly profess his deceit and fraud left us speechless. While we had ceased believing in his power more than a year ago, both of us still bore the psychic scars from his treatment. To have him acknowledge that the whole thing had been a lie was at once liberating and revolting. I felt angry thinking of all of the times he'd used my heart against me and the people he had praying for him back in Short Creek—the people he'd taken advantage of, who might never know the truth.

We wanted to reveal the footage to the FLDS people so they could make their own choice about the authenticity of their prophet, but the video recording would be ordered inadmissible at trial. In spite of Warren's wishes that it be distributed for mass consumption, the defense argued that releasing the tape would poison the potential jury pool and prejudice a jury. As such it was kept under wraps for the duration of the trial.

Several days after Warren's unexpected confession, we got word that he'd attempted to commit suicide by hanging himself in his cell. He was discovered by jail guards and taken to a local hospital for treatment and evaluation. Warren had long prophesized that he would die a martyr in an attempt to align with Joseph Smith, the founder of the Mormon Church, who died in prison terrorized by an angry mob. Authorities were adamant that they would not let this happen, and every precaution was taken to ensure his safety and well-being. During his lengthy incarceration at Purgatory, he'd been performing ritualistic fasts for days at a time and spent hour upon hour on his knees praying, leaving them cracked and bloodied.

All of these revelations instilled an unwavering certainty in Lamont and me that we were doing the right thing. God was sending us these signals to empower us with the confidence to move ahead.

CHAPTER TWENTY-NINE

THE TRIAL BEGINS

Opinion is a flitting thing, but truth outlasts the sun.
—EMILY DICKINSON

On September 13, 2007, I appeared in court to testify against Warren Jeffs. The preliminary hearing had ended nearly a year before; now it was time for the real thing. The man I had known all my young life as "Uncle Warren" was finally being put on trial as an accomplice to my rape.

Even before the trial began, I felt a sense of relief. At least my voice was going to be heard. I was no longer a vulnerable fourteen-year-old girl with someone else's convictions being shoved down my throat; I was a strong twenty-year-old woman, ready to confront the person who had squandered my childhood.

In the days after the preliminary hearing, word had quietly spread that the key witness in the case was me. Legally, my identity had to be revealed to Warren prior to the trial, and had been used in the preliminary. As a result, I went from being Jane Doe IV to being Elissa Wall more quickly than I had imagined. I received such an outpouring of affection and encouragement through a long chain of supporters. I realized that there must have been members of the FLDS who were secretly praying for me, and I could feel their silent support. I had even received word from friends of ours in Oregon who had begun an international prayer chain. To hear that so many people were praying for a fair outcome provided some much needed comfort. I no longer felt like Lamont and I were standing alone; rather, we had all these people to walk right beside us through the mud.

But we'd traveled a long and arduous road to finally arrive at this day. Over the previous year, Lamont and I had moved several times, taking our two small children to keep our identity and location from being compromised. To make matters more difficult, in the months after the charges against Warren were officially filed, members of both of our families shunned us. Lamont's relatives who were still in the FLDS were particularly thorny, and at times we felt as though we'd collapse from the unrelenting pressure and stress. On the other hand, some of our greatest support and encouragement came from my close family and Lamont's relatives no longer in the FLDS.

As in the preliminary hearing, arrangements had been made to bring us into the courthouse through an alternate door to protect us from the swarms of media gathering outside. In the previous months, I had experienced a small taste of this chaos, but now the media contingent had expanded further than I could have imagined. The rear parking lot of the courthouse was crammed with satellite trucks from local TV stations and major networks from across the country as well as from abroad. I worried about being subjected to the throngs of people shouting "Elissa!" and demanding responses to their questions.

Once inside the building, I worked to gather myself up. Glancing down at my outfit, I felt professional and well presented. I'd acquired some classy suits to wear, relieved not to have to hide under my tentlike maternity dresses anymore. Today I felt strong and free in a knee-length skirt, pin-striped blazer, and purple top. I wore my hair down with a thin black headband to keep it out of my face. I must have run through my hair with my straightening iron at least five times that morning, just to ensure that every strand looked perfect. Now, in these clothes, with my hair swinging defiantly across my back, I was ready to stand up to Warren Jeffs. I looked like the person I felt like inside, and this is a magical thing when it has been denied for so much of your life.

Whereas I'd been allowed to sit in the jury box at the preliminary hearing, now I was directed to take a seat among the spectators in the gallery. It had taken the lawyers three and a half days to pick the five men and seven women of the jury. Eight of the twelve would decide Warren Jeffs's fate. Soon they would be entering the courtroom and looking to me to testify for the prosecution in this very high-profile case. Among the jurors were at least two Mormons from the mainstream LDS church.

I was uneasy sitting in the second row squeezed between my husband and Roger. In the chairs in back of us and to our right, reporters and television journalists were sizing me up. Behind us, I felt the eyes of at least ten FLDS loyalists who'd come out to show their support to their prophet. As I waited for the proceedings to begin, I could feel their angry stares boring into the back of my head. I understood the full importance of a guilty verdict in this case; if Warren were to be set free, the implications for the girls of the FLDS community were grave. Winning a conviction, on the other hand, would send a message to the priesthood and hopefully slow or put a stop to the practice of underage marriage.

Unzipping my purse, I snuck a peek at the photo of Ally and Sherrie I'd tucked inside, drawing strength from their cheerful faces as I waited on pins and needles for the judge and jury to enter the courtroom. As soon as Warren was led in, we heard all the seats of the third row snap back as his followers stood in respect. They'd also done this during the preliminary hearing, but after this display, Warren's attorneys advised them to discontinue this practice. They apparently didn't want the jury to see this show of the obvious control that Warren had over his people.

Brock Belnap delivered the opening remarks for the prosecution, keeping his points short, not condemning Warren

Jeffs with any suggestive language or trying to sway the opinions of the jury before they heard the evidence. Instead, he simply stated that we were here because there was substantial evidence to support the fact that I was raped. He also illuminated for the jury that the prosecution was not there to make a case against the religion or even polygamy. Rather, it was strictly about accomplice to the rape of a minor.

Not surprisingly, Tara Isaacson made several comments in her opening statement that frustrated me, at one point telling the jury that in this case part of their duty was to put aside their personal feelings about whether or not fourteen was too young to have sexual intercourse. Their job as she described it was to determine if I was raped at all. Then she said, "For me, it would have been too young," as if to imply that it was too young for her, but not for me. She also said that in Utah, a child of thirteen engaging in sexual relations is considered to have been raped no matter what. A child of fourteen, though, is not being raped unless he or she is "not consenting."

In my mind, the difference between thirteen and fourteen is small. Images of forced encounters with Allen pulsed through my mind—him above me in bed, yanking my underwear off, forcing those stale kisses onto my mouth as I tried to keep it shut tight. If shouting "No," fleeing the scene for my mother's arms, crying beneath his body, and begging him to stop did not count as protest, what would? As far as I knew, and as far as I intended to show everyone in that courtroom, I was raped—even though at the time I had no understanding that what Allen was doing to me had a name. It had taken the past year working with members of law enforcement for me to accept what had really happened. But I knew in my soul that even though Allen had been told to do those things, and had been told by Warren Jeffs, he still chose to hurt me, and that when I sought help from Warren he turned a blind eye instead sending me home to repent and submit.

Isaacson's opening statement utilized a PowerPoint presentation complete with a "time line" of my marriage to

Allen. One caption read, "Pregnant with Lamont's Child and Left." It was clear that the defense was trying to establish that I was an adulterous wife, but I wasn't going to stand for blatant misrepresentations being shown on the projector. I tapped Brock on the shoulder and whispered that she had no right to present that caption to the jury. The judge had ruled that the testimony in this case be narrowed to a specific time frame, and here she was already violating the terms of the trial. After being respectfully asked to follow the court's ruling, Tara rolled her eyes and begrudgingly placed a piece of white paper over the projector to cover the words.

Her demeanor was cold and her exterior impeccable. She never had a strand of hair out of place, and her eyes reminded me of a villain from an old Superman movie who could shoot deadly laser beams at her enemies with a simple glance.

After the opening statements, I was called to the stand as the first witness in the trial. I was nervous, but I just worked to put one foot in front of the other as I walked toward the witness stand to be sworn in. I tried to prevent my voice from wavering as I promised to tell the truth, so help me God. It was ironic that I had to make that oath to God. I'd been telling God the truth for years; now it was time to share it with others.

I looked out into the packed courtroom and locked eyes with my husband. He was my anchor, the one true witness to my tumultuous parting from the FLDS. As I gave my testimony, Lamont would sit quietly stunned, learning for the first time about many of the most intimate and upsetting details of my previous marriage. While he'd long known that I had been abused, I had always tried to keep certain parts of my story buried. I hadn't wanted my connection with Lamont to be soiled or tarnished by the devastating details of that marriage.

Memories flooded my mind as the prosecuting attorney, Craig Barlow, rattled off his first few questions. Though I was not as comfortable with him as I was with Brock, I knew Craig to be a caring and gentle man, with teddy bear features and a calm, even tone. He had joined the legal team at Brock's request some months earlier. Craig was actually from the Utah Attorney General's Office in Salt Lake City, but his successful prosecution of an earlier case involving similar legal theories made him a valuable resource to the prosecution. Ironically, this Craig Barlow is a distant relative of Lamont's, but his family line was never a part of the FLDS Church. I found amusement in the fact that Warren was being confronted by members of the two family surnames he'd long detested: Wall and Barlow.

Craig crafted his questions to make me feel safe and secure. He spoke in an easy, conversational tone that allowed me to push some of my pain and anger to the background and answer clearly. He asked about the context in which I knew Warren Jeffs. I explained that he had been my principal and teacher at Alta Academy, later the first counselor and mouthpiece to our prophet, and ultimately the prophet himself. I knew that to the jury, much of this seemed strange, and in truth, much of it is. But somehow I found encouragement in the faces of these strangers. They were there to listen and I was there to tell the truth.

When my eyes fell on Warren Jeffs, I felt uneasy. While I'd seen him at the preliminary hearing, I couldn't get past the discomfort of being in the same room with him again after all of this time. His face had long been etched in my mind, one of many mental symbols of the pain I'd left behind. There had been so many times when I had gone to Uncle Warren seeking comfort and found nothing but scorn, punishment, or abandonment. Now his expression was just as I had expected it would be—stoic and unchanging. This person who had once represented God on earth to me had transformed himself into something totally different. As I spoke, I noticed that he was furiously scribbling notes on a pad of paper. I wondered why he was doing this, but then realized that he was not strong enough to cover up how uncomfortable he was hearing the details of what he had done. It seemed his only option was to bury himself in an activity.

Craig asked me in what context Warren Jeffs had taught me over the years. It was hard to articulate how a set of beliefs can consume your entire mind and everything you understand to be true. How could his words and the words of those before him have permeated my existence so absolutely? I explained about morning devotional, home economics classes, and all of those hours spent listening to Uncle Warren's sermons on tape. My pulse raced as I recalled walking around my home with a Walkman turned on, Warren Jeffs's flat, frightening voice trickling into my ears, telling me how to live my life. I explained that the tapes would play over the sound system at the Jessop home as we cleaned. As I spoke, I pictured myself at twelve and thirteen, sweeping or scrubbing or changing a diaper, all the while hearing the sound of that hypnotic voice. As a child it was all I had known. Now it seemed so foreign, so unsettling.

To hear myself speak about these customs in front of a roomful of people who had grown up in "normal" homes, outside of the FLDS, was strange. I felt conflicted about some of the things we discussed. Even though growing up in the FLDS had hurt me in so many ways, I still felt there was a lot of good in many of the church's followers. It was difficult and maybe a little embarrassing for me to explain how we had lived, how we had learned, and how we had loved when I knew that it was extremely foreign to almost everyone in the room. Although I realized that it was part of the professional atmosphere of the courtroom, the jurors' unchanging expressions made me a little uneasy. I couldn't read what they were thinking, and I tried to keep my focus on Craig Barlow so I wouldn't get flustered.

I was asked to explain how children of the FLDS were taught to treat people of the opposite sex, and I replied—"as snakes." I detailed how if someone was forced to leave the community, popular speculation was that they had behaved in an "unclean" way. That for all our reserved behaviors, people of the FLDS, like people in any other society, had never been free of gossip and social assumption. I tried to show the members of the jury what it was like to grow up in that world, illustrating that to touch or look at a boy in an "unclean" way was a major offense.

By the same token, I had to explain the immediate shift in male/female relations once marriage occurred. No matter the age of either party, a couple would spend their entire lives premarriage with no romantic or sexual contact with anyone. After the union, there was a drastic change, just as I had experienced. Suddenly, within as little as a few hours, a child would go from having absolutely no sexual understanding, experience, or basis of discussion to being told that it was time to lie down and make a baby. The point was made clear through Warren's teaching of "bars up, bars down." Before marriage, a woman is to keep the "bars" and her defenses up, and as soon as she is married, she is to let the "bars" down completely and give herself fully to her husband.

I blushed a little when I was asked what I'd been taught about female and male anatomy and about sex. Of course I had to tell them that we hadn't heard a word on either subject in any context. Once married, I explained, women and girls were to give themselves wholly to their husband and obey his every word. If you refused, eventually you lost your home, family, society, and everything else.

As I sat on the stand, the first pieces of evidence were presented. They played tapes of sermons Uncle Warren had utilized in our school curriculum as well as what we listened to at home. The first segment was from a recording made on November 23, 1997, of a home economics class, in which Warren explains the marriage covenant from *In Light and Truth*. His tone placed a soft lull over the entire courtroom, but the words were just as stunning as ever. When he arrived at the part when the bride takes her groom to be her "lawful and wedded" husband, he explained: "Do you give yourself to him completely? That means fully, no halfway, no going back. You are to obey him as you obey the law. Your covenant is to God and the prophet. Loyalty to them is expressed through obeying your husband." The next words stung even all these years after I'd been forced to marry Allen: "You are literally his property." And that was how it had truly been.

Reliving the times we had been torn from my father was especially difficult, but I knew this was important, so I went on to describe the afternoon when we'd been pulled from our classes at Alta Academy and sent to the Steed ranch. I also told them that Mom and her youngest kids had been sent to Fred Jessop's and that Mom had married him that following September, with no warning about what would happen to her next. The details of my shattered childhood were coming alive in front of a roomful of strangers. Everyone was listening, and most of them seemed to care. It felt good to say these things out loud and to hear my voice as I confessed the secrets that had ruled my existence for so many years.

Day two of the trial was more intense. As we approached the story of how I came to be married, my memories of all of those bitter, difficult conversations overwhelmed me, stirring up old emotions. I was asked to read from my journal, and I did trying not to let my voice crack. After reading the two entries from the evening of April 15, 2001—the original attempt followed by the one that I would make presentable for future generations to read—I was asked if there was anything more there.

I flipped absently for a moment through the butterfly-edged pages of the journal from my fourteenth year. I thought about what should have been written there. A young teenage girl should be scribbling furiously in the private pages of her journal about crushes, problems with friends, anticipation about high school. My journal was completely blank after those two entries. It was as if having heard my mother say that I needed to keep sweet in those writings, I had nothing more to write. From that week forward, my inner life had been suppressed. How could I keep a private record of my complicated emotions if I had to appear and behave like a good priesthood girl? Even if no one else here on earth was actually reading the words, God was. My prayers had done nothing to alleviate my situation. What good would putting it into a journal do?

A major hearsay issue arose when I brought up the afternoon I'd visited Rulon Jeffs at his home. The debate over whether or not I could repeat what Rulon had said to me wore on so long that the judge was kind enough to ask if I would like to step down from the stand. As a witness, I found the whole hearsay issue very difficult both to understand and to adhere to, but in the end the judge ruled that my recounting of Rulon's fateful words was not considered hearsay, since it was being used to establish my past mental state and not for the "truth of the matter."

With the issue resolved, I repeated for the jury: "He patted me on the hand and he said, 'Follow your heart, sweetie.'" In my mind I traveled back to that afternoon and recalled my all-consuming sense of relief. Of course, it had been cut extremely short. I could feel the silence blanket the courtroom as my voice broke, repeating the words that had shattered everything—when Warren Jeffs had told me that my heart was in the wrong place.

I was asked about my reaction when I went home and heard from Uncle Fred, my new father, that I was in fact to be married. Craig asked, "Did you consider other options?"

"I didn't have other options."

"Was there a bus stop in Hildale?"

"No, there wasn't."

"Did you have a friend with a car who could have—?"

"No, I did not."

"Did you have any money of your own?"

"No."

"Any credit cards?"

"No, I did not."

These were simple questions—even obvious. But they were necessary to establish that all these everyday options that people on the outside take for granted simply are not a part of life in Short Creek.

"What were your feelings when the dress was being made?"

I pictured myself in the floor-length lace-embellished dress. I was like a little girl playing dress-up—only it was terribly real. I remembered my sister at my ankles with her tiny piercing needle, weaving it in and out of the pristine white heavy fabric. I could see my mother's careworn face, the gray circles under her eyes. "That's a big question," I mustered the words, shaking my head. I tried again. "Despair. Betrayal. I was being betrayed by the people who I trusted the most."

"Why did you feel betrayed by Warren Jeffs?"

"He overlooked what I wanted, what I knew was important." This was, in fact, the heart of the issue. My voice had been silenced, my desires ignored. I was owned and always had been—now I was simply being passed to another set of hands.

Tears welled up in my eyes and my voice shook as I beheld the photographs projected on the court's viewing screen. In the pictures Kassandra and my mother had snapped during that night, my face was red and blotchy from crying. I remember their soft, sad voices, almost pleading with me to smile for the memory books. Now the images glared out over the entire room, filling me with the nausea that had plagued me in the wee hours of that tiring April morning in 2001.

"How did you feel when this photograph was taken?"

"I kept thinking—I felt like I was getting ready for death." It might have sounded dramatic to those assembled, but it was the most accurate description I could come up with.

"How long did it take to get to Caliente?"

"Forever." I heard the flutter of stifled giggles in the gallery at this response that might have been given by a child. I then relayed for the jury how I spent that whole trip to Caliente in silent panic, overwhelmed by the simple truth: *I can't do this.* "I could not believe I was in this situation. I felt like I had no control."

I could feel angst rising inside me and had to work to

keep it together on the stand. Craig Barlow continued his questions, focusing now on the ceremony itself. Envisioning myself in the lace overlay dress with the upswept hairdo and my splotchy, tear-stained face, I explained. "I couldn't stop crying."

"What kind of tears?"

"Despair . . . fear. I could not agree to do this." I choked on the words, unable to continue. I needed to get out of there, to take a minute to myself. "Can we take a break?" I managed. Luckily, my request was granted.

After the brief break, I was back on the stand for more. I relayed the story of my defiant and barely audible "Okay, I do" and the tiny peck I managed to deliver my husband upon Warren's demand to kiss him at the close of the wedding ceremony.

"Why did you do it?"

"He was my ticket into heaven. He was my leader. My future was with him."

"And did you have an understanding of when you would have children?"

"Other people got married, and then pregnant, and nine months later had a baby." It was crystal clear to me then, just as it is now, that the expectations had been strong. I was to marry and immediately start producing children. Child brides were not shielded from the demanding and mysterious world of sex in the FLDS, no matter what anyone in that courtroom would claim on the witness stand.

A second slide show illuminated the courtroom, and I detailed what the images were. A shot of the young bride with hands covering her face appeared. The next photo revealed Allen and my "honeymoon hideout" in the light of day. "This was the next morning," I said, mustering a clear voice, "My mother had come to take pictures of the decorations and . . . us." I was wearing a pink dress with strawberries in the pattern. Next came another photograph my mother had taken, in which Allen and I were the vision of new marital bliss, sitting together with his arm slung valiantly around me.

"How did you feel here?" Craig asked.

"Numb. That was a posed picture."

"Had you ever been physically that close to a boy?"

"No."

"How did that make you feel?"

"Extremely uncomfortable. For a girl who'd never experienced that . . . I felt wicked in a sense. I knew it was okay for us to touch, but I still didn't want to."

The subsequent piece of evidence was the brown paper bag I had held during my honeymoon with Allen and the two other couples. I had marked a time line of the the brief trip, to occupy myself and my hands. To an outsider it might appear that I had been keeping track of our travel as a memento, for the sake of the scrapbooks. But that couldn't have been farther from the truth.

"Why did you do it?"

"I didn't want to hold Allen's hand. It was a way to keep busy and I guess . . . to document the trip."

As I looked at the crumpled paper bag with dates and notes scribbled across it, something grew instantly clear to me. Just hours earlier, I had been asked to read my journal aloud to the jury. Despite the panic and uncertainty of the night I had written those two entries, I had been a mostly stable adolescent up to that point. The loopy cursive writing that had stretched across those butterfly-bordered pages was typical of a teenage girl—whimsical to a point, but still controlled and neat. The handwriting on this paper bag barely resembled my own. It was unruly, distracted, panicked. I could see the progression of my emotional breakdown evidenced in this simple contrast of the letters.

I described how when we got back to the hotel each night Allen kept touching me in a sexual way and refused to stop. I went on to detail the first time he exposed his genitals to me, that terrifying night in the park. "He told me that this is what we were supposed to do. 'Don't you want to have babies?' he asked, and I replied, 'Not with you.' "

Noon recess was a much-needed relief and a chance to gather my thoughts. I picked at my food idly as my mind catapulted back to those awful first days of my marriage to Allen.

The cross-examination began right after lunch and proved even more upsetting for me. At least the prosecution was on my side; Tara Isaacson was trying to paint me as a liar and a drama queen. She walked directly toward me, her face stony. The other witnesses would be questioned by only a male defense attorney, Wally Bugden, but Tara Isaacson would question me. They didn't want to make it seem like a male was badgering me for answers, so they used her to make it appear gentler on me. But I knew better. Her fierce, cutting demeanor and icy tone made her more intimidating than any male lawyer could ever be. Somehow the fact that we were both women and she was defending the man who had facilitated my rape made it difficult for her to look into my eyes. She was a classic bully, through and through, and it took everything in me to keep my anger in check.

I knew that her tactic would be to establish a rhythm with her questioning so she could trick me into responding in a way I would later regret. As we proceeded, I went over in my head the preparation I had done with the legal team. I had to remember to think carefully before responding to any question, so that I wouldn't fall into any traps. Furthermore, I had to make sure I truly understood each question before giving an answer. As she dug into every aspect of my story, I kept my responses as short and to the point as possible. I wanted to move through my testimony with clarity and efficiency.

"Did you ever specifically tell Warren Jeffs about your sexual relationship with Allen Steed?" Isaacson posed.

There was a heavy silence in the room as I contemplated how to answer. In this woman's understanding, of course, I hadn't specifically said anything, because I hadn't ever used the words "I'm being raped." But I knew in my heart that I had made the sexual abuse Allen inflicted upon me explicitly clear to Warren using the best language I could access. "Yes," I said.

"Did Warren Jeffs ever tell you directly that you had to submit to Allen Steed sexually?"

I tried to explain but got cut off.

"Yes or no, Miss Wall."

"No."

"Did you meet with Mr. Jeffs after returning from Canada?"

I knew she thought that with her tidy outfit and commandeering speech she could intimidate me into mixing up my story. But I was smarter than that, and I wasn't going to be rendered a fool on the stand. "I only spoke of one meeting with Warren Jeffs to the jury."

"Memory fades over time, right, Miss Wall?" she badgered. "You would agree that you can't remember every word in every meeting you've had with Warren Jeffs?"

"Ms. Isaacson," I replied, being sure to keep my voice clear, even, and composed, "that was a very difficult time for me. I was a scared fourteen-year-old little girl."

"I'd like to get back to what Warren said to you that day, that your heart was in the wrong place."

"Yes."

"On Friday you said that Warren Jeffs said that to you."

"That is correct."

She whipped out a document and placed it in front of me. "Read lines six through eight of what you said to the cops."

Cautiously, I did what I was told. A part of me wanted to leap out of that chair and shake this woman, to explain to her that these were difficult pieces of my heart and my memory to access. It was like opening a Pandora's box for me, with everything flooding out. Not only was I forced to face these painful details, I was also being asked to give lengthy accounts of my lifetime of experiences. No matter how jumbled they might have been when I first presented them, I always tried to tell the truth the best way I could at the time. Any inconsistency was due to nerves alone. I knew inside that I was not nearly the only victim of a sex crime to get confused about details in a preliminary police report.

The defense battled on. "Isn't it true that Warren asked you and Allen if you were trying for children?"

"Yes." I could feel her trying to break me, trying to make

me lose my credibility. I continued, "This was a long time ago for me . . . and it was a horrible time."

"I'm going to show you a copy of that transcript. Page 204, lines 17 through 18 and 19 through 20. He never told you to have intercourse with Allen."

"We didn't use the words 'sexual intercourse' in our society. He wouldn't tell me something we didn't say."

"He told you to pray, spend time together, and love your husband."

I nodded in response.

Shifting her questions to my sisters, she asked about my conversations with Teressa in the days before my wedding.

"You talked at length with your sister Teressa about getting married?"

"Yes."

"She also told you that you didn't have to do it."

"Women didn't have that kind of power," I replied.

With that, she took her place at the defense table and I was asked to stand down for the day. When I returned to my original seat and looked around, an uncomfortable feeling grew inside me. I had laid bare my story and my feelings for the lawyers, the judge, the jury, Warren—everyone knew what I had been through. It was liberating but I was also self-conscious. I had shared some of my darkest secrets with total strangers, yet none of them really knew who I was. There were members of the press there, and I had not spoken with them up to that point. I worried what they thought about me. But I resolved to keep my silence.

The following morning I was brought back to the stand for further interrogation by the defense.

"Isn't it true you never told your mother you were raped?" Tara Isaacson asked in her cutting tone.

"Yes," I said, doing my best to hold her gaze.

"One person in your life at the time was the mother of Allen Steed."

"I saw her from time to time."

"You said she was 'an angel.' "

My pulse raced. Were they trying to insinuate that I could have spoken to Mrs. Steed about my situation with Allen? "She was an angel," I confirmed. "But that still didn't mean I could have looked to her for help."

"Did you tell her what was going on with Allen?"

"She could see."

"You didn't tell your friends, either."

"No one could tell anyone they're being raped."

"Your father, Douglas Wall, is someone you could have told."

"Well, for starters," I retorted, "I had no phone number to reach him."

"You also had brothers who had left the church before your marriage."

"Yes, I did," I declared, "but I believed in the prophet."

"Did you agree to the marriage prior to the ceremony?"

I cleared my throat softly, frustrated by her continued insinuations that I had consented to the marriage. After facing off against her in the past, I'd promised myself that I would go toe to toe with her and stay strong no matter how hard she pushed me. I stared straight into her eyes as I firmly said, "As much as someone could agree to something against their will."

"So, Warren Jeffs was a teacher, principal, not the prophet?"

"Not at that time."

"So, you left the FLDS Church at the end of 2004, right?"

"Yes."

"Did you take those books and teachings with you when you left?"

"Yes."

"Since you left, who has played those tapes for you?"

"After I didn't listen to them," I responded.

The defense then took me on a complicated tangent, accusing me of wrongdoing by having my personal attorneys join me during the preceding meetings with the state. I made it clear that my lawyers Roger and Greg Hoole were in the court today, and had been by my side, supporting and protecting my rights throughout my entire legal journey.

After an examination of the many love notes that Allen had written me during the marriage, I was asked to stand down. I could feel the fury rising inside me as she tried to create a smokescreen by having me read these letters. I wanted to scream out that no letter from Allen, no matter how seemingly romantic or thoughtful, could undo the act of rape. I realized at that moment that the facts of this case were glaring: I was fourteen, forced into a marriage, and forced to have sex against my will. And they were using any shred of evidence they could to cover that up and muddy the water.

CHAPTER THIRTY

THE END IS IN SIGHT

Uncle Warren has done nothing wrong.
—ALLEN STEED

With my testimony completed, the State of Utah called my sister Teressa Wall Blackmore. She looked lovely with her soft blond hair cut in a stylish chin-length bob. It was immediately clear to the jury from her appearance that, like me, she was no longer confined by the rigid restrictions of the lifestyle we were born into.

"How are you familiar with the FLDS?" the state began its questioning.

"I was a part of it," my sister replied matter-of-factly. Just like at the preliminary hearing, her answers remained short and succinct.

"When did you leave?"

"A year and a half ago."

"Do you know Warren Jeffs?"

Teressa's eyes narrowed slightly as she replied that she indeed knew him, as a principal at Alta Academy, a counselor, a speaker in church meetings, and eventually as our prophet. She went on to explain that one of the central concepts of the FLDS faith was obedience. "We were raised our whole lives to be obedient no matter what. We were to 'keep sweet' and not ask any questions."

After describing her stint at Alta Academy from first through tenth grade, she explained how she, like so many other FLDS girls, including myself, had to leave school to get married. She described Warren Jeffs's role at Alta Academy not only as principal but as a teacher, especially to the high school students. "Warren taught all of the children in devotional and priesthood history," she went on. "He taught us to keep sweet."

"How did you take that teaching?"

"It was frustrating because inside I had questions and I couldn't ask. Deep down I didn't have this testimony, but I had to pretend I did."

Because she had already been sent to Canada, Teressa had not been present for the latter half of my childhood or our drastic and sudden move to Fred Jessop's. However, she did share her own distressing tale with the jury, explaining how she had been shipped off to Canada and pressured to marry at a young age.

Moving forward to the spring of 2001, Teressa described the initial tearful phone call she received from me while in Canada.

"Did you become aware of Elissa Wall's impending marriage?"

"She called me crying. I was very upset. But I was in Canada and there was nothing I could do. Even if I had been there, though, I couldn't have done anything."

"What did you tell her?"

"I told her she didn't have to do it."

"So she had options?" the prosecutor asked.

"To me, her option was to leave."

"Did you have any specific ideas of how she could leave?"

"Not really."

The state moved to my wedding, and Teressa recalled the countless phone calls between us during those tumultuous weeks. Even then I knew that she could do nothing to stop what was happening to me, but her comfort over the phone had been a true lifeline to me in those early days of my fated marriage. "I talked to her the day after her wedding," my sister told the court.

"What was her emotional state?"

"She was sobbing . . . sad, hopeless, depressed." Teressa shook her head slightly, remembering the desperation in my voice. She then went on to describe my visit with Allen to Canada.

"Did you talk about Elissa's relationship with Allen that week?"

"Yes, we did. He was touching her, doing things that she didn't want him to. In the FLDS we didn't know what sex is before marriage. We didn't use those words."

"How did Elissa behave around Allen Steed?"

"She hated to be near him. They were with us for four or five days, maybe a week. She was terrified of him, and standoffish."

"Did you go to Hildale in the winter of 2002?"

"Yes."

"Was there a change in Elissa's demeanor?"

"Only that it was worse than before. She was depressed and tired. She just wanted to sleep all of the time. She couldn't function. She was just a terrified little girl. I wanted her to come back to Canada and help me with my new baby." Teressa went on to detail the roller-coaster ride that our request for my trip had been, from asking Allen to the frustrating meeting with Warren. "And then Allen finally said if it was okay with Warren, then, fine, she can go. And we packed up and left within ten minutes."

"Why did you go this route instead of just leaving?"

"Roy would have gotten his family taken away," she explained. "You have to get permission for a trip or . . . anything you wanted to do. Everything went through Warren."

Not surprisingly, the defense had no questions for Teressa. She stood down from the witness stand, with Kassandra up next.

"Can you please describe the members of your family?"

Kassandra stifled a sweet, glittery laugh. "All of them?" she asked incredulously. "My father is Douglas Wall and my mother is Sharon Steed Wall. I have fourteen siblings from my mother. Elissa Wall is my younger sister by ten years."

As Kassandra spoke of our father, I took comfort in knowing that both my sisters and I had Dad's support. Although he hadn't come to the courthouse to be there for us in person, he'd been phoning me to offer private words of encouragement. He and Mother Audrey had treated my sisters and me to dinner on the eve of the trial, and would continue to share meals with us and two of my brothers, Brad and Caleb, in the coming days. I was heartened to see my brothers in the gallery offering their support. I was also grateful to Mother Audrey. Over time, I'd come to appreciate her dearly and had begun to understand so much more about our family life. It meant a lot to me to have at least one of my mothers still in my life.

"Have you lived in Salt Lake City your entire life?" Wally Bugden asked Kassandra.

"I moved when I was married at nineteen to Colorado City. Now I live in Idaho."

"Did you grow up in the FLDS Church?"

"Yes." Kassandra continued in her soft, bubbly voice. She was asked about Alta Academy and how she knew Warren Jeffs. Her story was somewhat different from mine and Teressa's, as she had been able to finish high school at Alta Academy. She then went on to teach fifth grade in the fall of 1994. As my sister opened the discussion of her time as a teacher at Alta, I shot back to that classroom in my mind.

"It was considered honorable," Kassandra explained of teaching. "Warren Jeffs was principal there. He would go to Father [Rulon] for the final decisions on everything."

"How long did you work as a teacher there?"

"Through September of 1995. Then I was married to Warren's father, Rulon Jeffs."

Kassandra's testimony delved deeper into the structure at Alta Academy, describing some of the facets I had only heard about and to which I had never been subjected, since my time there ended so much earlier than hers.

"Did the students at Alta Academy receive instruction from Warren Jeffs?" the state's attorney asked.

"Yes. He was the primary teacher. He taught devotional. He taught us math, chemistry, geography, history, and priesthood history. There were religious teachings every day. Every subject was based around priesthood history—stories of Christ and Joseph Smith."

"What materials were used?"

"Everything had to be approved by Warren Jeffs. We used the Book of Mormon, the Bible, and other discourses or lectures from prophets of the past. Priesthood history was taught every day. As years went on they removed world history and replaced it with doctrine only. Warren rewrote the entire curriculum based around priesthood stories. For instance, in a second-grade reading lesson, a Bible story would be used to teach the reading skills."

"How much of the teaching was based around Warren Jeffs?"

"At first not much. But later, quite a bit."

Kassandra corroborated what Teressa and I had said about viewing boys "as snakes" and explained why the school eventually closed as "Doomsday" neared.

"Who had the power to discipline?"

"Warren Jeffs."

"What was taught to girls about sex?"

"Nothing. Intimacy would be taught to a girl by her husband or parents. At nineteen I had no clue what that was."

"When did you find out?"

"Rulon Jeffs told me after I was married."

"Was the word *sex* ever used?"

"No."

"What if any term was used?"

"A . . . 'marriage relationship.' There was no real term."

It felt good to hear her words, validating what I'd said. While I'd always known that Kassandra's experience supported my own, watching her help the case against War-ren gave me confidence. I could almost feel the facts sliding into place.

"Are you familiar with the concept of a placement mar-riage?" the state continued.

"Yes. Girls were to keep bars up our entire lives. Never to let a man touch us or to go on a date. If you were clean and pure, God would tell the prophet. We put our lives in his hands. There was no other way to have a relationship; we couldn't make those choices."

Her answers were delivered flawlessly. I sat captivated as she described how people came to be married and what marriage in the FLDS was actually like.

"What was the role of women in a marriage?"

"The greatest thing a woman could become was a mother in Zion, to raise good children that would be loyal to the prophet and never question their priesthood head. After a woman was placed, she would give herself totally to her hus-band, 'body, boots, and britches.' If there was a conflict, you would pray to God to inspire the prophet to solve it, but you could never confront your husband."

When the attorney asked Kassandra for a description of the term "keep sweet," she responded, "Even when it hurts, you were to act happy. Even if you're uncomfortable. That was how you conquered the evil inside of you."

"What was your reaction when you heard about your sis-ter Elissa Wall's pending marriage to Allen Steed?"

"Disbelief," Kassandra answered slowly. "I was horri-fied." She described how she and Rachel had gone to Rulon in the hope that he would intercede on my behalf, and how she had instructed me to ask Uncle Fred for two more years.

"Why did you go to Rulon Jeffs?"

"Everyone else who had been confronted with our con-cerns had been turned down, so I went with Rachel and we explained to Rulon the situation and that our sister was up-set. He did not understand the situation. He was confused and looked to Warren Jeffs. He said, 'She is only fourteen.

What the hell is Fred thinking?' and Warren said, 'Well, because of who he is, we'd like to honor his request.' Rulon replied, 'There should be no rush.'" This was a whole new element that I had no idea ever existed. If this were true, and it was Uncle Fred who had really put this together, then why hadn't Warren listened to me? He'd been the one person who could have changed it, despite Fred's supposed insistence.

"After this meeting, how did you feel about your sister's situation?"

"I was hopeful."

The questioning shifted to the marriage itself.

"What was Elissa's emotional state the night before the wedding?"

"She was crying. She didn't care about the dress. Very emotional and just . . . sobbing. We took pictures and tried to get her to look happy."

Kassandra explained that my distress lasted long after those initial days and nights. "In the first few months she became very depressed. I saw her at Rulon's house just two to three months after the wedding. She told me she was there for an appointment with Warren."

"Did you meet her as she was leaving?"

"Yes, I did. And she said, 'Kassandra I can't talk to my sisters. I am supposed to go home and obey my husband.' Warren Jeffs then told me to encourage her to be happy where she was placed."

The state's final witness was Jane Blackmore, the midwife who had taken care of me in Canada after my stillbirth. It was smart thinking on the prosecution's part to include Jane's testimony of her treatment of me during my pregnancy and stillbirth so that the Walls didn't come across as some self-important troupe of sisters out to get the prophet for no solid reason. I appreciated Jane's participation; the stakes for her were quite high. Her life was very much entwined with the FLDS, and many of her children remained loyal to the sect. In publicly speaking out against the church she faced losing these children forever, but she did it because she knew it was right.

After Jane's testimony, we took a short break. Gathering in Brock's office, in the building next door to the courthouse, the prosecutorial team invited me in and we talked about how to proceed. We came to the decision that the state would rest. There was a lot more evidence and also more witnesses to give accounts of the FLDS culture, Warren Jeffs, and underage marriages. But we chose to keep it short and simple, and I had faith in the prosecuting attorneys. They had done their job well. We had presented the truth, and though we wondered if it was enough, we returned to the courthouse that afternoon and much to the surprise of the defense team, rested the state's case.

Even though we'd provided the defense with a lengthy collection of names to counter the list of seventy-seven potential witnesses they'd turned over, the prosecutors were confident that providing the jury with the simple facts would win a conviction. I'd been disappointed to see some of the people on the defense's list. They had pitted family against family. Every person that we had on our witness list was countered by that witness's family members, who would testify against the witness. The most troubling name was my mother's, although I was pretty confident it had been placed there more for intimidation. Still, I was saddened to think that Mom was possibly out there hurt by my actions, actions that I knew she didn't understand because the priesthood and even Warren Jeffs still had a solid hold on her mind. I was sure that others were looking down on her for the bad things that her children were supposedly doing against the church, and I imagined that she and my sisters were suffering as a result of their scorn.

The defense team had not expected our case to end so promptly, and Wally Bugden asked for a short break to prepare his witnesses. When we returned that afternoon, he called Jennie Pipkin, my FLDS friend who, along with her husband, had accompanied Allen and me on our camping trip in an attempt to perk up Lily. Jennie's anxiety was visible, and her knee bounced uncontrollably. We caught eyes for a moment, and I mouthed "Hi" to my old friend, but she promptly looked away. I watched in quiet empathy as Jennie was sworn in. Wearing a cobalt-blue pioneer-style gown, with her hair carefully coifed in a classic no-frills FLDS style and not a drop of makeup to conceal the exhaustion in her face, Jennie nervously took a seat in the witness box.

The contrast between her appearance and that of the Wall sisters must have alarmed the jury. She was a walking embodiment of the restriction that had been placed on my sisters and me during our lives as members of the FLDS. But as soon as Jennie's testimony began, I would realize that she, along with her fellow witnesses, had clearly been instructed to dress in this manner to appear innocent and unworldly—or, as outsiders would call it, uncultured. But I couldn't imagine her dressed any other way.

Even more transparent than Jennie's appearance was the degree of prep work she must have endured before standing trial. This was clear from the excessive manner in which she praised FLDS teachings and misrepresented its protocol, especially on the subject of marriage and sexual relationships.

"How old are you?" Wally Bugden asked her.

"Twenty-six."

"Have you been married?"

"Yes."

"When?"

"When I was seventeen years old." What followed was a shocking and painfully inaccurate-sounding account of the process by which Jennie Pipkin had been married. "I took the first step," she stated plainly. "I desired a placement marriage, and I turned myself in."

"Please explain."

"The woman indicates that she wants to get married," she said, "and my intent was to ask my father to pray for me."

"Did you have a choice? A part in the decision?"

"Oh, yes, of *course*," she declared smugly.

"And when did you 'turn yourself in' for marriage?"

"Four days after my high school graduation ceremony."

"What did your father say about your request to get married?"

"He said he would think about it. He asked me to get him something, and on my way back into the room, I picked up the phone. I really wanted him to make the call to Rulon Jeffs."

"Did you get married?"

"Well," she smiled slightly, "yeah. Warren said to Rulon, 'This is a young lady looking to be placed,' and Rulon asked, 'Who does she want to marry?' The prophet then contacted my father, and my father and I agreed that yes, we both wanted this. The marriage took place the next day."

At first I was a bit confused listening to Jennie's account. I had heard of girls turning themselves in to the prophet for marriage. It seemed contradictory that she'd desired a placement marriage and that then the prophet asked, "Who does she want to marry?" It didn't seem like there was anything placement about that. I was disturbed by Jennie's recounting of these events, and scribbled furiously on the legal pad that sat on my lap, "Turn yourself in 'First Step.' I *NEVER* TURNED MYSELF IN!! I was never asked if I had anyone in mind. . . . I never took the 'First Step' and asked to be married."

"During your wedding ceremony, was there any mention of the phrase 'to be fruitful and multiply'?"

"Well, that text is in the Scripture," she said. "It meant that I could have children."

As she spoke, Jennie refilled her water glass, and the object became a constant distraction from the questioning. I wondered if subconsciously she was creating a diversion from the subject at hand.

"Was there any expectation of when you were to have children?" the defense lawyer solicited.

"No, that was a girl's personal choice."

"And how many children do you have?"

"Five."

Her false confirmation that a young girl's progression into sexual activity was a matter of her own choice was aggravating, and she continued by launching into a statement that force in any way—sexual included—is not utilized or encouraged in the FLDS, let alone in a marriage.

When asked about her understanding of the concept of "obedience" and the duty of women of the FLDS, Jennie responded, "I wouldn't necessarily describe it as a duty. A man has learned and teaches his wife."

"Is a wife obligated to agree with her husband?"

"Absolutely not," Jennie said in a defiant tone. "That would be hypocritical." Jennie paused to take another sip of her water. "What if he went psycho or something?" Her rhetorical statement didn't fool me, and I searched the faces of the jury to determine if they felt the same. A few cracked smiles, but Jennie's jumpy body language seemed to betray her words.

"Would a husband command his wife what to do every day?"

Jennie laughed nervously and then responded, "No. Of course not."

"If a wife rules over her husband, is that considered a bad thing?"

"No," she answered firmly. "I do what I want whether we agree or not."

Her statement shocked me. She was outwardly defying so many teachings of the FLDS in a desperate attempt to prove a point for the defense.

"Can you please explain the husband's authority and the woman's right to say no?"

"Whatever she feels is wrong, she doesn't have to do," Jennie uttered the words staccato, then took another sip of her water.

"Did you learn that from Warren Jeffs?"

"Yes, I've learned this from Warren Jeffs and the supporting words of other church officials before him."

The more I heard, the more I grew flushed and agitated, but it wasn't until Jennie completely misconstrued my relationship with Allen that I was livid.

"After Allen and Elissa were married, do you remember seeing them together?"

"Yes."

"How did Elissa respond to Allen?"

"She was nasty to him. Once, on a trip to St. George, he bought her two dozen roses and she was still being rude."

I honestly didn't remember the shopping trip to St. George that she was speaking of, or the roses. Still, I was thinking, "Well, of course I was, he was hurting me. Anybody who's hurt lashes out."

"Was there a camping trip?" the defense lawyer asked, referring to the trip on which I'd been put in charge of encouraging Lily.

"Yes, and they were both smiling the whole time."

"They seemed very happy?"

"Yes, something had changed."

"Was Elissa standoffish?"

"No. She showed me a negligee she had purchased. She was excited; it was cute. They seemed to be communicating well." I looked back on that trip and found myself seething with anger at the way in which Jennie described it. I remembered how frustrated and uncomfortable I'd been the whole time, and I couldn't believe that she would deny that. We both knew that I'd been put in a position to show everyone on the trip that negligee because Allen had presented it to me in front of them all. Still, I tried to calm my anger toward her, knowing that she was under pressure.

Jennie explained the unraveling of her marriage, emphasizing that Warren Jeffs had granted her a release from her husband, Jonathan, when it was clear that things were not going to improve. I was furious that she had been granted a release, especially when she described her meeting with Warren; she had used the same language I had to explain my problems with Allen. I wrote Brock a note saying: "Didn't I use the same language? He didn't give me a release!"

Her cross-examination was irritating as well. She described coming across a passage in an old sermon that stated that it was a woman's job to invite her husband to have marital relations. At this point, her understanding of her own role changed.

"And would there be consequences if you refused him sexually?"

"There was none."

"Were there times when you had refused and then it happened anyway?"

"Yes. But only if I consented first."

"Were you aware there were husbands in the FLDS who would use force?"

"No. Force is against our religion."

When the prosecution asked about our shared camping trip, they intended to prove that I had been keeping sweet that week despite my pain, as I'd always been taught to do.

"Have you ever heard of 'keeping sweet'?" she was asked.

"I have heard that, yes, but it's not a central doctrine."

Of all her statements, this one shocked me the most. It was Rulon's favorite saying and he'd used it on every occasion. It was even printed on his funeral program. "Keep sweet, no matter what. It's a matter of life and death."

"One principle is if you suffer inside, you keep sweet, smile, and appear happy, right?" the prosecutor asked.

"It could be if you chose to smile," she answered.

"Warren Jeffs is the prophet?"

"I *choose* to see him as that, yes."

"Have you ever heard of the song 'We Love You, Uncle Warren'?"

"No, I've never heard that song."

After she had finished her testimony, Jennie Pipkin stepped down and crossed the courtroom to return to her original seat. I felt so bad that my honest friendship with her had been used to try to discredit me.

Several more FLDS women and their husbands followed with accounts of happy marriages, Warren's loving guidance, and inaccurate details of church teachings and expectations.

The most painful testimony for me to bear was that of my dear friend Joanna.

She was an older sister of my friend Natalie, and after my marriage, she too had been placed for marriage. We had bonded over the similarity of our experiences. I was surprised to see the defense use her as a tool, because I believed that her marriage had been much like mine. Interestingly, her testimony didn't touch on her problems; it only related the details of how Warren had guided her to happiness in her marital union. When asked about her relationship with me, she said that we'd gotten together many times to "complain" of the situations we were experiencing with our arranged husbands. She countered these admissions by testifying to how happy she and her husband were now, thanks to "Uncle" Warren. Her accounts of her meetings with Warren about her unhappy marriage differed greatly from those that I remembered in the moments that we'd sought each other for comfort.

Even after her testimony, I waited to hug her during one of the intermissions and was heartened when she whispered these words: "I'm sorry. I know you know what's right."

On September 19, my ex-husband, Allen Steed, took the stand. During the course of his testimony, I was overwhelmed by a dual sense of loathing and pity. Like Jennie, he had obviously been instructed to uphold a homespun image on the stand, and he appeared in an unpressed denim shirt and casual pants. I knew that Allen owned plenty of suits; I'd seen them hanging in his closet in the trailer. And he knew it was appropriate to dress more formally in court. The handful of FLDS supporters who'd come to court each day to show their support of Warren all donned black suits and ties.

Allen looked very self-conscious and like he was about to crumble. His meek, humble demeanor almost sickened me. I wasn't sure if it was an act or if in the years since I'd left him he'd become this pitiful. He had a glazed cloudiness to his eyes that matched the look I'd seen on my mother's face when the FLDS teachings had pushed every other thought from her mind. I was shocked along with many of those in attendance when Allen's questioning began with his lawyer present and the reading of his Miranda rights. He hadn't yet been formally charged with any crimes but by taking the stand and testifying he was waiving his right to self-incrimination.

Allen spoke so quietly throughout his testimony that it was almost impossible to hear him, and he was frequently reminded to speak up. Initially it seemed his nerves had gotten the better of him as he sat rattling off a chain of pro-FLDS statements and claiming for the jury that we had actually had a good marriage. As I listened to him speak, an image flashed briefly in my mind—Allen and me in the trailer during one of our painful nights when he forced sex on me. I was almost shocked to see him here at all, but then I knew what he was doing. He had to look good in front of the prophet, just like everyone else. Otherwise, he would have nowhere to turn. I felt a pang of sympathy for Allen; this was probably a last-ditch effort on his part to receive a new wife and start again on his path to heaven. He was willing to fall on the sword for Warren. Watching this whole legal process, I had seen Warren throw so many under the bus as he was now doing with Allen. In an effort to prove his innocence, he had thrown the blame at the feet of my mother, Uncle Fred, my sisters, my father, and even me. This act was a public statement that he was willing to condemn someone else to jail in order to win his freedom.

"Elissa Wall was your wife, is that right?"

"Yes."

"Are you related to her?"

"We have the same grandfather. Our grandmothers are separate," he said, as if that detail rendered our situation any more legal or justified.

The defense established that Allen and I had known each other and seen each other from time to time in Hildale at Uncle Fred's house.

"How did you get along before the marriage?"

For some reason, part of me expected Allen to admit that he had been cruel to me—a nasty tease. Instead, he responded, "I didn't do much with her, so . . ." It was left for the jury to intuit that we had no relationship either way.

"Did you do any dating growing up?"

"Absolutely not."

"Any dancing?"

"A little, mostly with my sisters."

"Any kissing?"

"No, sir."

Allen was then asked to explain his interpretation of placement marriage.

"I believe we have a God in heaven who looks down upon the earth. He sees his children and decides who should get married to each other, and then he tells his prophet, and he places the marriage together." A shudder ran up and down my spine.

"Did you understand there was anything illegal or wrong about your marriage because you had a shared grandfather?"

"No," Allen responded in a near whisper. At this time, his testimony was interrupted over and over again. He was so nervous he could not keep his volume up and he was constantly being stopped and asked to repeat what he'd said.

"So, did you propose to Elissa?"

"I believe I did. Yes, sir."

Now my agitation became palpable. Up until this point, Allen's testimony had been a series of misinterpretations and at best half-truths. With this line he began to spin a tale on Warren Jeffs behalf. Never was there anything even resembling a proposal between us. In fact the very idea that a man would propose to a woman ran counter to the concept of "placement marriage." The FLDS just didn't do that. Still, Allen rambled on, flying by the seat of his pants.

In discussing our wedding day, Allen was asked to detail his feelings, and the discrepancy between his and my own were glaring.

"I don't remember too much about it—I was kind of you might say on cloud nine."

"You were excited?"

"Very. Yes, sir."

His smile and the weird look in his eyes began to make me gag.

"Did you have an understanding about how men and women make a baby?"

"Not really," he responded. When the subject turned to our honeymoon, Allen continued to misconstrue the details.

"Did you become more comfortable with each other at that time?" Bugden asked.

"You could say that."

"Was there any hugging going on?"

"Yes."

"Kissing?"

"Yes."

"Sure," I thought, enraged. "If you call a one-hundred-dollar dare that I had been pressured to perform an actual kiss."

"In public or in private?"

"More so in private." Of course he would present it this way to make it seem as though I was cold with him in public and different when we were alone. When it came to the bedroom, it was his word against mine, and that was the best angle Allen could take. What followed was a grossly misrepresented tale of how Allen and I had learned about sex together, at first claiming that we hadn't had any intimate contact for the first three months of the marriage and saying that he had exposed himself to me in the park as a means of making me feel more comfortable around him.

When asked to describe our first sexual encounter, Allen's response cut through me like a knife. "She woke me up and asked if I cared about her," he recounted. "She rolled close to me, asked me to scratch her back, and one thing led to the next. I felt like she was ready to go forward."

As these words escaped his lips, I began to experience the symptoms of a classic panic attack; the pressure and pain had bottled up inside of me, and hearing this skewed interpretation of the sexual contact with Allen proved too much. Tears rolled down my cheeks, which were growing red hot with frustration. I became short of breath and my shoulders shook from my attempts to hold my sobs in. Suddenly I felt a hand on my shoulder. Looking up, I saw the kind face of the uniformed bailiff.

"Do you need to go out?" she whispered. She found her answer in my pleading eyes. I wasn't sure if I was permitted to leave the courtroom during the testimony and was grateful that she'd noticed my pain and given me an out. Jumping up from my seat in the second row of the gallery, I followed her to an empty courtroom, where Lamont and Roger immediately joined me.

The defense was trying to label me a lying, adulterous woman. Before the trial I honestly did feel a sense of sympathy for Allen. He was both a victim of Warren's power and a perpetrator, but after hearing Allen's revisionist history of our marriage, any remorse I'd felt evaporated. I was enraged by his sheer audacity and his unwillingness to take responsibility for what he'd done. The way he was speaking telegraphed that he didn't feel the least bit apologetic for how he'd treated me and the crimes he'd committed against a fourteen-year-old child.

While I was out of the room, Allen went on to testify about his counseling sessions with Warren, explaining how Warren had instructed him to get me to love him, so that I would obey out of love. He said that Warren had told him to "take things slowly."

"It was a rough and rocky road, then we learned to love one another," he told the court. "And I'm sure it wasn't easy, knowing what I didn't know then."

Allen admitted to the jurors that as much as he wanted to believe that he was in charge of the marriage, it simply wasn't true. "I tried to make decisions with wisdom and love, and a lot of times I didn't voice my decision, knowing there would be opposition.

"If she decided to do something I didn't want her to do, she would do it anyway," Allen muttered. He even told the court that although I was avoiding him and he was hearing rumors that I was seeing someone else, it had never crossed his mind to ask Warren for a release from the marriage.

When I finally felt composed enough to return to the courtroom, Craig Barlow was just beginning his cross-examination of Allen. I was glad I'd come back, because watching the state's attorney tear Allen to shreds was satisfying. Even under the questioning of the defense, Allen's testimony seemed shaky and hard to believe. Now that he was experiencing real pressure from the prosecution, cracks began to form in every other word he said. He was trapped, by his false testimony and the pattern of deception he had chosen to protect his prophet. Before Craig Barlow even asked his first question, Allen blurted out, "Uncle Warren has done nothing wrong."

Stopping in his tracks with a half grin, Craig informed Allen that usually the witness waits for a question before giving a response. Allen's oddly timed declaration of allegiance to Warren Jeffs suggested right away that he would do anything, even lie, for his prophet.

Craig immediately established that Allen's claims about his motivation behind the exposure incident in the park were ludicrous. Then he asked, "How did you communicate sex to her? What was the language you used?"

"We called it 'in-and-out.'"

My mouth was agape, and my stomach turned in anxious fury. He seemed to just make this up on the spot, compounding his deceitfulness by the minute. We never called anything "in-and-out." A hush fell over the room as spectators seemed to try to comprehend what he was saying. Even Craig Barlow revealed his astonishment in the line of questioning that followed Allen's outrageous claim. "So, when you wanted to do it, you would say, 'Let's do in-and-out'?"

"Yes, sir," he replied. At that moment, the only thing that crossed my mind was that Allen was the embodiment of a creep, and I swore never to eat at an In-N-Out Burger again.

Allen tripped over his own words when he claimed that, in an effort not to get pregnant, I had urged him, "Don't go in me."

It was clear to Craig that I wouldn't have had access to that kind of information about conception, nor would I use language like that. Furthermore, if members of the FLDS were only supposed to have intercourse as a means to reproduce, his testimony was hypocritical.

Allen grew so uneasy during the remainder of his cross-examination that at one point he asked to stand, explaining that he would feel more comfortable. It was a strange request, and I could feel a stir of amusement and confusion in the courtroom. It was painfully awkward for me to watch him. I shook my head in disbelief that I had ever been "married" to this odd man. After his testimony, my own musings were confirmed by the comments of people milling about in the hallway outside the courtroom. I heard someone refer to Allen as Forrest Gump.

Stepping down from the stand, his crumpled pants sagged slightly as he made his way toward the exit sign. It was clear from the way his shoulders matched his sagging pants that he knew he'd failed in his attempts to save the prophet. I knew that the defense had utilized Allen as the image of a soft-spoken, confused young man whose heart had been broken by a reckless teenage bride. In the end it seemed that Allen's testimony had done more harm than good. Even if the words he spoke had been believable, his behavior—his mumbling, his standing, his nervousness—seemed off-putting enough to alienate even the most objective juror. It was as though he was saying the first thing that came into his head, and there was little, if anything, that he was able to clarify.

I was confident that the prosecution had done a good job of scrutinizing the many holes in his story, but there remained a lingering fear in the back of my mind that somehow the jury would believe his version of our marriage and the one that Jennie had offered over my own. I knew that the truth was on my side, but for the first time I wondered if that was enough.

CHAPTER THIRTY-ONE

I AM FREE

Yea, that great pit which hath been digged
for the destruction of men shall be filled
by those who digged it.
—BOOK OF MORMON

Throughout the entire trial, Warren Jeffs remained
stone-faced and mute, refusing his right to testify in his
own defense. Sometimes he stared intently at the witnesses,
but mostly he scribbled furiously on the pad in front of him,
using silence as his only statement. In the court proceedings
before the trial even began, Warren stood with a yellow legal pad and had tried to speak directly to the judge. But at
the time his competency was in question and he was instructed that all communications must be made through his
attorneys. He was now in a system where he had to abide by
the laws of the land. At that moment, he was immediately
surrounded by his lawyers and gave up on his effort to read
whatever he had written.

Later a photo of the note that he was trying to read surfaced in a newspaper, revealing possible words that may
have indicated Warren's admission that he was not the
prophet. It was gratifying to see that the man who'd once
assumed absolute power over a people, and over me, was being humbled by the very laws he chose to ignore.

The closing arguments that Friday morning couldn't have

come soon enough. Getting to this final stage had been a journey of more than a year, and I was ready to move on. It would now be in the jury's hands to decide Warren's fate. Brock Belnap had taken something of a backseat during the questioning, cognizant of his strengths and humble enough to allow Ryan Shaum and Craig Barlow to carry that portion of the trial. Now Brock stood up to deliver the prosecution's closing remarks, facing the jury with a strong, sincere, and detailed statement. Rather than taking cheap shots at Warren, he simply redefined the law: "Did this man, Warren Steed Jeffs, solicit, request, command, encourage, or intentionally aid another to commit sexual intercourse with another person without the victim's—Miss Wall's—consent? That's all you have to decide." He paused for a moment to take a breath. "This is not a religious case," he explained. "You just need to decide if what the law states is what happened here.

"The evidence has shown that the only reason that Elissa Wall went into that bedroom and had sexual intercourse with Allen Steed is because that man there told her she was supposed to," Brock told jurors, pointing a finger at Warren Jeffs. "If Warren Jeffs had not performed that wedding ceremony, would Allen Steed ever had had sexual intercourse with Elissa Wall? If Warren Jeffs had never arranged the marriage or declared her his wife, would she have had sexual intercourse with him? He placed her in a position where she had no choice."

While Brock's statement was powerful and convincing, I wondered how the jurors were receiving it. The panel never once revealed any hint of how they were leaning, and there was no way to tell what they would ultimately decide.

Any ounce of respect I had tried to muster for Wally Bugden disintegrated minutes into his nearly two-hour closing arguments. He portrayed the state as out to prosecute religion and painted Warren as the victim of religious persecution. Again, he worked to portray me as the aggressor. "She is no shrinking violet," he remarked. Whipping out my medical records that had been provided by Jane Blackmore, he commented, "Let me show you something you don't know about Elissa Wall."

The courtroom fell silent in anticipation. I couldn't imagine what he was going to say and braced myself for this unexpected presentation. "Her medical records list the following items checked off: Nutrition, Alcohol, Drugs, OTC's and Vitamins, Smoking Before Pregnancy, Smoking Currently, Secondhand Smoke."

Flabbergasted, I shot Brock a look of panic. How could the defense paint me as such a monster, rattling off a list of lies? The judge requested a break, during which time I turned to Brock with tears of fury in my eyes. It was a feeling worse than being exposed—it was exploitation. I had no idea how they could have mustered those assertions about me, and I searched Brock's face for an answer.

"Don't worry, Elissa," he said to me softly. "I have it." I nodded.

Brock rose for a counterstatement. "I am about to do something that is very against my nature," he began, and I watched, stunned, as Brock's passion and emotion poured out of him. By the time he was finished, my respect and affection for him had only increased. He zoomed in on the medical record Bugden had tried to use against me, exposing a flaw in the defense's argument. Brock held up the paper for the jury to see, elucidating with an his pointer finger three little words printed above that fateful list of checked boxes: "Not a concern." Immediately, the courtroom was filled with gasps and murmurs. When it grew silent again, Brock continued.

"I'll tell you this," he said in conclusion. "No matter who it is—a preacher, a Buddhist, a friend, a parent—if they had done this to a young girl, they would be in here too." It was a phenomenal moment because this was not just a testament to me, nor was it about taking Warren down. It was not just about a high-profile trial and to add a feather to the prosecution's cap. Brock was simply defending the law of the land and what the prosecution knew was right. He was defending not only my honor but that of every young girl in the state of Utah.

The jury had much to discuss, and it wouldn't be an easy road for them. The panel of five men and three women went to the deliberation room to decide the case and remained there for about two hours that Friday before being dismissed for the weekend.

The jury reconvened on Monday, September 24, but by the end of the day there was a problem. One of the female jury members had not been completely candid in her juror questionnaire, failing to mention that she had been raped at thirteen. Apparently, at some point during the heated deliberations, she'd let the fact slip out, and as Monday's discussions wound to a close a note was sent to the judge alerting him to the situation, informing him that the jury was hung. They couldn't reach a unanimous verdict. The following morning, I learned of the problem. I assumed that the rape victim was the sole holdout for a guilty verdict. My heart sank as I tried to confront the idea that seven of the eight jurors wanted to acquit.

That morning Judge Shumate met with attorneys from both sides to determine how they would proceed. After some discussion, he instructed the juror to step down, but this left a larger question looming. The judge had not released the four alternate jurors from jury duty and had ordered them to refrain from watching TV, reading newspapers, going online, or doing anything that might compromise their oath. Since these jurors were all still on active jury duty, could the court proceed with an alternate juror or would the judge have to declare a mistrial?

The dismissal of the juror alarmed our team and made me worry that the jury was leaning toward a "not guilty" verdict. Furthermore, I felt deep empathy for the juror who'd been excused, knowing that if it weren't for me, her private story would not have been splashed across the daily news as a salacious update on the trial that was rocking Utah. Brock and I spoke about my concerns and he calmed me down by explaining that the last thing the prosecution wanted was to make us all go through this again, but if necessary they would argue for a mistrial and do it all over. This helps explain my deep respect for Brock and the rest of his team; they did not care about the time or money wasted. They were willing to go through with it again, just to do the right thing.

In a closed-door session with the judge, attorneys for both sides met to determine how the case would proceed. The prosecution hated to do so but still argued strenuously for a mistrial knowing that any conviction they achieved with this jury would give the defense grounds for an appeal. The defense saw the situation differently. They seemed confident that this jury would deliver them the not guilty verdict they were looking for and emphatically demanded to proceed with this jury.

After listening to both sides, Judge Shumate differed to the defense's request. He called in one of the alternates and sat her in the deliberation room. He instructed her and the other jurors to start from the beginning if necessary.

The situation was painfully difficult for me. I did not want to do this whole thing over again, but the idea that we could win a guilty verdict and then have it voided through a subsequent mistrial ruling was disconcerting. It was one thing to have a mistrial before we'd won anything; it would be quite different if we tasted victory only to have it taken away. But in the end the defense had gotten their wish to proceed with this jury, and now all we could do was wait.

Just three hours into deliberations with the alternate juror, word came that a verdict had been reached. I entered the courtroom that day in a cloud of anxiety and feeling sick to my stomach. My eyes met Brock's, seeking comfort. "It will be okay," he mouthed silently. As I took my seat behind the prosecuting team, I tried to take heart in the knowledge that we had done the best we could to show the truth. It was out of our hands now.

The prosecution had prepped me a bit on how to judge the jury's body language for clues about the decision. Sometimes, they explained, if the jury had ruled in favor of the victim, some of them might instinctively make eye contact with him or her. My heart sank into the floor as the jury filed into the courtroom and not one of them glanced in my direction. "Please, God, keep me strong," I asked. Then I thought of the people assembled in the back rows of the room and those waiting patiently in the still-intact FLDS communities, knowing that they were all praying for the release of Warren Jeffs. As much as I cared for them, on this day, I hoped that their prayers would go unanswered.

"Is there a verdict?" the judge inquired of the jury.

The jury foreman stood and replied, "Yes. We have a verdict."

The hearts of every person in that room pulsed frantically, each of us filled with hope and worry. Like a child, I squeezed my eyes shut to protect myself from what was to come.

"In the first count of rape as an accomplice, we the jury find the defendant, Warren Steed Jeffs, . . . guilty."

Guilty? Had I heard correctly? I looked at Warren's lawyers for their reaction and was able to confirm that the verdict had in fact been what I'd thought. Tears flowed to my eyes.

"In the second count of rape as an accomplice, we the jury find the defendant, Warren Steed Jeffs, . . . guilty."

I was paralyzed. A rush of emotions took hold of me. It wasn't just happiness, or a feeling of self-righteousness. It was bittersweet. On one hand, I felt grateful that the jury had been able to see past the confusion the defense had tried to create and vindicate the truth. And yet, I also felt a deep, sharp pain for every person who was still a part of the FLDS. I knew that everyone in that back row was so hurt. Mom and the other believers back home would be crushed once they heard the news.

Something changed in me then. While I'd long dreamed of this day, it wasn't the outcome I'd expected at all. Somehow deep down I'd always thought he would get away with it. Now that he hadn't, I didn't know how to feel. All I could think was that none of this would have happened if I hadn't had the reminder of all my sisters to give me strength to stand up to do what I knew was right. Even though no one would listen to me at first, in the end a group of eight jurors listened to me when it counted most. Ever since the day Uncle Fred informed me that I was to marry, I had been ignored and slandered by countless people—Warren, Fred, Allen, and now Warren's defense attorneys. But on this day, none of that mattered.

I looked at the faces of the prosecuting attorneys and didn't see a shred of arrogance or a loud display of triumph. Rather, they sat quietly as the room gradually emptied. In their eyes there was the satisfaction of knowing that justice had been served. Relief inflated me as I later was filtered into the back room to talk with the jury. I approached them, wondering what to say. "Thank you" would not be enough. I expressed my gratitude to them, but to this day I don't know if any of them will ever understand the depths of my admiration. I am so grateful for the their willingness and attentiveness, and for their taking the time out of their lives to hear the story of one young girl and the man responsible for her pain.

Throughout the gruelling trial process, I had purposely remained silent in the face of the press. My picture had been released, but I was apprehensive about saying anything, not wanting to be misunderstood. But a few people had approached me and suggested that I couldn't remain in the shadows anymore. It was hard to hear at first—I'd felt safe and comfortable there. Now I knew that they were right; I had to address the public.

I would make my statement brief despite the inner pull to speak for a full hour about how much I loved Mom, the girls, everyone in Colorado City, and even the people who had testified against me. I wanted them to know that I cared deeply about them all—even if we were on different sides— and that I knew they were in mourning. I wanted to urge the public to be kind to these people, and to let them come on their own. I wanted to say to the public, "If you see them in the grocery store, give them a kind word instead of a cruel one, because you never know if that one kind word would make the difference for them." All they know about people on the outside is what they have been taught; that they are evil, and the thing that had surprised me most in my transcendent journey from the FLDS to the life I live now is that good, honest, and respectful people lived out here and are nothing like what we'd been taught they are.

Brock reminded me that there would be safety risks involved with my facing the media, but I confirmed that this was something I needed to do. We remained in the quiet comfort of the courthouse when I turned to the bailiff and said, "Okay, I would like to give a statement, but I don't want to answer questions or be flooded." The bailiff was a spunky redhead with a strong will and loads of confidence. She marched right out front, and I could hear her through the glass doors as she faced the crowd that had assembled to hear Brock speak and declared, "All right, everybody. Elissa Wall is coming out here and she has words for you all. I am expecting a ten-foot distance to be upheld. She will not be answering any questions. If you can handle these rules, you can stay. If not, please leave."

I met Brock's eyes and beamed in a statement of "Here goes!" He started out first, heading down the stairs toward the press. As soon as I got outside, I wanted to turn in the other direction and run. There was a semicircle of people waiting—at least fifty reporters equipped with cameras and microphones. I froze in place, focusing on my breathing as I listened to Brock's brief, passionate statement. When he finished, he turned toward me and motioned for me to walk forward and begin. I was so self-conscious. All I could think was, "What happens if my heel breaks right now?" Timidly, I headed toward the swarm of media.

My voice was almost gone that day from the weeks of built-up stress and overextension. I worried that I wouldn't be able to speak. But once I arrived at the microphone, something strange happened. I glanced down at my paper and my eyes went directly to a line about my mother. A warm feeling stretched over me, putting my mind at ease. In that single moment I knew that though we were fighting on different sides and though we might never see or speak to each other again, the deep love my mother and I felt for each other could never be dampened or extinguished. In my heart, she was right there beside me, holding my hand.

My voice hardly wavered as I addressed the press.

"When I was young, my mother taught me that 'evil flourishes when good men do nothing.' This has not been easy. The easy thing would have been to do nothing. But I have followed my heart and spoken the truth.

"Lamont and I want to convey our love to our families. Mother, I love you and my sisters unconditionally, and will go to the ends of the earth for you. I understand and respect your convictions, but I will never give up on you. When you are ready, I am here.

"I have very tender feelings for the FLDS people. There is so much good in them. I pray they will find the strength to step back, reexamine what they have been told to believe, and follow their hearts.

"This trial has not been about religion or a vendetta. It was simply about child abuse and preventing further abuse.

"I hope that all FLDS girls and women will understand that no matter what anyone may say, you are created equal. You do not have to surrender your rights or your spiritual sovereignty. I know how hard it is, but please stand up and fight for your voice and power of choice. I will continue to fight for you.

"To those who have been there to support and keep Lamont and myself encouraged, words cannot begin to express our gratitude. I hope the FLDS people will feel the same kindness as they make their difficult journey.

"I would like to thank Brock Belnap and the prosecuting legal team for all their kindness and hard work."

I took a breath and closed my statement with the quote: " 'Opinion is a flitting thing. But truth outlasts the sun.'

Emily Dickinson." I looked into the flash of clicking cameras and the microphones that danced up and down, each clamoring to get closest. I nodded once and turned away.

Lamont and I left the courthouse that day hand in hand, filled to the brim with a sense of hope and renewal. The late-September sun beamed down upon us as we faced the beginning of a new and beautiful chapter of our lives. That night, I snuggled with two-year-old Tyler and baby Emily, relishing their sweet smiles and soft sounds. My own childhood had been racked with pain and confusion, stunted too quickly by sexual abuse and a complete loss of innocence. But now I had the chance to start over.

Tyler and Emily are my precious blank slates. They have been my healing, my salvation, and a fresh opportunity to have—and feel safe within—the construct of a family. Each day that I look at them I see a future, a future that until recently I didn't even think was possible. The thought that their tiny bodies will grow up never knowing the confines of the FLDS Church makes me realize now, perhaps more than ever, the true presence of God. In the end, he's the only reason that I made it. Sometimes that's the only thing we have. Whether you call it God, or hope, faith—whatever word you use—the fact is, I couldn't have survived if I hadn't believed in something. It was the one part of me that neither Warren nor Allen could touch, and no matter what happens, as long as I have that, I've won.

Epilogue

On November 20, 2007, almost two months after Warren's guilty verdict, Lamont and I walked into the courthouse for the sentencing of Warren Jeffs, unsure of what was going to happen. Outside, the sun shone brightly as one last time we were ushered through the back door of the courthouse. Oddly, this arena had become a part of my reality and I'd grown strangely comfortable within its walls surrounded by the people who had caringly walked beside me throughout this grueling process.

I was concerned that Warren might receive a sentence as light as eighteen months and return to the community to start all over again with his "work." I had been offered the opportunity to address the court one last time before Judge Shumate rendered Warren's sentence. I agonized over whether saying more would complicate things for the judge. We had all heard the evidence, and the closing arguments. Warren had already been found guilty; now it was just about deciding the consequence. I'd already spelled out my final thoughts in a Victim Impact Statement for the court. As I took my seat in the second row of the gallery that morning, I was still undecided, but as I listened to Wally Bugden talk of "religious persecution" and try to remove the blame from his client, I decided I had to speak up. This wasn't just about me; I owed it to all young girls, especially those of the FLDS still holding onto their innocence.

When both sides had presented their arguments with regard to Warren's sentence, the judge turned to the prosecution to learn if I would exercise my right to make a statement. I walked slowly toward the front of the courtroom, placing one wobbly foot in front of the other. I could feel my emotions taking hold as I stood at a podium directly before the judge. In that instant, the events of the past years flashed before me. Here was the man who had inflicted such pain and sorrow on so many people. Here was the moment when God would answer prayers. While I wanted to see justice served, I also felt the grief and sadness of Warren's thousands of supporters, praying that God would show his hand. I knew they were in mourning and that they didn't understand; they couldn't risk having such thoughts. But I felt like God was showing us mercy and he was answering prayers. I thought of Lamont and my children and all those who'd worked hard to get to this moment, and I knew without a doubt it had all been worth it. As I cleared my throat to speak, I was still unsure what words could be said to show the judge what was in my heart.

"I have thought of this day and how it would go for a very long time," I began, my voice quivering but filled with resolve. "Warren Jeffs and his influence over me as a fourteen-year-old girl affected me and my family in so many ways. I am so grateful for the justice system that you would see the truth and believe in me." I could already feel myself healing from the inside out. It was a powerful moment for me, even though the end had not yet arrived.

"I know from fact that whatever I do today will not make it better," Judge Shumate told me, his voice laced with sympathy and concern. "You live under a life sentence. Your courage in carrying on is laudable, but you don't have to do it alone."

I nodded, comforted that he cared and seemed to understand how much pain I had endured. I had spent a lot of time
delving into my past but I'd never focused on the fact that
these scars would be with me forever. It felt good to be vali-
dated like that; Judge Shumate made me feel fathered in a
way. Granting me this new perspective lifted a weight off
my shoulders and I will always be grateful to him for that.

I was trying to keep my emotions in check as Judge
Shumate explained to me that I was entitled to monetary
compensation from Warren for therapy and other services. I
thought for a moment, and then shook my head and replied,
"I do not seek restitution, nor would I accept it from him.
There is nothing he can give me that could change the past.
My restitution is knowing that I spoke the truth and you and
the justice system have done your job."

After a brief recess, the judge returned to the bench to
render his decision. The courtroom fell completely silent.
Behind me in the last row of the gallery sat a handful of
Warren's most devoted supporters. We were completely different now, even though I had been raised as one of them. I
cared for them all, and hoped that having sat through the
court proceeding maybe they could begin to look deeper
and examine what they had built their lives around.

In the end, Judge Shumate delivered the sentence he felt
necessary and appropriate—two consecutive terms of five
years to life in prison. This meant under Utah law that Warren would serve at least ten years and would be fined by the
court. As the judge addressed Warren, I felt grateful to see
him being held accountable for his actions. Judge Shumate
called it "poetic justice" that Warren had been captured by
authorities in the same state in which he had conducted my
wedding ceremony with Allen.

"First cousins of any age cannot marry lawfully in the
state of Utah," the judge said, confirming that Warren un-
doubtedly knew this, intentionally breaking the law.

But true to character, Warren stood before the court that
day seemingly unaffected. I don't know what I expected, but
it surprised me that such a loaded moment could unfold with

so little reaction from him. The courtroom was eerily silent as Wally Bugden rose to request that his client be allowed to remain at the Purgatory Correctional Facility in Hurricane for a week while he prepared an appeal. I was secretly glad when the judge refused and ordered that Warren be immediately transferred to the Utah State Prison in Draper, where he would undergo a five-week observation to determine his eventual placement.

It seemed that this would be the final moment in the struggle that had begun two years earlier, but this culminating event would not mark the end of the road for either Warren Jeffs or me. The prophet now faces similar criminal charges in Arizona. Jeffs has also been indicted by a federal grand jury in Salt Lake City on a single count of unlawful flight to avoid prosecution, stemming from his time on the FBI's Ten Most Wanted list. As for Allen, prosecutors in Washington County filed rape charges against him and his case is pending.

On April 24, 2008, a hearing was held to determine whether the juror substitution in The State of Utah vs. Warren Jeffs was appropriate. The defense claimed that their insistence on adding an alternate juror to the original jury was such a bad mistake that Warren should be given a new trial. The prosecution argued that by pressing for the alternate juror, the defense waived the possibility of a new trial. The presiding judge ruled that, in fact, the juror substitution was allowable and ignored the defense's request for a new trial. As of this writing, attorneys for Warren Jeffs have yet to appeal the ruling.

Life after the trial has not been perfect for any of us, especially my sister Teressa who is currently facing an incredibly distressing ordeal. In response to Teressa's testimony against Warren, her ex-husband, who is still a member of the FLDS and lives in Bountiful, filed for sole custody of their three children. The most distressing element of Teressa's battle for custody arose in January 2008, when we learned that my mother, my sister Sabrina and others still in the church had signed affidavits on Teressa's ex-husband's behalf. Their statements were hurtful and alleged and Teressa was a neglectful mother, who snuck out to drink and left the children in the care of others. While an affidavit from our mother was unexpected, and we still doubt that the words are even hers, Sabrina's, stung the most. As fellow transplants in Canada for years, Teressa and Sabrina shared a very deep mutual understanding, and Teressa felt understandably betrayed.

The FLDS Church has been pitting family members against one another for a long time, but in recent years it has gotten worse than ever. Teressa is a prime example, and so are Lamont and myself. In December 2007, Lamont's aunt passed away. Since losing his mother, Lamont had forged a strong bond with her sister and she had become like a mother to him. Her loss impacted him deeply and we wanted to attend her funeral in Short Creek. To our dismay, Lamont and I were promptly informed that if we were present, the service would be canceled and she would just be buried with no memorial service. Two of her children who had removed themselves from the FLDS were even hindered greatly from attending their own mother's funeral. It's sad to see how church leaders are willing to use people's emotions and sincere love against them as a way to punish them for holding a different point of view.

A part of me had secretly hoped that Warren being in prison might open the eyes of some of the devoted people of the FLDS. Maybe without Warren's presence and influence, some doors would open and ties to loved ones shoved out along the way might be permitted again. I had even allowed myself to dream of the day when my mother and I would be reunited and allowed a chance at a relationship, despite our differing views.

To my disappointment, little has changed in the community, and life continues on much as it did under Warren. Ultimately, these systems are much bigger than just one man. They were in place long before he took power and they will carry on until more people stand up against these injustices. I still haven't heard a word from Sherrie or Ally in years, and I have not seen my mother since we parted following Uncle Fred's funeral. In late March of 2008, I received word that they might surface long enough to clear the missing persons report that Kassandra filed after their initial disappearance. The news came after lengthy communications between David Doran, the sheriff of Schleicher County, Texas, and the leaders of the Yearn for Zion Ranch (YFZ) that Warren Jeffs and others had constructed in Sheriff Doran's jurisdiction in Eldorado.

Remarkably, Sheriff Doran is the only member of law enforcement who has ever been able to open a friendship and line of communication with the people of the FLDS, and because of this relationship church elders agreed to entertain the possibility of a meeting with my mother. Sadly, we learned that the men in charge of Mom, Sherrie, and Ally would not allow one to take place if any of my mother's apostate children were in attendance. Eventually my father, my mother, Sherrie and Ally, and members of law enforcement met in Washington County, Utah, but the meeting did not produce any new information about where they were living.

While I am sure my mother may feel disrespected and hurt by my actions, I hope she understands that coming forward was something I had to do. Her staunch support of the religion and inability to extract herself from that mindset put me in a position where she couldn't protect me. It is for this reason that I have resolved to make it my mission to help my little sisters and others like them in any way possible.

In early April 2008, I got that opportunity when a young girl reached out from the inside the FLDS to a crisis hotline in Texas. The caller claimed that she was sixteen years old, eight months pregnant, and wanted help to get out of the FLDS community. In response, members of Texas law enforcement entered the compound on Thursday, April 3, in hopes of locating her. During their initial search, and over the next few days, they were unable to find a girl fitting that description but observed many underage girls who were visibly pregnant. This prompted officials to embark on a more thorough investigation that led to the removal of hundreds of women and children from the ranch.

Suddenly faced with this newly daunting task, officials in Texas needed an understanding of this culture and its people, and so they invited my sister Kassandra and me to Texas to assist them in their communication with the FLDS people. My desire was to ensure that the men, women, and children were treated with kindness, understanding, and respect. I knew the fear and anxiety that they were experiencing all too well. I was also hoping that I would see Sherrie and Ally there, but they were not among the women and children bused from the ranch.

The experience of being on the scene proved extremely emotional for me. At points, I found it incredibly difficult to be reminded of how conditioned the people—especially the women—were. Even with our help, the questioning proved extremely difficult for the investigators. Some women refused to speak altogether, and those who did comply provided fake names and declined to give concrete answers to the questions asked of them. I had the perspective to understand that the authorities were there to provide assistance and investigate and protect the innocence of young women and children, but the people, locked in the church's grasp, were devastated by what was happening to them. Once, long ago, I would have felt the same way. I observed one young mother in particular with a baby in her arms and a small boy holding on to her finger as she made her way past the phalanx of uniformed Rangers toward the awaiting buses. She walked with her head held high and a silent tear cutting down the side of her cheek. As she reached the bus, she turned and looked one of the officers directly in the eye, saying, "I want you to know I truly forgive you for this." Within that simple statement, I could see the difficult road ahead. These poignant words made it apparent that she, like many of the women, felt victimized by the police and the Texas government. She was unable to see that the few men in charge of the FLDS had placed these girls in harm's way and made matters worse by refusing to cooperate with authorities.

Beneath these hardships, however, I was able to witness firsthand the outpouring of kindness, respect, and dignity given to the FLDS people involved in Texas's investigation. From Texas law enforcement to Child Protective Services, and every other department involved, each made an incredible effort to reach out and understand the people of the FLDS, their culture, and how they could best approach them and communicate with them. It was clear that this investigation was not about religion. It was about child abuse, sanctioned and directed by the FLDS men in authority.

As hard as it has been to watch the events of Eldorado unfold, they prove that there are still so many young girls and women who don't yet realize that they, too, have the right to cry out against injustice. I hope this book reaches the many young girls and women around the world whose faces I'll never see and whose names I'll never know, and that perhaps in some way my words will help them to use their strength to reclaim what is rightfully theirs—the power of choice.

Afterword

It's been almost six months since the drama at Eldorado captivated the country, but the passing of time has done little to ease the difficulty of the situation or my own struggle with the issues that the events in Texas raised.

In the weeks following the raid on the YFZ ranch, I continued to work with Texas Child Protective Services, offering my assistance whenever possible. In late May 2008, the State Supreme Court of Texas upheld an earlier decision by an appeals court and ruled that the children had to be returned to their FLDS families almost immediately. Along with this ruling, the Texas Supreme Court mandated that Texas maintain its investigation into charges of alleged child abuse at the ranch—even after the children returned to their parents. As part of the court's decision, the FLDS families were required to cooperate fully with the state's investigation into the alleged abuses, and CPS was allowed to have regular access to the kids, particularly those it deemed at risk for underage marriage. The FLDS families would have to work with CPS to prove that the children were not vulnerable to underage marriages. Despite the lingering resentment and distrust that the FLDS members held toward CPS, they would have to cooperate with CPS if they were going to keep their children.

A few days after the Texas Supreme Court's ruling, the children went back home to their FLDS families. But there was still a nagging question beneath all of this: should the court have allowed the children to return to the YFZ ranch?

It's an understatement to say that this is a tough question. Children belong with their parents, and FLDS members understandably want their kids back. But the simple truth was that there were a range of child abuse issues that CPS encountered and it was vital for the kids' safety that these issues be investigated. The most pressing of these issues were the young girls in the compound who were at risk of being forced into marriage. Based on what the Texas officials had seen of the young girls from the compound, there were many reasons to be concerned for the girls' safety as well as that of many of the other children.

CPS's concerns were supported at the end of May when photos of Warren Jeffs intimately hugging and kissing two different young teenage girls were revealed to the world. The fact that the spiritual leader of the FLDS also was engaged in inappropriate behavior with underage girls bolstered CPS's claims that the practice of underage marriage and sexual relationships was far more widespread than the FLDS would admit. These photos would eventually contribute to Texas's investigation into events at the YFZ Ranch, as the images—along with other evidence that Texas officials collected—showed that underage marriage was being practiced at all levels of the church.

Seeing these photos was an incredibly painful experience and a clear reminder that what I had gone through was not a rare occurrence. The fact that Warren was himself a part of this lent an even greater sense of urgency to Texas's efforts. What worried me the most was how the FLDS would comply with the new court order to allow CPS access to the children. Prior to the events in Texas, many of these children had absolutely no contact with the outside world. Now they would be forced to allow their children to have regular interaction with state officials. While in some ways this solution seemed reasonable, I understood their fears of outsiders, which made me very concerned about the practicalities of how it would play out.

It didn't take long for some of the FLDS's cooperation with CPS to deteriorate, feeding my worries that Texas's fight was just beginning. At various points over the following months, numerous court-appointed CPS officials reported instances of interference by leading adult FLDS members. Though the FLDS was bound by the original court order to comply with Texas's investigation, they seemed to put a number of roadblocks in the way to prevent the investigation from moving forward. It was clear that Texas was gathering evidence against them, and so certain FLDS members used tactics both procedural and behavioral in their attempt to disrupt those efforts.

In spite of these roadblocks, Texas officials and CPS advocates were able to collect a substantial amount of evidence during their investigation. In late June, the state convened a series of grand jury hearings to evaluate the evidence that had been gathered. While the first of these hearings ended without any indictments, the subsequent two grand jury hearings produced a total of six brand-new indictments against FLDS members, including one for Warren Jeffs.

In the coming months and years, these indictments and perhaps others will result in trials. As painful as this is for all sides, I hope these future developments allow much more to come to the surface so that the truth can be seen and issues can be dealt with. Though it will most likely take years for the complete story of the YFZ temple to come out, I have little doubt that in the end, justice will be served.

What's harder to predict is how the legacy of the YFZ raid will be written within the confines of FLDS society. One thing I know from my experience is that the leaders will use this as justification for why the outside cannot be trusted. Behind the walls of the YFZ compound and throughout the dusty red streets of Short Creek, FLDS members will use the actions of Texas to justify their claims of religious persecution. They'll most likely say that this was about polygamy and religious freedom, and it has nothing to do with keeping the children safe. Discussing the events surrounding the YFZ Ranch will become the new scare tactic—a story that participants will tell for generations to come to prove the wickedness of the outside world.

Personally, the months since *Stolen Innocence* was published have been a mixture of highs and lows. I was astounded and encouraged by the outpouring of support I received from people around the world. That support came in the form of letters and e-mails from people on all sides of the discussion who were eager to learn as much as possible about the issues I raised. To be honest, I didn't know how people would react when I first decided to write my story, and I was completely overwhelmed by how many worldwide responded with thoughts of goodwill.

Many people were anxious to learn what had happened with my sister Teressa and her child custody battle. Unfortunately, it has been an uphill battle for her, one that is ongoing to this day. As our family members still in the FLDS sided with Teressa's husband's claim for custody, Teressa fought back the only way she could—acquiring her own affidavits from people who had witnessed her as a parent. Meanwhile lawyers for her ex-husband tried to convince the court that the church's influence in the children's lives was irrelevant to the case. They argued the only thing that mattered was determining who was the better parent.

The proceedings were messy and emotional, but after much sparring, the court granted Teressa temporary full custody until further developments could be made in the case. As a single mother, she struggled to gain a solid footing and faced the overwhelming problem of money. Fighting the FLDS does not come cheaply and they have a lot of money at their disposal to pursue a case against Teressa. Simply put, she did not have enough in the bank to bring the case to trial in hopes of gaining permanent custody of her three children.

Without the money to move forward, she was forced to come to a less-than-perfect agreement, where she had to make many compromises to retain her full custody status, giving Roy a lot of visitation and even allowing him to take the children for the summer. Though I am sure she would not want to have her children kept from their father, her concern for them is clear, and she is still working to raise the money she needs to continue her legal fight against her ex-husband and the FLDS.

In addition to questions about Teressa, other people wrote me eager to understand life in the FLDS and voice their concerns about the allegations of abuse that have been brought to light. It was so encouraging and fulfilling to hear that so many were touched by my story. I felt a kinship with those who wrote me and voiced their own personal tragedies, telling me how my book had helped them rethink disturbing events in their past. I was comforted by those who offered solace and reassurance, always taking the opportunity to remind me that while the path I had chosen was hard, I had made the right choice. I gained strength from those who encouraged me to persevere in my causes and offered an unexpected web of support during the moments when I needed it the most.

At the same time that I was receiving such positive messages of hope, much of my optimism was tainted by the events in Eldorado. Though I was helping the Texas officials in any way that I could, it was an incredibly difficult time for me as I was forced to revisit my fears about what was happening with Sherri and Ally. During the weeks after the raid, I knew they were close and I was trying desperately to find a line of contact to them and my mother. Initially, I had high hopes that the events in Eldorado would help me uncover their whereabouts and gain some form of communication with them, but that chance slipped away. Despite the dust settling from the raid, I still have had no contact with them or found a record of where they've been. With all that's been

learned and the indictments since the children were returned, I've become increasingly worried about whether
they were forced into underage marriages as well. But no
matter how much time has passed, I still refuse to give up
hope and am actively taking steps to find them.

One of the greatest tragedies of Eldorado was that it demonstrated how entrenched the FLDS is in its ways. Before
Texas, I'd been hopeful that my court testimony against Warren would help motivate the FLDS against underage marriages, that by raising my voice, I could spare other girls my
fate if the men behind it knew that it carried the risk of
prison. The raid on the YFZ ranch illustrated that this behavior has yet to stop. While the actual number of underage
brides and mothers has yet to be accurately determined,
there is no mystery that the practice continues to occur despite Jeffs's conviction.

Today it is not apparent that the practice of underage
marriage has stopped and the FLDS continues to stand in
the way of people who try to expose this issue. In their campaign against those who oppose them, they've gone to great
lengths to use the media as their weapon, employing a multi-
faceted, smoke and mirrors PR campaign that distracts the
public from what's really going on. They talk in circles and
obscure the truth, all in the hope that people won't poke
holes in their flawed defense of the indefensible.

Indeed, what they do publicly does not even compare to
their tactics in private, as the leaders of the FLDS have gone
to great lengths to prevent the issues at hand from being
brought to light. They've repeatedly attacked anyone who
vocally opposes them, while making outrageous claims and
filing affidavits against those who have stood up to them.
Using the same strategies that they often used against my
family and me, the FLDS still turns individual members
and families against one another as they try to preserve their
version of reality.

Despite all that has happened since my journey began, I
remain committed to exposing what I went through and
what girls still go through in the FLDS. The stakes are too

high for us to ignore what's been occurring behind the closed doors of FLDS life. As I write this, I am preparing for more trials this fall, with one involving Allen Steed in Utah and another against Warren in Arizona. I have little doubt that as these new trials take place more will be revealed about the FLDS and their practices. They will try to spin their way out of this mess, lobbing accusations and trying to drag people's pasts through the mud in an effort to obscure the facts.

While the events of these last several months have tested me, to this day I am thankful that so many people in my life helped me find the courage to come forward and tell my story. This experience has allowed me to discover a reservoir of support from people that I've never met and probably never will. Even though my journey on the outside world has just begun, their words have touched and changed me in ways that I didn't know were possible, and for that I will always be blessed.

This is my story. The events described are based upon my recollections and are true. I have changed the names of some individuals to protect their privacy.

In this book, I have used the terms "FLDS" or "priesthood" to describe the religious system in which I was raised. I have also made brief mention of "The Work"—later more commonly known as the FLDS Church, as well as the UEP—the trust through which the priesthood owns and controls all the property and homes of the FLDS people. I have usually combined The Work, the FLDS, and the UEP into the terms "FLDS" or "priesthood" for simplicity, but also because they are one and the same—inseparable parts.

After I began working with law enforcement, I brought a lawsuit against the FLDS system, naming as defendants Warren Jeffs, the FLDS Church, and the UEP Trust. In conjunction with that case, I have set up a fund, the MJ Fund, to provide girls and women with options that I did not have and help them start lives for themselves. It is my intention to use proceeds from that lawsuit, a portion of my profits from this book, and donations to start and operate the MJ Fund. There are so many people that need help, and it is my hope that I will be able to provide the necessary services that these people will need to get their lives back.

ACKNOWLEDGMENTS

This has been a long and difficult journey for me and I have been blessed with the support, friendship, and love of so many wonderful people.

To Lisa Pulitzer, whose dedication to learning my past inside and out and helping me to get it down on paper will never be forgotten. Your visits to Utah and our long speaker-phone conversations were always a breath of fresh air and a source of comfort as I explored many painful memories. Our friendship has impacted me profoundly and I will always admire your talent, drive, and caring manner. And thank you to Lisa's husband, Douglas Love, who supported us and entertained their two daughters, Francesca and Juliet, so Lisa and I could work. And to Jenny Studenroth, whose role as editorial assistant helped us to stay on track and sunny voice kept me encouraged.

To Matt Harper, my editor at HarperCollins, thank you for your tireless work and effort and for finding the humor when things went awry. I cannot even imagine how many late nights you suffered, and your skill has enhanced and shaped this book in a way I never could have anticipated. And to

Lisa Sharkey at HarperCollins for realizing I had a story to tell and for helping to make it happen. Much appreciation and gratitude to our meticulous copyeditor, Margaret Wimberger, and the many others at HarperCollins whose hard work and dedication under these incredible deadline pressures shone through.

My father and three mothers, especially my biological mother—I appreciate your love every day. Mom and Dad—no matter what has happened in the past and what faces us in the future, you will always be dear to my heart. My love for you transcends everything else between us. Thank you for instilling in me my strength to know what's right. To my little sisters Sherrie and Ally, thank you for being there for me through the most difficult time of my life, and for helping me to stay strong. Mother, Sherrie, and Ally, please know that I will always be here for you, and my love and devotion will remain forever bright.

Thank you to my eleven brothers and twelve sisters, all of whom I love deeply. I pray for you all and will never give up on any of you, especially those of you who have been there for me in this very difficult time. While our past has not always been rosy, I take great comfort in knowing that despite any distance, we've done it together. To Mother Audrey, you know who you are, thank you for not abandoning me, and for continuing to love me as one of your children.

To Lamont, you are indeed my guardian angel. Without you by my side, I would not be who I am today. Your love, understanding, patience, and willingness to listen and share my tears are only a few of the reasons why I hold you so dear. It is with certainty that I say that God sent you to rescue and strengthen me so that I may do this important work. The road has and always will be fraught with hurdles, and even when the horizon may look bleak, we have the greatest gift of all and that is one another and our beautiful family.

Lamont and I could not have survived without the support from our many incredible friends. Merintha and Melvin, you are such dear friends and have been so helpful and caring. Merintha, you were my first friend outside of the

FLDS, and you have remained by my side all along, without judgment. Thank you for loving my children as if they were your own. Knowing Lamont and I could count on you to take care of our family throughout this incredible journey made what had to be done that much easier.

We extend our deep gratitude to Dan and Lennie Fischer; thank you for everything you have done to help this effort. We could never have done it without you. You have helped hundreds and we all owe our greatest thanks. To Shem and Lisa Fischer and family, we appreciate and love you more than you know.

Thanks also to our other friends Diane and Jack McSarland, author John Krakauer, Kirby Bistline, David and Cammy Southam, Jethro Barlow, Jerry and Leanne Denman, Roseanne and Les Young, Jane Blackmore, Steven and Dorothy Sheffield, John Morley and Polly Black, T.R. and Leysi Dockstater, Hyram and Melinda Dockstater, Rick and Jacquelyne White, and so many others.

For all the women who have touched my life in so many ways, Natalie Dutson, Joanna Dutson, Sarah Duston, Lori Barlow, Ashlee Bistline, Shirley Draper, Becka Jessop, Lorraine Fischer, Margaret Fischer, Adrienne Quinton, Meg Wight, Kathy Jessop, Martha Barlow, Jennie Steed, and Leah Dockstater, and to those stepsisters of mine who were kind and caring, I love you all dearly.

A special thank-you to Buzz and Anne Woods for enabling us to get where we are today and helping us to stand on our own. Gratitude to Dr. Steven and Yasmin Miller, Robert and Alex Campbell, Kent Nelson, Doug and Linda Moore, Lester and Janet Perry, Troy Evans, Doug Hunt, Maureen Crump of Utah Safe Passages, Peggy Powell, Dr. Ralph Bradley, Dr. Derek Muse, and the Diversity Foundation and Utah State Attorney General's Office for their dedication to this cause.

To Roger Hoole—there are not enough words to express how grateful I am. You have been more than an attorney to me; you have become a dear friend. You and Sharon have helped me so much, and I will be forever grateful. To Roger's law partner and brother Greg and his wife, Kelly Hoole, thank you for your friendship, hard work, and support. To both Roger and Greg and your families, thank you for believing in us, and for sacrificing so much of your time to this cause. To legal assistant Shellie Manzanares, you have been a quiet soldier, and private investigator Sam Brower, thank you for your many efforts and encouragement.

Heartfelt gratitude to the dedicated members of the Washington County Attorney's Office, Ryan Shaum, Bryan Felter, Roger, and all the many others who gave their time and hard work to this case. You were all amazing and so utterly impacting on me. A special thank-you to Brock and Shaunty Belnap—you encouraged me to come forward and you always believed in me. To Jerry Jaeger, for your extensive investigation and for helping us to survive the many trials and tribulations of the witness protection program. You and so many others were there to guide and protect us, and we are forever grateful. Thank you to the Washington County Sheriff's Office: Kirk Smith, Jake Schultz and all the deputies who helped investigate and keep us safe.

To Sheriff David Doran of Schleicher County for his untiring efforts to understand the FLDS people. To Capt. Barry Caver, Sgt. L. Brooks Long, and all the Texas Rangers for taking time to listen and learn about the FLDS.

To the Mojave County Attorney's Office, and Gary Engels, you have forged the path for these cases, and so many people owe you their gratitude. Matt Smith, your efforts do not go unnoticed. To everyone else who worked hard to help me, you are appreciated.

And to all of you who have been there and touched our lives in some way, no matter how small, your kindness and efforts have not gone unnoticed. Your hard work and dedication in this case will surely change the destiny of so many girls and young women that you may never know.

Most important, I thank my loving children, who give me a reason to look forward to each new day with happiness and anticipation. It is my hope that you will someday understand why I needed to write this book. As your mother, I will strive to be an example in your lives and show you the difference between right and wrong. I hope I've shown you to stand up for your beliefs and defend your rights. Always remember that no matter where you go in life or what you choose to do, my love will always follow you.

ABOUT THE AUTHORS

ELISSA WALL, a former member of the FLDS Church, was forced into marriage at age fourteen. She left the FLDS church at age eighteen, and she currently resides with her two children.

LISA PULITZER is a former correspondent for the *New York Times* and author of more than a dozen nonfiction titles, including *Portrait of a Monster: Joran van der Sloot, A Murder in Peru*, and the *Natalee Holloway Mystery*.